October 19–26, 2012
Tucson, Arizona, USA

**Association for
Computing Machinery**

Advancing Computing as a Science & Profession

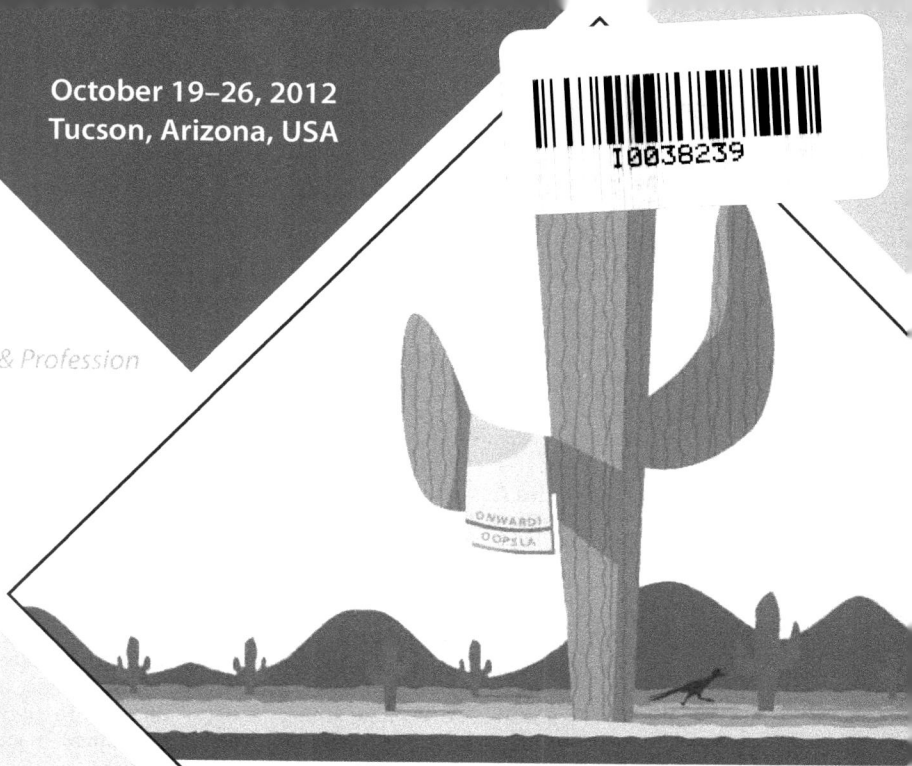

SPLASH

TUCSON, ARIZONA | OCTOBER 19-26, 2012

SPLASH'12

Proceedings of the 2012 ACM Conference on
Systems, Programming, and Applications:
Software for Humanity

Sponsored by:
ACM SIGPLAN

Supported by:
**Microsoft Research, Cisco, Oracle Labs, IBM Research,
Google, & Dejan Research**

**Association for
Computing Machinery**

Advancing Computing as a Science & Profession

The Association for Computing Machinery
2 Penn Plaza, Suite 701
New York, New York 10121-0701

Notice to Past Authors of ACM-Published Articles
ACM intends to create a complete electronic archive of all articles and/or other material previously published by ACM. If you have written a work that has been previously published by ACM in any journal or conference proceedings prior to 1978, or any SIG Newsletter at any time, and you do NOT want this work to appear in the ACM Digital Library, please inform permissions@acm.org, stating the title of the work, the author(s), and where and when published.

ISBN: 978-1-4503-1563-0 (Digital)

ISBN: 978-1-4503-1926-3 (Print)

Additional copies may be ordered prepaid from:

ACM Order Department
PO Box 30777
New York, NY 10087-0777, USA

Phone: 1-800-342-6626 (USA and Canada)
+1-212-626-0500 (Global)
Fax: +1-212-944-1318
E-mail: acmhelp@acm.org
Hours of Operation: 8:30 am – 4:30 pm ET

Printed in the USA

Welcome from the SPLASH General Chair

Welcome to Tucson, Arizona and the 2012 *Systems, Programming, Languages, Applications: Software for Humanity (SPLASH)* conference! This is the third annual *SPLASH* conference. *SPLASH* is an umbrella conference containing *OOPSLA*, *Onward!*, and *Wavefront*. This year we also have the *Dynamic Languages Symposium (DLS)* and *Pattern Languages of Programs (PLoP)* co-located with us. The *SPLASH* conference grew out of *OOPSLA*, which started in 1986 and eventually grew to a *SPLASH*-like set of conferences (including *Onward!*) in 2009. Thus 2012 can be considered the 27th year of this great tradition.

The rebranding of the conference as *SPLASH* recognizes the growth of this area beyond object-oriented programming. However, the conference as a whole retains a similar set of interests. These interests span many areas of programming, programming languages, and software engineering. I invite you to dive into the research papers at *OOPSLA*, find out about cutting-edge industrial ideas at *Wavefront*, and expand your horizons at *Onward!* This year we have continued making 5 day registrations available, so that you can easily sample all these conferences as well as a variety of workshops and the *DLS*.

This year we are fortunate to have four keynote speakers who span different parts of the *SPLASH* tradition. Barbara Simons's keynote addresses the timely application area of electronic voting. Jim Coplien's keynote about the Data, Context, and Interaction paradigm will add to the *SPLASH* tradition of software design as well as offering a new perspective on how to design software for humanity. Rustan Leino's keynote promises to be at the intersection of programming languages and software engineering. Rob Pike's keynote on the Go language will address both programming language design and cutting-edge applications at Google.

The organization of this large conference is a task that cannot be completed by one person: it requires a village worth of dedicated volunteers. I want to particularly thank William Cook, the *SPLASH* steering committee chair and our treasurer, for guiding me through the process of organizing the conference as well as watching the budget. Richard Gabriel also provided lots of helpful advice, and took on the herculean task of producing all the publications in a compressed amount of time. Henry Baragar, assisted by Chuck Matthews, handled the website and its content, which was a great help. Rebecca Mebane of MeetGreen handled interfacing with the hotel and managed many of the details of the arrangements. Besides these, I want to warmly thank all the other committee chairs: Matt, Jonathan, Julia, Ademar, Ulrik, Sushil, Eli, Hridesh, Igor, Chris, Dennis, Max, Alex, Rochelle, and Ferosh. It has been my honor and privilege to work with all these great people.

Thanks to our generous supporters for their contributions to *SPLASH*. Thanks also to the University of Central Florida their support of my work, and for providing space for the *OOPSLA* program committee meeting.

I sincerely hope that the conference and the ideas in these proceedings stimulate you to provide great software for humanity.

Gary T. Leavens
University of Central Florida
Orlando, Florida

Welcome Message from the OOPSLA Chair

SPLASH

TUCSON, ARIZONA | OCTOBER 19-26, 2012

Welcome to the 2012 *ACM SIGPLAN Conference on Object-Oriented Programming, Systems, Languages, and Applications (OOPSLA)*. We believe that we have selected an interesting and high-quality program of research papers. As you will see, *OOPSLA* continues to expand beyond the conference's 1986 roots in object-oriented programming. This year's papers discuss many topics, including: concurrency, verification, program analysis, types, fault detection, program understanding, dynamic languages, compilation, and a variety of approaches that support the program development process. As you can see from this topic list, this instance of *OOPSLA* continues to explore core issues in programming languages and reaches out to connect with broader issues in software engineering.

Papers were reviewed by a combination of the *OOPSLA* program committee (PC), consisting of 31 experts in the field, and the *OOPSLA* external review committee (ERC), also consisting of 31 experts. Each paper was assigned to at least three committee members to review; submissions from PC members were treated specially as discussed below. The reviews were made available to authors who were then able to write a response providing clarification to reviewers. Author responses were read and, in some cases, used to identify papers for which an additional fourth review was needed. The program committee meeting, which was held on June 29–30, 2012 at the Harris Center of the University of Central Florida, in Orlando, was attended by all of the *OOPSLA* PC members. I would like to thank Gary Leavens and Rochelle Elva for all of their assistance with the organization and operation of the program committee meeting.

OOPSLA is a healthy research conference. This year a record number of papers, 228, were submitted and 59 were accepted. This 25.8% acceptance rate is slightly higher than the historical average of 24.4%.

The *OOPSLA* conference allows committee members to submit papers. Papers co-authored by program committee members were reviewed by the ERC. Discussion of those submissions and acceptance decisions were made separately from the program committee meeting. The papers were all evaluated individually and held to a slightly higher standard than non-PC submissions. This year, 21 papers were submitted with program committee co-authors, and 5 were accepted.

It is an honor and a privilege to serve as research program chair for *OOPSLA 2012*. It is also a pleasure to work with the many dedicated professionals who comprised the PC and ERC for *OOPSLA*. I thank them for all of the time and effort they contributed to help build a strong program. As those who have served on PCs know, the amount of work that goes into reviewing papers is significant and it is often quite impressive to see the quality and depth of feedback that fellow reviewers provide to authors. This year I decided to consult with the PC to identify a member of the PC who did a particularly noteworthy job in reviewing papers, responding to author feedback and the feedback of other reviewers, and advocating for papers during the PC meeting. Seven individuals were nominated, which indicates the breadth of quality in the conduct of the PC this year. Isil Dillig received the most nominations and she has the honor of being named *2012 OOPSLA Distinguished Reviewer*.

I hope that you find the papers that we have accepted for inclusion in *OOPSLA 2012* to be both of current interest and of long-term significance to the *OOPSLA* community.

Matthew B. Dwyer
University of Nebraska - Lincoln

Table of Contents

Student Research Competition

Wavefront Technical Papers

Wavefront Experience Reports

Workshop Summaries

SPLASH 2012 Conference Organization

General Chair:	Gary T. Leavens, *University of Central Florida*
***OOPSLA* Program Chair:**	Matthew B. Dwyer, *University of Nebraska – Lincoln*
***Onward!* Program Chair:**	Jonathan Edwards, *MIT*
***Onward!* Essays Chair:**	Julie Steele, *O'Reilly Media, Inc.*
***DLS* Program Chair:**	Alessandro Warth, *Google*
***Wavefront* Chair:**	Christopher O'Connor, *University of Michigan*
***Wavefront Experience* Chair:**	Dennis Mancl, *Alcatel-Lucent*
Workshops Committee Chairs:	Ademar Aguiar, *U. Porto* Ulrik Pagh Schultz, *University of Southern Denmark*
Demonstrations Chair:	Igor Peshansky, *Google*
Panels:	Gary T. Leavens, *University of Central Florida* Michael Ernst, *University of Washington*
Posters and ACM SRC Chairs:	Eli Tilevich, *Virginia Tech* Sushil Bajracharya, *Black Duck Software*
Doctoral Symposium Chair:	Hridesh Rajan, *Iowa State University*
Proceedings:	Richard P. Gabriel, *IBM Research*
Treasurer:	William Cook, *University of Texas at Austin*
Advertising and Social Media:	Michael Maximilien, *IBM Research*
Content Management:	Henry Baragar, *Instantiated Software Inc.* Charles Matthews, *Fifth Generation Systems*
Student Volunteer Chairs:	Rochelle Elva, *University of Central Florida* Ferosh Jacob, *University of Alabama*
RPG 2012:	Richard Gabriel, *IBM Research*
***Pattern Languages of Programs*:**	Eduardo Guerra, *Aeronautical Institute of Tech.* Joseph Yoder, *The Refactory*
Graphic Artist:	Victor Davila, *University of Central Florida*
Steering Committee Chair:	William Cook, *University of Texas at Austin*

SPLASH 2012 Sponsor and Supporters

Sponsor:

Supporters:

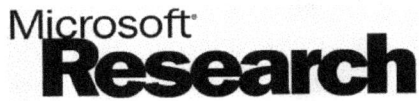

™ Microsoft is a trademark of the Microsoft group of companies and is used under license from Microsoft

Oracle Labs

Internet Voting: An Idea Whose Time has Not Come

Barbara Simons

IBM Research (Retired)
San Jose, California
simons@acm.org

Abstract

Properly designed and engineered computerized voting systems can facilitate voting and increase the security and reliability of our voting systems. Unfortunately, in their eagerness to have the most modern and best election equipment and to take advantage of almost $4 billion in federal funding, well meaning election officials were quick to accept accuracy and security claims of computerized voting system vendors. Few questions were asked about crucial issues. How secure, accurate, and reliable are these machines? How easy are they to use, especially by people with disabilities? How could an election audit or recount be conducted? There was little or no consultation with independent technical experts on these questions, and remarkably little scientific research. Standards and regulations were inadequate to nonexistent. The implicit assumption appears to have been that no recount would ever be needed, because the new systems were so completely secure and accurate that there would no longer be any reason to challenge an election result.

There is now a widespread perception that Internet voting is the wave of the future and the way to save money while increasing voter participation, especially participation of young people. (I can bank online; why can't I vote online?) Not having learned from previous mistakes and against the advice of essentially all computer security experts, Internet voting is currently being used in several countries and in some U.S. States. There is also strong pressure to adopt Internet voting in the U.S. for members of the military and civilians living abroad. In this talk I examine some of the threats of Internet voting in the hope of encouraging the technical community to oppose Internet voting unless and until these threats can be eliminated.

Categories and Subject Descriptors J.7 [Computers in Other Systems]

General Terms Computer Applications

Keywords Voting, Internet, Security, Elections

1. Bio

An expert on electronic voting, Dr. Barbara Simons recently published Broken Ballots: *Will Your Vote Count?*, a book on voting machines co-authored with Douglas Jones. She is on the Board of Advisors of the U.S. Election Assistance Commission, and she was a member of the workshop, convened at the request of President Clinton, that produced a report on Internet Voting in 2001. She also co-authored the report that led to the cancellation of Department of Defense's Internet voting project (SERVE) because of security concerns. Simons, a former ACM President, co-chaired the ACM study of statewide databases of registered voters, and co-authored the League of Women Voters report on election auditing.

Simons earned her Ph.D. in computer science from the University of California, Berkeley. Her dissertation solved a major open problem in scheduling theory. Her main areas of research have been compiler optimization, algorithm analysis and design, and scheduling theory. Her work on clock synchronization won an IBM Research Division Award. She holds several patents and has authored or co-authored two books and numerous technical papers.

Staged Program Development

K. Rustan M. Leino

Microsoft Research
Redmond, WA, USA
leino@microsoft.com

Abstract

A major issue facing software development and maintenance is the sheer complexity of programs. Even software designs that start off simple often evolve into programs that are both brittle and hard to understand.

In this talk, I advocate programming in *stages*, where the programming language allows the program design to be described at varying levels of abstraction. Higher levels of abstraction focus on the intent of the design, whereas lower levels of abstraction introduce optimizations and other details. Since the layering is expressed in the programming language, the stages are preserved as part of the program text. Therefore, the stages help break down the program's complexity not only during development but also during maintenance.

I will describe some language features, both old and new, that encourage staged development. To help communicate the vision, I will demonstrate Dafny, a research programming system whose language blends specifications, imperative programming, and staged program refinements and whose development environment is powered by an automatic program verifier that constantly analyzes the program to help the programmer get details right.

Joint work with Jason Koenig.

Categories and Subject Descriptors D.2.2 [*SOFTWARE ENGINEERING*]: Design Tools and Techniques

General Terms staged development, varying levels of abstraction, programming language design, program verification

Keywords abstract specifications, concrete representations, program refinement, preconditions, invariants, verification, Dafny

References

[1] J.-R. Abrial, M. Butler, S. Hallerstede, T. S. Hoang, F. Mehta, and L. Voisin. Rodin: An open toolset for modelling and reasoning in Event-B. *International Journal on Software Tools for Technology Transfer*, Apr. 2010.

[2] R.-J. Back and J. von Wright. *Refinement Calculus: A Systematic Introduction*. Graduate Texts in Computer Science. Springer-Verlag, 1998.

[3] ClearSy. Atelier B. http://www.atelierb.eu, 2009.

[4] E. W. Dijkstra. A constructive approach to the problem of program correctness. *BIT*, 8:174–186, 1968.

[5] Escher Technologies, Inc. Getting started with Perfect. http://www.eschertech.com, 2001.

[6] D. Gries and J. Prins. A new notion of encapsulation. In *Proceedings of the ACM SIGPLAN 85 Symposium on Language Issues in Programming Environments*, number 7 in SIGPLAN Notices 20, pages 131–139. ACM, July 1985.

[7] C. A. R. Hoare. Proof of correctness of data representations. *Acta Inf.*, 1(4):271–281, 1972.

[8] J. Koenig and K. R. M. Leino. Getting started with Dafny: A guide. In T. Nipkow, O. Grumberg, and B. Hauptmann, editors, *Software Safety and Security: Tools for Analysis and Verification*, volume 33 of *NATO Science for Peace and Security Series D: Information and Communication Security*, pages 152–181. IOS Press, 2012. Summer School Marktoberdorf 2011 lecture notes.

[9] K. R. M. Leino. Dafny: An automatic program verifier for functional correctness. In E. M. Clarke and A. Voronkov, editors, *LPAR-16*, volume 6355 of *LNCS*, pages 348–370. Springer, Apr. 2010.

[10] C. Morgan. *Programming from Specifications*. Series in Computer Science. Prentice-Hall International, 1990.

[11] J. T. Schwartz, R. B. K. Dewar, E. Dubinsky, and E. Schonberg. *Programming with Sets: An Introduction to SETL*. Texts and Monographs in Computer Science. Springer, 1986.

[12] N. Wirth. Program Development by Stepwise Refinement. *Commun. ACM*, 14:221–227, 1971.

Go at Google

Rob Pike

Google, Inc.
Mountain View, California, USA
r@google.com

Abstract

The Go programming language was conceived in late 2007 as an answer to some of the problems we were seeing developing software infrastructure at Google. The computing landscape today is almost unrelated to the environment in which the languages being used, mostly C++, Java, and Python, had been created. The problems introduced by multicore processors, networked systems, massive computation clusters, and the web programming model were being worked around rather than addressed head-on. Moreover, the scale has changed: today's server programs comprise tens of millions of lines of code, are worked on by hundreds or even thousands of programmers, and are updated literally every day. To make matters worse, build times, even on large compilation clusters, have stretched to many minutes, even hours.

Go was designed and developed to make working in this environment more productive. Besides its better-known aspects such as built-in concurrency and garbage collection, Go's design considerations include rigorous dependency management, the adaptability of software architecture as systems grow, and robustness across the boundaries between components.

This talk will explain how these issues were addressed while building an efficient, compiled programming language that feels lightweight and pleasant. Examples and explanations will be taken from the real-world problems faced at Google.

Categories and Subject Descriptors   D3.3 [*Programming Languages*]: Language Constructs and Features

General Terms   Design, Languages

Keywords   *Composition, Concurrency, Go, Programming in the large.*

1. Biography

Rob Pike is a Distinguished Engineer at Google, Inc. He works on distributed systems, data mining, programming languages, and software development tools. Most recently he has been a co-designer and developer of the Go programming language. Before Google, Rob was a member of the Computing Sciences Research Center at Bell Labs, the lab that developed Unix. While there, he worked on computer graphics, user interfaces, languages, concurrent programming, and distributed systems. He was an architect of the Plan 9 and Inferno operating systems and is the co-author with Brian Kernighan of The Unix Programming Environment and The Practice of Programming. Other details of his life appear on line but vary in veracity.

Reflections on Reflection

James O. Coplien

Gertrud & Cope
cope@gertrudandcope.com

Abstract

Though it usually makes its appearance only as a footnote in the broader discourse of object design, reflection is a recurring and sometimes noisily divisive topic in object-orientation. Glimmers of reflection pervade even the darkest corners of the tapestry of object orientation's history. In fact, the broader notion of code's self-knowledge, such as run-time method dispatch, goes to the heart of what differentiates objects from other paradigms.

Object orientation, at its roots, was about people and human mental models. It is impossible to make serious headway in these models without reasoning about the system outside of its simple imperative expression. By analogy, the silent movie era of film held that by removing speech, the media of film could both appeal to broader audiences and to tap into the broader human universals that speech obfuscates.

Programs are the silent films that connect much of humanity today. The silent experience plays out at the screen; the Internet is the deep hardware on which it runs, and our software illuminates and articulates the connections between them. To make software fulfil any social agenda of human problem-solving requires a link between the reflections of the individual and those of the software; to rise to social phenomena requires a computational model that accommodates reflection at the social and societal layers.

The DCI (Data, Context, and Interaction) paradigm provides a world model whose reflection allows program structure to shift with the dynamics in the context of application while featuring new ways to clearly present program structure to faithfully capture end-user mental models of uses cases and data. DCI and other recent post-modern approaches offer breakthroughs that raise reflection to its proper place as a first-class programming concern.

Categories and Subject Descriptors C.0 [**System Application Architecture**]

General Terms Algorithms, Design, Human Factors, Languages, Theory, Verification.

Keywords DCI; aspect-oriented programming; reflection; object-oriented programming; use case; silent movies; social discourse.

1. The Vision

For me, the high point of the past 27 years of OOPSLA was Dave Thomas' (originally Jerry Archibald's) tutorial on "The behavior of behavior" at OOPSLA '91. George Bosworth, Adele Goldberg and other notables interjected key technical and historic insights during the talk. The talk was an example of the potential of reflection to accomplish great work with little effort, but the very "gee-whiz" timbre of the talk revealed its arcane nature. In fact reflection has had difficulty gaining a footing over the years, due in large part to a lack of understanding of how to constrain it.

We can better appreciate the need for through its namesake in the human domain, and use that understanding to create better apologies for reflection and better-tuned computational models for its application. In this talk I will show that reflection is crucially fundamental to the success of any program that enjoys use in a human context, and will suggest ways in which technology can smooth the way to better reflection in design and programming.

2. Meta is fundamental

The object vision of programming is rooted in a belief that we can go beyond formal logic to tap into human cognition, while the trappings of polymorphism and encapsulation are largely derived afterthoughts from software engineering. If we want programming languages to support human endeavour, we must revisit and reflect on how we think. Human discourse unfolds along ever deepening, alternating layers of extemporization and reflection. To communicate literally, while excising the contextual underpinnings, is not to communicate effectively. The silent movie era of film was in fact rooted in a belief that pictures opened a rich interchange that could tap into the broader human contexts that speech obfuscates, with no lesser aspiration than to head off what ultimately became World War I [7]. Written scripts underpinned the unspoken scenes; the scripts built on timeless human concerns.

Programs are the silent films that connect much of humanity today. The silent experience plays out at the screen; the Internet is the deep hardware on which it runs, and our software illuminates and articulates the connections between them. To make software fulfil any social agenda of human problem solving requires a link between the reflections of the individual and those of the software; to rise to social phenomena requires a computational model that accommodates reflection at the social and societal layers.

Hofstadter's *Gödel-Escher-Bach* [1] playfully makes a strong argument that having a concept of self is the essence of intelligence. Individual objects can represent information as data, and can interpret that data in their methods. But intelligence is more than knowledge. We need a computational model that lifts us above semantics and epistemology into hermeneutics: the ability to reason. That means reflection at the level of network computation: connections *between* objects. This doesn't mean the kind of unconstrained reflection that gave it a reputation as a "dangerous" technique, or the kinds of surprises one finds with Aspects [2]. We need a computational model whose code self-organizes around mental models. That's roughly how objects started. [3]

Human beings of all sorts figure into this issue. I as a programmer must reflect more about the interaction between users and their program and less about my interaction with the program or about the end user's interaction with me during requirements. Agile is about the latter and user experience (UX) work is about the former. Reflection is about all three together, but we have matured to deal with these issues only pair-wise.

This view of system construction implies that "going meta" is not an option, or a distraction, or a deferrable phase. Meta is where it starts. Meta provides the foundation on which non-meta stands. We need to move beyond program semantics to epistemology — a theory of knowledge — and interpretive hermeneutics. We need the meaning of meaning; the behaviour of behaviour.

Aspects were one noble attempt to open the dialog on reflection and to move away from the imperative expression of program logic to more conceptual building blocks. As has been described elsewhere, this reflects a shift from the modern school of thought to a more post-modern framework. However, Aspects were based on overly find units of behaviour, focusing on class-granularity features instead of use cases. And they create serious challenges for comprehensibility of the program flow at that.

3. Reflection and the Programming Model

Reflection is to program dynamics as architecture is to program statics. There has classically been strong focus on the design of the source structure of an object-oriented program: choosing the right classes (CRC cards, designing class hierarchies) and capturing them in the code. Most object-oriented programming languages focus on classes as their primary building block. Most object testing regimens claim to focus on testing individual classes (though the actually just test class methods).

Object-oriented programmers have long held similar models, knowing that there are general recurring properties that recur place-wise in multiple enactments of business and social transactions. Base classes have traditionally served as the home for such recurring business logic. Programmers also know that no two enactments ensue in exactly the same way. While the general form of the use case may be formalizable in closed form, its details cannot. Designers and programmers represent those details as different values in the objects involved in the computation. Some variants can best be understood by structuring the data different or by adding data values, as an investment account is different than a deposit account in the presence of an interest value. Programmers organize these data differences using classes, and organize them as hierarchies. Method specialization has followed, happily building on the basic programming language facilities for structuring data variations through inheritance, to express method variations using the same mechanism.

No one talks about the dynamics of object relationships. No one designs objects. Use cases rarely survive beyond analysis: their identity disappears, scattered across the network of interacting objects. If they are not explicit in the code you cannot understand them from the code. Class method design is difficult because the code of one class's methods cannot be cognisant of the method it may invoke in another class: Dynamic object bindings and polymorphism, which try to compensate for an overly complex source code structure, make this impossible.

The polymorphism of Smalltalk, C++, .Net, and Objective-C today implement an impoverished kind of reflection that is more general than is necessary. It is reminiscent of the early visions of reflection as "a dangerous technique" in the spirit of changing class Behavior or re-wiring the virtual machine of a symbolic language. This leads to a paradox between accidental complexity of unconstrained rebindings and overly restrictive coupling between program use cases and data. We want the program to be able to reason about itself in a way that reflects how end users think about the program. Today's code reflects a static worldview that strips out on much of the end user model of the workflow, and attempts to compensate for it by dynamically dispatching methods on classes that the language forces to be designed in isolation, without regard for the interactions between them.

3.1 DCI

DCI, which Trygve Reenskaug and myself have been developing over the past ten years, provides a model of reflection that allows the program to create a new set of program structures for each new use case enactment, while capturing the common recurring rhythms of both system behaviours and of recurring data configurations. Regarding the latter, DCI still has classes, but they are reduced to managing the way the computer represents information in storage. DCI gives system activities full first-class standing as algorithms, expressed in terms of the roles [5] involved in a use case. Each use case lives within another programming construct called a Context. Program interactions always take place in the context of some configuration of social actors, and the Context is the locus of that aspect of the human mental model.

The Context is the main unit of reflection. A Context corresponds to a use case, whose roles it encapsulates. For each use case enactment it changes the program structure to create a network of objects suitable to carry out the use case. All the same, those aspects of structure that are static in the end user mental model — such as the use case itself — remain static in DCI code and statically can be reasoned about in during program construction.

By adding this form of structured reflection to the computational model, we slice the program dynamics so the code clearly expresses the use case structure. Paradoxically, this selective reflection greatly aids code comprehensibility. The use case becomes a primary structure in its own right, with the data class structure another. Compile-time inheritance forces use cases to be split across class layers whose run-time dynamics cannot be reasoned about in the code. DCI's reflection gives the behavioural part its own expression apart from the data structure.

4. Conclusion

Reflection has had a checkered history as a technique in its own right, though by definition every OO program expresses some form of it. Reflection has stumbled and struggled for a lack of discipline and for a lack of concern for human mental models, and for the difficult task of tying together the triangle of relationships between the programmer, the end user, and the program.

Many thanks to Thore Bjørnvig and Trygve Reenskaug.

References

[1] Hofstadter, Douglas. Gödel-Escher-Bach: An eternal golden braid. Basic Books (1979).

[2] Kiczales, Gregor. Et al. "An overview of AspectJ." Proceedings of ECOOP (2001).

[3] Kay, Alan. "The Early History of Smalltalk." http://gagne.homedns.org/~tgagne/contrib/EarlyHistoryST.html (2007).

[4] Reenskaug, Trygve. http://heim.ifi.uio.no/~trygver/1979/mvc-1/1979-05-MVC.pdf (1978)

[5] Reenskaug, Trygve. Working with objects: The OORAM Software Engineering Method. Prentice-Hall (1996).

[6] Coplien, James, and Bjørnvig, Gertrud. Lean Architecture for Agile Software Development. Wiley, 2010.

[7] Bjørnvig, Thore. The Holy Grail of Outer Space: Pluralism, Druidry, and the Religion of Cinema in *The Sky Ship*. In *Astrobiology*, October 2012, http://www.liebertpub.com/ast.

Welcome Message from the Demonstrations Chair

TUCSON, ARIZONA | OCTOBER 19-26, 2012

Welcome to the SPLASH 2012 Demonstrations track. We all know that it's better to see something once than to hear about it a hundred times. Live demonstrations show the impact of software innovation in a dynamic and highly interactive setting. This track is an excellent opportunity for companies and universities to share their latest work with an experienced and technically savvy audience – you.

We have received many interesting and diverse demonstration submissions from both industry and academia, and have compiled an exciting demonstration program consisting of tools, applications, and languages in various stages of development – from prototypes and proofs of concept to mature tools and systems. Each of them contains interesting and relevant technology and should appeal to the SPLASH community.

These demonstrations are not product sales pitches, but rather an opportunity for the authors to highlight, explain, and present interesting technical aspects of running applications. The sessions are intended to be two-way interactions with the audience, which has the opportunity to share ideas, interact with the authors in a small scale venue, and learn techniques used in developing innovative and high quality software. Presenters are encouraged to actively solicit feedback from the audience, which should lead to very interesting and entertaining demonstration sessions.

I would like to thank this year's demonstration presenters for their hard work in bringing live demonstrations to SPLASH 2012. I am also grateful to this year's demonstrations subcommittee for their efforts to shape the 2012 demonstrations program.

Demonstrations Committee Members:
Filip Pizlo (Apple)
Michael Ernst (University of Washington)
Nathaniel Nystrom (University of Lugano

Igor Peshansky
Google
demos@splashcon.org

Truffle: A Self-Optimizing Runtime System

Christian Wimmer   Thomas Würthinger

Oracle Labs

christian.wimmer@oracle.com   thomas.wuerthinger@oracle.com

Abstract

We present Truffle, a novel framework for implementing managed languages in Java™. The language implementer writes an AST interpreter, which is integrated in our framework that allows tree rewriting during AST interpretation. Tree rewrites incorporate type feedback and other profiling information into the tree, thus specializing the tree and augmenting it with run-time information. When the tree reaches a stable state, partial evaluation compiles the tree into optimized machine code. The partial evaluation is done by Graal, the just-in-time compiler of our Java VM (a variation of the Java HotSpot VM). To show that Truffle supports a variety of programming language paradigms, we present prototype implementations of JavaScript (a dynamically typed programming language) and J (an array programming language).

Categories and Subject Descriptors   D.3.4 [*Programming Languages*]: Processors—Run-time environments, Optimization

General Terms   Algorithms, Languages, Performance

Keywords   Java, JavaScript, J, Truffle, Graal, dynamic languages, virtual machine, language implementation

1. Introduction

An abstract syntax tree (AST) interpreter is a simple and natural way to implement a programming language. However, it is usually also considered the slowest approach because of the high overhead of virtual method dispatch. Language implementers therefore define bytecodes to speed up interpretation, followed by a just-in-time compiler that is needed to reach excellent peak performance. In addition, a high-performance garbage collector is necessary for automatic memory management, together with a runtime system to form a complete virtual machine (VM) The algorithms for all these components are well known. However, VM code is rarely reused when implementing a VM for a new language. This makes the process of developing new high-performance languages expensive and tedious.

Truffle is a novel approach to implement AST interpreters in which the syntax tree is modified during interpretation to incorporate type feedback [5]. This tree rewriting is a general and powerful mechanism to optimize many constructs common in dynamic programming languages. Our system is implemented in Java and uses the static typing and primitive data types of Java elegantly to avoid a boxed representation of primitive values in dynamic programming languages.

The just-in-time (JIT) compiler of our Java VM, named Graal [3], is extensible and accessible from the AST interpreter. The Truffle compilation system uses Graal on top of the Java HotSpot VM to create optimized machine code snippets for parts of a Truffle AST. The main idea is to exploit that the AST changes rarely after it has reached a stable state. We use partial evaluation and assume that the current AST node structure remains constant. We inline the `execute` methods of all AST nodes into one big compilation unit. This compilation unit is then optimized by Graal. If there is a control path that would change the Truffle AST, we remove it from the compiled code and instead replace it with a runtime call that triggers deoptimization [2], i.e., the optimized machine code is discarded and execution continues in the AST interpreter. This way, we are able to create optimized machine code for a Truffle sub-tree that only contains the fast path for every node. This results in an executable version of the sub-tree that is valid as long as no AST rewriting needs to be performed. Such rewriting should be relatively rare as an AST will only be scheduled for optimization when profiling indicates that it is stable.

The source code of our system is available as open source from [3].

2. Related Work

The system most closely related to Truffle is PyPy [4]. Truffle shares with PyPy the main mission: automatically deriving an efficient implementation of a language by using an interpreter of that language written in a statically typed language. The difference between PyPy and Truffle is that PyPy uses a trace-based JIT compiler [1], while Truffle uses a traditional method-based JIT compiler. Because of the dynamic AST replacements in Truffle, we can leverage the best of a trace compiler, i.e., only compiling the specialized fast paths, while at the same time avoiding many of the problems of trace compilers, e.g., handling or recursive method calls, complications from trace tree merging to avoid code explosion, or trace recording overhead.

3. Demonstration Outline

- Motivation for a modular language framework and re-use of VM components.
- System architecture: Truffle runs on the Graal VM, a modified version of the Java HotSpot VM with the Graal JIT compiler. We present the basic architecture of Graal.
- Overview of Truffle: core classes that form the AST and the framework for AST rewriting.
- AST interpreter cookbook: implementation of an AST interpreter for a simple language. We will implement a language and integrate it with the Truffle framework to get a high-performance implementation of this language.
- Overview of the existing language implementations that are under development: JavaScript (a dynamically typed programming language) and J (an array programming language).

4. Presenters

Christian Wimmer is a researcher at Oracle Labs, working on the Maxine VM, the Graal compiler, the Truffle dynamic language infrastructure, as well as on other projects that involve dynamic compilation and optimizations. His research interests span from compilers, virtual machines, and secure systems to component-based software architectures. He received a Dr. techn. degree in Computer Science (advisor: Prof. Hanspeter Mössenböck) and a Dipl.-Ing. degree in Computer Science, both from the Johannes Kepler University Linz, Austria. Before the time at Oracle, he was a postdoctoral researcher at the Department of Computer Science of the University of California, Irvine, working with Prof. Michael Franz.

Thomas Würthinger is a researcher at Oracle Labs in Austria. He works on the Graal compiler, the Truffle dy-

namic language infrastructure, and other projects in the area of virtual machines. His research interests include compilers, virtual machines, and graph visualization. He received a Dr. techn. degree in Computer Science (advisor: Prof. Hanspeter Mössenböck) and a Dipl.-Ing. degree in Computer Science, both from the Johannes Kepler University Linz, Austria.

Acknowledgments

Truffle and Graal would not be possible without the efforts of our academic collaborators, especially the Institute for System Software at the Johannes Kepler University Linz. We would also like to thank all members of the Virtual Machine Research Group at Oracle Labs for their support and contributions.

Oracle and Java are registered trademarks of Oracle and/or its affiliates. Other names may be trademarks of their respective owners.

References

[1] C. F. Bolz, A. Cuni, M. Fijałkowski, and A. Rigo. Tracing the meta-level: PyPy's tracing JIT compiler. In *Proceedings of the Workshop on the Implementation, Compilation, Optimization of Object-Oriented Languages and Programming Systems*, pages 18–25. ACM Press, 2009. doi: 10.1145/1565824.1565827.

[2] U. Hölzle, C. Chambers, and D. Ungar. Debugging optimized code with dynamic deoptimization. In *Proceedings of the ACM SIGPLAN Conference on Programming Language Design and Implementation*, pages 32–43. ACM Press, 1992. doi: 10.1145/143095.143114.

[3] Oracle. OpenJDK: Graal project, 2012. URL http://openjdk.java.net/projects/graal/.

[4] A. Rigo and S. Pedroni. PyPy's approach to virtual machine construction. In *Companion to the ACM SIGPLAN Conference on Object Oriented Programming Systems, Languages, and Applications*, pages 944–953. ACM Press, 2006. doi: 10.1145/1176617.1176753.

[5] T. Würthinger, A. Wöss, L. Stadler, G. Duboscq, D. Simon, and C. Wimmer. Self-optimizing AST interpreters. In *Proceedings of the Dynamic Languages Symposium*. ACM Press, 2012.

A Semantic Integrated Development Environment

Francesco Logozzo, Michael Barnett,
Manuel Fändrich

Microsoft Research
{logozzo, mbarnett, maf}@microsoft.com

Patrick Cousot

ENS, CNRS, INRIA, NYU
pcousot@cims.nyu.edu

Radhia Cousot

CNRS, ENS, INRIA
rcousot@ens.fr

Abstract

We present SIDE, a Semantic Integrated Development Environment. SIDE uses static analysis to enrich existing IDE features and also adds new features. It augments the way existing compilers find syntactic errors — in real time, as the programmer is writing code without execution — by also finding semantic errors, e.g., arithmetic expressions that may overflow. If it finds an error, it suggests a repair in the form of code — e.g., providing an equivalent yet non-overflowing expression. Repairs are correct by construction. SIDE also enhances code refactoring (by suggesting precise yet general contracts), code review (by answering what-if questions), and code searching (by answering questions like "find all the callers where $x < y$").

SIDE is built on the top of CodeContracts and the Roslyn CTP. CodeContracts provide a lightweight and programmer-friendly specification language. SIDE uses the abstract interpretation-based CodeContracts static checker (cccheck/ Clousot) to obtain a deep semantic understanding of what the program does.

Categories and Subject Descriptors D. Software [*D.3 Programmimg Languages*]: D.3.3 Language Constructs and Features; F. Theory of Computation [*F.3 Logics and meanings of Programs*]: F.3.1 Specifying and Verifying and Reasoning about Programs, F.3.2 Semantics of Programming Languages; I. Computing Methodologies [*I.2 Artificial Intelligence*]: I.2.2 Automatic Programming

General Terms Design, Documentation, Experimentation, Human Factors, Languages, Reliability, Verification.

Keywords Abstract interpretation, Design by contract, Integrated Development Enviroment, Method extraction, Program Repair, Program transformation, Refactoring, Static analysis

1. Introduction

Integrated Development Environments (IDEs) provide a cohesive view of the software development environment in which many tools are unified under a common and uniform user interface. The ultimate goal of an IDE is to assist and improve programmer productivity by simplyfing and rationalizing program development. Routinely, IDEs include a source editor, build automation tools, debuggers and profilers. Modern IDEs, like Eclipse or Visual Studio, provide additional functionalities like real-time compilation, type checking, IntelliSense, refactoring, class browsers, quick fixes for *compile-time* errors, *etc*. Existing IDEs have only a very partial and *syntactical* understanding of the program. We believe that in order to provide further value to the programmer the IDEs should get a deeper, more *semantic* understanding of what the program does. In the demo we show a working prototype of a Semantic Integrated Development Environment (SIDE).

2. SIDE

SIDE is a smart programmer assistant. It statically analyzes the program in real time, while the programmer is developing it. Unlike similar program verification tools, our static analysis infers loop invariants, significantly reducing the annotation burden. The information gathered by the static analysis is used to verify the absence of common *runtime* errors (*e.g.*, division by zero, arithmetic overflows, null pointer exceptions, and buffer overruns) as well as user-provided assertions and contracts [1].

If SIDE detects a potential runtime error, it suggests a fix in the form of code. The suggested fix is valid in that it guarantees that no good execution is removed: only bad ones are [7]. Since the fix is based on a static analysis, SIDE can suggest fixes for partial or even syntactically incorrect programs. No test runs are needed. Examples of fixes include object and constant initializations, arithmetic overflows, array indexing, wrong guards, missing contracts — *e.g.*, preconditions [4].

SIDE helps the programmer in other common tasks, such as refactoring. For instance, when the programmer extracts a method, SIDE proposes a contract (precondition, postcondition) for the extracted method [5]. The proposed contract is valid, safe, complete, and general. In particular, completeness implies that the contract is precise (strong) enough to carry on the proof in the method from which the code was extracted. Generality guarantees that the contract can be called from other calling contexts *i.e.*, it does not just project of the state of the analyzer, which encodes the local context of the extracted method.

SIDE exploits the inferred semantic information to answer non-trivial queries on the program execution. For instance, SIDE supports *what-if* scenarios: The programmer adds extra-assumptions on the program state at some points and then she asks, *e.g.*, if some program point is reachable, or a certain property holds. The assumption and the queries are arbitrary Boolean expressions in the target language. SIDE enables semantic search, too. The programmer can ask if a certain method is invoked in a certain state. Examples of semantic searches are callers such that: $x \neq null$, $a.f > b.c + 1$, or a Boolean combination thereof. Overall, the semantic queries targets common scenarios in the code-reviewing phases.

3. The Architecture

Our target language is C# or VB, the two most popular .NET languages. We implemented SIDE on the top of the Roslyn CTP and of CodeContracts. The Roslyn CTP exposes the VB and C# compilers as services. We leverage Roslyn for the user interaction, *e.g.*, the squiggles for warnings and the previews for applying fixes, as well as to get basic services as "standard" refactoring. We use the CodeContracts API as the specification language for the preconditions, postconditions and object invariants. The CodeContracts API is a standard part of .NET. The CodeContracts static checker (cccheck [6]) is the underlying semantic inference and reasoning engine for SIDE. cccheck is a static analyzer based on abstract interpretation [3]. To enable real-time analysis, cccheck drawes on a SQL database to cache the analysis results, so that unmodified code is not re-analyzed. CodeContracts has been publically available for 3 years and has been downloaded more than 60,000 times.

4. The Demo

We show how SIDE acts as a smart programmer assistant, quickly catching tricky bugs, explaining them, and proposing fixes. In particular we show how the interaction is very natural for the user, despite the complex analyses and reasoning performed underneath.

In the first part of the demo, we code an Insert method, which inserts an element into a list represented as an array. SIDE points out several errors in a trivial implementation (a buffer overrun and a null dereference) and it proposes some preconditions to fix them. Then we add some code to resize the array when an insertion into a full array occurs. SIDE points out that the new code is unreached. Once the bug is

fixed, it finds some other weaknesses in the code: an arithmetic overflow and a buffer overrun. In both cases it suggests a code repair — actually more than one: we will see and discuss in the demo that there are several different ways of fixing a program. In the case of the buffer overrun, we use the query system of SIDE to understand the origin of the warning ("*what happens when ...*"). Then we apply one of the (non-trivial) fixes proposed by SIDE. Finally, we realize that the code for resizing is more general than the usage made in the Insert body. Therefore we decide to refactor it into a new method. SIDE generates a new method, Resize, and the corresponding contracts. In particular: (i) the inferred precondition is more general than the simple projection of the original abstract state, enabling more calling contexts; (ii) the inferred postcondition is strong enough to ensure the safety in the refactored Insert method, *i.e.*, no imprecision is introduced by the assume/guarantee reasoning. We conclude this part of the demo by asking SIDE some semantic queries (*e.g.*, "*which callers insert an empty string into the list?*").

In the second part of the demo, we consider a slightly more complicated example, a buggy implementation of the binary search algorithm. Discovering the bug(s) and presenting the fixes require the analysis to perform complex reasoning, *e.g.*, inferring a complex loop invariant. However, we will show how all this machinery is totally transparent to the user. For instance we show how SIDE naturally suggests a (verified!) repair for the famous Java arithmetic overflow bug [2].

5. Presenters

F. Logozzo is a researcher in the RiSE group at MSR Redmond. He is the co-author of the CodeContracts static checker and of SIDE. His main interests are abstract interpretation, program analysis, optimization, and verification.

References.

[1] M. Barnett, M. Fähndrich, and F. Logozzo. Embedded contract languages. In *SAC'10*, pages 2103–2110. ACM, 2010.

[2] J. Bloch. Nearly all binary searches and mergesorts are broken, 2008. http://googleresearch.blogspot.com/2006/06/extra-extra-read-all-about-it-nearly.html.

[3] P. Cousot and R. Cousot. Abstract interpretation: a unified lattice model for static analysis of programs by construction or approximation of fixpoints. In *POPL*, pages 238–252, 1977.

[4] P. Cousot, R. Cousot, and F. Logozzo. Contract precondition inference from intermittent assertions on collections. In *VMCAI*, pages 150–168, 2011.

[5] P. Cousot, R. Cousot, F. Logozzo, and M. Barnett. An abstract interpretation framework for refactoring with application to extract methods with contracts. In *OOPSLA*, 2012.

[6] M. Fähndrich and F. Logozzo. Static contract checking with abstract interpretation. In *FoVeOOS*, pages 10–30, 2010.

[7] F. Logozzo and T. Ball. Modular and verified repairs. In *OOPSLA*, 2012.

The Storyteller Version Control System
Tackling Version Control, Code Comments, and Team Learning

Mark Mahoney

Carthage College
Kenosha, WI
mmahoney@carthage.edu

Abstract

This demonstration shows the Storyteller version control system. The tool aims to change the way software developers learn by opening up for examination how they do their work. The tool has traditional version control functionality (branching and merging) but in addition it records how development work is done, organizes it, and allows it to be played back for others. Most importantly, the tool allows developers to tell stories about what they did and why. It captures and organizes institutional knowledge that would otherwise be lost.

Categories and Subject Descriptors D.2.7 [**Software Engineering**]: Distribution, Maintenance, and Enhancement - Documentation, Version Control.

Keywords   software evolution; storytelling

1. Author Biography

Mark Mahoney is the chair of the computer science department at Carthage College in Kenosha, WI. Before that he was a software engineer at Motorola. Dr. Mahoney leads groups of undergraduate researchers examining how to make it easier for software developers to *learn* from their code repositories.

2. Demonstration Proposal

Performing work on a computer is a mostly solitary activity. Because of this, one can generally only reflect on one's own experiences. It is difficult to get inspiration from others. Some people consider developing software to be a craft. Apprentice craftsmen learn by watching and working with more experienced craftsmen. Experienced craftsmen have to be able to tell stories. This is why people become apprentices- to watch, to hear stories, to discuss, and to get feedback from masters. However, because of the nature of our work and the tools we use it is as if we software developers go out of our way to hide how we do our work. In the software development world it is expensive and time consuming for masters to teach others. This tool aims to reduce the cost for developers to teach and learn from each other.

Traditional version control systems, while invaluable for concurrent development, were not built to promote *learning* among a development team. They store snapshots of code. These snapshots cannot easily be animated to tell an interesting story. Moving pictures do a better job of telling a story [3].

Commit logs could help tell a story about the development of a piece of software if developers wrote good commit messages. Unfortunately, they do not. Writing a truly descriptive commit message takes a great deal of effort to recall and describe all the changes made to a set of files in between commits. Most developers are not willing to put in the effort to *animate* the changes using the commit log.

The Storyteller version control system [16], in addition to providing basic branching and merging capabilities, captures textual, change-based software evolution information in order for a developer to create a new type of documentation about program development. The tool was not developed to revolutionize how concurrent development gets done, but to promote *learning* among team members. This learning takes place by truly animating the changes stored in the version control system and then allowing comments to be written about the animation. Others can watch the code being developed along with the comments about its evolution. Developers can point out how they leveraged their good decisions and recovered from the bad ones.

SPLASH'12, October 19–26, 2012, Tucson, Arizona, USA.
ACM 978-1-4503-1563-0/12/10.

This demonstration will show the tool being used with an Eclipse IDE plug-in. The tool records all the changes made and the order they were made in. With this information one can 'playback' the interesting parts of a coding session so a developer can tell a *story* about how their code was created. These stories form a new type of program documentation that can be viewed by team members to learn about the systems they are working on and how to become better developers.

Next, the evolution of a more significant chunk of source code will be played back. A complex narrative about the evolution will be created and recorded. The comments recorded in the story are context sensitive in the sense that they can be used to describe a series of programming decisions related to each other that span many files. It is more likely that important institutional knowledge will make it in these stories than in source code comments. This is the type of information that usually stays in our heads for a little while but eventually escapes or walks out the door.

This tool was designed to preserve the order that changes are made in a repository. These orderings are lost using traditional line-oriented, delta-based version control systems. This is similar to the difference between a sorted and unsorted phone book. Even though both contain the same information one is more valuable than the other.

3. Related Work

Software evolution research has been done to statistically analyze systems to predict future changes in related sections of code [1][2][10][11]. The work described in this paper is related to change-based software evolution [5][6][7][8][9]. In these works, information is stored about changes to a program's abstract syntax tree. The approach used in the tool being described in this paper is text based. The problems with relying on a program's abstract syntax tree are that the tools are programming language and paradigm dependent. Further, the tools can only be used on source code. Non-source code documents, like specification documents, design documents, and web pages also have interesting histories.

There have been some examples of visualizing historical information gathered from version control systems. The Code Swarm project [13][4] shows the history of commits in a version control system. Developers and files are represented as moving elements. When a developer commits a file, it lights up and flies towards that developer.

There are commercial editors that store and replay all keystrokes [12][14][15], however, they do not offer the same level of filtering options nor record comments associated with the evolution of the edits.

4. Conclusion

The demonstration will show a working tool that provides version control functionality, but in addition allows developers to replay their work and create narratives about it. These narratives are often more valuable than code comments alone since they are in context of how the code was created. The most important aspect of the tool is that team members can learn from each other about the systems they work on and how to become better developers. The tool reduces the cost and effort for team members to teach their peers.

References

[1] Gall, H., Hajek, K., Jazayeri, M. Detection of Logical Coupling Based on Product Release History. In Proceedings of the International Conference on Software Maintenance 1998.

[2] Gall, H. Jazayeri, M., Klosch, R., Trausmuth, G. Software evolution observations based on product release history. In Proceedings International Conference on Software Maintenance (ICSM'97), pages 160–166, Los Alamitos CA, 1997.

[3] Mahoney, M., "Software Evolution and the Moving Picture Metaphor", Onward! Conference Co-located with OOPSLA '09, Orlando, FL October 2009.

[4] Ogawa, M., Kwan-Liu Ma. code_swarm: A Design Study in Organic Software Visualization. In Proceedings of the IEEE Information Visualization Conference October, 2009.

[5] Robbes, R., Lanza, M. A Change-based Approach to Software Evolution. Electronic Notes in Theoretical Computer Science (ENTCS) archive Volume 166, January, 2007.

[6] Robbes, R., Lanza, M. SpyWare: a change-aware development tool-set. ICSE '08 Proceedings of the 30th international conference on Software engineering ACM New York, NY, USA 2008.

[7] Robbes, R., Lanza, M. Versioning Systems for Evolution Research. In Proceedings of IWPSE 2005, pp 155-164. 2005.

[8] Robbes, R., Lanza, M. Towards Change-aware Development Tools. Tech Report, University of Lugano, 2008.

[9] Sharon, Y., EclipsEye - Spying on Eclipse. Bachelor Project University of Lugano, 2007.

[10] Zimmermann, T., Sunghun Kim, Whitehead Jr., E. J., Zeller, A. Mining Version Archives for Co-changed Lines. Proc. of the Third International Workshop on Mining Software Repositories, pp 72-75, May 2006.

[11] Zimmermann, T., Weißgerber, P., Diehl, S., Zeller, A. Mining version histories to guide software changes. in ICSE. IEEE Computer Society, 2004, pp. 563–572.

[12] https://www.stypi.com/

[13] http://vis.cs.ucdavis.edu/~ogawa/codeswarm/

[14] http://etherpad.com/

[15] http://docs.google.com

[16] http://www.storytellersoftware.com

The ALIA4J Approach to Efficient Language Implementation

Christoph Bockisch

Software Engineering group
University of Twente
P.O. Box 217, 7500 AE Enschede, the
Netherlands
c.m.bockisch@cs.utwente.nl

Andreas Sewe

Software Technology group
Technische Universität Darmstadt
Hochschulstr. 10, 64289 Darmstadt, Germany
sewe@st.informatik.tu-darmstadt.de

Abstract

New programming languages are frequently designed to improve upon other languages or to simplify programs through domain-specific abstractions. They are often implemented as transformations to an established (intermediate) language (IL). But while many new languages overlap in the semantics of their core concepts, re-using the corresponding transformations is limited by existing compiler implementation frameworks. In the ALIA4J approach, we have identified *dispatching* as fundamental to most abstraction mechanisms and provide a meta-model of dispatching as a rich, extensible IL. Based on this meta-model, the semantics of new atomic language concepts can be implemented in a modular and portable fashion. For the execution of the IL, we provide both platform-independent and platform-dependent Java Virtual Machine extensions, the latter of which allows the modular implementation of machine code optimizations.

In this demo, participants get an overview of advanced dispatching and the ALIA4J approach. By the example of a language for text-based adventure games, they will see the usage of ALIA4J as back-end for a language developed in a modern Language Workbench. Finally, the implementation of new atomic language concepts and their optimization is demonstrated.

Categories and Subject Descriptors D.3.4 [*Programming Languages*]: Processors—Run-time environments

Keywords Advanced dispatching, language implementation, modular optimization

SPLASH'12, October 19–26, 2012, Tucson, Arizona, USA.
ACM 978-1-4503-1563-0/12/10.

1. The Demonstrated Technology

Addressed Problems Typically, implementations of new languages build on the back-ends of established languages, re-using the implementation of the concepts native to that intermediate language. But not all concepts of the new languages map directly to the established intermediate language (e.g., Java bytecode), which was tailored to a different source language (e.g., Java). This task is further complicated when one element in the source program affects the behavior of multiple elements in the intermediate representation (requiring so-called local-to-global transformations).

Compiler frameworks assist in generating low-level code, and even enable to re-use non-trivial code generation logic. Open compilers for aspect-oriented languages, such as the AspectBench Compiler even support modularizing local-to-global transformations. But these technologies require the new language to be a syntactic extension of an existing one. Moreover, the knowledge about the source language concepts is lost during the transformation and cannot, e.g., drive specific virtual-machine-level optimizations.

Technology of Our Solution The ALIA4J[1] architecture realizes our approach to implementing programming languages with advanced dispatching. At its core sits a meta-model of advanced dispatching declarations, called LIAM, and a framework for execution environments that handle these declarations, called FIAL. LIAM hereby defines a *language-independent meta-model* of atomic concepts relevant for dispatching. For example, dispatch may be ruled by predicates which depend on values in the dynamic context of the dispatch. When mapping the concrete advanced-dispatching concepts of an actual programming language to it, LIAM either has to be *refined* with the *language-specific* semantics or suitable,

---

[1] The Advanced-dispatching Language Implementation Architecture for Java. See http://www.alia4j.org/.

existing refinements have to be re-used. The dispatch declarations defined in terms of this meta-model, are partially evaluated by the FIAL framework and automatically re-written into an execution model for the dispatch sites in the program.

Uniqueness in Design and Implementation In ALIA4J, there are three ways of modularly implementing a meta-model refinement (and as such an atomic language concept): (1) The most abstract way is implementing a plain Java method that realizes the semantics of an atomic language concept through *interpretation*. This allows easy experimentation and is targeted at designers of the semantics of language concepts. (2) Control over the generated code is gained by implementing a Java method that compiles the concept to *Java bytecode*, allowing context-dependent bytecode generation; this allows language implementers to improve runtime performance in a portable way. (3) The most control is gained by implementing a method that compiles the concept to *machine code*. While losing platform-independence, this allows to achieve optimal runtime performance.

Interesting Details The STEAMLOOM^{ALIA} JVM extension, which enables the machine code optimization, is an extension of the Jikes Research VM (RVM), a high-performance Java VM. It can bypass bytecode generation for LIAM entities to directly generate native machine code for them, using the two JIT compilers of the Jikes RVM, the baseline compiler and the optimizing compiler. The generation can access all VM internals and rich information about the generation context to produce the most specific machine code.

The implementation of a concept's semantics *and* optimization is modular. Implementations of different strategies can even co-exist; the best strategy is picked at runtime. This is very useful to implementers of optimizations who can use the—less efficient but by definition correct—implementation produced by the language designer as a test oracle. Overall, we provide re-usable implementations of more than 75 atomic language concepts, the majority of which offers at least bytecode-level optimizations.

We use an extensive integration test suite to assure the high quality of ALIA4J. The integration tests use our intermediate representation as interface; thus, all FIAL-based JVM extensions are subject to the same test suite which ensures compatibility between different execution environments. Almost all of the 4,083 tests are systematically generated to cover all relevant variations of dispatch sites and LIAM entities. Our build process is fully automated with the Maven build manager and our integration test suite is automatically executed using the Jenkins continuous integration server.

Over the past years, four PhD projects and more than 20 master and bachelor student projects have contributed to ALIA4J. The technologies applied in ALIA4J are presented more than 10 peer-reviewed journal, conference, and workshop papers.

2.   Content of the Demo

The demo contains an explanation of the predicate dispatching and aspect-oriented programming paradigms, which have shaped the ALIA4J approach, followed by an introduction to ALIA4J's meta-model and its execution semantics. By the example of a domain-specific language for defining text-based adventure games, it is demonstrated how an EMFText-based language implementation can use ALIA4J as an execution back-end. The participants will see how the example language is transformed into ALIA4J's intermediate representation by re-using provided atomic language concepts; and how to implement the execution semantics of new, specific language concepts. The concepts will be implemented in a platform-independent, high-level way and supplanted by bytecode and machine code optimizations.

3.   Presenter

Christoph Bockisch is an assistant professor at the University of Twente, the Netherlands. He received his doctoral degree from Technische Universität Darmstadt, Germany in 2008. To provide optimizations of new language mechanisms, Christoph researches extensions to high-performing Java virtual machines based on just-in time compilation. He initiated the ALIA4J project as part of his PhD studies and is now one of two project supervisors and lead programmers. He is co-founder and co-organizer of the workshop series on Virtual Machines and Intermediate Languages (VMIL) and Free Composition (FREECO), both held at the SPLASH conference.

4.   Presentation History

The demo builds on material that has been used in:

- the academic course "Advanced Programming Concepts" (University of Twente, the Netherlands) in 2010/11 and 2011/12,

- the tutorial "Efficient Implementation of Efficient (Domain-Specific) Languages" held at the Brazilian Conference on Software: Theory and Practice (CB-Soft) 2010, and

- the journal paper: C. Bockisch, A. Sewe, H. Yin, M. Mezini, and M. Aksit. An in-depth look at ALIA4J. *Journal of Object Technology*, 11(1):1–28, Apr. 2012.

Upload your Program, Share your Model

Jens Dietrich

Massey University, Palmerston North, New Zealand

j.b.dietrich@massey.ac.nz

Abstract

We demonstrate the Massey Architecture Explorer (MAE), a browser-based application to visualise and analyse the architecture of JVM applications. The MAE extracts a graph-based model from Java byte code, and visualises it using a force directed layout on an HTML5 canvas. A novel scalable algorithm is used to detect architectural antipatterns. The antipatterns detected focus on problems software architects face when trying to refactor applications into OSGi or similar dynamic component models.

A unique feature of this system is that the state of the application is encoded in the URL ("URL memento"). These URLs can be shared and bookmarked, facilitating the sharing of architectural knowledge amongst software engineers.

Categories and Subject Descriptors D.2.8 [*Metrics*]: Complexity measures; D.2.9 [*Management*]: Software quality assurance (SQA); D.2.11 [*Software Architectures*]: Patterns; D.3.3 [*Language Constructs and Features*]: Modules, packages, patterns; E.1 [*Data Structures*]: Graphs and Networks; G.2.2 [*Graph Theory*]: Network problems

Keywords software architecture recovery, software as a service

1. Introduction

There are a number of applications to extract architectural models from Java applications and visualise and analyse these models, including Structure101, Lattix and Sonargraph. These are desktop applications, and lack the ability or scalability to analyse programs for certain types of structural antipatterns which impact on the modularisation of programs, including **subtype knowledge** (a super type uses one of its subtypes, violating the dependency inversion principle), **degenerated inheritance** (the existence of multiple inheritance paths from a subtype to one of its super-

types), **strong circular dependencies between packages and jars** and **abstraction without decoupling** (a class references an abstract type (service description) as well as one of its implementation types (service implementation)). A detailed description of these antipatterns can be found in [2]. These antipatterns are critical when refactoring applications into module systems such as OSGi and its extensions that require the separation of namespaces and abstract and implementation types.

Furthermore, the above-mentioned tools are desktop-based, either as standalone applications or plugins for integrated development environments. The tool presented here is web-based, and has the usual advantages of web based tools such as low cost of maintenance.

The MAE uses the fragment identifier (aka hash part) of the URL to encode application state, similar to the approach used by applications like Gmail. This means that users can use browser navigation and directly bookmark and share these URLs. With these URLs, the application state is transferred, and the user opening this URL gets full access to the model. A URL shortener is used to compact long URLs.

2. Relevance

Firstly, the need for tools like MAE stems from fact that software engineering is becoming a more and more social activity and there is greater need to share modelling artefacts. While the sharing of code artefacts is well-supported through platforms such as github and a new generation of web-based IDEs, there is no adequate support for sharing modelling artefacts. Secondly, the MAE focuses on supporting analysis tasks related to breaking up monolithic applications and refactoring them into dynamic component models such as OSGi. This is a very timely issue, as some of the most complex systems, including the Java Development Kit itself are currently being modularised. Our work is partially motivated by our collaboration with an industry partner from New Zealand facing this very problem.

3. Unique Features

3.1 Navigation Model, Selections and Filters

In general, the number of nodes and edges in the models extracted from programs is large. The *base model* is the graph where the nodes (vertices) represent classes and the edges represent dependencies (extends, implements and uses) between classes. From the base graph, further *derived models* (also called *perspectives*) are computed by means of aggregation - nodes represent aggregated artefacts such as top-level classes, packages, jars and package and class tangles.

The size of these models can be significant. For instance, the base model for JRE 1.6.0_17 contains 11708 vertices and 139362 edges.To visualize graphs of this size is challenging for two reasons. Firstly, the computation of graph layouts is computationally expensive. Secondly, even if the layout can be computed quickly, it is difficult to render large graphs in a way that can convey useful information to the user.

We address this problem by using filters and a selection model. The selection model is based on the idea that the user often analyses only a few artefacts and their dependencies. By selecting previously unselected artefacts (either nodes or edges) in the neighbourhood of currently selected artefacts, the user can navigate through the model. We call this feature *horizontal navigation* as the user stays within the current perspective. *Vertical navigation* is also supported through the OLAP-style *rollup* and *drilldown* functions in the context menus of selected artefacts. These operations preserve selection.

3.2 Mode of Deployment

The use of the tool is very simple: the user just has to upload a jar file containing java byte code, and the model will be built on the server and made available for analysis in a browser session. There is a large number of models pre-built from popular open source programs, including the programs from the Qualitas Corpus v20101126 [3], and several versions of the Java runtime environment.

3.3 Antipattern Detection

Antipattern detection is a special case of the subgraph isomorphism problem that is known to be NP-complete. This makes scalable antipattern detection difficult. MAE uses the novel GUERY graph query engine [1] for this purpose.

3.4 Critical Edge Analysis

Nodes and edges are labelled with several metrics known from software design and network analysis, including the antipattern score proposed in [2]. There are several built-in queries to compute the edges with the highest score. The antipattern score is similar to a number of widely used graph scoring algorithms such as Page Rank and betweenness centrality. But instead of traversing only the shortest paths in the dependency graph, only paths that are part of motifs representing antipatterns are visited while scoring edges.

We have shown that edges with a high score represent high impact refactoring opportunities in our previous work [2]. This means that if these dependencies can be broken (for instance, by using dependency injection, service locators or inlining), the number of structural antipatterns in the program will strongly decrease.

3.5 Tangle Analysis

There are two views ("perspectives") that show strongly connected components (aka tangles) in the class and package graph, respectively. This allows the software engineer where clusters are formed that need refactoring. The computation of tangles is straightforward due to the availability of scalable algorithms and many other architecture recovery tools also feature tangle analysis.

3.6 URL Mementos

The application state is stored in the fragment identifier part of the URL which is continuously updated while the user interacts with the application. We call this feature "URL mementos".

4. Underlying Technologies Used

The MAE is a client-server application. The server is written in Java J2EE (servlets and JSPs) and uses the GUERY library for antipattern detection. GUERY uses an observer based API that produces a result stream. The results are then JSON-encoded and streamed to the client using server-sent events. The computation is done in background threads on the server. This keeps the user interface very interactive and minimises latency - results are usually received and displayed faster than the user can consume (i.e., inspect) them.

5. Techniques Used to Build the Software

The application relies on the features provided by extra libraries that are not available in standard web technology stack, such as modern UI components, list comprehensions, and data structures like maps and sets. The force directed layout implementation of arbor.js is used. To manage the complexity and size of the client-side part of the application, the Google closure component model was used. In this model, JavaScript objects are used as namespaces with managed dependencies. However, this results in many relatively small JavaScript files that slow down application loading. For this reason, the application is designed to run in two different modes - a development (debug) and a deployment mode. When the deployed version is built, these files are merged and compressed. The application was built using the NetBeans and the Chrome IDEs, and hosted on BitBucket.

References

[1] J. Dietrich and C. McCartin. Scalable motif detection and aggregation. In *Proceedings ADC'12*, 2012.

[2] J. Dietrich, C. McCartin, E. Temero, and S. M. A. Shah. On the existence of high-impact refactoring opportunities in programs. In *Proceedings ACSC'12*, 2012.

[3] E. Tempero, C. Anslow, J. Dietrich, T. Han, J. Li, M. Lumpe, H. Melton, and J. Noble. Qualitas corpus: A curated collection of java code for empirical studies. In *Proceedings APSEC'2010*, 2010.

Citisense: Mobile Air Quality Sensing for Individuals and Communities

Celal Ziftci   Nima Nikzad   Nakul Verma   Piero Zappi   Elizabeth Bales   Ingolf Krueger
William Griswold

Department of Computer Science and Engineering, University of California, San Diego
{cziftci,nnikzad,naverma,pzappi,earrowsm,ikrueger,wgg}@cs.ucsd.edu

Abstract

Air quality has great impact on individual and community health. In this demonstration, we present Citisense: a mobile air quality system that enables users to track their personal air quality exposure for discovery, self-reflection, and sharing within their local communities and online social networks.

Categories and Subject Descriptors D.2.11 [*[Sofware Engineering] Software Architectures*]: Service-oriented architecture (SOA)

General Terms Design, Reliability, Security, Human Factors

Keywords ubiquitous systems, air pollution, mobile systems

1. Background

During daily activities, we are exposed to many invisible environmental hazards, such as pollutants from automobile exhaust, ozone, and methane. According to the EPA, in 2007, 158.5 million people across the US lived in counties which had air conditions worse than the national ambient air quality standard [1]. These pollutants, such as diesel exhaust, are not uniformly distributed across locations and time. Similarly, residents are often not equally active during the day and some individuals may be especially susceptible to pollution related risk due to asthma or heart disease.

In this demonstration, we present CitiSense: a new kind of "citizen infrastructure" to monitor environmental conditions and pollution that users are exposed to [2]. CitiSense is developed at UCSD (University of California, San Diego). It gives real-time feedback to everyday people about the pollutants they are exposed to during the course of their day.

The architecture of CitiSense is shown in Figure 1. The system includes affordable, small sensors carried by users, Android mobile phones, and a backend cyber-infrastructure that stores the collected data and performs analysis, modeling and learning. The results of this analysis helps other stakeholders of the system better understand how diseases such as asthma develop and coordinate efforts within a user's community to improve conditions.

2. Demonstration Description

In this demonstration, we present how the CitiSense system works end-to-end. Pollution and sensor data, such as ozone, carbon monoxide, and temperature, are collected with the portable sensor-board we developed. The sensor-board has small velcro straps that make it easy to attach to a belt or backpack. The collected data is tagged with the location of each user as she moves.

Each user also carries an Android phone. The data collected by the sensor-board is transmitted, over bluetooth, to the Android phone that is coupled with the sensor-board. The phone has an application that analyzes the data as it arrives and provides real-time feedback to users about the ambient air pollution (see Figure 2). The main screen of the application, in Figure 2(a), shows the current pollution inside a cloud using the air-quality-index (AQI). When the air is clean, the cloud is green. As it gets worse, the color of the cloud changes to reflect the detected air pollution. The color scheme for AQI has been developed by EPA to provide easy-to-understand information to non-expert users. Our application has a link to the color chart prepared by the EPA.

The Android application also provides more fine-grained information about the pollution detected at the user's location (see Figure 2(b)), and a plot of the maximum AQI recorded during the past hours of the day. The application also has buttons to share the current AQI on the popular social networks.

The Android application transmits the data to the backend cyber-infrastructure (CI). The CI performs modeling and analysis of the data, and provides a web interface to show users their personal data collected over the day on a Google map (see Figure 3). Each bubble on the map is colored according to the EPA AQI color scheme, and numbered to show how a user moved during the day, eg. from home to work.

Furthermore, users are provided a timeline of the AQI values recorded, to see when they were exposed to more pollution. This timeline has more detail than the one provided on the phone.

3. CitiSense Development Challenges

There have been many challenges in the development of the CitiSense system. The system collects real-time data, performs real-time analysis on it, and also provides a web interface to view the data. We have run user studies with human participants who carried the sensor-board and the Android phone.

The first challenge was the large amount of data transmitted from the sensor-boards to the backend during user studies. The CI summarizes and aggregates the data in real-time and caches the results. This dramatically improves page loads and the user experience for user-facing web pages.

Another challenge was the battery usage of the mobile components. Our sensor-board can run for a week on a single recharge. Since the Android phones use GPS, it was challenging to optimize the application to allow the battery to last throughout the work day.

Another challenge was the security of user data, and making some of that data publicly available over social networks. We designed a permissioning system that allow users to configure publicly accessible time windows of their data.

4. Presenters

Celal Ziftci is a PhD student at UCSD, where he conducts research and participates in the development of the CitiSense project. He oversees the end-to-end system development, and was part of the development efforts on the Android platform, the backend CI and the web interface.

Acknowledgments

This work was supported in part by NSF Grants CNS-0932403 and 0729029, as well as a generous donation of phones by Qualcomm.

References

[1] E. P. Agency. National Air Quality Status and Trends through 2007, Highlights, 2007. URL Highlights. http://www.epa.gov/air/airtrends/2008/report/Highlights.pdf.

[2] E. Bales, N. Nikzad, N. Quick, C. Ziftci, K. Patrick, and W. Griswold. Citisense: Mobile Air Quality Sensing for Individuals and Communities. In *Pervasive Health 2012*, 2012.

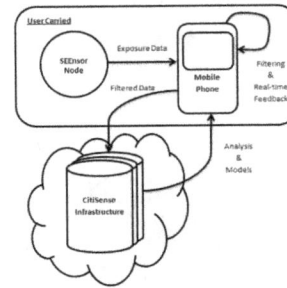

Figure 1. The CitiSense system architecture. Portable sensor-boards collect pollution data and transmit them to the Android phone. The phone provides real-time feedback, and transmits the data to the backend cyber-infrastructure (CI). The CI performs modeling and analysis on the collected data.

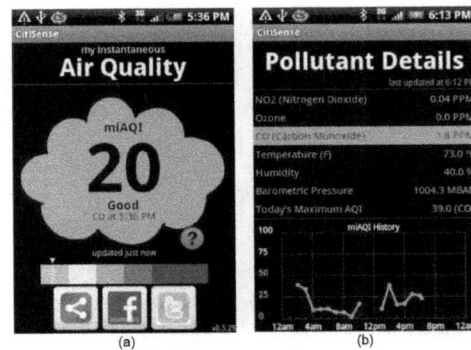

Figure 2. The Android application. The application shows real-time feedback about the pollution at the current location, as well as details about the detected AQI value, and a plot of the historical data for the day's AQI. There are also buttons to share the AQI on the popular social networks.

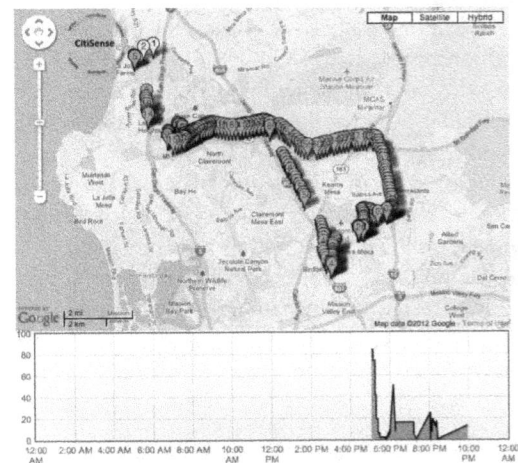

Figure 3. The map to view the data collected during the course of day. The bubbles have information about the pollution collected at a specific location. The timeline below shows the AQI over the course of day.

Analyzing Ultra-Large-Scale Code Corpus with *Boa*

Robert Dyer   Hoan Nguyen   Hridesh Rajan   Tien Nguyen

Iowa State University
{rdyer,hoan,hridesh,tien}@iastate.edu

Abstract

Analyzing the wealth of information contained in software repositories requires significant expertise in mining techniques as well as a large infrastructure. In order to make this information more reachable for non-experts, we present the *Boa* language and infrastructure. Using *Boa*, these mining tasks are much simpler to write as the details are abstracted away. *Boa* programs also run on a distributed cluster to automatically provide massive parallelization to users and return results in minutes instead of potentially days.

Categories and Subject Descriptors D.1.3 [*Concurrent Programming*]: Distributed programming

General Terms Experimentation, Languages

Keywords MapReduce, software repository mining

1. Background

Repositories such as SourceForge, GitHub, and Google Code contain over 250,000 projects each. Together, these represent an enormous amount of software, as well as related project and bug information, just waiting to be analyzed. Such a task however is much easier said than done. There are at least three problems to mining such repositories: 1) researchers must have significant knowledge about how to access and mine such data, including all of the libraries needed to implement the required infrastructure; 2) analyzing such a large amount of data using traditional methods takes a significant amount of time, thus also potentially requiring knowledge and implementation complexity of parallelizing the analysis; and 3) reproducing another research result is almost impossible, due to the burdens imposed by the first two problems.

Consider a relatively simple example that wishes to answer the question "how many revisions are there for all Java projects using Subversion in SourceForge?" A typical approach to this would write a program that does (at a minimum) the following: downloads/scrapes project metadata from the repository, parses this metadata, determines which projects are Java and use Subversion, accesses the Subversion repository to obtain the revision count, and accumulates the results into a final answer. Such a solution would require using several libraries (to parse the metadata and access Subversion) and contain upwards of 60 lines of code. This analysis would also take a significant amount of time, as it runs sequentially and accesses hundreds of thousands of remote repositories.

2. *Boa*

To solve these issues, we present the *Boa* language and supporting infrastructure. *Boa* is inspired by the Sawzall language [3] but adds several domain-specific types to ease software mining tasks. These types represent the mined data from the repository and abstract the details of how to mine that data from the user. *Boa* also abstracts away the details of the MapReduce framework [2], which allows the programs to run in a distributed environment without requiring users to explicitly mark parallelism in their code.

An example program is shown in Figure 1 which answers the previous question of how many revisions exist for Java programs using Subversion. Note how simple this code is - it is only 5 lines of code! There is also no notion of mining the software or parallelizing the code, as these are completely abstracted from the user.

```
1 total_revisions : output sum of int;
2 p: Project = input;
3 when (i: some int; match('^java$', p.programming_languages[i]))
4    when (j: each int; p.code_repositories[j].repository_type ==
          RepositoryType.SVN))
5       total_revisions << len(p.code_repositories[j].revisions);
```

Figure 1. Program in *Boa* answering "How many revisions in Java projects using Subversion?"

To run such programs, our infrastructure builds on the Sizzle compiler [4], which generates programs that run on the Hadoop MapReduce framework [1]. We add support for our domain-specific types as well as several language features not previously implemented, such as quantifiers and

SPLASH'12,   October 19–26, 2012, Tucson, Arizona, USA.
ACM 978-1-4503-1563-0/12/10.

when statements. An example use of these features is shown in Figure 1 on lines 3 and 4. These statements allow easily filtering the data, which is then sent as output to a table (line 5). The table provides an aggregation function (several are built into the language, such as sum, mean, min/max, etc.) to collect the results and reduce them to a final answer.

3. Benefits of *Boa*

Boa aims to lower the barrier to entry for researchers wishing to perform software mining tasks. It also aims to provide efficient support for performing these tasks on very large scale repositories.

Task	LOC		Time	
	Java	*Boa*	Java	*Boa*
Counting revisions	60	4	331m	<1m
Counting committers	69	6	1,596m	<1m
# Multi-lingual projects	32	4	10m	<1m

Figure 2. Three mining tasks implemented in Java and *Boa*.

Some early results are shown in Figure 2, where we implemented three software mining tasks in both Java and *Boa*. These results show significant improvements in lines of code, requiring only 5 lines of code on average for *Boa* programs. They also show considerable speedup in execution time on an input size of 620k+ projects. The *Boa* versions finish in under one minute, whereas the Java versions take up to 27 hours (a speedup of over 1,500x)! Even in the simplest case *Boa* shows speedups of 10x.

In summary, *Boa* provides the following key benefits:

- simple to write programs (usually around 5 lines),
- details of repository mining abstracted away from users,
- no need to learn libraries to perform repository mining,
- extremely efficient - runs in a fraction of the time of standard approaches, and
- scalable to ultra-large code repositories.

4. Demonstration Overview

This demonstration showcases the benefits of the *Boa* language and infrastructure via several realistic examples. Software engineering questions are proposed and answered using *Boa* programs. These example programs are then run on the *Boa* web-based infrastructure (see Figure 3), demonstrating how researchers can successfully answer research hypotheses using *Boa*.

5. Presenter Biographies

Robert Dyer and Hridesh Rajan have prior experience in developing new programming languages. Rajan developed the Ptolemy event-based language as well as the aspect-oriented language Eos. Dyer worked on the implementations

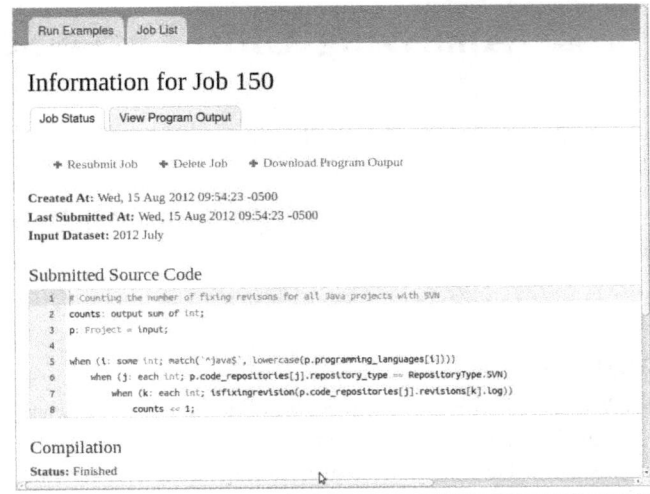

Figure 3. *Boa*'s web-based interface

and evaluation of the Ptolemy language. They have successfully given previous demonstrations at AOSD'10, FSE'10, ECOOP'11, and SPLASH'11.

Hoan Nguyen and Tien Nguyen are experts in software evolution and mining software repositories. Their work includes mining research in clone and API usage evolution, bug prediction and localization, and traceability link recovery. They are also experts in version control systems with work on novel infrastructures for semantics-based version control and configuration management.

All four authors worked on the design of the *Boa* language and infrastructure. Robert Dyer and Hoan Nguyen also developed the frontend compiler, backend caching mechanisms, and additional supporting infrastructures.

Acknowledgments

Dyer and Rajan are funded in part by NSF grant CCF-10-17334. Tien Nguyen and Hoan Nguyen are funded in part by NSF grant CCF-1018600.

References

[1] Apache Software Foundation. Hadoop: Open source implementation of MapReduce. http://hadoop.apache.org/.

[2] J. Dean and S. Ghemawat. MapReduce: simplified data processing on large clusters. In *Proceedings of the 6th Symposium on Opearting Systems Design & Implementation - Volume 6*, OSDI'04, 2004.

[3] R. Pike, S. Dorward, R. Griesemer, and S. Quinlan. Interpreting the data: Parallel analysis with Sawzall. *Sci. Program.*, 13(4):277–298, 2005.

[4] A. Urso. Sizzle: A compiler and runtime for Sawzall, optimized for Hadoop. https://github.com/anthonyu/Sizzle.

OpenRefactory/C

An Infrastructure for Developing Program Transformations for C Programs

Munawar Hafiz

Auburn University

munawar@auburn.edu

Jeffrey Overbey

National Center for Supercomputing Applications

overbey2@illinois.edu

Abstract

This demonstration will provide an overview of OpenRefactory/C, an infrastructure for developing source-level program transformations for C programs. OpenRefactory/C is platform independent; however, the demonstration will be on the Eclipse platform. We will highlight the features of the infrastructure, outline the problems it solves, show the program analyses support that we have built for this infrastructure, and show traditional refactorings as well as advanced security-oriented program transformations that cannot be developed in any other C IDEs.

Categories and Subject Descriptors D.2.3 [*Software Engineering*]: Coding Tools and Techniques; D.2.7 [*Software Engineering*]: Distribution, Maintenance, and Enhancement

General Terms Languages, Security

Keywords Program Transformation, C, Preprocessor

1. The Problem

IDEs for modern languages, e.g., Java and C#, have support for maintenance and code evolution using automated refactorings. C, in spite of its popularity, has IDEs with a limited portfolio of program transformations, with limited static analysis capabilities, limited scalability, and limited applicability to real-world programs—particularly ones that make extensive use of the C preprocessor.

There are two major challenges that make it hard to build practical tools for transforming C programs.

(1) C programming IDEs ignore multiple configurations of C preprocessor because of its complexity; most IDEs provide program analysis and transformation support based on a single configuration. The resulting program transformations are inaccurate.

(2) IDEs for C do not support sophisticated static analyses even on preprocessed C code, e.g., Eclipse CDT only supports name binding, type analysis and limited control flow analysis. Without data flow analysis, it is impossible to implement any non-trivial program transformation. Preprocessors and multiple configurations make static analysis even more complicated.

2. The Demonstration

Existing tools have attempted to repurpose compiler- or IDE-based language infrastructures for refactoring. In contrast, OpenRefactory/C was built, from the beginning, with the goal of correctly refactoring C. It is based on a well-established infrastructural and API design, and it is being designed to support a sophisticated suite of static analyses while respecting the full semantics of the C preprocessor.

The demonstration will contain these parts.

(1) Problem explanation, and an illustration of the limitations of refactorings in current IDEs for C.

(2) Basic features of OpenRefactory/C highlighting the program analyses supported by the infrastructure.

(3) Advanced security-oriented program transformations [3, 4] that prevent various security vulnerabilities, most importantly integer overflow and buffer overflow vulnerabilities, that are implemented on OpenRefactory/C.

(4) The big picture and the plans ahead.

3. Features of OpenRefactory/C

The motivation behind OpenRefactory/C is our work on security-oriented program transformations [3]—complex transformations, that cannot be implemented by existing infrastructures with limited support for sophisticated analyses.

Our current infrastructure supports name binding analysis, type analysis, control flow analysis and static call-graph analysis. Name binding analysis information is encoded in the abstract syntax tree (AST). Any AST node representing a name reference can be queried to return the corresponding declaration node. Control flow and type information are computed as a query to the AST. Control flow analysis follows Morgenthaler's [7] algorithm of AST nodes dynamically computing which other AST nodes constitute its con-

SPLASH'12,   October 19–26, 2012, Tucson, Arizona, USA.
ACM 978-1-4503-1563-0/12/10.

trol flow successors and predecessors. Type analysis uses the results of name binding analysis to compute types of variables and functions. Call graph analysis uses the results of both the name binding and control flow analyses to annotate the AST with call graph edges. We have been working on integrating pointer analysis, specifically Anderson's points-to analysis [2], by interfacing with a points-to analysis implementation [6] based on Hardekopf's [5] algorithm.

4. Under the Hood

OpenRefactory/C is a plug-in for OpenRefactory, a framework for building source-level program analyses and transformations. OpenRefactory is so named because it is designed to be extensible both in terms of the refactorings it supports as well as the languages it can refactor. OpenRefactory/C adds C language support to OpenRefactory.

The refactoring infrastructure in OpenRefactory/C is based on the design of Photran [1], an Eclipse-based integrated development environment and refactoring tool for Fortran. Photran's refactoring infrastructure and source rewriting APIs were refined over the course of several years: Photran 8 contains 39 refactorings for Fortran programs, many of which were developed by third-party contributors. Thus, Photran's refactoring API has proven to be both general and reasonably easy for new contributors to learn, making it a good starting point for a C refactoring tool.

Like Photran, OpenRefactory/C's internal program representation is a rewritable abstract syntax tree generated by Ludwig [8]. The syntax tree is augmented with preprocessor information as described by Overbey, Michelotti, and Johnson [10]. Semantic checks are based on a differential precondition checking infrastructure [9]. Our infrastructure currently handles a *single preprocessor configuration*, i.e., it assumes that C Preprocessor macros take only one, fixed value; thus, it ignores some code in #ifdef regions.

Photran is based on Eclipse, but most of its underlying infrastructure is platform-independent. Our demonstration will also be based on Eclipse, but the infrastructure is platform-independent; it could be plugged in to other IDEs such as Visual Studio, or Vim.

5. Future Plans

The C preprocessor poses a particular challenge because most C programs use multiple preprocessor configurations: Through the use of macros and #ifdef directives, programmers vary what code is included in the executable, e.g., in debug vs. release configurations, $x86$ vs. $x86\_64$, etc.

Almost all existing C program transformation tools present in IDEs work on a single configuration of preprocessed code. While this is normal behavior for a compiler, and generally good enough for an IDE, it is insufficient for a refactoring tool. For example, a tool that applies a rename refactoring to a variable in one configuration but ignores other configurations may change the behavior of a program.

OpenRefactory/C will eventually support *multiple preprocessor configurations*. This means that it will be able to transform un-preprocessed source code, exactly as the programmer sees it, and will analyze and transform code with respect to *all possible* macro configurations.

References

[1] Photran - An Integrated Development Environment and Refactoring Tool for Fortran. http://www.eclipse.org/photran/.

[2] L. O. Andersen. *Program Analysis and Specialization for the C Programming Language*. PhD thesis, DIKU, University of Copenhagen, May 1994. (DIKU report 94/19).

[3] M. Hafiz. *Security On Demand*. PhD thesis, University of Illinois at Urbana-Champaign, 2010.

[4] M. Hafiz. An 'Explicit Type Enforcement' program transformation tool for preventing integer vulnerabiliites. In *Companion of OOPSLA '11*, pages 21–22. ACM, 2011.

[5] B. Hardekopf and C. Lin. The ant and the grasshopper: fast and accurate pointer analysis for millions of lines of code. In *Proceedings of the ACM Conference on Programming Language Design and Implementation, 2007*. ACM, 2007.

[6] M. Méndez-Lojo, A. Mathew, and K. Pingali. Parallel inclusion-based points-to analysis. In *OOPSLA*, 2010.

[7] J. Morgenthaler. *Static Analysis for a Software Transformation Tool*. PhD thesis, UCSD, 1997.

[8] J. Overbey and R. Johnson. Generating rewritable abstract syntax trees. In *Software Language Engineering: First International Conference, SLE 2008. Revised Selected Papers*, volume 5452 of *Lecture Notes in Computer Science*, pages 114–133, Berlin, Heidelberg, 2009. Springer-Verlag.

[9] J. Overbey and R. Johnson. Differential precondition checking: A lightweight, reusable analysis for refactoring tools. In *26th IEEE/ACM International Conference on Automated Software Engineering (ASE 2011), 2011*. IEEE, 2011.

[10] J. Overbey, M. D. Michelotti, and R. Johnson. Toward a language-agnostic, syntactic representation for preprocessed code. In *WRT '09: Proceedings of the 3rd Workshop on Refactoring Tools*.

Presenter Biography. Munawar Hafiz is an Assistant Professor at Auburn University, AL. He leads the program analysis and program transformation aspects of OpenRefactory/C, especially how complex program transformations can be built on this infrastructure [4]. Munawar has presented his research in various forms at previous SPLASHes, e.g., as part of a tutorial, as a poster, and as a finalist project in ACM student research competition.

Jeffrey Overbey, currently a postdoc at National Center for Supercomputing Applications (NCSA), is the chief designer of OpenRefactory/C infrastructure. He is co-lead of Photran [1], an open source project hosted by the Eclipse Foundation. It is widely used by the scientific community (approximately 20,000 users worldwide). Photran influences many design decisions in OpenRefactory/C.

SCuV: a Novel Software Clustering and Visualization Tool

Xiaomin Xu   Sheng Huang   Yanghua Xiao *   Wei Wang

School of Computer Science, Fudan University, Shanghai, China

{10210240041,shhuang,shawyh,weiwang1}@fudan.edu.cn

Abstract

Decomposing a software system into smaller, more manageable clusters provides an insight for better comprehension of large systems for software engineers. However, invocation-awareness and dynamic view are two features which are not supported by existed software clustering visualization tools. In this paper, we presents a novel tool, named SCuV, to partition the *S*oftware into invocation-aware clusters, *Clu*ster them with nested containment & invocation hierarchy and *V*isualize the clustering result in granularity-adjustable way.

Categories and Subject Descriptors   D.2.7 [*Software Engineering*]: Distribution, Maintenance, and Enhancement

Keywords   software clustering, static source code analysis

1. Introduction

Software clustering is widely used to gain insight into the softwares' architecture, which is critical for software maintenance activities such as architectural module reuse, legacy system reengineering and modification impact analysis.

In general, current related works on software clustering could be roughly classified into two groups according to the data source from which the clusters are extracted. The first group is documentation based approaches which extract clusters from design documentation such as UML graphs [1]. These approaches have an obvious drawback since they rely on existing design conventions. The second group is based on source code analysis which extracts system modules according to the dependency graph built from source code files. Dependencies considered include function invocation [2, 4], variable reference or directory structure of source code files [5] etc. Then, top-down or bottom-up clus-

tering frameworks are usually adopted to build clustering hierarchy. Generally speaking, source code based approaches are more promising when system design documentations are unavailable. However, there still exists a number of challenges remaining unsolved for software clustering.

1. Previous works aren't aware of the invocation order among modules. For example, given a target module, users may be interested to find out which modules are invoked by it and how they are invoked. Unfortunately, existed visualization tools for clustering result make it difficult for users to obtain such information directly.

2. In real applications, dynamic views of clustering result are preferred. A good visualization tool should support zoom-in and zoom-out operations to explore modules of interest. In this way, users can not only have an overview of the system but also gain the insight into the detailed invocation relations between modules.

In this work, we developed SCuV, which is invocation aware and supports granularity-adjustable visualization of clusters. The tool can easily be ported to iPAD or large touch-screen system for better interactive usability in individual software comprehension and better software engineering experience in team discussion.

2. . Clustering Approach Implementation

The architecture of our tool consists of three parts: the Source Code Analyzer, Hierarchical Clustering and Visualization. Our approach takes source code as input, clusters source code on-line and provides users with a granularity-adjustable and hierarchical view of modules.

2.1 Source Code Analyzer

The source code analyzer extracts call graph of function from source code. It serves as the input of the clustering procedure. Currently, the tool only support java and it could be easily extended to support other programming languages. Notice that we just consider explicit function call when building call graph in this version. In the next version, implicit dependencies such as classloading dependencies and reflection will be considered.

2.2 Hierarchical Clustering

In this part, functions in the call graph are clustered into higher-level modules on which module invocation-dependency graph (MIDG) is built level by level iteratively until a single

* Correspondence author. We thank Tao Yu for implementing visualization of this demo. This work was supported by NSFC under grant Nos 61003001, 61170006 and 61033010. Specialized Research Fund for the Doctoral Program of Higher Education No. 20100071120032.

cluster is formed. Our clustering approach has two phases: *partition* and *clustering*. In the partition phase, we sperate the input call graph into connected components, each of which will be fed into the clustering phase. In the clustering phase, a hierarchical cluster is generated for each connected component. The clustering phase contains two steps: *Entry-based clustering* and *PageRank-based clustering*.

In *Entry-based clustering* phase, the following steps are executed iteratively for each connected component C. We first detect the *entry* functions in C. Then, for each entry function f, we find all functions only invoked by f, which form the *dominated set* of f and merge them into a larger module. Then we delete these functions from C iteratively until there is no more entry functions. After functions in C are merged into larger modules, we build module invocation-dependency graph $MIDG_C$ as follows. $MIDG_C(V, E)$ is a weighted directed graph with each $v \in V$ representing a module and each directed edge $e_{i,j} \in E$ representing the dependency of module i on module j. The edge weight, $w_{i,j}$ on $e_{i,j}$ represents the coupling degree between the two endpoints and is defined as the fraction of inner-modules in v_i that invoke at least one inner-module in v_j.

In *PageRank-based clustering* phase, for each $MIDG_C$, we run a variation of the PageRank algorithm [3] on $MIDG_C$ to determine the coupling cost for each vertex $v \in MIDG_C$ by $PageRank(v)$. Then we process each vertex in the decreasing order of vertices' PageRank score as follows: We find its k out-neighbors with the largest coupling degree to merge them into a higher-level module and then delete them from $MIDG_C$. Then we build a higher-level MIDG on these newly merged modules by the approach described in *Entry-based clustering* phase. The above two clustering steps are executed alternatively and iteratively until $MIDG_C$ are merged into a single cluster. Next, we introduce the naming strategy of new modules.

Naming Strategy We use package and class names to name new modules. First, functions are labeled by their signatures which include names of packages and class as prefix. Modules generated in *entry-based clustering* phase are named by the labels of their *entry* functions. For each module generated in *PageRank-based clustering* phase, its name is derived from names of its internal lower-level modules by adopting textural mining techniques proposed in [1].

2.3 Visualization

Visualization of the clustering result provides users with a hierarchical and dynamic adjustable view of the software systems. The left part of Fig. 1 shows the highest level of the cluster result of Java based system Weka[1](ver. 3.0) which contains 10 packages, 147 class files with a total of 95 KLOC of source code. In this view, rectangles represent the currently visible internal modules contained in higher-level modules represented by shadow parts. The label on rectangle is module name derived by our naming strategy.

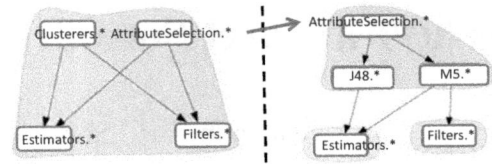

Figure 1. Screenshot of Clustering Result for Weka.

The arrows reveal invocation dependency between modules. Visible modules are displayed in a top-down fashion according to their invocation order. For example, in the left part of Fig. 1, because module labeled by *"AttributeSelection.*"* invokes module labeled by *"Estimators.*"*, the former is displayed on top of the latter one. When the user zoom in to the module labeled by *"AttributeSelection.*"*, its internal modules will be displayed in the right part of Fig. 1.

3. Demonstration

The goal of demonstration. Through the demo, we plan to show the following two aspects of SCuV : (1) our tool can produce meaningful invocation-aware hierarchial clustering; (2) our tool supports dynamic visualization with the flexibility to navigate clustering in different granularity.

The way of demonstration. We will let participants use SCuV to understand the target java project-Weka, with the comparison to understand Weka by using IDE like Eclipse. First of all, the presenter will introduce the implementation of SCuV with a deck. Then the Weka project will be loaded into Eclipse. The presenter will show participants how to understand the Weka project using Eclipse. In contrast, the presenter will load Weka into SCuV and show the comprehension process: (1)navigate from higher level modules for a global view of cluster result; (2)zoom in to explore the detailed invocation & containment relationship; (3)zoom out to hide the detail and display the higher level clustering. Meanwhile, we encourage participants to browse the visualized result to experience the benefits of SCuV. Besides, we hope to discuss with participants to see how the implementation of SCuV can be improved.

References

[1] N. Anquetil and T. C. Lethbridge. Recovering software architecture from the names of source files. *Journal of Software Maintenance*, pages 201–221, 1999.

[2] S. Mancoridis, B. S. Mitchell, C. Rorres, Y. Chen, and E. R. Gansner. Using automatic clustering to produce high-level system organizations of source code. In *IWPC '98*, page 45.

[3] C. McMillan, N. Hariri, D. Poshyvanyk, J. Cleland-Huang, and B. Mobasher. Recommending source code for use in rapid software prototypes. In *ICSE*, pages 848–858, 2012.

[4] C. Patel, A. Hamou-Lhadj, and J. Rilling. Software clustering using dynamic analysis and static dependencies. CSMR '09, pages 27–36, 2009.

[5] V. Tzerpos and R. C. Holt. Acdc : An algorithm for comprehension-driven clustering. WCRE '00, pages 258–267.

---

[1] http://www.cs.waikato.ac.nz/ml/weka/

Welcome Message from the Doctoral Symposium Chair

The main goal of the SPLASH Doctoral Symposium is to provide students with guidance for completing their dissertation research and beginning their research careers. A typical doctoral student who attends this symposium is in one of two phases:

- Apprentice, who is just beginning their research, are not ready to actually make a research proposal, but are interested in learning about structuring research and getting some research ideas; and,

- Proposer, who has progressed far enough in their research to have a structured proposal, but will not be defending their dissertation in the next 12 months.

At the symposium, all students give a two-minute overview of their research describing the most critical issues (the "elevator talk"). Proposers also give a 20-minute description of their research, including its purpose, goals, and technical approach. The doctoral symposium committee then provides each student with constructive feedback on his or her research.

This year, the committee consisted of Michael Ernst, Milind Kulkarni, Christina V. Lopes, and Hridesh Rajan (chair). The committee reviewed the 6 proposer and 1 apprentice submissions to the doctoral symposium. After reading each submission, I decided to accept all 7 submissions.

Special thanks to Iowa State University for providing needed resources. I hope you enjoy their papers in this volume. In my opinion, they are representative of the broad range of topics in the area of SPLASH, and the energy and creativity that students bring to the conference!

Hridesh Rajan
Iowa State University

Generic Adaptable Test Cases for Software Product Line Testing

Suriya Priya R Asaithambi*
School Of Computing; National University of Singapore
suria@nus.edu.sg

Stan Jarzabek
Associate Professor
School Of Computing; National University of Singapore
stan@comp.nus.edu.sg

Summary

This research study is about constructing **"generic adaptable test cases"** to counter test case libraries explosion problem. Our work focuses on effort reduction via systematic reuse of generic test assets by taking advantage of common aspects and predicted variability in test cases. We envision that the proposed approach to organizing test case libraries will be particularly useful in the context of Software Product Line Testing (SPLT). By exploring strategies for generic test cases, I hope to address problems of domain-level testing. Our work will investigate existing testing (SPLT) practices in variability management context by conducting empirical studies. We plan to synthesize principles for "generic test case" design, identify gaps between required and exiting techniques, and finally propose new approach for *generic adaptive test case construction*.

Categories and Subject Descriptors   D.2.13 [**Reusable Software**]: Domain Engineering, Reusable Libraries, Software Product Line Testing

Keywords   Generic adaptable test cases; software product line testing

1. Motication

"A **software product line (SPL)** is a set of software-intensive systems that share a common, managed set of features satisfying the specific needs of a particular market segment or mission and that are developed from a common set of core assets in a prescribed way" [SEI Definition (McGregor 2001)]. SPL is a family of systems designed to take advantage of their *common aspects and predicted variability*.

The essence of Software Product Line (SPL) (Pohl, Böckle et al. 2005) approach is to systematically analyze system variants and build so-called SPL core assets from which system variants can be developed and maintained in cost-effective way. Test cases form an important part of SPL core asset. Further, testing of core assets is considered critical because a fault within certain functionality can spread over thousands of products which reuse this functionality. Thus, it is important to prioritize and thoroughly

test SPL core assets by taking advantage of reusability.

In (Myers 2011) single system development, testing consumes between 35% and 50% of the development costs. In SPL context, testing core assets is a challenge. SPL testing (SPLT) is executed at two levels namely: domain and application testing. **Domain testing** is responsible for the validation and verification of reusable components (SPL core assets). Properties validated at the core asset level would also apply to system variants, eliminating the need to re-test them for individual system variants. The challenge is to test parameterized software components without instantiation. Thus domain testing has many open challenges. *Application testing* will reuse the test assets created from domain testing heavily; it focuses on testing individual products with all needed variability bounded to appropriate product variant choices.

Our work focuses on test effort reduction through the systematic reuse of generic test assets by taking advantage of product line common aspects and predicted variability. As generic test cases reflect properties of SPL core assets, by exploring strategies for generic test cases, I hope to address problems of domain-level testing.

2. Problem Description

In single system engineering, test artifacts [Ref: IEEE 1998] are deliverables from the testing process. *Test artifacts* can be classified as non-executable artifacts (such as test plans, test model, test strategies and test reports) and executable artifacts (such as test cases, test data sets and test scripts). A *test case* typically validates whether certain aspect of system specification is correctly realized in the implementation. *Result* is a verdict (pass or fail) documented inside test result report. In SPL domain testing context, test plan enumerates testing activities, elicits plan for effort/resource consumption and importantly selects which common and variable test cases are to be executed based on accumulated variants information. The test summary report includes additional information such as variant description, its relation to test cases and a classification (domain or application defect). Thus test plan and test summary reports are less impacted by variability management in comparison to test cases.

Derivation of test case for core assets product families is difficult owing to presence of variability. Each variation point presents multiple behaviours to be tested. Industry projects can easily incorporate thousands of variable features and configuration parameters. With continuous evolution of projects, features gets added, modified and removed over time – maintenance of such test case libraries is a research problem worth investigation. In domain testing the key challenge is to test unbound variant points. In application testing the challenge is testing correct binding of variant points against selected product.

For example, if SPL contains 16 feature variants, then it is theoretically possible to derive $2^{16} = 65536$ variant combinations. Thus even a small number of feature variants can results in combinatorial explosion of variants. ***Combinatorial explosion of test case libraries*** is caused by the need to test individual variants. This need can be reduced if we could exploit the fact that test cases for different product variants are similar, in the same way as respective products are similar.

The example shown above is a simple acceptance test written in selenium tool for testing a particular scenario

```
public class OpenHomePage {
. . .
WebDriver driver = new FirefoxDriver();
driver.get("http://www.mycompany.com/home");
WebElement query = driver.findElement(By.name("q"));
. . .
}
```
Example: Acceptance test for firefox browser

inside Firefox browser. Similar test are used to ensure compatibility for other browsers. Maintaining this test case as multiple copies is complicated. SPLT artifacts comprises of representation such as natural language, programming language and scripting language. Thus _managing variants among SPL Test artifacts using a language neutral mechanism is a key success factor._

Generic adaptive test case design attempts to directly exploit the fact that test cases for system variants form groups of similar test cases. Our design promotes parameterization techniques for building generic, reusable and modifiable generic test cases. For example, replace the driver variant point above with appropriate frame ***<<Browser>>***. The mechanism complements and extends mechanisms supported by SPL's programming language.

From literature survey on SPLT, limitations of current approaches are: (1) Existing approaches are more focused on non-executable test artifacts. (2)There is no formal classification of test artifacts in terms of nature of variability. (3)Very few specific techniques are available for executable test artifacts.

2.1 Motivating research questions (RQs)
RQ1: How to save time and increase productivity using generic test artifacts? In SPL Variation points are often source of faults. Testing all variants of SPL core assets a priori is usually impossible for all but the simple cases. Formulating effective "generic test cases" that would minimize efforts and increase productivity is essential.

RQ2: How do we assemble generic test artifacts, that tests commonalities and preserve variation in domain testing? The study (Engström and Runeson 2011) highlights need for new techniques addressing variability preservation and commonality testing. The study also reveals a trend in increase of test automation recently.

RQ3: How is generic test artifacts managed at different levels and phases? Our research will focus on generic test case construction parallel to core asset creation and before application engineering.

The intent of our research work is to propose a new approach that avoids combinatorial explosion via use of generic adaptive (domain) test cases that preserves variability. Related Work

2.2 Summary of current generic test cases research:
- *Kolb and Muthig (Kolb and Muthig 2006) discuss the importance and complexity of testing a SPL and component based systems. They promote the need for generic test cases.*
- *McGregor (McGregor 2001) creates generic test cases from the use-case scenarios. The variability combination is resolved using orthogonal arrays technique.*
- *For legacy systems, (Geppert, Li et al. 2004) obtained a family of generic test cases by generalizing(using decision tree) existing (or new) test cases driven by the parameters of variation of the commonality analysis.*
- *In model driven SPLT (Reuys, Kamsties et al. 2005), state chart describes a generic test case with variant point as Boolean expression.*
- *CAFÉ project (Bayer, Flege et al. 1999) presents a method called ScenTeD (Scenario based Test Derivation for product family testing) that addresses generic test cases with respect to system and integration testing. It supports the derivation of generic test case from requirements and architecture information at the domain engineering level.*

Thus current research lacks language neutral techniques to address generic test case. The understandings and challenges are well established. But contibutions are either ideas or partial implementations targeted on specific modeling language or notations. Research (Engström and Runeson 2011) shows that empirical evaluations are sparse in the context of industrial projects.

3. Proposed Work
Our proposed technique works in two steps. The first step is to analyze and craft appropriate generic test case artifacts. Additional inputs inferring the type of core asset and nature of variant points are provided to help choosing suitable mechanism(s). The outcome will be a 'generic test case specification' constructed preserving the variations present. The second step is to derive product specific test cases from the generic test artifacts with appropriate variation points being bound.

Our approach primarily contributes to the first step of constructing generic adaptive test cases as shown in figure 1. The _novelty_ of our approach is that generative technique we propose being language/application/domain independent. Our approach can manage variations, propagating changes across all the artifacts. Singular mechanisms have their own merits and limitations and handles only one type of variability. Such mechanisms are simple, cost-effective and work well only for small feature sets. In reality, test artifacts are complex to be dealt using single technique. There are customizations at file level, domain level and method level. Thus mixed techniques are more appropriate.

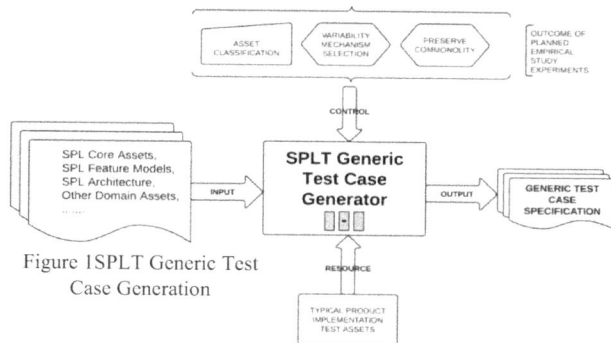

Figure 1SPLT Generic Test Case Generation

3.1 Generic Test Cases under Study

Test cases approaches could be black-box or white-box and implementation could be manual or automated. We select two kinds of test case specifications and provide relevant techniques for generic test case. (1) Unit Testing: conducted by developer on individual code components, usually automated white box testing. (3)Acceptance Test conducted by business user on final product, usually manual and black box testing.

4. Methodology

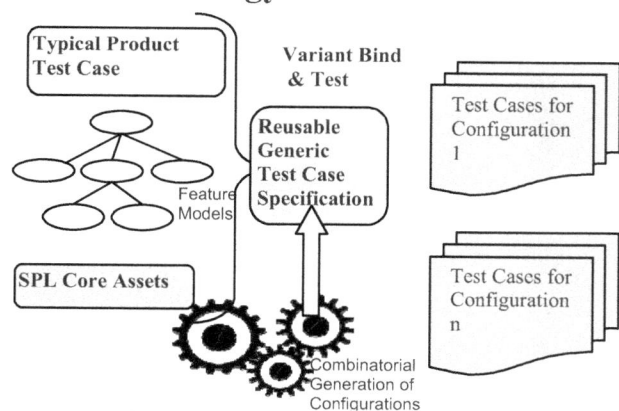

Figure 2: Overview of our contribution

Literature survey involved intensive review of journals, proceedings, projects, and Internet resources related to the SPLT literature. The main research idea in product lines testing is to reuse test case and related artifacts throughout the entire product lines instead of testing every application as an independent software product. It is therefore, impor-

tant to create proper testing artifacts in SPL as core assets using reuse principles.

Our research study is planned to be conducted in three phases. *Phase one:* Conduct empirical studies identified sets of test artifacts. Observe different types of variability occurring in domain testing, document the variant point representation and draw conclusion regarding generic test artifacts possiblity. *Phase two:* Classify and propose possible variability management techniques for different test artifacts. Propose a systematic method that identifies test case clones, understands the nature of variability and treats with mixed-strategy based reuse approach. The generic adaptive test cases will be built and maintained using generative reuse technique. *Phase three:* Evaluate the approach in qualitative and quantitative ways, by conducting controlled experiment. Discuss its strengths and weaknesses.

The following are needful activities: (1) Define research question (2) Detailed Literature Study: to find out what is already known before trying to answer research goal. (3) Create Theoretical Model to conceptualize the problem stated in research question. (4) Identify possible open source projects. Perform initial empirical studies and identify research gaps. Depending on gaps, one research method will be selected [RQ2]. (5) The researcher injects practices directly into pilot project and observes before and after reactions. Data is collected with research instrument, for example test artifacts review [RQ3]. (6) Conclusions can be drawn statistically or analytically. Consideration will be given to reliability, validity and threats to validity (internal, external) [RQ1].

References

[1] Bayer, J., O. Flege, et al. (1999). PuLSE: a methodology to develop software product lines. Proceedings of the 1999 symposium on Software reusability. New York, NY, USA.

[2] Engström, E. and P. Runeson (2011). "Software product line testing – A systematic mapping study." Information and Software Technology.

[3] Geppert, B., J. Li, et al. (2004). Towards Generating Acceptance Tests for Product Lines. Software Reuse: Methods, Techniques, and Tools. J. Bosch and C. Krueger, Springer Berlin, Heidelberg.

[4] Kolb, R. and D. Muthig (2006). Making testing product lines more efficient by improving the testability of product line architectures. Proceedings of the ISSTA 2006 workshop on Role of software architecture for testing and analysis. New York, NY, USA, ACM.

[5] McGregor, J. (2001 & 2010). "Testing a Software Product Line" Software Engineering Institute.

[6] Glenford J. Myers, Corey Sandler, Tom Badgett (2011). "The Art of Software Testing." John Wiley andSons.

[7] Pohl, K., G. Böckle, et al. (2005). Software Product Line Engineering: Foundations, Principles, and Techniques, Birkhäuser.

[8] Reuys, A., E. Kamsties, et al. (2005). Model-Based System Testing of Software Product Families. Advanced Information Systems Engineering. O. Pastor and J. Falcãoe Cunha, Springer.

Using Software Quality Standards to Assure the Quality of the Mobile Software Product

Luis Corral

Luis Corral

Free University of Bozen/Bolzano
Piazza Domenicani 3, 39100 Bolzano, Italy
Luis.Corral@stud-inf.unibz.it

Abstract

Due to the high relevance gained by mobile software applications, software developers require a way to measure and track the quality of their mobile products from a domain-specific, quantitative point of view. Currently, there is no a link between the general quality goals set by the mobile ecosystem and the practices that have to be exercised to develop a compliant application. In this work, we pursue the implementation of a strategy to extend software quality standards to supply mechanisms to measure the quality of mobile software products from the point of view of developers and users, in the context of mobile execution environments and mobile application markets.

Categories and Subject Descriptors D.2.0 [**Software Engineering**]: General, Standards

Keywords ISO 9126; Markets; Metrics; Mobile; Process; Product; Quality; Standards

1. Introduction

The impact of the mobile software product is growing every day, and has reached a point in which mobile devices have become one of the most important platforms for the distribution and utilization of user-oriented software. Smartphone sales outnumber those of PCs [1], and application markets represent a primary channel for the dissemination of end-user software products, hosting thousands of apps and reporting millions of downloads per day. Handset terminals have experienced a shift from being simple communication devices to become high-end, multipurpose computer equipment. Smartphones are driven by powerful operating systems that allow users to add and remove applications, and they employ architecture that is similar to a regular personal computer. However, these applications have to cope with several constraints inherent to the mobile ecosystem that are not present in conventional desktop computing. These constraints include wireless communication problems, mobility issues, diversity of standards and operating platforms, limited capabilities of terminal devices, security, and many others.

The quality of mobile applications is usually regulated by application market policies, and the perception of quality may also be affected by "word of mouth" via customer's ratings and reviews. Several software lifecycles have been proposed to assist developers in the process of creating successful mobile applications. However, published mobile software lifecycles fail to establish a clear link between the general quality goals imposed upon mobile applications, and specific characteristics that can be measured to determine, the fulfillment of those quality goals quantitatively.

The high relevance gained by mobile software applications triggers the need for a method to measure the quality of mobile software products from a specific point of view.

2. Research Problem

Software applications for mobile devices are created through development practices the objective of which is to create products that are able to perform satisfactorily in a resource-limited environment, while delivering value to the end-users. Additionally, developers must also consider the regulations imposed by distribution channels, which must be met in order to include a product in the application store.

Thus, mobile software engineers should put into practice a development strategy that considers several quality drivers: the mobile environment itself, the expectations of the end-user, and the restrictions set by application markets. A number of software development processes have been proposed to guide software engineers to produce high-quality mobile applications. These processes are typically based on Agile methods, which some consider to be the most effective way to address the diverse and evolving requirements of the mobile environment [2-4].

Nevertheless, none of these development lifecycles provide an appraisal model that delivers goals, methods and metrics to directly assess the software product in light of the conditions and constraints given by the mobile execution and marketing environments. Currently, mobile software lifecycles fail to establish an environment-specific measurement plan that links the overall quality goals of the mobile software market, the processes that have to be conducted to develop applications that fulfill such expectations, and the metrics that have to be calculated to quantitatively assure such compliance. We propose to learn from traditional and innovative quality frameworks that have proven their value in other environments and to tailor them to incorporate specific requirements that determine the quality of the mobile product, building upon solid knowledge of the environment, markets and customers.

2.1 Goals of the Research

The objective of this work is to develop the capability to associate the market requirements and success factors of a mobile product with quality characteristics that can be measured. Our work hypothesis states that the mobile software product can be analyzed to relate measurable parameters of the software product with user expectations and market compliance criteria, thus delivering an accurate approximation of the product quality (Figure 1). To achieve these objectives, three research questions were established:

RQ.1: What are the most relevant quality requirements for a mobile application? In other words, what is typically expected from a mobile application from the viewpoint of the involved stakeholder?

RQ.2: What is the impact of the mobile environment on the quality of the software product? This is, what conditions exist in the mobile ecosystem that have a significant impact on the product quality?

RQ.3: How can the quality of a mobile software product be measured and appraised? To determine this, we can utilize the answers from the previous research questions to define a collection of metrics that help to approximate the quality of a mobile product quantitatively.

3. Proposed Approach

Our technical approach is organized in three stages that focus on providing answers for each question established in Section 2.1: First, to identify the most important quality requirements relating to mobile apps, a comprehensive survey of the publishing guidelines of major application stores will be carried out (e.g., iOS store, Google Play, Nook Store, etc.). Publishing guidelines represent the minimum quality expectations for an application to be included in the distribution platform. These conditions make these requirements highly influential factors in the development of mobile applications. We recognize them as instrumental assets in defin-

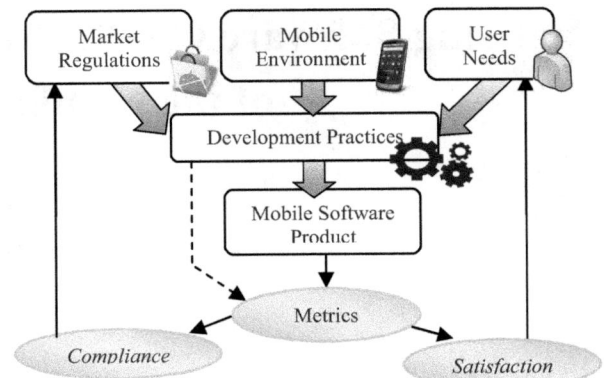

Figure 1. Metric-based Approach to Measure the Quality of Mobile Software Applications

ing what a mobile application should aim to be, what constraints it should observe, and how it should perform. The initial effort concentrates on reviewing and comparing diverse publishing guidelines to extract commonalities, quality factors, and measurable requirements. The next step will be to conduct an analysis that allows us to relate mobile-specific characteristics with their corresponding measurable quality requirements. The mobile-specific target constraints will be studied (e.g., slow processor, limited quantity of memory, limited power resources, etc.). Such study will be carried out through literature review and experimentation (e.g., benchmarking, performance analysis, etc.). This will allow us to isolate additional needs, and track how the mobile environment, by itself, affects the quality of mobile applications. Finally, with the information obtained from the previous stages, the Goal-Question-Metric (GQM) methodology [5] will be used to propose an effective strategy for product quality measurement. So far, a preliminary sketch of our goal has been defined: "To analyze the mobile software product for the purpose of evaluating it with respect to quality; from the view point of developers and customers, in the context of the mobile execution environment and mobile application markets". To describe this goal through questions and to determine the corresponding metrics, the selection of a mature software quality standard is considered, to provide a framework that can be applied to the mobile markets and the mobile ecosystem.Our choice is to revisit ISO/IEC 9126, already suggested for similar domains [6, 7], and to analyze its quality characteristics, focusing on those applicable to the mobile software product, in the given context. ISO/IEC 9126 groups quality characteristics into two orthogonal dimensions: developer's viewpoint (internal and external quality) and customer's viewpoint (quality in use), making it very suitable for the proposed approach. After combining the custom attributes with the core standard characteristics, a robust, mobile-specific quality framework will be available to define quality metrics that can be calculated directly to analyze the mobile software application. In this way, the essential software quality characteristics of ISO/IEC 9126,

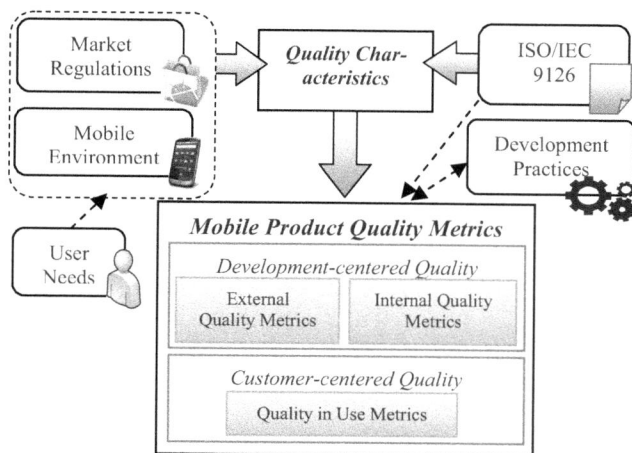

Figure 2. An Approach for Approximating Mobile Software Product Quality Based on ISO/IEC 9126

combined with those identified by us, will be related to metrics capable of delivering quantitative values that accurately approximate the quality of the product in the required contexts, and also to provide information for feedback to the development processes, for continuous improvement (Figure 2).

4. Evaluation Methodology

In accordance with our work hypothesis, we seek to know whether the mobile software product can be analyzed to relate measurable parameters of the software product (i.e., product metrics) with user expectations (e.g., ratings) and application market compliance criteria. To validate our approach, an experiment will be deployed, consisting of the retrieval of an initial sample of 500 assorted applications from Google Play and calculating from them the mobile software quality metrics defined with the GQM methodology. Then, an automatic evaluation will be performed using a non-invasive measurement framework able to analyze the Android-native Java code and calculate user-defined metrics [8, 9]. Using an automatic measurement framework will allow us to execute a multi-dimensional evaluation of the code without adding human-operator noise or bias.

The selected applications should represent a variety of categories (e.g., entertainment, health, lifestyle, etc.) to cover a wider range of user and developer profiles, and they must be distributed under Open Source licenses, so that access to the source code and code repositories can be guaranteed, first to retrieve the code to perform the automatic analysis, and second to study the behavior and evolution of the project (e.g., number of commits, number of releases, etc.) [10]. For each studied application, the product quality metrics obtained after the automatic analysis will be compared to the number of downloads and to the user's rating obtained by the product in the application store, and also with the number of commits and the number of releases stated in the code repository. This evaluation effort will be extended to other mobile operating platforms, in order to analyze the impact of the target platform on the quality of a mobile application, and to understand how the quality metrics of a given mobile app may relate to the constraints imposed by the corresponding application.

5. Conclusions

In this doctoral work, we propose a standard-based strategy for assessing the quality of mobile applications through metrics built upon the demands imposed by application stores and execution environments. Further work will concentrate on isolating the critical quality characteristics from markets and environments to later determine, the metrics that will be used to approximate the quality of the mobile software product. The conduction of the experiment will supply the empirical data required to validate the accuracy of this approach, through the automatic calculation of the metrics and the correlation with product assessment parameters already existing in application stores and code repositories. This study aims to contribute to state-of-the-art providing mechanisms to assess the quality of the mobile software product, based on real-world user expectations and real-world market awareness.

References

[1] International Data Corporation. 2011. Nearly 1 Billion Smart Devices Shipped in 2011. *Release,* retrieved June 7th, 2012. http://www.idc.com/getdoc.jsp?containerId=prUS22917111

[2] Rahimian, V. Ramsin, R. 2008. Designing an Agile methodology for mobile software development: A Hybrid Method engineering approach. *In Proc. 2nd Intl. Conf. on Research Challenges in Information Science.*

[3] Scharff, C., Verma, R. 2010. Scrum to support mobile application development projects in a just-in-time learning context. *In Proceedings of CHASE '10 (ICSE 2010)* pp. 25-31.

[4] Cunha, T.F.V., Dantas, V.L.L., Andrade, R.M.C. 2011. SLeSS: A Scrum and Lean Six Sigma integration approach for the development of software customization for mobile phones, *In Proc. 25th Brazilian Symposium on Software Engineering,* pp. 283-292.

[5] Basili, V. 1993. Applying the goal question metric paradigm in the experience factory. In *Proceedings of the 10th Conference of Software Metrics and Quality Assurance in Industry.*

[6] Spriestersbach, A., Springer, T. 2004. Quality attributes in mobile web application development. *In Proceedings of the 5th PROFES 2004.* LNCS vol. 3009, pp. 120-130.

[7] Mantoro, T. 2009. Metrics evaluation for context-aware computing. *In Proceedings of MoMM2009.* pp. 574-578.

[8] Sillitti, A., Succi, G., Vlasenko, J. 2011. Toward a better understanding of tool usage. *Proceedings of ICSE 2011*

[9] Sillitti, A., Succi, G., Vlasenko, J. 2012. Understanding the impact of pair programming on developers attention: a case study on a large industrial experimentation. *Proceedings of ICSE 2012.*

[10] Sillitti A., Janes A., Succi G., Vernazza T. 2004 Measures for mobile users: an architecture. *Journal of Systems Architecture,* Elsevier, Vol. 50, No. 7, pp. 393-405.

Reifying and Optimizing Collection Queries for Modularity *

Paolo G. Giarrusso

Philipps University Marburg

Abstract

Conventional collection libraries do not perform automatic collection-specific optimizations. Instead, performance-critical code using collections must be hand-optimized, leading to non-modular, brittle, and redundant code.

We propose SQUOPT, the Scala Query Optimizer, a *deep embedding* of the Scala collection library performing collection-specific optimizations automatically without external tools or compiler extensions.

Categories and Subject Descriptors H.2.3 [*Database Management*]: Languages—Query languages; D.1.1 [*Programming Techniques*]: Applicative (Functional) Programming; D.1.5 [*Programming Techniques*]: Object-oriented Programming

Keywords Deep embedding; query languages; optimization; modularity

1. Introduction

In-memory collections of data often need efficient processing. For on-disk data, efficient processing is already provided by database management systems (DBMS), thanks to their query optimizers which support many optimizations specific to the domain of collections. However, moving in-memory data to DBMSs does not typically improve performance [10], and query optimizers cannot be reused separately, since DBMSs are typically monolithic and their optimizers are deeply integrated. A few collection-specific optimizations, such as shortcut fusion [5], are supported by compilers for purely functional languages such as Haskell, but the implementation techniques do not generalize to many other optimizations, such as support for indexes. In general, collection-specific optimizations are not supported by the

---

* Extended version of [4].

SPLASH'12,   October 19–26, 2012, Tucson, Arizona, USA.
ACM 978-1-4503-1563-0/12/10.

general-purpose optimizers used by high-level (JIT) compilers. Therefore, when collection-related optimizations are needed, programmers perform them by hand.

Some optimizations are not hard to apply manually, but in many cases become applicable only after manual inlining [8]. But manual inlining modifies source code by combining distinct functions together, while often distinct functions should remain distinct to preserve modularity, for instance to separate different concerns or to allow reusing a code fragment. In this case, manual inlining will reduce modularity.

To sum up, developers have to choose between modularity and performance when writing queries. We propose instead an automatic optimizer supporting both inlining and collection-specific optimizations, combining performance and modularity. In particular, our optimizer automatically performs various collection-specific algebraic optimizations, such as map fusion, selection pushdown, automatic indexing and query unnesting. Some of these optimizations can reduce the complexity class of a query. Moreover, the optimizer supports general-purpose optimizations, such as inlining and various algebraic simplifications, to allow collection-specific optimizations to trigger more often. We show a few examples in the next subsection.

1.1 Motivating Example

Let us consider for instance map fusion, which combines multiple map operations to avoid intermediate results.

Consider this Scala function definition in module M1:

```
def firstPart(someColl: List[Int]) = someColl.map(x ⇒ x + 1)
```

This code defines function `firstPart` which maps function $\lambda x.x + 1$ on some collection of integers `someColl`. Suppose now that module M2 contains:

```
val theColl: List[Int] = ...
def secondPart = M1.firstPart(theColl).map(x ⇒ x + 2)
```

This code defines function `secondPart` which maps function $\lambda x.x + 2$ on the result of `M1.firstPart`. We assume that these functions are part of different modules, for instance because they are related with different concerns and `firstPart`'s implementation should be hidden behind an abstraction barrier.

This code is inefficient: Executing this code will build a collection to represent the result of `firstPart`, and then consume it immediately to build a new collection; this intermediate step is unnecessary and expensive. Moreover, we sum each number with first 1 and then 2; adding 3 directly would be faster.

To improve performance we can write, in module `M2`, just `def secondPart = theColl.map(x ⇒ x + 3)`. However, this code combines code fragments which belong to different modules, which is undesirable in our example. An alternative would be to rely on an automatic optimizer. Automating this optimization requires inlining the call to `firstPart` (which in general might be a virtual call, hence resolved only at run-time) and then performing collection-specific optimizations (here, map fusion). While most general-purpose automatic optimizers can handle inlining, they cannot handle collection-specific optimizations: They do not understand the semantics of collections, and in general these optimizations require complex tracking of side effects, which must be avoided in programs using SQuOpt. Furthermore, inlining virtual calls is hard because virtual calls typically cannot be resolved statically, and hence they can only be inlined at run-time by JIT compilers. Hence, collection-specific optimizations like map fusion cannot be performed automatically by a typical optimizer, especially not by a compile-time one.

There are many other optimizations that are possible to improve performance, but that require implementation overhead or lead to nonmodular solutions; one example is maintaining indexes to speed up queries. Consider an address book application, which manipulates a collection of people. To find people by their name, this application will probably maintain an index mapping names to people. Each time a person is added or removed, both the collection of people and the index need to be updated: Keeping in sync these operations by hand is error-prone. Automatic index maintenance, as done by databases, would make such inconsistencies impossible, once again reconciling modularity and performance. This optimization is however not in scope for general-purpose optimizers: Among other things, converting a collection scan to an index lookup means synthesizing a different algorithm.

2. Our Solution

To provide automatic collection-specific optimizations and thus address these problems, we introduce SQuOpt, the Scala Query Optimizer, which consists of:

1. An embedded domain-specific language (EDSL) for queries on collections. This EDSL corresponds to the purely functional portion of the Scala collection API and inherits its advantages [7]. This EDSL can be regarded as a query language. As such, it subsumes naturally database concepts such as views, indexes (which become simply queries of dictionary type) and user-defined functions; being object-oriented, the language also naturally supports nested collections. Moreover, this EDSL is designed to be as close as possible to the standard Scala collection API; translating the code shown in the previous example requires only changing a type annotation:

```
def firstPart(someColl: Exp[List[Int]]) = someColl.map(x ⇒ x
  + 1)
// ...
def secondPart = M1.firstPart(theColl).map(x ⇒ x + 2)
```

2. A Scala implementation of the above EDSL. Queries written in this EDSL produce explicit representations of themselves, termed expression trees; in other words, ours is a *deeply embedded* DSL. Crucially, the produced representation includes Scala expressions and arguments of query operators like `map` or `filter`. This library requires no compiler extensions, unlike LINQ. To this end, we extend existing techniques based on Scala implicit conversions [9] to cope with operations on collections. Moreover, the produced program representation is fully typed and is easier to manipulate than the one used by LINQ [2]: Query operations are reduced to a small number of operators which are polymorphic over the collection type. Each included operator supports uniformly all appropriate collections included in the Scala library and any additional one implemented according to the same rules [7]. As a result, programs manipulating expression trees and new collection types can be added independently from one another.

3. A run-time compiler to convert queries to runnable code.

4. A run-time optimizer which transforms queries into faster ones before compilation. Since optimizations happens at run-time, handling virtual calls precisely is possible. Since the query representation represents faithfully the arguments of query operators, each optimization has all the information needed to verify that its side conditions apply. While the optimizer is not yet complete, the speedups it achieves are already promising, as detailed subsequently.

5. An indexing component, which allows creating indexes on collections manually (as in typical DBMSs) and applying them automatically. Thus query authors need not choose which indexes to use. Indexes are simply standard queries which use aggregation operators (`groupBy`) to build a dictionary. Since objects can contain other collections (that is, our data model is not *relational* like in relational databases but *hierarchical*), we use hierarchical indexes [1].

6. A prototype implementation of incremental view maintenance, which will allow to materialize and update the results of any view, including indexes, so that the materialized results can be reused in other queries.

Our current implementation is available online.[1]

Overall, our approach seems a promising solution to combine performance and modularity.

---

[1] `http://www.informatik.uni-marburg.de/~pgiarrusso/SQuOpt`

3. Initial evaluation

We are evaluating SQUOPT by re-implementing several code analyses of the Findbugs tool [6] and comparing performance of different implementations of the same query.

Our primary hypothesis is that it is possible to write more modular code while still getting good performance; a secondary hypothesis is that the optimizer removes the entire abstraction overhead introduced by writing modular code— in other words, modular code should perform as well as the manually inlined and optimized version of the same code.

Another secondary hypothesis is that the optimizer recognizes when it can apply indexes, and that it can rewrite queries to use indexes where appropriate.

To evaluate these hypotheses, we choose code analyses from FindBugs through a mixture of convenience and random sampling, and we compare four variants of each analysis query.

1. We first implement the considered query in Scala using the standard collection library non-modularly, that is, as a single query.[2] This implementation is our performance baseline.

2. We split the considered query into different subqueries, trying to make each one reusable if possible. This implementation is more desirable, but potentially slower because it introduces abstraction overhead.

3. We copy and adapt the first variant to use our framework.

4. We copy and adapt the second variant to use our framework.

Moreover, we create indexes corresponding to the queries and evaluate whether they are used whenever appropriate, and what are the speedups.

Currently we do not yet have modular variants for all queries. The current results suggest that the optimizer provides promising speedups and that it should be straightforward to extend it to remove remaining abstraction overheads. Results about indexing are also encouraging, with order-of-magnitude speedups achieved by simply adding appropriate indexes. Overall, around half of the queries can be optimized, and speedups range from 2.5x to 2000x.

3.1 Threats to validity

Our first threat to validity is our selection of benchmarks— in our case, the individual queries—because speedups are quite different depending on the particular query. We plan to address this by enlarging the benchmark suite and by investigating the choice of different benchmarks.

Since we measure runtime performance, we must deal with measurement error. To do so, we use rigorous benchmarking techniques [3].

Our performance baseline is created by us and not externally validated; therefore, it might contain performance

bugs which limit the validity of the results. To address this concern, we tried to use the original implementation in Find-Bugs as a performance baseline. However, measuring performance of individual queries in FindBugs is difficult because they are not intended to be executed independently, and not optimized for this use case. Moreover, the differences between FindBugs and our implementation are quite extensive, and each of these implementation differences might be the reason for any performance difference between us and Find-Bugs.

Acknowledgements The author would like to thank Eli Tilevich for encouraging me to submit at this venue, Klaus Ostermann, Michael Eichberg, Tillmann Rendel and Christian Kästner for collaboration in this research project and Sebastian Erdweg and the OOPSLA anonymous reviewers for their helpful comments. This work is supported in part by the European Research Council, grant #203099.

References

[1] E. Bertino and W. Kim. Indexing techniques for queries on nested objects. *IEEE Trans. Knowledge and Data Engineering*, 1(2):196–214, 1989.

[2] O. Eini. The pain of implementing LINQ providers. *Commun. ACM*, 54(8):55–61, 2011.

[3] A. Georges, D. Buytaert, and L. Eeckhout. Statistically rigorous Java performance evaluation. In *Proc. Int'l Conf. Object-Oriented Programming, Systems, Languages and Applications*, OOPSLA '07, pages 57–76. ACM, 2007.

[4] P. G. Giarrusso, K. Ostermann, M. Eichberg, T. Rendel, and C. Kästner. Reifying and optimizing collection queries for modularity. In *SPLASH'12 Conference Companion—Poster Abstracts*, 2012.

[5] A. Gill, J. Launchbury, and S. L. Peyton Jones. A short cut to deforestation. In *Proc. Int'l Conf. Functional Programming languages and Computer Architecture*, FPCA '93, pages 223–232. ACM, 1993.

[6] D. Hovemeyer and W. Pugh. Finding bugs is easy. *SIGPLAN Notices*, 39(12):92–106, 2004.

[7] M. Odersky and A. Moors. Fighting bit rot with types (experience report: Scala collections). In *IARCS Annual Conference on Foundations of Software Technology and Theoretical Computer Science*, volume 4, pages 427–451, 2009.

[8] S. Peyton Jones and S. Marlow. Secrets of the Glasgow Haskell Compiler inliner. *Journal of Functional Programming*, 12(4-5):393–434, 2002.

[9] T. Rompf and M. Odersky. Lightweight modular staging: a pragmatic approach to runtime code generation and compiled DSLs. In *Proc. Int'l Conf. Generative Programming and Component Engineering*, GPCE '10, pages 127–136. ACM, 2010.

[10] M. Stonebraker, S. Madden, D. J. Abadi, S. Harizopoulos, N. Hachem, and P. Helland. The end of an architectural era: (it's time for a complete rewrite). In *Proc. Int'l Conf. Very Large Data Bases*, VLDB '07, pages 1150–1160. VLDB Endowment, 2007.

---

[2] Syntactically, by a single Scala for-comprehension.

Developing a New Computer Music Programming Language in the 'Research through Design' Context

Hiroki Nishino

NUS Graduate School for Integrative Sciences & Engineering, National University of Singapore
CeLS, #05-01, 28, Med. Drive, Singapore 117456
g0901876@nus.edu.sg

Abstract

The development of computer music languages seems to be considered from outside the computer music community just as contributions in practice rather than in research. Yet, the emerging approach of 'Research through Design (RtD)' in HCI also casts a significant question as to how the academic contribution can be made through the design of such DSLs. We describe our practice in the development of a computer music language from the perspective of the RtD.

Categories and Subject Descriptors D.3.3 [**Programming Languages**]: Language Classifications – Specialized application languages

Keywords   computer music, research through design

1. Motivation

Computer music programming languages have been playing a significant role both in research and artistic creation in the field. However, the development of such DSLs itself has been considered as the development of practical tools rather than academic contributions from outside the computer music community; at the same time, the development of programming languages with such domain-specific needs is becoming a topic of interest in HCI as end-user programming gets more popular. Blackwell argues, *"the study of unusual programming contexts such as Laptop music may lead to more general benefits for programming research"*, as seen in the spreadsheet, which *"was invented in response to the needs of business school students"* [1].

Such a situation for computer music languages also corresponds well to the concept of 'Research through Design (RtD)', an approach in HCI research that recently emerged within the community. In RtD, designers and researchers are expected to develop *"a product that transforms the world from its current state to a preferred state"* and *"the*

artifacts produced in this type of research become design exemplars, providing an appropriate conduit for research findings to easily transfer to the HCI research and practice communities" and RtD focuses on *"producing a contribution of knowledge"* as academic research rather than *"more immediately inform the development of a commercial product"* through design practices [14].

This doctoral symposium proposal emphasizes this aspect of 'Research through Design' in the development of a new computer music language.

2. Background and Problems

In this section, we briefly describe the background knowledge in computer music, which we discuss later in the problems that we aim to solve in our RtD practice.

2.1 The Unit-Generator Concept

The unit-generator concept, one of the most significant abstractions in computer music, was established around 1960 and even today many computer music languages are still based on these abstractions. A unit-generator is a software module considered to perform *"conceptually similar functions to standard electronic equipment used for electronic sound synthesis"*[7], e.g. oscillators and filters. A sound synthesis model is described as a network of such unit-generators; figure 1 below is a pictorial representation of the unit-generators and the synthesis model definition in *CSound* computer music language [4].

Figure 1. A synthesis model definition in *CSound* [4,p.27]

2.2 Microsound Synthesis Techniques

Generally speaking, microsound synthesis techniques [10] involve many short sound particles (microsound) that overlap-add each other to constitute the entire sound output.

Copyright is held by the author/owner(s).
SPLASH'12, October 19–26, 2012, Tuscon, Arizona, USA.
ACM 978-1-4503-1563-0/12/10.

Such concept significantly differs from the traditional unit-generator concept, which originates in electronic sound synthesis that assumes the signal s is a function *s(t)* of time *t*. Figure 2 describes an example of *synchronous granular synthesis*, a kind of microsound synthesis that schedules microsounds, which are called *grains*, with a regular interval. Figure 2(a) shows 3 grains scheduled with relatively large intervals. As the intervals get shorter from (a) to (f), the overlap-add of microsounds results in the different waveforms with various pitches, even when they all schedule the identical grains with the regular interval.

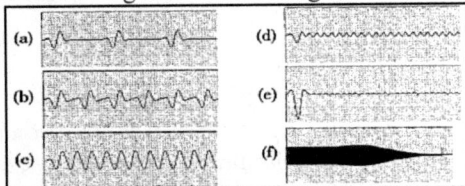

Figure 2. Influence of grain density on pitch (a) 50 grains/sec (b) 100 grains/sec (c) 200 grains/sec (d) 400 grains/sec (e) 500 grains/sec (f) Plot of a granular stream sweeping from the infrasonic frequency of 10 grains/sec to the audio frequency of 500 grains/sec over 30 seconds [10, p.95].

2.3 Problems Related to Microsound Synthesis

While there are a number of different microsound synthesis techniques, it is necessary to schedule each microsound in precise timing with sample-rate accuracy for the accurate sound rendering; yet many computer music languages are incapable of such precise timing behavior as seen in most general purpose programming languages. Furthermore, some previous works argue difficulty in realizing microsound synthesis techniques solely in computer music languages and how to implement microsound synthesis has been one of significant concerns in computer music [5,12].

3. Approach

3.1 RtD and Computer Music Language Design; Beginning wit the Existing Problems

RtD aims to produce academic contributions through designing a product that results in 'a preferred state' to users. In the development of a new computer music language as a RtD practice, we interpreted 'a preferred state' as an issue in the usefulness of a programming language; usefulness *"concerns the degree to which a product enables a user to achieve his or her goals"* [11, p.4]; thus, we begin with identifying the existing problems in computer music as the problems in usefulness, and expect the design process for solving such problems to lead to academic contributions.

In our practice, we primarily focus on the difficulty in implementing microsound synthesis techniques, which we consider '*unpreferable*' in computer music programming. We interpreted this difficulty as the issues in usability and functionality of computer music languages; thus this RtD practice contextualizes this problem in HCI (usability) and

software engineering/programming language design (functionality). Such contextualization enables to the investigation of the problem in the frameworks provided by the previous study in each field.

3.2 The usability issue and incompatible abstraction in the sound synthesis frameworks

The first problem in this RtD practice is how to discuss such 'usability' problems such as readability and simplicity in programming language design. Markstrum even argues that a language designer throw *"together some convincing looking examples and skirt the effort involved in administering a user study or a long-term development study"* [6].

As for usability aspects of this RtD practice, our interest is in reducing difficulty in implementing microsound synthesis techniques in a computer music language. We consider this as a problem in the abstraction of the underlying sound synthesis software framework in a computer music language design, as it is generally considered that incompatible abstractions with the users' conceptualization of the domain can lead to significant usability problems. Blandford provides a valuable view to such issues in her CASSM (Concept-based Analysis of Surface and Structural Misfits") framework, *"the purpose of which is in the identification of misfits between the way the user thinks and the representation implemented within the systems"* [3].

We borrowed such perspectives and frameworks from the previous study in HCI so to better analyze and discuss the usability problems for a new language design. We primarily used the Cognitive Dimensions of Notations framework (CDs) developed for *"broad-brush analysis"* of usability problems in notation [2] and analyzed the usability problems in the existing languages regarding to microsound synthesis, and then assessed the gap between the user's conceptualization of computer music sound synthesis and the representation implemented within the language designs, as CASSM approach suggests. For this assessment, we consider nine musical time-scales by Roads [10] as the conceptualization of time in computer music. We found that the traditional unit-generator-based synthesis frameworks entirely lack the counterpart entities and the manipulations for microsounds, which exist in the user's conceptualization. Thus, the usability issues led to a new abstraction of sound synthesis framework that integrates microsound objects and manipulations, which we developed for our new sound synthesis language. The details are described in [8].

3.3 The functionality issue and mostly-strongly-timed programing concept

The other problem proposed in computer music languages related to microsound synthesis is imprecise timing behaviors. Generally speaking, lack of precise timing behaviors can easily lead to inaccurate sound rendering in computer music, which is audible to human ears; Wang's *strongly-timed programming* is a variation of synchronous programming that integrates explicit control of logical synchronous time into an imperative programming language and thus achieves precise timing behaviors in logical time [13]. Such a feature of *strongly-timed programming* is suitable for timing issues in microsound synthesis. Together with the novel abstraction of sound synthesis framework described above, our new computer music language can provide precise timing behaviors with terse programming model.

However, since as a variation of synchronous programming, strongly-timed programming is based on the *synchrony hypothesis*, which is *"interpreted to imply the system must execute fast enough for the effects of the synchronous hypothesis to hold"* [6]. In practice, the presence of time-consuming tasks that invalidate this assumption can cause a system to fail to meet the deadline for real-time sound rendering; yet time-consuming tasks can be often seen in computer music, e.g. loading and processing of the large amount of sound data. This problem also led us to propose *mostly-strongly-timed programming*, a programming concept that integrates asynchronous behaviors and the explicit switch between a synchronous context and asynchronous context, as an extension of strongly-timed programming. The underlying scheduler can suspend and resume time-consuming tasks so as not to let them cause the failure in meeting the dead-line for real-time sound rendering; such extension can help solving the practical problem as above in audio programming. More information on *mostly-strongly-timed programming* can be seen in [9].

4. Evaluation Methodology

Basically, we follow Markstrum's classification of three types of claims in programming language design, which are *novel features*, *incremental improvement* (*of existing features*) and *desirable language properties* [6]. We can follow the established evaluation methods for the claims in the first two types, such as comprehensive survey of the previous study, performance analysis and comparative approaches with the existing languages.

Yet, as Markstrum also argues, programming language study has been significantly lacking an appropriate framework for the claims in *desirable language properties*, such as readability and simplicity; since we integrated the HCI frameworks such as Cognitive Dimension of Notations in the design phase for the identification and assessment of the usability problems, these frameworks are also introduced in the evaluations phase and used for the heuristic evaluations by external experts; thus, by introducing the

same HCI frameworks during the design and evaluations, we can provide good *claim-evidence correspondences* for desirable language properties by comparing the designer's claims and the evaluation result by external during in the iterative design process.

5. Conclusion

We described our 'Research through Design (RtD)' approach in the development of a new computer music language, with a focus on the problems in microsound synthesis in the existing languages, which resulted in a novel abstraction of sound synthesis framework and programming concept for computer music. As is expected of a RtD practice, our study led to 'contribution of knowledge' through the design process of a product.

References

[1] A.F. Blackwell and N. Collins. The Programming Language as Musical Instrument, In *Proc.of PPIG'05*, 2005

[2] A.F. Blackwell et al. Notational Systems–the Cognitive Dmensions of Notation Framework. In *HCI Models, Theories and Frameworks: Toward a Multidisciplinary Science*, Morgan Kaufmann, 2003

[3] A. Blandford et al. Evaluating System Utility and Conceptual Fit Using CASSM. In *Int'l J. of Human-Computer Studies*, *Vol.66*, 2008

[4] R. Boulanger et al. *The CSound Book*, The MIT Press, 2000

[5] E. Brandt. *Temporal Type Constructors for Computer Music Programming*. Ph.D Thesis, Carnegie Melon University, 2002

[6] S. Markstrum. Staking Claims: A History of Programming Language Design Claims and Evidence. In *Proc. of PLAT-EAU'10*, 2010

[7] M.V. Mathews. et al. *The Technology of Computer Music*. The MIT Press, 1969

[8] H. Nishino. and N. Osaka. LCSynth: A Strongly-Timed Synthesis Language that Integrates Objects and Manipulations for Microsounds. In *Proc. of Sound and Music Computing'12*, 2012

[9] H. Nishino. Mostly-Strongly-Timed Programming. In *Proc. of SPLASH'12, 2012*

[10] C. Roads. *Microsound*, The MIT Press, 2004

[11] J. Rubin. *Handbook of Usability Testing: How to Plan, Design, and Conduct Effective Tests*. Wiley, 1994

[12] G. Wakefiled and W. Smith. Using Lua for Audio Visual Composition, In *Proc. of ICMC'07*, 2007

[13] G. Wang. *The ChucK Audio Programming Language: A Strongly-timed and On-the-fly Environ/mentality*. PhD Thesis, Princeton University, 2008.

[14] J. Zimmerman et al., Research through design as a method for interaction design research. In *Proc. of SIGCHI'07*, 2007

Automated Behavioral Testing of Refactoring Engines

Gustavo Soares

Federal University of Campina Grande, Campina Grande, PB, Brazil

gsoares@dsc.ufcg.edu.br

Abstract

Refactoring is a transformation that preserves the external behavior of a program and improves its internal quality. Usually, compilation errors and behavioral changes are avoided by preconditions. However, defining and implementing preconditions is a complex task. As a result, even mainstream refactoring engines contain critical bugs. We propose an automated approach for testing of Java refactoring engines based on program generation.

Categories and Subject Descriptors D.1.5 [*Programming Techniques*]: Object-oriented Programming; D.2.5 [*Software Engineering*]: Testing and Debugging

Keywords Refactoring, Testing, Program Generation

1. Motivation

Refactoring is a transformation that preserves the external behavior of a program and improves its internal quality. Each refactoring may contain a number of preconditions needed to guarantee behavioral preservation. For instance, to pull up a method m to a superclass, we must check whether m conflicts with the signature of other methods in that superclass. In practice, testing refactoring preconditions involves manually creating an input program to be refactored and specifying a refactoring precondition failure as expected output.

However, developers choose input programs for checking just the preconditions they are aware of. Since specifying preconditions is a non-trivial task, developers may be unaware of preconditions needed to guarantee behavioral preservation. When the implemented preconditions are insufficient to guarantee behavioral preservation, we call it as *overly weak preconditions*. Additionally, some implemented preconditions may be *overly strong*, that is, it leads the engine to refuse to apply a behavior preserving transformation. Producing tests for checking refactoring preconditions by

hand is not simple due to the complexity of the test inputs and the analysis of the refactoring output, which may result on a test suite with a low coverage level, potentially leaving many hidden bugs.

2. Problem

Although refactoring engine developers have invested in testing (Eclipse's test suite has more than 2.000 unit tests for checking refactoring correctness), their test suites still fail to detect a number of bugs. For instance, take class A and its subclass B as illustrated in Listing 1. The B.test() method yields 1. If we use Eclipse 3.7 to perform the Pull Up Method refactoring on m(), the tool will move method m from B to A, and update super to this. A behavioral change was introduced: test yields 2 instead of 1. Since m is invoked on an instance of B, the call to k using this is dispatched on to the implementation of k in B.

Listing 1. Pulling up B.k() by using Eclipse 3.7 or JRRTv1 changes program behavior.

```
public class A {
    int k() {return 1;}
}
public class B extends A {
    int k() {return 2;}
    int m() {return super.k();}
    public int test() {return m();}
}
```

Researches have tried to handle this problem by formally specifying refactorings. For instance, Schäfer and Moor [5] specified refactorings for Java, and proposed a tool called JastAdd Refactoring Tools (JRRT) [5]. However, proving refactoring correctness for the entire language is still a challenge [6]. The same problem occurs when we apply this previous transformation by using JRRTv1[1].

As we mention, refactoring engine developers may also implement overly strong preconditions. For instance, consider the A class and its subclass B in Listing 2. A declares the k(long) method, and B declares methods n and test. Suppose we would like to rename n to k. If we apply this transformation by using Eclipse 3.7, it will show a warning

---

[1] The JRRT version from May 18th, 2010

message. However, we can apply this transformation by using JRRTv1. It performs an additional change to make the transformation behavior-preserving by adding a `super` access to the method invocation `k(2)` inside `test`.

Listing 2. Eclipse 3.7 prevents renaming B.n to B.k but JRRTv1 correctly applies the transformation.

```
public class A {
    public long k(long l) {return 1;}
}
public class B extends A {
    public long n(int i) {return 2;}
    public long test() {return k(2);}
}
```

To help developers on testing refactoring engines, Daniel et al. [1] proposed an approach to automate this process. They used a program generator (ASTGen) to generate programs as test inputs. ASTGen allows users to directly implement how the program will be generated. Also, they implemented test oracles to evaluate engine outputs. They have identified a number of bugs that introduce compilation errors on the user's code. Later, Gligoric et al. [2] proposed (UDITA), a Java-like language that extends ASTGen allowing users to specify what is to be generated (instead of how to generate), and uses the Java Path Finder (JPF) model checker as a basis for searching for all possible combinations.

3. Approach

We propose an automated approach for testing of Java refactoring engines. Its main novelties are its technique for generating input programs and its test oracles for checking behavioral preservation based on dynamic analysis. The approach performs four major steps. First, a program generator automatically yields programs as test inputs for a refactoring. Second, the refactoring under test is automatically applied to each generated program. Then, the transformation is evaluated by test oracles in terms of overly weak and overly strong preconditions (Step 3). In the end, we may have detected a number of failures, which are categorized in Step 4.

Test input generation. To perform the test input generation, we propose a Java program generator (JDOLLY [9]). It contains a subset of the Java metamodel specified in Alloy, a formal specification language. It employs the Alloy Analyzer, a tool for the analysis of Alloy models, to generate solutions for this metamodel. Each solution is translated into a Java program. In JDOLLY, the user can specify the maximum number (*scope*) of packages, classes, fields, and methods for the generated programs. The tool exhaustively generates programs for a given scope. In this way, it may generate input programs capable of revealing bugs that developers were unaware of. Furthermore, JDOLLY can be parameterized with specific constraints. For example, when testing a refactoring that pulls up a method to a superclass, the input programs must contain at least a subclass declaring a method that is subject to be pulled up. We can specify these constraints in Alloy.

Test oracles. We propose SAFEREFACTOR [7], a tool for checking behavioral changes, as oracle for weak preconditions. First, the tool checks for compilation errors in the resulting program, and reports those errors; if no errors are found, it analyzes the results and generates a number of tests suited for detecting behavioral changes. SAFEREFACTOR identifies the methods with matching signature before and after the transformation. Next, it applies Randoop [4], a random unit test generator for Java, to produce a test suite for those methods. Finally, it runs the tests before and after the transformation, and evaluates the results. If results are divergent, the tool reports a behavioral change.

We propose an oracle to detect overly strong preconditions based on differential testing [8]. When the refactoring implementation under test rejects a transformation, we apply the same transformation by using one or more other refactoring implementations. If one implementation applies it, and SAFEREFACTOR does not find behavioral changes, we establish that the implementation under test contains an overly strong condition since it rejected a behavior-preserving transformation.

Test clustering. Since our technique exhaustively generates input programs, it may produce a large number of failures. Jagannath et al. [3] propose an approach to split failures based on oracle messages (Oracle-based Test Clustering - OTC). They used it to classify refactoring engine failures that introduce compilation errors in the output program. The failures are grouped by the template of the compiler error message, so that each group contains a distinct fault. We adopt this approach to classify this kind of failure.

However, we cannot use this approach for classifying failures related to behavioral changes since there is no information from our oracle (SAFEREFACTOR) that could be used to split the failures. Instead, we propose an approach to classify them based on *filters* that check for structural pattern in each pair of input and output programs. For example, there are filters for transformations that enable or disable overloading/overriding of a method in the output program, relatively to the input program.

We also use OTC to categorize the overly strong precondition failures. However, to split the failures, we use the template of the warning message thrown by a refactoring engine.

4. Evaluation Methodology

Our goal is to evaluate our approach with respect to efficiency in the context of testing of real refactoring engines. In particular, we address four research questions:

- **Q1**: Can our approach identify bugs in refactoring engines with reasonable effort to configure and perform it?

- **Q2**: By using a dynamic analysis (SAFEREFACTOR), will we be able to detect bugs not detected by previous oracles [1]?

- **Q3**: Do failures related to behavioral changes with the same structural pattern represent the same fault?

- **Q4**: Do failures related to overly strong preconditions containing the same template of warning message reveal the same strong precondition?

Experiment planning. To evaluate our first research question (**Q1**), we plan to choose refactoring implementations from state-of-art academic and industrial refactoring engines to be tested by using our technique. As metrics, we are going to use the number of identified bugs, the specification size for generating programs for each refactoring, and the time to perform the technique. Based on our primary results, we plan to evaluate the other research questions. For **Q2**, we are going to check whether each bug identified by our approach can be identified by previous oracles. Finally, for **Q3** and **Q4**, we are going to use an external developer to analyze whether each group of failure contains the same fault and all distinct groups of failures contain distinct faults.

Threats do validity. We check overly strong conditions by comparing two or more refactoring engines. These engines may not share the same concept with respect to the evaluated refactoring. We plan to confirm with the engine developers whether the bugs identified by our technique are indeed related to overly strong conditions. With respect to internal validity, constraints specified for JDOLLY may be too restrictive with respect to the program generation, which may hide possibly detectable bugs. We must be cautious when creating these constraints. Concerning the external validity, we are going to select a representative set of refactorings, which should include refactorings that are applied to different structures of the program.

5. Research Status

Preliminary results. We evaluated our approach by testing refactoring engines from Eclipse JDT 3.7, NetBeans 7.0.1, and two versions of JRRT [9]. We evaluated two versions of JRRT. First, we tested the refactorings implemented by JRRTv1, and reported the bugs we found. Later, a new version was released with improvements and bug fixing (which we call JRRTv2); this new version was also subject to our analysis. We evaluated a total of 27 refactoring implementations.

Concerning overly weak preconditions, we identified 34 bugs in Eclipse. All of them were accepted by the Eclipse developers, but 16 of them were labeled as duplicated. So far, they have fixed just two of them. In NetBeans, our technique identified 51 bugs. NetBeans team has already accepted 30 of them and fixed 7 bugs. Meanwhile, we reported 24 bugs to JRRTv1, from which 20 were accepted and fixed (4 of the bugs were not considered bugs due to a closed-world assumption of JRRT developers). We reported more 11 bugs to JRRTv2, from which 6 were accepted and fixed.

Our technique also identified 17 overly strong preconditions in Eclipse JDT [8]. We have not received feedback about them from Eclipse developers prior to this submission. Moreover, it identified 7 overly strong preconditions in JRRTv1, from which three were fixed in JRRTv2.

Future work. So far, we have specified a subset of the Java metamodel in JDolly, which allows us to deal mainly with testing refactorings that operate at or above the level of methods. The method bodies contain just one return statement, such as the example in Listing 1. Additionally, our current Java metamodel does not include some structural Java elements such as interface and inner classes. We are going to extend our Alloy specification in order to test the evaluated refactorings with more elaborated input programs, and also test other refactorings, such as Extract Method.

Additionally, we plan to conduct the experiments to evaluate our research questions **Q2-Q4**. With respect to the test clustering technique for classifying behavioral change failures, we have already defined 13 filters. We used them to manually classify the behavioral change failures that we found in our preliminary experiment [9]. We plan to define more filters and provide a tool support.

Acknowledgments

I gratefully thank Rohit Gheyi, Max Schäfer and the anonymous referees for useful suggestions. This work was partially supported by the National Institute of Science and Technology for Software Engineering (INES).

References

[1] B. Daniel, D. Dig, K. Garcia, and D. Marinov. Automated testing of refactoring engines. In *ESEC/FSE '07*. ACM, 2007.

[2] M. Gligoric, T. Gvero, V. Jagannath, S. Khurshid, V. Kuncak, and D. Marinov. Test generation through programming in udita. In *ICSE '10*, pages 225–234, New York, NY, USA, 2010. ACM.

[3] V. Jagannath, Y. Y. Lee, B. Daniel, and D. Marinov. Reducing the costs of bounded-exhaustive testing. In *FASE '09*, pages 171–185, Berlin, Heidelberg, 2009. Springer-Verlag.

[4] C. Pacheco, S. K. Lahiri, M. D. Ernst, and T. Ball. Feedback-directed random test generation. In *ICSE '07*, pages 75–84, Washington, DC, USA, 2007. IEEE Computer Society.

[5] M. Schäfer and O. de Moor. Specifying and implementing refactorings. In *OOPSLA '10*, pages 286–301, New York, NY, USA, 2010. ACM.

[6] M. Schäfer, T. Ekman, and O. de Moor. Challenge proposal: verification of refactorings. In *PLPV '09*, pages 67–72. ACM, 2008.

[7] G. Soares, R. Gheyi, D. Serey, and T. Massoni. Making program refactoring safer. *IEEE Software*, 27:52–57, 2010. ISSN 0740-7459.

[8] G. Soares, M. Mongiovi, and R. Gheyi. Identifying overly strong conditions in refactoring implementations. In *ICSM '11*, pages 173–182, 2011.

[9] G. Soares, R. Gheyi, and T. Massoni. Automated behavioral testing of refactoring engines. *IEEE TSE*, 99(PrePrints), 2012.

Understanding Communication within Pair Programming

Mark Zarb

School of Computing
University of Dundee
Dundee, UK
markzarb@computing.dundee.ac.uk

Abstract

Communication occurs constantly within a pair whilst they are programming. As examples, a navigator might grunt in approval to a new method the driver has just created, or the pair could have a long conversation discussing requirements and coding strategies. This paper presents a brief background study exploring communication within pair programming, and an investigation which results in the creation of a general analytic coding scheme for expert-expert pair programming. Finally, an experiment is detailed that aims to further explore this field.

Categories and Subject Descriptors D.1.5 [**Programming Languages**]: Object-oriented Programming.

Keywords pair programming; communication; video analysis; grounded theory; collaboration; analytic coding

1. Motivation

Pair programming is an agile software development activity during which two programmers work together and collaborate continuously, usually sharing one keyboard and one computer. Each member of the pair takes on a different role: the driver has full control of the keyboard, whereas the navigator is in charge of reviewing the code and performing continuous analysis and design [1]. The pair is expected to switch roles frequently.

It is widely understood that pair programming is beneficial as it encourages programmers to talk to each other – this 'pair pressure' adds benefits such as greater enjoyment of the work and increased knowledge distribution [2], as well as output quality improvements.

Beck [3] stated that communication is one of the most important values for extreme programming (of which pair programming is a key practice), whereas Lindvall et al. [4] assert that the most important success factors for agile methodologies are cultural support, competent team mem-

bers and support for rapid communication., which in itself is "a vital aspect of pair programming".

Further research indicates that the subject matter of communication "is integral to pair programming" as it helps people to work better when partnered [5], and is an important topic of research interest, with several frameworks proposing advances within this field of study [6]. Gallis et al. [7] state that communication is "one of the most important factors" within software engineering. This statement is acknowledged by Ally et al. [8], who state that pair programming improves communication skills in the team, and improves team interaction.

However, we don't know what the communication within the pair contributes, or how this is linked to success. If we can understand this, it can lead to improved teaching and training about pair programming, and may help identify obstacles to successful pairing. This research aims to investigate which aspects of communication are critical to the success of the pair activity, and to gain a wider understanding of the communication that occurs within the pair.

2. Problem

Many programmers venture into their first pair programming experience sceptical about the social aspects of the added communication that shall be required of them [1]. In a pilot experiment, roughly 50% of first-time pair programmers noted that due to the various forms of communication difficulties within the pair, "communication" was the main problem with the pair programming process [9].

There are existing studies which show that pairs who experienced a high rate of communication did not necessarily experience a high level of satisfaction, nor a high level of confidence with the final outcome of their work [10]. This shows that it is not enough for the members of the pair to simply communicate between themselves – it is also important that their communication stays on-topic, and that it is used to drive the work forward.

The overall aim of the PhD is to further explore the links between communication and pair programming, in particular, types of communication that lead to successful pairing.

This should lead to a robust scheme for creating communication patterns that shall help with understanding pair programming success at various levels of skill. The knowledge gained from these experiments will then be applied in the form of guidelines to assist novice pair programmers to communicate properly when programming.

3. Approach

The author initially carried out a literature review to fully understand current issues within pair programming, and the impact of communication in this area. The findings from this review are discussed in section 2 above, and highlight the importance of communication within pairs. However, little is known about the nature of this communication.

An initial investigation was carried out to understand the various types and topics of communication that occur within a pair of highly skilled programmers. To this effect, a set of 60 videos showing a pair of expert programmers working on a software project (referred to as *pairwith.us* [11]) have been acquired for the use of this project. The main advantage of using videos for this research is that they can be a great resource due to the wealth of layers embedded in the information – the researcher has access not only to the participants, but to their setting, their speech, their gestures, and their actions [12].

All sixty videos showcase the same two programmers working for an average of 30 minutes in each video on an incremental software project. The video consists of the following potential data sources:

- The code, which updates live as the programmers are working;
- A low-resolution video, showing the programmers' facial expressions and gestures;
- An audio feed, which allows the viewer to listen to the conversations between programmers.

Due to the natural, unstructured setting of these videos, and the research question's concern with the words, actions, and points of view of the participants, a qualitative research method was chosen for this study.

Following a detailed review of various qualitative methodologies, including ethnography, narrative research and phenomenology [13, 14], the author decided to use Grounded Theory for data analysis during this evaluation, as it promotes constant refinement and comparisons of the data gathered. This allows for researchers to analyse text-based transcripts created from raw video data, using analytic coding methods to generate evidence.

Grounded Theory is a systematic methodology that has become the most widely-used framework for analysis of qualitative data [12], involving analysis of data through observations, interactions and materials gathered by researchers. Whereas most other qualitative methods allow researchers free reign in following up on potentially interesting data, grounded theory provides methods that have explicit guidelines indicating how the research should proceed. Furthermore, these methods can complement other approaches to qualitative data analysis, rather than stand in opposition to them [15]. According to Myers [16], grounded theory is "very useful in developing [...] descriptions and explanations of organizational phenomena".

3.1 The Use of Grounded Theory

A plan for the investigation was created in separate stages inspired by Grounded Theory, as follows [15, 17]:

- *Open coding, and the gathering of rich data*
  Following an initial viewing of the videos, the author observed various verbal and non-verbal (mouse pointing, gesturing, finger-drumming, grunting) instances of communication, as well as several notable behaviours (such as the programmers' constant awareness of their goals, and use of jokes to lighten the mood and regain focus).
  A smaller sample of videos were randomly selected, re-watched and analysed, with field notes being taken for each pair programming session.
  The field notes were compared with the list of behaviours observed in the earlier stage, to create a list of eight common analytic codes (keywords that categorise segments of the audio-visual data) that could be seen to occur throughout all the *pairwith.us* videos.

- *Development of concepts, and theory formation*
  A sample of five videos was selected at random to be used to test the coding scheme created. All videos were fully transcribed and coded using the initial set of analytic codes. During this process, the codes were continuously refreshed, with some codes being added, and others being merged together. Inter-rater reliability tests were used to assess the codes generated, and this, in turn, was used to refine the set of codes.
  These codes shall then be applied to videos obtained from other expert pairs to verify their validity. The researcher aims at creating theories and guidelines from the generated data; this shall allow for an improved understanding of communication patterns and trends within pairs.

4. Evaluation Methodology

The author is currently in the process of recruiting other pair programmers to validate the coding scheme. It is expected that all programmers recruited shall be experts in pair programming, ideally working in the industry.

4.1 Hypotheses

The primary hypothesis is that novices can be trained in using certain communication patterns in order to improve their satisfaction and coding quality.

The secondary hypothesis is that the understanding of communication between pair programmers can lead to more successful pair programming.

4.2 Experiment Setup

It is expected that the author shall be able to gain access to expert programmers to record videos of their pair programming sessions. With managerial consent, the author expects to be able to allow the pair to work in their usual environment. The camera would be placed in an unobtrusive location, and the author shall not be present in the room during filming, so as not to disturb or distract the pair's usual working process. The programmers shall be asked to work as they would normally.

Following the recording, it is expected that the pair shall be informally interviewed, and presented with a brief questionnaire that shall ask them to note down several points, including but not limited to the following:

- their individual levels of experience (e.g. years spent in the industry);
- for how many years they have been pair programming overall;
- for how many years/months they have been programming specifically with each other.

Once the videos are gathered, they shall be transcribed, and coded. Using the completed set of *pairwith.us* analytic codes discussed above. The data obtained shall be compared and contrasted with the initial *pairwith.us* data to determine similarities and differences, which in turn will allow the author to gather more data and gain a greater understanding into the way expert pairs communicate.

Acknowledgements

The research work disclosed in this publication is funded by the Strategic Educational Pathways Scholarship (Malta). The scholarship is part-financed by the European Union – European Social Fund (ESF) under Operational Programme II - Cohesion Policy 2007-2013, "Empowering People for More Jobs and a Better Quality of Life".

The author would like to thank Dr Janet Hughes and Prof John Richards, for their attention and support.

References

[1] Williams, L., et al., *Strengthening the Case for Pair Programming.* IEEE Software, 2000. **17**(4): p. 19-25.

[2] Bryant, S., P. Romero, and B. du Boulay, *The Collaborative Nature of Pair Programming*, in *Extreme Programming and Agile Processes in Software Engineering*, P. Abrahamsson, M. Marchesi, and G. Succi, Editors. 2006, Springer Berlin / Heidelberg. p. 53-64.

[3] Beck, K., *Extreme programming explained: embrace change.* 2000: Addison-Wesley Professional.

[4] Lindvall, M., et al., *Empirical Findings in Agile Methods*, in *Proceedings of the Second XP Universe and First Agile Universe Conference on Extreme Programming and Agile Methods - XP/Agile Universe 2002.* 2002, Springer-Verlag. p. 197-207.

[5] Cockburn, A. and L. Williams, *The costs and benefits of pair programming*, in *Extreme programming examined.* 2001, Addison-Wesley Longman Publishing Co., Inc. p. 223-243.

[6] Stapel, K., et al., *Towards Understanding Communication Structure in Pair Programming*, in *Agile Processes in Software Engineering and Extreme Programming*, A. Sillitti, et al., Editors. 2010, Springer Berlin Heidelberg. p. 117-131.

[7] Gallis, H., E. Arisholm, and T. Dyba. *An initial framework for research on pair programming.* in *International Symposium on Empirical Software Engineering.* 2003.

[8] Ally, M., F. Darroch, and M. Toleman. *A Framework for Understanding the Factors Influencing Pair Programming Success*, in *Extreme Programming and Agile Processes in Software Engineering*, H. Baumeister, M. Marchesi, and M. Holcombe, Editors. 2005, Springer Berlin / Heidelberg. p. 1305-1308.

[9] Sanders, D., *Student Perceptions of the Suitability of Extreme and Pair Programming*, in *Extreme Programming Perspectives*, M. Marchesi, et al., Editors. 2002, Addison-Wesley Professional. p. 168-174.

[10] Choi, K.S., F.P. Deek, and I. Im, *Pair dynamics in team collaboration.* Computers in Human Behavior, 2009. **25**(4): p. 844-852.

[11] Marcano, A. and A. Palmer. *pairwith.us.* 2009 [cited 2012 31 July]; Available from: http://vimeo.com/channels/pairwithus.

[12] Bryman, A., *Social Research Methods.* 2012: Oxford University Press.

[13] Wertz, F.J., et al., *Five Ways of Doing Qualitative Analysis: Phenomenological Psychology, Grounded Theory, Discourse Analysis, Narrative Research, and Intuitive Inquiry.* 2011: Guilford Press.

[14] Ritchie, J. and J. Lewis, *Qualitative research practice: a guide for social science students and researchers.* 2003, London: Sage Publications Ltd.

[15] Charmaz, K., *Constructing grounded theory: a practical guide through qualitative analysis.* 2006: SAGE.

[16] Myers, M.D., *Qualitative research in business & management.* 2008, London: Sage Publications Ltd.

[17] Lazar, J., J.H. Feng, and H. Hochheiser, *Research methods in human-computer interaction.* 2009: Wiley.

Welcome Message from the Panels Chair

SPLASH

Welcome to the panels sessions for SPLASH 2012. It is these sessions that most strongly bring out this year's theme of "Software Tools."

This year we are pleased to offer two panels, each with a great set of panelists. Both panels were put together by Steven Fraser of Cisco Research, who has been a great asset to this part of the SPLASH program.

The first panel, on software tools research, addresses fundamental and practical questions surrounding software tools. The second panel on trade-offs in software design and delivery addresses key issues in engineering evolving software systems. This second panel builds on a workshop "What Drives Design?" which is occurring earlier during the conference.

Special thanks to Steven Fraser for proposing and organizing both of this year's panels. Thanks also to Michael Ernst of the University of Washington for serving on the Panels committee this year.

Please enjoy the panels and ask questions!

Gary T. Leavens
University of Central Florida

Panel

Software Tools Research:
A Matter of Scale and Scope – or Commoditization?

Steven Fraser

Director, Cisco Research Center
Cisco Systems, San Jose
sdfraser@acm.org

Kendra Cooper

Associate Professor
UT Dallas
kendra.m.cooper@gmail.com

Jim Coplien

Software Architecture and Agile Consultant
Gertrude & Cope
jcoplien@gmail.com

Ruth Lennon

Lecturer, Letterkenny
Institute of Technology
ruth.lennon@lyit.ie

Ramya Ravichandar

Software Engineer
Cisco Systems, San Jose
raravich@cisco.com

Diomidis Spinellis

Professor, Athens University of
Economics and Business
dds@aueb.gr

Giancarlo Succi

Dean and Professor
Free University Bolzano-Bozen
Giancarlo.Succi@unibz.it

Abstract

Tools emerge as the result of necessity – a job needs to be done, automated, and scaled. In the "early days" – compilers, code management, bug tracking, and the like – resulted in mostly local home-grown tools – and when broadly successful - spawn (from either industry or university origins) independent tools companies – for example Klocwork from Nortel and Coverity from Stanford University. This panel will bring together academics and industry professionals to discuss challenges in tools research.

Categories and Subject Descriptors
K.0 Computing Milieux

General Terms   Management, Design, Economics, Experimentation, Standardization.

Keywords   Tools, Process, Research

1. Steven Fraser

STEVEN FRASER joined the Cisco Research Center as Director in July 2007 with responsibilities for fostering university research collaborations, managing PhD recruiting, and nurturing technology transfer. Prior to joining Cisco Research, Steven was a Senior Staff member of Qualcomm's Learning Center in San Diego, leading software learning programs and creating the corporation's internal technical conference (the QTech Forum). Steven held a variety of technology strategy roles at BNR and Nortel including: Process Architect, Senior Manager (Disruptive Technology and Global External Research), and Advisor (Design Process Engineering). In 1994 he spent a year as a Visiting Scientist at the Software Engineering Institute (SEI) collaborating with the "Ap-

plication of Software Models" project on the development of team-based domain analysis (software reuse) techniques. Fraser is the Panels Chair for XP2013 and the Publicity Chair for ESEC 2013. He was the Corporate Support Chair for OOPSLA'08 and OOPSLA'09. He was the Tutorial Chair for XP2008 and the Tutorial Co-Chair for ICSE'09. Fraser holds a doctorate in EE from McGill University in Montréal – and is a senior member of the ACM and the IEEE.

Based on the SPLASH 2012 theme of "New Tools for Software" topics for panel discussion are likely to include:
- What are the principal challenges in tools R&D?
- What are the challenges assessing and improving user satisfaction (e.g. small sample populations, or populations lacking requisite variety)?
- What are the appropriate measures of tool value (usability, configurability, support, cost, stability, etc.).
- How quickly can tools be commoditized – and does this tend to improve (or reduce) tool capability?

2. Kendra Cooper

KENDRA COOPER is an Associate Professor in the Department of Computer Science at The University of Texas at Dallas; she has an Adjunct faculty position at the University of Calgary. She received her Ph.D. in Electrical and Computer Engineering from The University of British Columbia. She has published extensively in journals, conferences, symposia, and workshops and serves on numerous program committees and editorial boards. Cooper has worked in the early phases of the software and systems engineering of large-scale, complex systems in industrial and academic settings. Her research interests center on modularization and re-use issues in requirements engineering/architecture for adaptive systems and engineering education. She has investigated these issues using a variety of paradigms including component-, aspect-, agent-, and recently cloud-based engineering. Software tools research is a matter of scale and scope (in other words, what is the tool research supposed to accomplish?). It is also a matter of the development environment – where and by whom is the tool research being conducted?

Software tools research is conducted in a variety of settings, including academia, research labs, industry, and open source projects. In academia tools are often developed by research students as proof of concept prototypes; they are used in the validation effort for their proposed solution to a problem. The students need the tool as part of their research and are motivated to develop them: the tool is needed for validation; validation is needed to demonstrate the value of their solution; demonstrated value is needed for a successful defense, graduation, and then "getting a life". The scope and scale of these prototypes are often quite narrow - they are usually intended to provide specific capabilities; they are unlikely to be extensible, scalable, easy to use, and so on. Tool teams in industry or research labs are staffed with experienced, paid professionals, who create larger, more general tools in a team-based, managed environment. Open-source tools are developed by volunteers – enthusiasts seeking to extend and contribute their expertise to the broader community.

If we want to go beyond proof of concept, prototype tools for individual research projects in academia, for example, to establish their place in the community as The School That Developed Tool X, is it possible to move towards team-based, managed development or an open-source approach? I've been trying the former on the R&D of a tool. The students (M.Sc. in computer science) work on the project as team members to gain practical development experience and improve their resumes. The students are not paid with salaries; they sign up for the course as an elective. Over the last five terms, a number of challenges have become clear when trying to adopt a more industry-like model in academia. For example:

Some of the challenges seem relatively straightforward to address. For example, graded homework assignments to build technical and soft skills have been included in the course; research assistants have been hired to reduce the impact of the turnover by becoming a repository of knowledge about the project. Overall, however, the productivity of the industry-like teams has not been strong. Recently, I've been trying a more open-source like approach, where an individual student works on one specific problem.

3.   Jim Coplien

JIM COPLIEN is an old C++ shark who now does world-wide consulting on Agile software development methods and architecture. He is one of the founders of the software pattern discipline, and his organizational patterns work is one of the foundations of both Scrum and XP. He is a Certified Scrum Trainer and a Member Emeritus of the Hillside Group.

He currently works for Gertrud & Cope in Denmark, is a partner in the Scrum Foundation, a Director of Scrum Tide and the Product Owner for Scrum Knowsy®. Together with Gertrud Bjørnvig, he has written a book on Lean Software Architecture and Agile Software Development.

When I visited the temples in Nara several years ago I learned that the craftsmen who built them, and those who still maintain them, start their work by building their own tools. I have found that the same has been true in the most memorable of my software experiences over the years, because general-purpose tools are often only suitable for general-purpose work and are never ideal for any job in particular. In Bell Labs we wrote our own compilers

because there were no commercial compilers that could scale to our needs or that were of high enough quality to meet the stringent engineering constraints of continuous-running software. We all have frequently built our own tools for custom tasks. These are the tools worthy of dialog and focus; commodity tools form an important but uninteresting backdrop. And most tools are commodities.

Most Agile tools suffer generation rot. Many of the tools that are the darlings of upstart Scrum teams are based on pre-Agile building blocks and pre-Agile thought. Few of the household name Agile support tools truly support what Agile development needs. While trumpeting support for communication they in fact get in its way. The tools are often used in under-engineered environments whose sluggish performance frustrates users until they are lulled into submission and resignation to poor performance. Few of them are able to capture the complex requirement relationships discovered during the elaboration of user stories. Capturing user stories is almost useless; capturing their detailing is important; structuring requirements in a way that drives high-ROI backlogs is crucial; mapping them onto a tool ideologically suited to capturing old-fashioned requirements is just stupid; believing that one metaphor and organization fits all or that it easily can be parameterized is naïve. Every Agile shop is compromised by the lack of an ideal fit between its goals and its tools, but instead of working to improve the tools, Agilists seem to celebrate their quirkiness. The great tools are home-grown.

In the Toyota Production System traditions at the roots of Scrum, high-order tools are used only to automate proven manual processes. Few Agile tools used in contemporary software shops emerge from optimized manual processes; they more often replace earlier dysfunctional processes. What's worse is that because of organizational politics or "formal envy," these tools often replace perfectly good manual processes. We're an industry that uses tools for tools' sake, in large part because almost all of us build tools. But a fool with a tool is still a fool.

A commodity tool bought off a shelf and brought into a development context is either de-contextualized or primitive by necessity. We in fact need commodity tools: the compilers, editors, and operating systems are the saws and hammers of our trade. Most of what was called a "tool" in the past generation is a commodity tool today: True power tools are generally done in-house because they rely heavily on business expertise. It's interesting to note that commodity tools are becoming increasingly invisible and that our need for tools as such is decreasing. As a user of XCode and it storyboarding facility, I haven't directly used a compiler or configuration management tool in years. XCode, while a tool, probably doesn't fit the category of being a commodity; such animals in the burgeoning tool zoo are particularly worthy of discussion. Beyond that, I fail to appreciate why SPLASH would have a panel that revolves around commodity items. I rarely see organizations get in trouble for what are tool problems.

There are some "tools" that transcend groups and organizations, and among them are games. A game is a tool that can support reflection, growth, and the proper *esprit de corps* in an Agile organization. We have recently launched a tool called Scrum Knowsy® designed to assess and build alignment within a Scrum team and to allow each team to assess its collective alignment to community norms. If you've got to have a tool, it might as well be fun and support the Agile agenda.

4.   Ramya Ravichandar

RAMYA RAVICHANDAR is currently leading the *Agile Lean at Cisco* program at Cisco Systems, Inc. She is focused on evangelizing emerging software practices, researching on enterprise-level initiatives, and fostering an Agile Lean community in Cisco. Related to this she has presented in Agile 2010, and XP 2012 conferences. Her other interests span software quality, processes, change-tolerant systems, and requirements engineering. She has a Ph.D. in Computer Science from Virginia Tech and is a member of IEEE Computer Society.

Oh so appealing is the nifty blazingly fast in-house tool! Compare it with the magnificent full-featured enterprise-level solution. What you choose, depends on where you sit in the food chain. Therein lies the crux of the argument about tooling in our industry.

In this distributed environment where teams are connected through tools, there is a danger of the tools becoming the sole connectors. They are often used in lieu, and not as an aid to good software engineering. And can you blame the engineer, for using the aggressively marketed silver bullet? A tool's success should be driven by its effectiveness and not measured by a fixed deployment schedule; a challenge in this metrics-driven environment of instant gratification.

Tools are bound to influence the process. It is a possibility that when both become so intertwined we are in the danger of overlooking other innovations. Perhaps what we need is a tool litmus test. How do we decide that a tool is right? Is it a trade-off between: hidden costs vs. productivity gains, or resolving singular issues vs. one-size-fits-all approach? The answer lies somewhere in between.

5. Ruth Lennon

RUTH LENNON has worked for Letterkenny Institute of Technology for over 14 years in lecturing and research activities. Prior to joining LYIT, Ruth worked with a software company developing software in Delphi. Ruth is currently working on research on *Software As A Service* and BYOD. Ruth is one of the Directors of InfoSecurity Ireland. Ruth has been an active participant in the ACM's OOPSLA workshops and BOF's since 2005. Ruth is a member of the ACM and IEEE and actively encourages women to work in all aspects of engineering.

I represent an important part of the "software tools research" community -- a "user" of the tools. In the work I describe in my BYOD and Cloud paper, my institution is trying to use a wide variety of commercial and open source tools in a challenging environment. We are trying to keep costs down, we are dealing with wide variations in experience levels among learners and staff, and many of the existing tools create some difficult and unnecessary obstacles to deployment. The range of specifications of PCs in our institute leads to the need to consider issues such as ease of deployment, deployment in a cloud environment, deployment on a low end PCs and legacy operating systems, interoperability with other tools, documentation, training, ability to export useful data in a standard data format, etc. I represent a unique body of system users in that some are computer experts while others simply want to use the tools with the greatest level of simplicity. The software and hardware tools requirements for users and systems administrators can be quite disparate and this can prove challenging. Take as one example the need to provide access to Fire Modelling Software which has not changed much in the last 10 years. Some software still restricts licenses via dongles and may be significantly processor heavy. The Fire laboratory equipment software exports data onto a Windows 95 PC and has not yet be upgraded to keep with modern systems.

One problem with industry-academic research partnerships: they are often narrowly focused on research areas that are less likely to produce a real paradigm shift. There are some new innovative ideas that are "easy to launch" as a new product, such as web apps, open-source toolkits, and other products that are centered around new innovative algorithms but in relatively conventional packaging. The most creative and different new ideas are the most difficult for established industry product groups to embrace. It is already difficult for most product development groups to accept an "escaped from the lab" product idea from an internal corporate research organization, it is doubly difficult to build on the work of graduate students in a corporate environment. On the other hand, if a partnership is done right, there are plenty of benefits going in both directions. In particular, both sides of an industry-academic partnership will usually bring in useful ideas about how to convert an innovation into a marketable product.

6. Diomidis Spinellis

DIOMIDIS SPINELLIS is a Professor in the Department of Management Science and Technology at the Athens University of Economics and Business, Greece. From 2009 to 2011 he served as the Secretary General for Information Systems at the Greek Ministry of Finance. His research interests include software engineering, computer security, and programming languages. He has written two award-winning, widely-translated books: *Code Reading* and *Code Quality: The Open Source Perspective.* He is a member of the *IEEE Software* editorial board, authoring the regular "Tools of the Trade" column. Spinellis is the author of many open-source software tools, packages, and libraries. Some tools he has developed include the *UMLGraph* declarative UML drawing engine, the *CScout* refactoring editor for huge complex systems written in C, and the *ckjm* tool, which efficiently calculates Chidamber and Kemerer object-oriented metrics in Java programs. His implementation of the Unix *sed* stream editor is part of Apple's Mac OS X and all BSD Unix distributions. Spinellis holds a M. Eng. in Software Engineering and a PhD in Computer Science, both from Imperial College London. He is senior member of the ACM and the IEEE.

The development of production-quality software tools is becoming an increasingly difficult task for individual researchers. First, the application domains are becoming more complex. This includes language specifications, interfaces, and development frameworks. Kernighan and Ritchie's *The C Programming Language* (1988) was 274 pages long, whereas Stroustrup's *The C++ Programming Language* (2000) stands at a hefty 1030 pages. This rising complexity is reflected in the size of the corresponding tools. The 7th Edition Unix C compiler consisted of about 14k lines of code, whereas GCC 4.2, at 1.5 million lines, is two orders of magnitude larger. We can find at least one order of magnitude difference between the original tools and their current ancestors across the board; consider for instance RCS (1982, 25k lines) versus the current version of git (2012, 449k lines). Distribution and support is nowadays also more demanding. Whereas Ken Thompson mailed Unix source code magnetic tapes to his friends, labeling them simply "Love, ken", nowadays researchers developing tools are expected to maintain a project web site, support binary packages for diverse operating system distributions, provide a bug tracking service, answer questions on a forum, and respond to patch pull requests.

Thankfully, a number of countervailing factors help us keep the situation in balance. Modern software frameworks, like Java and .NET, and libraries, like Boost, make modern code considerably more expressive. Mature open-source offerings can dramatically reduce the implementation effort required for a tool's front-end (e.g. LLVM), processing (MiniSat), and presentation (GraphViz). Robust package management systems enable the painless installation of tools with complex dependencies on external software. Cloud offerings, like GitHub, Google Groups, and StackExchange, simplify collaboration, bug tracking, wiki maintenance, and end-user support. The open source software community often stands ready to embrace a useful tool, offering extensions, bug fixes, and support. Finally, nowadays tool developers can often create plugins for a larger framework, like Eclipse, rather than build a tool from scratch.

The challenge for software tool researchers is to avoid being intimidated and turned-off by the large scope and complexity associated with modern tool development, learn how to harness the available countervailing factors, and benefit from them. Curriculum developers and mentors can help budding researchers by bringing them in contact with modern tool development practices.

7. Giancarlo Succi

GIANCARLO SUCCI is Professor and Dean of the Faculty of Computer Science and Director at the Center for Applied Software Engineering at the Free University of Bozen-Bolzano. Before moving to Bolzano he held several academic appointments around the world and is a global consultant for software companies and public institutions. Giancarlo Succi is a Fulbright Scholar.

The evolution in the software industry has been possible because of the presence of smart software development tools, which enabled the production or more complex systems and of better tools. For instance, it would be unimaginable today to develop the simplest native Android application writing the code using vi and running by hand or via some sort of make the compilation process. Moreover, it would not be conceivable to have an IDE like Eclipse without first having the experience of emacs, which in turn draws from the experience of vi.

Still, the research done on how people use tools is very limited and the design of new tools does follows more personal tastes and fads rather than a systematic empirical process. A major im-

provement toward a better understanding of how tools are used has been the introduction of AISEMA (Automated In-Process Software Engineering Measurement and Analysis) systems, which track non-invasively the activities of developers, including the tools they use [1]**Error! Reference source not found.**. However, so far it has still remained an open question how to actually analyze data coming from AISEMA systems on tools usage, especially trying to understand the usefulness and the usage of each tool together with the mutual interactions between tools. To this end specific visualization techniques could be employed, like the ones proposed in [2]. Such visualization enables the immediate understanding of the roles that specific tools have in software development and how people then use such tool, evidencing for instance that Pair Programming increases significantly the permanence in tools before doing context switching triggering higher level of attention, which then result in better work [3]. This visualization also evidences in a case study a fact always known in the software engineering community but never rigorously experimented: that only a small fraction of the installed tools are effectively used [4].

Altogether, more systematic, empirical, let me say "scientific" research has to done in this direction, determining empirically the impact of software tools, and also trying to understand how different tools mutually interact and contribute, as a cluster and not just individually, to the production of software systems.

References
[1] Ilenia Fronza, Alberto Sillitti, Giancarlo Succi, Jelena Vlasenko, Does Pair Programming Increase Developers' Attention? Industrial Track of ESEC/FSE2011, Szeged, Hungary, Sept 2011
[2] Alberto Sillitti, Andrea Janes, Giancarlo Succi, and Tullio Vernazza. Collecting, integrating and analyzing software metrics and personal software process data. In EUROMICRO '03: Proceedings of the 29th Conference on EUROMICRO, page 336, Washington, DC, USA, 2003. IEEE Computer Society.
[3] Alberto Sillitti, Giancarlo Succi, Jelena Vlasenko, Toward a better understanding of tool usage (NIER Track), Proceedings of the ICSE2011 Conference, Honolulu, Hawaii, May 2011.
[4] Alberto Sillitti, Giancarlo Succi, Jelena Vlasenko, Understanding the impact of Pair Programming on Developers Attention, Proceedings of the ICSE2012 Conference, Zurich, Switzerland, June 2012.

Trade-offs in Software Design and Delivery

Steven Fraser

Cisco Research Center
Cisco Systems, San Jose
sdfraser@acm.org

Richard Gabriel

IBM Research
Redwood City
rpg@dreamsongs.com

Gail E. Harris

Web Development Manager
and Architect
TV Ontario, Toronto
gail.e.harris@gmail.com

Ricardo Lopez

Software Architect and Consultant
San Jose
rjlopez@acm.org

Dennis Mancl

Distinguished Member of Technical Staff
Alcatel-Lucent, New Jersey
dennis.mancl@alcatel-lucent.com

William Opdyke

Architecture Lead
Corporate Internet Group
JP Morgan Chase, Chicago
opdyke@acm.org

Abstract

There are many design and delivery trade-offs that engineers face in creating or evolving software systems. Challenges in accelerating delivery, offering more features, providing better more reliable systems, or managing costs – whose optimization are just some of the hurdles that contribute to system success (or failure). This panel will discuss the heuristics of trade-offs, the inherent risks – and plans to build on the success of the 2012 SPLASH workshop "What Drives Design".

Categories and Subject Descriptors
K.0 Computing Milieux

General Terms Design, Experimentation, Standardization

Keywords Innovation, Creativity, Design Trade-Offs

1. Steven Fraser

STEVEN FRASER joined the Cisco Research Center as Director in July 2007 with responsibilities for fostering university research collaborations, managing PhD recruiting, and nurturing technology transfer. Prior to joining Cisco Research, Steven was a Senior Staff member of Qualcomm's Learning Center in San Diego, leading software learning programs and creating the corporation's internal technical conference (the QTech Forum). Steven held a variety of technology strategy roles at BNR and Nortel including: Process Architect, Senior Manager (Disruptive Technology and Global External Research), and Advisor (Design Process Engineering). In 1994 he spent a year as a Visiting Scientist at the Software Engineering Institute (SEI) collaborating with the "Application of Software Models" project on the development of team-based domain analysis (software reuse) techniques. Fraser is the Panels Chair for XP2013 and the Publicity Chair for ESEC

2013. He was the Corporate Support Chair for OOPSLA'08 and OOPSLA'09. He was the Tutorial Chair for XP2008 and the Tutorial Co-Chair for ICSE'09. Fraser holds a doctorate in EE from McGill University in Montréal – and is a senior member of the ACM and the IEEE.

2. Richard Gabriel

RICHARD P. GABRIEL received a PhD in Computer Science from Stanford University in 1981, and an MFA in Poetry from Warren Wilson College in 1998. He has been a researcher at Stanford University, company president and Chief Technical Officer at Lucid, Inc., vice president of Development at ParcPlace-Digitalk, a management consultant for several start-ups, a Distinguished Engineer at Sun Microsystems, and Consulting Professor of Computer Science at Stanford University. He is a researcher at IBM Research, looking into the architecture, design, and implementation of extraordinarily large, self-sustaining systems as well as development techniques for building them. Until recently he was President of the Hillside Group, a non-profit that nurtures the software patterns community by holding conferences, publishing books, and awarding scholarships. He is on Hillside's Board of Directors. He helped design and implement a variety of dialects of Lisp. He is author of four books ("Performance and Evaluation of Lisp Systems," MIT Press; "Patterns of Software: Tales from the Software Community," Oxford University Press; "Writers' Workshops and the Work of Making Things," Addison-Wesley Press; and "Innovation Happens Elsewhere: Open Source as Business Strategy," Morgan Kaufmann), and a poetry chapbook ("Drive On," Hollyridge Press), with two books of poetry in preparation: "Leaf of my Puzzled Desire" and "Drive On." He has published more than 100 scientific, technical, and semi-popular papers, articles, and essays on computing. He has won several awards, including the AAAI/ACM Allen Newell Award. He is the lead guitarist in a rock 'n' roll band and a poet.

Design in the future will have two distinct and mutually contradictory challenges. Remember: the future.

First, all the programs that can be written by a single person or a team working together have already been written, and every interesting new program cannot be subject to whole-system design. Neither requirements nor design will be consistent. Every designer will be limited to a narrow part of the program's interface or to its interstitial glue. In the past, design was like creating Esperanto - control of every aspect - while now design is like adding a new slang phrase to English - something akin to "Shatner texting." One way to do this is like Siri: a small interface on the iPhone designed by designers (using guidelines from Apple and subject to their approval), plus a raft of code in the cloud (put together over a decade or more by a team originally scattered and now long gone). This could be called iceberg architecture.

Second, all the crap that goes with finding, acquiring, installing, maintaining, upgrading, and using software and that is not about the actual task (let's call it) the software's user wants to accomplish has to be scraped away from view, must be invisible to the buyer, user, and everyone on that end of the whole transaction - this is a designer's task. Some have called this "ready-to-hand." It's a kind of whole-system design. More recently some corporations have taken to calling this "consummability." Siri is a way to accomplish consummability by hiding all the crap in the cloud, but can all software be cloudy?

3. Gail E. Harris

GAIL E. HARRIS was recently appointed Web Development Manager and Architect at TVOntario (TVO), the Province of Ontario's public educational media organization. Gail is responsible for all technical aspects of TVO's web and mobile presence, including long term strategy and development methodologies. Prior to joining TVO, Gail was a Principal and co-owner of Instantiated Software, a company that applied agile methodologies and open source technologies to successfully deliver custom applications to start-up companies. Previous to Instantiated, Gail worked for several larger organizations including the Department of National Defence, and Deloitte Consulting. For the past fifteen years Gail has been a regular contributor to SPLASH/OOPSLA. Gail was the OOPSLA Conference Chair in 2008.

Not too long ago, on a modest sized system that had been running for a few years, a customer requested a seemingly simple change to the text on a certain web page. The complexity, and hence the design challenge and trade off, showed up while doing the analysis. While the text needed to vary according to the data being displayed, more importantly, the web page in question was displaying an invoice. In addition to the required text change, there was also an underlying constraint that an old invoice needed to be presented exactly as it would have appeared at the time it was issued. A backward compatibility requirement. Backward compatibility may not be a new topic, nor a cool topic. It does however force designers to think strategically about the compromises they make. Should I put time and effort (money) into programming the strategy pattern or the facade pattern? Can I limit compatibility to no more than X major historical releases? How will I maintain code readability and repair-ability?

In this particular example something interesting occurred. Near the very beginning of the project the designers had decided that all invoice data would be retrieved from the business model objects and copied into a completely separate set of read only database tables, allowing for historical trend analysis. These tables would be queried to display invoices, not the core model tables. Furthermore, the text in question existed in the invoice template in the view layer. Two main options were considered:

- detect the version in the view layer and generate the appropriate text for invoices of different ages

- add a database field for the text, modify the view to display it, modify the core model to generate the text based on version, and populate all the old invoices.

The trade-off here is between effort (cost) and separation of concerns that keeps business logic separate from view logic. After consulting with the customer the designers chose the former option, because the nature of the business suggested that it would be highly unlikely to have another change. This meant that the changes would not require backward compatibility of the core classes; the programming changes were isolated in the view layer. The less nice observation is that the view layer now has a smell: date pollution. In a few places the code includes some conditionals about the version needed for the invoice being presented. The residual design dilemma is how much effort to put into removing that smell, if it's even possible.

The views expressed in this position statement are those of Gail E. Harris and do not represent those of her employer.

4. Ricardo Lopez

RICARDO LOPEZ is a software architect and consultant. Formerly he was a Principal Engineer at Qualcomm CDMA Technologies and adjunct to the Office of the Chief Scientist at Qualcomm. He was responsible for software architecture, software process, and sometimes Just Good Old Fashioned Software – AKA Code. Architecting and designing Software for over thirty-five years (too old for Google), he has been an evangelist for OO technology for the last twenty-five years and he has the arrow heads to prove it (time to become an early adopter of the next great orientation)...

5. Dennis Mancl

DENNIS MANCL works for Alcatel-Lucent, where he is involved in applying software modelling approaches, agile development practices, and legacy software development techniques to the development of large telecom systems. He has worked with technologies from C++ to UML to Scrum, with a preference for simple designs, simple tools, and simple metrics.

Software design and software delivery are difficult. The design process, which builds up the structure of a proposed solution to a real world problem, requires a combination of experience and creativity from the designer. The delivery process, which reshapes the design and its implementation to closely fit the current customer expectations, requires patience and attention to detail.

How can we coordinate the design process and the delivery process, especially in a world of rapidly evolving customer needs? A number of design approaches and process models have been proposed over the years, from Object Oriented Design to Extreme Programming, with some success. Maybe any organized design approach will work, as long as the developers believe in it.

6. William Opdyke

BILL OPDYKE has spent much of his career focusing on the technical and organizational issues related to transitioning advanced software technologies and software engineering techniques into product development. He is currently on staff at JP Morgan Chase. Previously, at Motorola, he was part of an advanced technology team focusing on home networking related middleware and on techniques for improving productivity and reducing costs of software developments. While at Bell Labs, he was technical lead on several advanced development projects where he gained a keen appreciation for the challenges in leveraging emerging technologies and in extending existing products to meet emerging market needs. He also spent several years as a faculty member at North Central College. His doctoral research at the University of Illinois focused on object-oriented refactoring (supporting the process of change to object-oriented software).

Posters & ACM Student Research Competition Co-Chairs' Welcome

SPLASH Posters provide an excellent forum for authors to present their work in an informal and interactive setting. Posters are ideal to showcase speculative, late-breaking results or to introduce interesting, innovative work. Poster sessions are highly interactive. They allow authors and interested participants to connect to each other and to engage in discussions about the presented work. Posters provide authors with a unique opportunity to draw attention to their work during the conference. Therefore, authors in other SPLASH technical tracks are strongly encouraged to complement their submissions with posters about their work.

After its remarkable success in previous years, SPLASH is again hosting an ACM SIGPLAN Student Research Competition. The competition, sponsored by Microsoft Research, is an internationally recognized venue that enables undergraduate and graduate students to experience the research world, share their research results with SPLASH attendees, and compete for prizes. The ACM SIGPLAN Student Research Competition shares the Poster session's goal to facilitate students' interaction with researchers and industry practitioners, providing both sides with the opportunity to learn about ongoing research. Additionally, the ACM SIGPLAN Student Research Competition affords students with experience in both formal presentations and evaluations.

On the following pages, you will find the abstracts for both SPLASH Posters and the ACM SIGPLAN Student Research Competition that cover an exciting mix of topics from the domains of systems, applications, and programming languages. It is worth noting that students participating in the ACM SIGPLAN Student Research Competition submit their abstracts as sole authors. You can use the abstracts to receive a brief introduction to posters from both SPLASH Posters and the ACM SIGPLAN Student Research Competition on display during the poster session, or to find further information about the authors and their work. The ACM SIGPLAN Student Research Competition abstracts can also be used to get a general overview of what the competitors will be presenting during their formal presentations in the competition's second round.

At this time, we would like to take the opportunity to thank everyone who has helped make SPLASH Posters and the ACM SIGPLAN Student Research Competition a success. In particular, we would like to acknowledge the contribution of the Program Committee members. Their insightful reviews provided valuable feedback to the authors and helped us considerably in selecting the most worthy submissions for both SPLASH Posters and the ACM SIGPLAN Student Research Competition. Finally, we would also like to acknowledge Microsoft Research for sponsoring the ACM SIGPLAN Student Research Competition.

We look forward to seeing you in Tucson, Arizona at SPLASH.

Eli Tilevich
Virginia Tech

Sushil Bajracharya
Black Duck Software Inc.

Programming Language Abstractions
for Self-Reconfigurable Robots

Ulrik Pagh Schultz

Modular Robotics Lab, University of Southern Denmark
ups@mmmi.sdu.dk

Abstract

Self-reconfigurable, modular robots are distributed mechatronic devices that can change their physical shape; modules are programmed individually but must coordinate across the robot. We present dynamic distributed scope as a programming language abstraction for modular robots, and show how it provides a unified abstraction for the domain.

Categories and Subject Descriptors   D [*3.2*]: Specialized application languages

General Terms   Languages

Keywords   Language design, robotics, distribution, roles

1. Introduction

Modular robotics is an approach to the design, construction and operation of robotic devices aiming to achieve flexibility and reliability by using a reconfigurable assembly of simple subsystems [9]. Robots built from modular components can potentially overcome the limitations of traditional fixed-morphology systems because they are able to rearrange modules automatically, a process known as self-reconfiguration, and are able to replace unserviceable modules without disrupting the system's operations significantly. Programming reconfigurable robots is however complicated by the need to adapt the behavior of each of the individual modules to the overall physical shape of the robot and the difficulty of handling partial hardware failures in a robust manner.

In earlier work, we have investigated a role-based, geometrically aware distributed language for programming modular robots [1–3, 8]. We are currently working on generalizing the language based on a robust notion of distributed state inspired by spatial computing [6], and on exploiting reversibility as an error recovery mechanism [7]. This poster presents the latest evolution in the design of programming language abstractions for modular robots, with a focus on how the notion of a dynamic distributed scope can provide

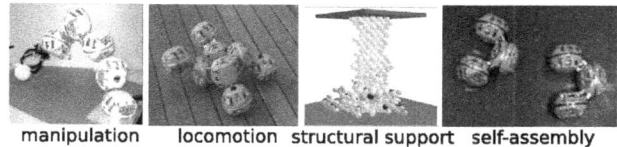

Figure 1. The ATRON modular robot; various applications

a unified abstraction for the various components of the language. We believe the language design principles to be generally useful for programming distributed robotic systems.

2. Modular Robots

There are numerous kinds of modular robots [9]. The ATRON self-reconfigurable modular robot (Fig. 1) is our primary experimental platform [5]. Each unit is composed of two hemispheres rotating relative to each other, giving the module one degree of freedom. Connections are performed by using eight mechanical connectors, positioned at 90 degree intervals on each hemisphere. The likewise positioned infrared ports are used to communicate among neighboring modules and to sense distance to nearby objects. Each module is in principle an autonomous robot, but for the robot as a whole to provide useful functionality the actions of the individual modules must be coordinated.

Self-reconfiguration concerns the spatial transformation of the robot morphology from one shape to another [9]. Off-line planning of self-reconfiguration has been studied for a large number of different robotic systems, whereas on-line algorithms only are feasible for modules with relatively few motion constraints, making them less useful for the ATRON [4]. We assume that the goal of the program is to control a modular robot by specifying sequences of actions that should be performed by the robot; such action sequences can be written by the programmer or generated automatically by a planner, in both cases abstractions for expressing control and an underlying runtime system providing robust, distributed execution is needed. The key challenge is to enable the programmer to express the overall behavior of the system in a high-level, fault-tolerant manner.

3. Language Design

We propose the RoCE (Robust Collaborative Ensembles, pronounced "rose") language for robust, general-purpose

```
ensemble Car {
  state obstacle { None, Left, Right, Center } = None;
  when (obstacle==None) Wheel.drive.Forward
  else { Wheel.drive.Evade; sleep(3); }
}
role Front within Car {
  require connected(COMPASS_ANY)==2;
  when (isProximity(FRONT_LEFT) &&
        isProximity(FRONT_RIGHT)) obstacle.Center;
  when (isProximity(FRONT_LEFT)) obstacle.Left;
  when (isProximity(FRONT_RIGHT)) obstacle.Right;
  else obstacle.None;
}
role Wheel within Car {
  require connected(COMPASS_ANY)==1;
  int MY_SIDE, FWD;
  when connected(COMPASS_EAST==1) {
    MY_SIDE = Left; FWD = 1;
  } else when connected(COMPASS_WEST==1) {
    MY_SIDE = Right; FWD = 0;
  }
  state drive {
    Forward { rotateContinuous(100,FWD); }
    Evade { if(obstacle==MY_SIDE)
              rotateContinuous(50,!FWD);
            else rotateContinuous(100,!FWD); } } }
```

Figure 2. Obstacle evasion program in RoCE

control of modular robots. The language has two primary abstractions: ensembles and roles. An *ensemble* is a dynamic, distributed scope the covers a number of modules and introduces shared state and proactive, distributed behaviors into these modules. A *role* applies to a single module, and introduces local state and reactive behaviors into the module, in the form of a statemachine. A module can be a member of any number of ensembles at a given time. Ensembles and roles together are referred to as *entities*. Declarative rules are used to control the activation of entities based on spatial constraints, the active entities of neighboring modules, local state from roles, and shared state from ensembles. Entities can be specialized with a semantics resembling standard object-oriented inheritance: members can be added and existing members can be overridden.

One of the primary design goals of RoCE is to allow modular robots to be controlled in a robust manner based on a global description of the behavior. As an example, consider obstacle avoidance for the small ATRON cars from Fig. 1 implemented by the program shown in Fig. 2. The ensemble Car encapsulates the overall behavior of the robot, and consists of a shared state variable obstacle and a conditional behavior that executes continuously. Depending on the value of the shared state, the behavior is to either drive forwards or perform an evasive behavior for 3 seconds. Roles are assigned to modules that satisfy the require clauses (such clauses can also be used to activate ensembles), and can similarly introduce states and behaviors but only locally to the given module. The role Front applies to modules *within* the Car ensemble that have the required two connections

(uniquely identifying the front module). The role checks the front sensor and updates the shared state obstacle correspondingly (the shared state is visible here due to the within declaration). The role Wheel acts differently depending on its connections (the left and right wheel must rotate in opposite directions), and the state drive expresses the actions to take when driving forwards or evading (the wheel closest to the obstacle rotates slower to turn away from the obstacle).

The RoCE language as described here is currently being implemented [6, 7]. Compiling a program produces a number of robust distributed state machines that execute in parallel on the modular of the robot, an approach which has been experimentally demonstrated to work well in practice [8]. Each state machine continuously diffuses state (describing shared variables and behavior execution) to neighboring modules which are then responsible for merging this state with their own; this approach decouples communication from execution and enables modules to automatically route around failing communication paths and recover from spontaneous loss of state.

References

[1] M. Bordignon, K. Stoy, and U. P. Schultz. A Virtual Machine-based Approach for Fast and Flexible Reprogramming of Modular Robots. In *Proc. IEEE Int. Conf. on Robotics and Automation (ICRA'09)*, pages 4273–4280, 2009.

[2] M. Bordignon, U. P. Schultz, and K. Stoy. Model-based Kinematics Generation for Modular Mechatronic Toolkits. In *Proc. 9th ACM SIGPLAN/SIGSOFT Int. Conf. on Generative Programming and Component Engineering (GPCE'10)*, 2010.

[3] M. Bordignon, K. Stoy, and U. Schultz. Generalized programming of modular robots through kinematic configurations. In *Proc. IEEE/RSJ Int. Conf. on Intelligent Robots and Systems (IROS)*, pages 3659–3666, 2011.

[4] D. Brandt and D. J. Christensen. A new meta-module for controlling large sheets of atron modules. In *Proc. IEEE/RSJ Int. Conf. on Intelligent Robots and Systems*, 2007.

[5] E. Østergaard, K. Kassow, R. Beck, and H. Lund. Design of the ATRON lattice-based self-reconfigurable robot. *Autonomous Robots*, 21(2):165–183, 2006.

[6] U.P. Schultz. Towards a robust spatial computing language for modular robots. In *Proc. of the 2012 Workshop on Spatial Computing (AAMAS)*, 2012.

[7] U.P. Schultz. Towards a general-purpose, reversible language for controlling self-reconfigurable robots (work-in-progress). In *Preliminary Proc. of the 4th Workshop on Reversible Computing (RC)*, pages 101–107, 2012.

[8] U.P. Schultz, M. Bordignon, and K. Stoy. Robust and reversible execution of self-reconfiguration sequences. *Robotica*, 29:35–57, 2011. Video at http://www.youtube.com/watch?v=SYizuooEs7s.

[9] M. Yim, W.-M. Shen, B. Salemi, D. Rus, M. Moll, H. Lipson, E. Klavins, and G. S. Chirikjian. Modular Self-Reconfigurable Robot Systems [Grand Challenges of Robotics]. *IEEE Robot. Automat. Mag.*, 2007.

JaDaRD: Java Data-Race Detector

Filip Voráček

Faculty of Information Technology
Czech Technical University in Prague
Czech Republic
voracfil@fit.cvut.cz

Zdeněk Troníček

Faculty of Information Technology
Czech Technical University in Prague
Czech Republic
tronicek@fit.cvut.cz

Abstract

When two threads access a shared variable, at least one thread writes, and there is no ordering of the accesses, a data race occurs. We deal with the problem of data-race detection. We present a JVM agent that monitors the application and reports data races as soon as they occur. The agent was evaluated on Java2Demo for which it reported more than 2500 data races.

Categories and Subject Descriptors D.2.5 [**Testing and Debugging**]: Debugging aids, Diagnostics

Keywords Data race, synchronization, happens-before relation, Java, JVM

1. Introduction

When two concurrent threads access a shared variable, at least one access is write, and these accesses are not ordered by a happens-before relation, a *data race* occurs. A data race usually means an error that is hard to detect and can have fatal consequences. Accesses to a shared variable can be ordered in several ways [1]. In this paper, we consider only synchronization by the `synchronized` keyword (used as modifier or statement), the `Lock` interface from `java.util.concurrent`, and methods `start()` and `join()`.

Algorithms for data-race detection are either static or dynamic. Static algorithms search for data races without program execution, by inspecting the source code or bytecode. Dynamic algorithms gather data when program is running and use them to search for data races. They are based either on locksets or on happens-before relation. Lockset-based algorithms assume that each shared variable is guarded by a lock and checks whether all threads follow the same locking policy. They monitor accesses to shared variables and report as a data race each access that does not have a common lock with previous accesses. This is easy to implement but leads to many false positives. Algorithms based on happens-before relation monitor events such as thread start or thread join and use them to order accesses to shared variables. They are more precise than lockset-based algorithms but also more demanding as for implementation and runtime overhead. The hybrid algorithms are combinations of these two approaches.

In this paper, we deal with the problem of detection of data races in Java Virtual Machine (JVM). We present a JVM agent [8][9] that implements a hybrid algorithm for data-race detection. JVM agent is a dynamic library that is linked when JVM starts and that can receive JVM events, such as Field Access and Field Modification, which are generated when the program reads from and writes to a field, respectively.

2. Java Data-Race Detector

The agent monitors accesses to shared variables, the `start()` and `join()` methods on the `Thread` instances, and the `lock()` and `unlock()` methods on the `Lock` interface. Each thread has the logical time, which is an integer value. The logical time is incremented upon each `start()` and `join()` calls. The thread instructions that are executed with the same value of logical time form a thread segment. Two segments may have the happens-before relation. The agent monitors the `start()` and `join()` methods and when either of them is called, it stores the happens-before relation between the two thread segments and increments the logical time in both threads. Furthermore, the agent monitors the `lock()` and `unlock()` methods on the `Lock` interface to have information on locks that are currently locked. Whenever a thread reads from or writes to a field, the agent figures out the monitors hold by the thread and stores them for use later. At each field access, the agent evaluates the gathered information to decide whether the access may be a data race. The evaluation is done in three steps: (a) checking if there is a common monitor hold during this access and previous accesses. The read and write accesses are treated separately. If the current access is read, it is not compared with previous reads because two reads cannot form a data race. (b) If there is a pair of accesses that are conflicting (i.e. read-write, write-read, or write-write) and do not have a common monitor, the locks are checked the same way as monitors. (c) If the pair does not have a common lock either, the happens-before relation is checked. If there is no happens-before relation between these two accesses, they are reported as a data race.

3. Implementation

The agent exploits the Java Virtual Machine Tool Interface (JVM TI) [2] to access the JVM infrastructure. Each object whose field is accessed is given a unique tag. The tag is used to identify the object when an event Field Access or Field Modification occurs. For each object, the agent stores a list of fields that have been accessed and for each such field it builds a trie [5]. The trie has edges labeled by the monitor and lock tags. In vertices, there are two lists: one for reads and one for writes. The lists contain thread segments and stack traces.

The happens-before relation is implemented using the *vector clocks* [6][7]. For each thread, a vector clock is maintained, which is indexed by thread id. The value in thread A's vector on position that corresponds to thread B is the lowest segment of B that does not influence the current segment of A (i.e. there is no happens-before relation between these two segments). The value in thread A's vector on position that corresponds to thread A is the current logical time in A. For the start() and join() method calls, the logical times of both threads are incremented and the vectors are merged. When thread A calls start() on thread B, the merged vector is stored as vector for B and when thread A calls join() on thread B, the merged vector is stored as vector for A.

4. Evaluation

We evaluated JaDaRD on well-known Java2Demo from Oracle Java Development Kit, which demonstrates various features of Java 2D, and the agent reported more than 2500 data races. The vast majority of them are due to initialization of the Swing components from the main thread instead of via the SwingUtilities.invokeLater method. Another type of data races found was between threads that share the Runnable instance. Other common types were leaking constructors and setting non-final fields in constructor without synchronization. These fields are accessed from different threads (mainly from the Swing event-dispatch thread) and this causes data races.

5. Related Work

There are several competitors of JaDaRD. Here we mention only two of them. Eraser [3] was probably the first implementation of the lockset-based algorithm. Its advantage, in comparison to algorithms based on happens-before relation, is that it does not depend on thread timing. A drawback is that it reports many false positives.

Racer [4] implements a hybrid algorithm similar to our algorithm but the implementation is very different. Racer uses the AspectJ framework enriched by three new pointcuts: lock(), which corresponds to monitor enter, unlock(), which corresponds to monitor exit, and maybeShared(), which addresses fields that may be shared between threads. The maybeShared() pointcut is implemented by static analysis.

6. Conclusion

We described the JVM agent, called JaDaRD, that implements a hybrid algorithm for data-race detection. The main advantages of JaDaRD are (i) ease of use, (ii) precision – it gives very few false positives and rarely any false negatives, and (iii) configuration capabilities – we can select fields that are to be monitored.

References

[1] The Java Language Specification. Java SE 7 Edition.

[2] The Java Virtual Machine Tool Interface. http://docs.oracle.com/javase/7/docs/platform/jvmti/jvmti.html.

[3] S. Savage, M. Burrows, G. Nelson, P. Sobalvarro, and T. Anderson. Eraser: a dynamic data race detector for multi-threaded programs. *ACM Trans. Comput. Syst.* 15, 4 (Nov. 1997), pp. 391-411.

[4] E. Bodden and K. Havelund. Aspect-Oriented Race Detection in Java. *IEEE Trans. Software Eng.* 36, 4 (2010), pp. 509-527.

[5] J. D. Choi, K. Lee, A. Loginov, R. O'Callahan, V. Sarkar, M. and Sridharan. Efficient and precise datarace detection for multithreaded object-oriented programs. *SIGPLAN Not.* 37, 5 (May 2002), pp. 258-269.

[6] C. J. Fidge. Timestamp in message passing systems that preserves partial ordering. *Australian Computing Conference*, pp. 56–66, 1988.

[7] F. Mattern. Virtual time and global states of distributed systems. *Parallel and Distributed Algorithms Conference*, pp. 215–226, 1988.

[8] F. Voráček. *Dynamic detection of data races in JVM: Master thesis.* Czech Technical University in Prague, Faculty of Information Technology, 2012.

[9] JaDaRD: Java Data-Race Detector. http://java.net/projects/jadard.

From Actors to Agent-Oriented Programming Abstractions in simpAL

Alessandro Ricci

University of Bologna, Italy
a.ricci@unibo.it

Andrea Santi

University of Bologna, Italy
a.santi@unibo.it

Abstract

simpAL is a programming language introducing an agent-oriented programming abstraction layer on top of actors, with the the aim of simplifying the development of programs that need to integrate aspects related to concurrency, interaction, reactivity, distribution.

Categories and Subject Descriptors D.3.3 [*Programming Languages*]: Language Constructs and Features; D.1.3 [*Programming Techniques*]: Concurrent Programming

Keywords agent-oriented programming; actors

1. Introduction – "The Free Lunch is Over"

The fundamental turn of software towards concurrency that we are witnessing in recent years – effectively summarized by the sentence *the free lunch is over* by Sutter and Larus in [10] – calls for devising effective programming abstractions that would "help build concurrent programs, just as object-oriented abstractions help build large component-based programs" in every-day programming.

Actors and Object-Oriented Concurrent Programming

To this purpose actors [2] and Object-Oriented Concurrent Programming (OOCP) [1, 4] are main references. The actor model unifies objects and concurrency and nowadays is the foundational model on which many recent languages and frameworks are based – Erlang, Scala Actors, AmbientTalk, Axum to mention some.

Looking for High-Level Programming Abstractions

Actors are a powerful, elegant yet very simple model—based solely on concurrent (re)active entities communicating by asynchronous message passing. This makes pure actor pro-

gramming quite hard, in particular as soon as large concurrent and distributed programs are considered. Different kinds of ad hoc programming mechanisms have been proposed in literature to tackle specific problems–e.g., direct support for RPC-like interactions, local synchronization constrains and pattern-based receive primitives to select messages to receive, etc. Besides ad hoc mechanisms, which are often hard to combine and lack of generality, we are looking forward a single coherent programming abstraction layer, that would make as simple and natural as possible the design and development of concurrent and reactive programs.

2. Agent-Oriented Programming & the simpAL Programming Language

To that purpose, we propose a rich set of programming abstractions inspired from agents and multi-agent systems [3, 5, 9], orthogonal to the data abstraction layer. It can be defined *human-inspired* since humans and human organizations are the background metaphor. simpAL is a statically typed programming language based on these first-class abstractions [8].

A program in simpAL is modeled as an organization of agents working in a shared environment, possibly distributed into multiple workspaces. Agents model autonomous entities fulfilling pro-actively tasks, using and observing their environment and talking with other agents. The agent programming model is inspired from the BDI (Belief-Desire-Intention) model [7]. Main concepts of the model include:

- *Tasks* - description of the job to do. An agent "moves" because it has at least one task to do. Tasks are grouped into roles, defining the type of agents.

- *Plans* – define how to accomplish tasks. They are similar to procedures, but more flexible: they are composed by a set of *action rules*, specifying *when* doing *which* actions. Plans are grouped into scripts. Agents can dynamically load scripts to get the expertise to play roles and fulfill tasks.

The execution semantics of an agent is given by a *reasoning cycle*, which is an extension of actors' event loop. At every cycle, an agent first (*sense* stage) updates its *beliefs* (i.e., its internal state variable) about the state of the environment which is using, then (*plan* stage) it selects the actions to do in that moment using the action rules described in plans given its internal beliefs and the tasks to accomplish, and finally (*act* stage) it executes the selected actions.

The environment on the other side is used to explicitly define a shared context of agents' work. It can be programmed and modularized in terms of *artifacts*, as basic programming blocks, dual with agents. Artifact can be used to directly model non autonomous resources and tools that agents can dynamically create, share, use, part of their context [6]. They are more similar to passive objects (or, better, monitors), encapsulating:

- a set of *operations* that agents can execute (as actions). Operations are executed atomically, avoiding race conditions in the case of concurrent requests;

- a set of *observable properties*, i.e. information items that are eventually changed by actions and that are directly perceived by all the agents using such artifacts, as observers that possibly need to react to them.

3. Highlights

Like actor based approaches, simpAL allows for naturally exploiting concurrency and parallelism—agents and artifacts are logically parallel entities, mapped onto the physical OS threads and processors by the runtime. The key point with respect to actors is the programming model, which aims at being rich enough to handle the typical programming complexities arising with a flat actor model with a single uniform high-level approach.

A main example is the capability provided by the agent programming model to easily express active behaviors that need to integrate autonomy and reactive behavior [4], keeping modularity and abstraction, and to realize event-driven programming without callbacks. Another example is to recover the benefits of shared-memory models in synergy with direct communication, without exposing to the programmers (and agents) the complexity of locks and related low-level synchronization mechanisms. This is given by the environment programming model, devised to simplify the programming of artifacts functioning as coordination media, from a simple bounded buffers to tuple spaces, exploiting the basic native synchronization features of the artifact model.

Finally, a main aim of the programming model is to *keep abstractions alive from design to runtime*, making them first-class when programming, in particular. A main example in simpAL are *tasks*, which are created, assigned, manipulated by agents at runtime.

4. The simpAL Platform

simpAL comes with a Java-based platform[1] embedding a compiler, a distributed runtime infrastructure and an Eclipse-

---

[1] Available as open-source project at http://simpal.sourceforge.net

based IDE, based on xtext, including also a minimal debugger that allows for executing agents cycle by cycle, and to inspect dynamically their state as well as the artifacts' state. simpAL programs can be distributed, i.e. organization of agents distributed among workspaces running on different network nodes. The platform provides a native support to handle distribution, so that the deployment, running and debugging of distributed programs is the same of those programs that are not distributed (being all the workspaces hosted in the same node).

5. Road-map

simpAL aims at being just a starting point for exploring the value of programming models based on agent-oriented abstractions. Many important issues are still to be explored, including: *(i)* formalization of the approach, by devising a proper core language/calculus – to formally define and reason about the behavior of simpALprograms; *(ii)* mechanisms for re-use and extensibility – sub-typing (e.g., defining new roles from existing roles), inheritance/composition (e.g. defining new agent scripts by composing existing plans of existing scripts); *(iii)* performance analysis and optimizations – in particular concerning the optimized execution of the agent reasoning cycle.

References

[1] G. Agha. Concurrent object-oriented programming. *Commun. ACM*, 33(9):125–141, Sept. 1990.

[2] G. A. Agha, I. A. Mason, S. F. Smith, and C. L. Talcott. A foundation for actor computation. *J. Funct. Program.*, 7(1): 1–72, Jan. 1997.

[3] R. H. Bordini, M. Dastani, J. Dix, and A. El Fallah Seghrouchni. Special issue on multi-agent programming. *Autonomous Agents and Multi-Agent Systems*, 23 (2), 2011.

[4] J.-P. Briot, R. Guerraoui, and K.-P. Lohr. Concurrency and distribution in object-oriented programming. *ACM Comput. Surv.*, 30(3):291–329, 1998.

[5] N. R. Jennings. An agent-based approach for building complex software systems. *Commun. ACM*, 44(4):35–41, 2001.

[6] A. Omicini, A. Ricci, and M. Viroli. Artifacts in the A&A meta-model for multi-agent systems. *Autonomous Agents and Multi-Agent Systems*, 17 (3), Dec. 2008.

[7] A. S. Rao and M. P. Georgeff. BDI Agents: From Theory to Practice. In *First International Conference on Multi Agent Systems (ICMAS95)*, 1995.

[8] A. Ricci and A. Santi. Designing a general-purpose programming language based on agent-oriented abstractions: the simpAL project. In *Proc. of AGERE! Workshop at SPLASH*, pages 159–170, New York, NY, USA, 2011. ACM.

[9] Y. Shoham. Agent-oriented programming. *Artificial Intelligence*, 60(1):51–92, 1993.

[10] H. Sutter and J. Larus. Software and the concurrency revolution. *ACM Queue: Tomorrow's Computing Today*, 3(7):54–62, Sept. 2005.

The Nature of Order: From Security Patterns to a Pattern Language

Munawar Hafiz

Auburn University

munawar@auburn.edu

Paul Adamczyk

paul.adamczyk@gmail.com

Categories and Subject Descriptors   D.2.11 [*Software Engineering*]: Software Architectures—Patterns

General Terms   Design, Security.

Keywords   Security Patterns, Pattern Language.

1. Introduction

Christopher Alexander [1] was the first to introduce the concept of a pattern language. He has inspired many computer scientists to develop pattern languages for software, but so far we have not produced a result that is as impressive as his. This paper describes our experiences of developing a pattern language for security [6]. We describe the mechanism of growing this pattern language: how we cataloged the security patterns from books, papers and pattern catalogs, how we classified the patterns to help developers find appropriate patterns, and how we identified and described the relationships between patterns in the pattern language. Ours is the first pattern language that covers patterns of an entire problem domain; to our best knowledge, it is also the largest in software. But the most significant contribution of this work is the story behind how the pattern language is grown, as the mechanism can be adapted to other domains.

2. Growing a Pattern Language

Security patterns capture security knowledge. We have been maintaining a comprehensive catalog of all security patterns published in the last 15 years (the first security pattern paper [14] appeared in 1997). It is a union of all security patterns that appear in many books [7, 11, 12], catalogs [2, 8–10], and papers [3, 4, 14]. It accumulates the experience of the entire security pattern community and is a fair representation of the solution domain of security.

The pattern sources describe 174 security patterns, but with many overlaps. After removing the overlaps, the current catalog contains 96 security patterns.

We started by evaluating various classification schemes that break up the large catalog into smaller clusters of related patterns. Second, we created small pattern languages, one for each cluster of patterns. Third, we combined the small diagrams into one large diagram, adding more inter-group relationships. We describe these three steps here.

2.1 Categorize Security Pattern Catalog

Our previous work [5] organized the security patterns. We tried several classification schemes; and found that a hierarchical scheme using threat models works the best. A tree-based scheme allows us to classify a pattern by placing it on a leaf node (low-level patterns) as well as internal nodes (high-level patterns), therefore creating the hierarchy. Patterns at the root of the tree are applicable to multiple contexts. The application contexts (core, perimeter, and exterior) are in the internal nodes. Each context is further classified using threat models; we use the STRIDE threat model [13].

To illustrate the classification, consider SADE DATA STRUCTURE [4] that suggests that strings should be represented with a separate data structure that keeps information about allocated and used memory. This is a *core* pattern that prevents *tampering*, and it is classified at that leaf node. On the other hand, SECURITY NEEDS IDENTIFICATION FOR ENTERPRISE ASSETS [11] describes a process for asset evaluation. This is clearly more general, and applies to all contexts and all threat models. It is classified at the root node of the tree.

2.2 Build Category-specific Pattern Languages

A pattern language offers the reader a guidance in selecting the next pattern to consider. It shows all the closely related patterns. But how does one determine that there exists a relationship between patterns? In Alexander [1], the pattern at the head of the connecting arrow is typically mentioned in the Context section of the pattern that appears at the end of the arrow. Alternatively, the pattern at the end of the arrow is mentioned in the Resulting Context of the pattern at the head of the arrow. Unfortunately, most of the security patterns were not written in that format, so we had to re-create those relationships by carefully considering the typical order in which they would be applied. We listed them in that temporal order, and then described their relationships.

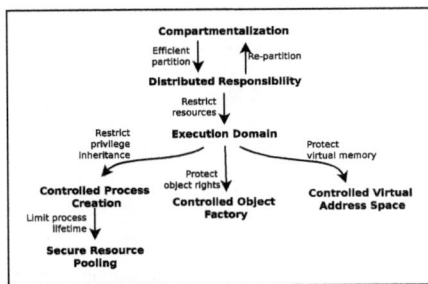

Figure 1. Core Patterns for Preventing Privilege Escalation

Figure 1 shows the relationship between 7 core patterns that prevent privilege escalation. The first step of preventing privilege escalation is partitioning an application, described by two patterns. We relate them by an arrow from COMPARTMENTALIZATION [4] to DISTRIBUTED RESPONSIBILITY [4], meaning that the latter follows the former. In practice, these two patterns typically go hand in hand. A user compartmentalizes a system, then checks whether the responsibilities are properly distributed, and may compartmentalize again and so on. So, we add an arrow in the reverse direction. EXECUTION DOMAIN [11] specializes DISTRIBUTED RESPONSIBILITY [4] by restricting access to resources available to a process.

It is important to check process creation (CONTROLLED PROCESS CREATION [11]), object creation (CONTROLLED OBJECT FACTORY [11]), and memory usage (CONTROLLED VIRTUAL ADDRESS SPACE [11])—all three follow EXECUTION DOMAIN [11]. SECURE RESOURCE POOLING [4] eases process creation by pre-forking a process pool; it also adds control on process lifetime to prevent privilege escalation vulnerabilities in long-running processes.

2.3 Unify Pattern Languages

The small pattern languages created are relatively self-contained; each contains patterns for a type of security problem. But if we consider the pattern language for high level security patterns, they will explain how to approach solving any security problem, but stop short of solving any. They will leave off where all the other figures for small pattern languages start. Figure 2 presents a relationship between the small pattern languages. It sketches the unification step.

3. Conclusion

A pattern language communicates *the nature of order* by describing the way patterns relate to one another. Our current pattern language is a work in progress. It has not yet been used on a large project, been reviewed by more than a few security experts, or been used to teach students how to make

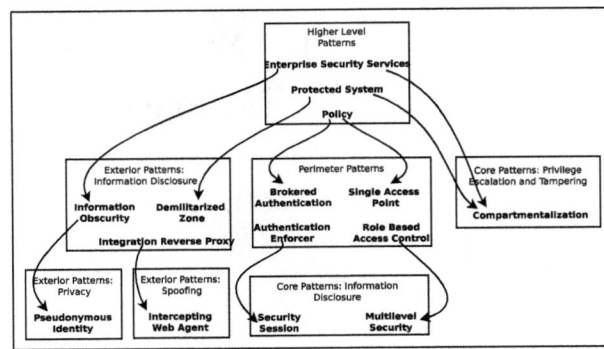

Figure 2. Unifying the Pattern Languages

secure systems. Doing these things will undoubtedly point out ways to improve it. However, its current version is already an improvement on the state of the art.

A. Location of Security Pattern Catalog

http://munawarhafiz.com/securitypatterncatalog/index.php.

References

[1] C. Alexander, S. Ishakawa, and M. Silverstein. *A Pattern Language: Towns, Building and Construction.* Oxford University Press, New York, 1977.

[2] B. Blakley and C. Heath. Security design patterns technical guide–Version 1. Technical report, Open Group(OG), 2004.

[3] M. Hafiz. A Pattern Language for Developing Privacy Enhancing Technologies. *To be published in Software—Practice and Experience*, 2012.

[4] M. Hafiz and R. Johnson. Evolution of the MTA architecture: The impact of security. *Software—Practice and Experience*, 38(15):1569–1599, Dec 2008.

[5] M. Hafiz, P. Adamczyk, and R. E. Johnson. Organizing security patterns. *IEEE Software*, 24(4):52–60, July/August 2007.

[6] M. Hafiz, P. Adamczyk, and R. Johnson. Growing a pattern language (for security). In *OOPSLA*, 2012.

[7] J. Hogg, D. Smith, F. Chong, D. Taylor, L. Wall, and P. Slater. *Web Service Security: Scenarios, Patterns, and Implementation Guidance for Web Services Enhancements (WSE) 3.0.* Microsoft Press, March 2006.

[8] D. Kienzle, M. Elder, D. Tyree, and J. Edwards-Hewitt. Security patterns repository version 1.0, 2002.

[9] S. Romanosky. Security design patterns part 1, Nov 2001.

[10] S. Romanosky. Enterprise security patterns, 2002.

[11] M. Schumacher, E. Fernandez-Buglioni, D. Hybertson, F. Buschmann, and P. Sommerlad. *Security Patterns: Integrating Security and Systems Engineering.* John Wiley and Sons, December 2005. ISBN 0-470-85884-2.

[12] C. Steel, R. Nagappan, and R. Lai. *Core Security Patterns : Best Practices and Strategies for J2EE(TM), Web Services, and Identity Management.* Prentice Hall PTR, Oct 2005.

[13] F. Swiderski and W. Snyder. *Threat Modeling.* Microsoft Press, 2004.

[14] J. Yoder and J. Barcalow. Architectural patterns for enabling application security. In Proceedings of the 4th Conference on Patterns Language of Programming (PLoP'97)., 1997.

Reifying and Optimizing Collection Queries for Modularity

Paolo G. Giarrusso
Klaus Ostermann
Philipps University Marburg

Michael Eichberg
Software Technology Group,
Darmstadt University of Technology

Tillmann Rendel
Christian Kästner
Philipps University Marburg

Abstract

Conventional collection libraries do not perform automatic collection-specific optimizations. Instead, performance-critical code using collections must be hand-optimized, leading to non-modular, brittle, and redundant code.

We propose SQUOPT, the Scala Query Optimizer, a *deep embedding* of the Scala collection library performing collection-specific optimizations automatically without external tools or compiler extensions.

Categories and Subject Descriptors H.2.3 [*Database Management*]: Languages—Query languages; D.1.1 [*Programming Techniques*]: Applicative (Functional) Programming; D.1.5 [*Programming Techniques*]: Object-oriented Programming

Keywords Deep embedding; query languages; optimization; modularity

Introduction

In-memory collections of data often need efficient processing. For on-disk data, efficient processing is already provided by database management systems (DBMS), thanks to their query optimizers which support many optimizations specific to the domain of collections. However, moving in-memory data to DBMSs does not typically improve performance [6], and query optimizers cannot be reused separately, since DBMSs are typically monolithic and their optimizers are deeply integrated. A few collection-specific optimizations, such as shortcut fusion [1], are supported by compilers for purely functional languages such as Haskell, but the implementation techniques do not generalize to many other optimizations, such as support for indexes. In general, collection-specific optimizations are not supported by the general-purpose optimizers used by high-level (JIT) compilers. Therefore, when collection-related optimizations are needed, programmers perform them by hand.

Some optimizations are not hard to apply manually, but in many cases become applicable only after manual inlining [4]. But manual inlining modifies source code by combining distinct functions together, while often distinct functions should remain distinct to preserve modularity, for instance to separate different concerns or to allow reusing a code fragment. In this case, manual inlining will reduce modularity.

To sum up, developers have to choose between modularity and performance when writing queries. We propose instead an automatic optimizer supporting both inlining and collection-specific optimizations, combining performance and modularity. In particular, our optimizer automatically performs various collection-specific algebraic optimizations, such as map fusion, selection pushdown, automatic indexing and query unnesting. Some of these optimizations can reduce the complexity class of a query. Moreover, the optimizer supports general-purpose optimizations, such as inlining and various algebraic simplifications, to allow collection-specific optimizations to trigger more often. We show a few examples in the next subsection.

Motivating Example

Let us consider for instance map fusion, which combines multiple map operations to avoid intermediate results.

Consider this Scala function definition in module M1:

```
def firstPart(someColl: List[Int]) = someColl.map(x ⇒ x + 1)
```

This code defines function firstPart which maps function $\lambda x.x + 1$ on some collection of integers someColl. Suppose now that module M2 contains:

```
val theColl: List[Int] = ...
def secondPart = M1.firstPart(theColl).map(x ⇒ x + 2)
```

This code defines function secondPart which maps function $\lambda x.x + 2$ on the result of M1.firstPart. We assume that these functions are part of different modules, for instance because they are related with different concerns and firstPart's implementation should be hidden behind an abstraction barrier.

This code is inefficient: Executing this code will build a collection to represent the result of firstPart, and then consume it immediately to build a new collection; this intermediate step is unnecessary and expensive. Moreover, we sum each number with first 1 and then 2; adding 3 directly would be faster.

To improve performance we can write, in module M2, just `def secondPart = theColl.map(x ⇒ x + 3)`. However, this code combines code fragments which belong to different modules, which is undesirable in our example. An alternative would be to rely on an automatic optimizer. Automating this optimization requires inlining the call to `firstPart` (which in general might be a virtual call, hence resolved only at run-time) and then performing collection-specific optimizations (here, map fusion). While most general-purpose automatic optimizers can handle inlining, they cannot handle collection-specific optimizations. Furthermore, virtual calls typically cannot be resolved statically, hence can only be inlined at run-time by JIT compilers. Hence, this optimization cannot be performed automatically by a typical optimizer, especially not by a compile-time one.

There are many other optimizations that are possible to improve performance, but that require implementation overhead or lead to nonmodular solutions; one example is maintaining indexes to speed up queries. Consider an address book application, which manipulates a collection of people. To find people by their name, this application will probably maintain an index mapping names to people. Each time a person is added or removed, both the collection of people and the index need to be updated: Keeping in sync these operations by hand is error-prone. Automatic index maintenance, as done by databases, would make such inconsistencies impossible, once again reconciling modularity and performance.

Our Solution

To provide automatic collection-specific optimizations and thus address these problems, we introduce SQuOPT, the Scala Query Optimizer, which consists of:

1. An embedded domain-specific language (EDSL) for queries on collections. This EDSL corresponds to the purely functional portion of the Scala collection API, inherits its advantages [3] and naturally supports advanced features of database query languages.

2. A Scala implementation of the above EDSL. Queries written in this EDSL produce explicit representations of themselves, termed expression trees. Crucially, this representation includes Scala expressions and arguments of query operators like map or filter. This library requires no compiler extensions, unlike LINQ. To this end, we extend existing techniques based on Scala implicit conversions [5] to cope with operations on collections.

3. A run-time compiler to convert queries to runnable code.

4. A run-time optimizer which transforms queries into faster ones before compilation. Since optimizations happens at run-time, handling virtual calls precisely is pos-

sible. Since the query representation represents faithfully the arguments of query operators, each optimization has all the information needed to verify that its side conditions apply. While the optimizer is not yet complete, the speedups it achieves are already promising, as detailed subsequently.

5. A prototype implementation of incremental view maintenance, which will allow to materialize and update the results of any view, including indexes, so that the materialized results can be reused in other queries.

Our current implementation is available online.[1]

Overall, our approach seems a promising solution to combine performance and modularity.

Initial experiments

To evaluate our optimizer, we reimplemented some queries (sampled from FindBugs [2]) in Scala. At run-time, we create indexes and measure the optimization speedup on different queries, compared with native queries in Scala. Around half of the queries can be optimized, and speedups range from 2.5x to 2274.9x. In other cases, the optimizer does not improve query performance significantly. Moreover, we study the overhead introduced by dividing queries into smaller functions to increase reuse; our optimizer prototype seems to already reduce this overhead significantly.

Acknowledgements The authors would like to thank Sebastian Erdweg and the OOPSLA anonymous reviewers for their helpful comments. This work is supported in part by the European Research Council, grant #203099.

References

[1] A. Gill, J. Launchbury, and S. L. Peyton Jones. A short cut to deforestation. In *FPCA*, pages 223–232. ACM, 1993.

[2] D. Hovemeyer and W. Pugh. Finding bugs is easy. *SIGPLAN Notices*, 39(12):92–106, 2004.

[3] M. Odersky and A. Moors. Fighting bit rot with types (experience report: Scala collections). In *IARCS Conf. Foundations of Software Technology and Theor. Comp. Science*, volume 4, pages 427–451, 2009.

[4] S. Peyton Jones and S. Marlow. Secrets of the Glasgow Haskell Compiler inliner. *JFP*, 12(4-5):393–434, 2002.

[5] T. Rompf and M. Odersky. Lightweight modular staging: a pragmatic approach to runtime code generation and compiled DSLs. In *GPCE*, pages 127–136. ACM, 2010.

[6] M. Stonebraker, S. Madden, D. J. Abadi, S. Harizopoulos, N. Hachem, and P. Helland. The end of an architectural era: (it's time for a complete rewrite). In *Int'l Conf. Very Large Data Bases*, pages 1150–1160. VLDB Endowment, 2007.

---

[1] http://www.informatik.uni-marburg.de/~pgiarrusso/SQuOpt

The Spoofax Name Binding Language

Gabriël D. P. Konat, Vlad A. Vergu, Lennart C. L. Kats, Guido H. Wachsmuth, Eelco Visser

Delft University of Technology, The Netherlands

g.d.p.konat@student.tudelft.nl, {v.a.vergu, l.c.l.kats, g.h.wachsmuth, e.visser}@tudelft.nl

Abstract

In textual software languages, names are used to identify program elements such as variables, methods, and classes. Name analysis algorithms resolve names in order to establish references between definitions and uses of names. In this poster, we present the Spoofax Name Binding Language (NBL), a declarative meta-language for the specification of name binding and scope rules, which departs from the programmatic encodings of name binding provided by regular approaches. NBL aspires to become the universal language for name binding, which can be used next to BNF definitions in reference manuals, as well as serve the generation of implementations.

Categories and Subject Descriptors D.2.1 [*Requirements-/Specifications*]: Languages; D.3.2 [*Language Classifications*]: Very high-level languages

Keywords name binding, name resolution, declarative, meta-language, Spoofax

1. Introduction

Name binding is concerned with the relation between definitions and references through identifiers in textual software languages, including scope rules that govern these relations. Classical approaches to name binding provide definitions in terms of programmatic encodings that carry environments through tree traversals. Attempts at abstractions such as attribute grammars (3; 4) or dynamic rewrite rules (2) reduce the overhead of such programmatic encodings, but are still algorithmic in nature. Our goal is a *declarative* domain-specific language for name binding that can be used to explain the binding rules of a language *and* and from which an efficient name resolution algorithm can be automatically derived, much like grammar formalisms (EBNF) abstract from the programmatic encoding of parsers.

In this poster, we present the Spoofax Name Binding Language (NBL) (6), a declarative meta-language for the specification of name binding in terms of namespaces, definitions, references, scopes, and imports. From definitions in NBL, a compiler generates a language-specific name resolution strategy in the Stratego rewriting language (1) by parametrizing an underlying generic, language independent strategy. Name resolution results in a persistent symbol table for use by semantic editor services such as reference resolution, consistency checking of definitions, type checking, refactoring, and code generation. NBL is integrated in the Spoofax Language Workbench (5), but should be reusable in other language processing environments.

2. Name Binding and Scope Rules

We discuss the core concepts of NBL and illustrate their usage for a subset of C#.

Definitions and References The essence of name binding is establishing relations between a *definition* that *binds* a name and a *reference* that *uses* that name. Each class in a C# program defines the name of a class. Figure 1 defines the classes Env, Expr, BinOp, Plus and Let. Base class declarations are references to class definitions. For example, class Plus has a reference to its base class BinOp.

An NBL specification consists of a collection of rules of the form pattern : clause*, where pattern is an abstract tree (term) pattern and clause* is a list of name binding declarations about the language construct that matches with pattern. Figure 2 shows the NBL specification for name analysis of the C# subset. The first rule declares that a node matching the pattern Class(x,_,_) defines a class with name x. The second rule declares that the term pattern Base(x) is a reference to a class with name x. Thus, : BinOp is a reference to class BinOp.

Namespaces Definitions and references declare relations between named program elements and their uses. Languages typically distinguish several *namespaces*, i.e. different kinds of names, such that an occurrence of a name in one namespace is not related to an occurrence of that same name in another. The Let class in the example has a method *and* a field with name eval; methods and fields have their own namespace in our C# subset.

Scopes *Scopes* restrict the visibility of definitions. Scopes can be nested and name resolution typically looks for definitions from inner to outer scopes. The example includes three definitions for a method `eval`. These definitions are not distinguishable by their namespace `Method` and their name `x`, but, they are distinguishable by their scope, i.e. their containing class. The **scopes** ns clause in NBL declares a construct to be a scope for namespace ns. The `Class` rule in the NBL specification scopes all names in the `Field` and `Method` namspaces. Methods in turn scope local variables in the `Variable` namespace.

Imports An *import* introduces definitions from another scope into the current scope, either under the same name or under a new name. An import that imports all definitions can be *transitive*. Inheriting from a base class corresponds to (transitively) importing methods and fields from the base class into the super class. For example the `Plus` class imports the fields `l` and `r` from `BinOp`, `BinOp` imports `eval` from `Expr`. The second rule in the NBL specification declares that a base class reference to class `x` transitively imports all elements from the `Field` and `Method` namespaces of that class into the surrounding scope.

Types Types also play a role in name resolution. When calling a method `e.m(e*)`, the resolution of the method depends on the type of the target `e` and the types of the arguments `e*`. For example, `l.eval(env)` refers to the `eval` method of the `Expr` interface, since `l` has type `Expr` and `env` has type `Env`. In NBL, the **of type** t clause of a **defines** declaration indicates a type assignment. The **where** e **has type** t clause can be used to retrieve the type of an expression. For example, the rule for `Call` computes the types of the arguments and target of the method call.

Editor services Modern IDEs provide a wide range of editor services where name resolution plays a crucial role. Traditionally, each of these services is handcrafted for each language supported by the IDE. We automatically generate a name resolution algorithm and editor services from an NBL definition. Reference resolution, constraint checking and code completion are automatically generated from an NBL specification. Figure 3 shows an example of the generated constraint checking editor service; error markers are shown for unresolved references. An example of the generated code completion can be seen in Figure 4.

References

1 M. Bravenboer, K. T. Kalleberg, R. Vermaas, and E. Visser. Stratego/XT 0.17. A language and toolset for program transformation. *SCP*, 72(1-2):52–70, 2008. 1

2 M. Bravenboer, A. van Dam, K. Olmos, and E. Visser. Program transformation with scoped dynamic rewrite rules. *FUIN*, 69(1-2):123–178, 2006. 1

3 T. Ekman and G. Hedin. Modular name analysis for java using jastadd. In *GTTSE*, pages 422–436, 2006. 1

```
interface Env { Env add(string name, int val); }
interface Expr { int eval(Env env); }
class BinOp : Expr { Expr l; Expr r; }
class Plus : BinOp {
 int eval(Env env) {
  return l.eval(env) + r.eval(env);
} }
class Let : Expr {
 string name; Expr eval; Expr body;
 int eval(Env env) {
  return body.eval(env.add(name, eval.eval(env)));
} }
```

Figure 1. Expression evaluation classes in C# subset.

```
namespaces Class Method Field Variable
rules
 Class(x, _, _) :
  defines Class x of type Type(x)
  scopes Field, Method

 Base(x) :
  refers to Class x
  imports Field, Method from Class x {transitive}

 Method(t, x, p*, _) :
  defines Method x of type (t*, t)
  scopes Variable
  where p* has type t*

 Call(exp, x, a*) :
  refers to Method x of type (t*, _) in Class c
  where a* has type t*
  where exp has type Type(c)

 Field(t, x) :
  defines Field x of type t

 Param(t, x) :
  defines Variable x of type t

 VarRef(x) :
  refers to Variable x
  otherwise refers to Field x
```

Figure 2. NBL specification for a subset of C#.

```
18   class Let : Exp {
19     sting name;
20     Expr t;
21     Expr body;
22
23     int eval(Env env) {
24       Env newEnv = env.add(nam, t.eval(env));
25       return body.eval(newEnv);
26     }
27   }
```

Figure 3. Constraint checking for C# subset.

```
12     Expr r;
13     int eval(Env env) {
14       return l.e(env) + r.eval(env);
15     }
16   }
17
           eval
```

Figure 4. Code completion for C# subset.

4 U. Kastens and W. M. Waite. Modularity and reusability in attribute grammars. *ACTA*, 31(7):601–627, 1994. 1

5 L. C. L. Kats and E. Visser. The Spoofax language workbench: rules for declarative specification of languages and IDEs. In *OOPSLA*, pages 444–463, 2010. 1

6 G. Konat, L. C. L. Kats, G. Wachsmuth, and E. Visser. Language-parametric name resolution based on declarative name binding and scope rules. In *SLE*, 2013. 1

Applying Aspect Mining Techniques to Understand an Existing Program

Fernanda Campos   Yadran Eterovic

Pontificia Universidad Católica de Chile

{mfcampos,yadran}@ing.puc.cl

Abstract

Research in magnetic resonance imaging requires reprogramming the software that controls the scanner -a difficult task. We have successfully applied three aspect mining techniques to obtain information about several properties of this complex, non object oriented program.

Categories and Subject Descriptors   D.2.7 [*Software*]: SOFTWARE ENGINEERING—Distribution, Maintenance, and Enhancement

Keywords   Program understanding, Aspect Mining, Execution relations, Event traces, Concept analysis, Random Walks.

1.   Introduction

Program comprehension is a practical field in software engineering concerned with understanding existing code for reuse, maintenance and refactoring. Research in magnetic resonance imaging (MRI), requires reprogramming the software that controls the scanner, which in turn requires identifying the functions and parameters that must be changed.

Our focus is understanding the program used to control a Philips scanner; a large, complex, non object oriented, almost not modularized and poorly documented code. It contains over 300,000 lines of code written in GOAL-C, a special-purpose programming language. A typical execution trace obtained by executing a pulse sequence in the scanner may contain more than 30,000 function calls. Therefore, identifying the changes that have to be made, usually takes a very long time. We hypothesized that by applying aspect mining to the program we could obtain information about its properties (not necessarily it's aspects), which could help us perform the changes required by MRI researchers

SPLASH'12,   October 19–26, 2012, Tucson, Arizona, USA.
ACM 978-1-4503-1563-0/12/10.

2.   Aspect Mining

Aspect mining is a reverse engineering process, which consists in finding crosscutting concerns hidden in existing software. Techniques have been tested mainly on small scale experiments in object oriented languages. We are interested in the application of these techniques to real, non object oriented code, where they may help understand the program's organization, behavior and important features.

We chose three techniques, that give us different information about the program. **Event traces** finds recurring execution traces, indicating general execution patterns in the code. **Formal concept analysis** looks for those functions from the same module that are present in all traces, i.e., scattered code. It computes the list of functions only present in a certain trace, i.e., what functions are more related to a specific trace type. **Modified random walks** identifies the most popular and less significant functions; it can also point out functions that crosscut the system. Since to obtain the crosscutting concerns we need to compute the popularity and significance of each function, this will also give us the list of most significant functions.

3.   Applying diferent techniques

To apply **Event traces**, we search for specific relations between functions [1] in the traces. The *outside before* relation: for an execution of function a, function b is executed just before a; the *inside first* relation: for execution of function a, the first function called inside it is function b; *outside after* and *inside last* relations, with the obvious meanings. Two properties are defined over these relations, a relation is *uniform*, if it exists always in the same composition and *crosscutting*, if it occurs in more than one calling context in the trace. In the original paper execution relations that are both *uniform* and *crosscutting* are considered *aspect candidates*. For our purposes, these candidates show us information regarding the order in which functions call each other.

By applying this technique to different traces, we obtained a list of relations between functions. We see multiple repetitions of some functions in the relations, called from different modules, from at least 20 files, and from many other functions. This suggests the code is coupled.

Multiple types of validations are found among the most common relations in all traces; with this technique we can obtain which functions are common to the system validations, ie: functions called in various validation phases. We also found functions belonging to the scan simulation interface, called when a user selects a protocol page in the simulator; for instance, *MPIEX_softkey_screen* masks enabled parameters during validation. Thus, given that the program consists of a parameter definition part (PDF) and a measurement part (MPF), this information shows which functions belong to the PDF part of the program: those concerned with the setup and validation of the parameters. What is interesting is that most relations found in most traces are from this part of the program. Only four relations were found which belong to the MPF.

Formal concept analysis technique [2] consists in obtaining a concept lattice from traces. The use case associated with an execution trace is an object whose attributes are the functions in the trace. A concept is the object plus its attributes. Aspect candidates are obtained when different functions from the same module are executed for more than one concept or when a concept has functions from different modules (although this is not sufficient to identify a *crosscutting concern*).

This technique gives us a list of functions that appear on all traces. This means each candidate function is executed at least once in each trace. The fact that it repeats in different executions indicates scattered code, but also refers to functions that are part of the base of the program, like user interface or validation functions. We find among the aspect candidates functions related to the specific absorption rate restrictions; this makes sense since it is a factor that should always be computed before a scan.

Some common functions that execute scans may be considered part of the core of these traces, since they perform the measurements necessary for obtaining the sequences (MPF). For example *MPIMN_scan_exec* is part of these candidates. If we take a closer look we see it is in charge of executing the PDF for the scan, after the "start scan" button is pressed and before the scan starts it calls certain initializations and sets up some parameters for the scan.

We executed heart scan traces and brain scan traces, comparing the results from applying the technique only to *heart traces* with those from applying it to *brain traces*, we obtain candidates that appear in one of the types of sequences and not in the other. This identifies functions that are specific to certain procedure types.

Modified random walks, is the application of a page rank algorithm to compute possible *concerns* by determining which elements are more popular and significant [3]. We modified the original technique by performing the calculations over actual traces. *Popularity* is the number of times an element is visited from different elements. *Significance* is the number of distinct elements an element visits. These ranks help us obtain potential *crosscutting concerns* in two ways. *Homogeneous crosscutting:* popularity is higher than significance by a certain threshold. Other possible concerns are *Heterogeneous crosscutting:* elements with much higher significance than popularity.

Analyzing the results we found that some *concerns* are functions that are also concerns in previous techniques. Thus, these functions are not only crosscutting and uniform relations but they are also the most popular and least significant functions. Only one *concern* is unique to each type of trace. For the heart scans, *MPICOIL_get_app_sar_limit*, a function that gets the maximum amount of specific absorption rate allowed. For the brain scans, *MPGGEO_m_matrix-_to_sg_matrix*, a function that stores a matrix structure.

All candidates for traces of a specific sequence type are the same, and even between different type of traces most of them are repeated. Since they don't vary with the sequence, and since they are called multiple times, they can be considered part of the application's core. Because this technique requires the candidates to have low significance, the results are very simple functions, much like getters and setters.

4. Conclusions

The application of all three techniques, combined with the scarce documentation available, allowed us to understand different properties of the program's execution. Event traces reveals function call sequences found in all traces. Results from concept analysis gives us a list of the functions most likely to be related to general parts of the execution, such as parameter setup and validations. Finally random walks identifies more general functions that are called for both types of traces.

The combined application of several aspect mining techniques, based on dynamic analysis, can reveal important information about the execution of a complex program. Whether this information is related to actual aspects is not as important for us, as is understanding the code: relative execution order, function significance and popularity, function roles and their relationship to specific sequence types.

Overall the information obtained regarding the programs execution is very valuable to improve our understanding of the program. While as software engineers we interpret this information syntactically, an MRI researcher can infer at least part of the programs functionalities.

References

[1] S. Breu and J. Krinke. Aspect mining using event traces. In *Proc. of the 19th IEEE int. conf. on Automated software engineering*, 2004. ISBN 0-7695-2131-2.

[2] P. Tonella and M. Ceccato. Aspect mining through the formal concept analysis of execution traces. In *Proc. 11th Working Conf. on Reverse Engineering*, 2004. ISBN 0-7695-2243-2.

[3] C. Zhang and H.-A. Jacobsen. Efficiently mining crosscutting concerns through random walks, 2007.

Migration and Execution of JavaScript Applications between Mobile Devices and Cloud

Xudong Wang   Xuanzhe Liu   Ying Zhang   Gang Huang

Key Laboratory of High Confidence Software Technologies (Peking University), Ministry of Education
{wangxd10, liuxzh, huanggang, zhangying06}@sei.pku.edu.cn

Abstract

Currently, mobile devices might suffer from their own limited resources to support complex Web applications. We present a framework that can offload JavaScript applications to cloud. Based on dynamic analysis and profiling, our approach partitions the computation-intensive tasks for remote execution and efficiently improves performance.

Categories and Subject Descriptors D 2.7 [*Distribution, Maintenance, and Enhancement*]: Restructuring,reverse engineering and reengineering

Keywords Cloud computing, JavaScript, offloading

1. Introduction

Currently, the JavaScript language is capable of realizing complex computation logics in advanced applications. Meanwhile, with the advance of mobile computing, the mobile Web applications become very popular on various devices, including laptops, smartphones, and tablet computers. Since Web applications become more complicated, they recruit increasing amounts of computation, storage and communications from constrained supply on mobile devices.

To alleviate the performance overhead on mobile devices, it is a natural idea to migrate the computation intensive and consuming code fragments from "weak" devices to powerful server with plentiful resources[3]. For example, recently popular Amazon Silk Browser leverages the cloud resources to improve end-user experiences on the mobile devices. However, compared with most popular Object-Oriented programming language like C++ and Java, JavaScript stakes a rather extreme position in the spectrum of dynamic features[1]. Everything might be modified, including the fields and methods of an object or its parents.

This is a challenge for existing static analysis techniques.

This paper proposes a JavaScript offloading framework, called *ExtremeJS* (*EX*tensive *TR*ansformation and *E*lastic *M*igration and *E*xecution of JavaScript) for seamlessly use of ambient computation to augment JavaScript Web applications on mobile devices, making them fast and resource efficient.

2. Contributions

The contributions of our work can be summarized as follows:

- We present a framework for enabling the elastic migration and execution of JavaScript Web applications between mobile devices and cloud, without any modification of original applications.

- We provide a partitioner for automatically identifying costs of computation intensive and time consuming portion in the application, through static and dynamic code analysis.

- We experimentally validate our approach by exercising a prototype implementation of ExtremeJS framework based on series of experiments. The evaluation results show that ExetremJS can adapt JavaScript based application partitioning to different computing and communication environments, and can help some applications achieve as much as almost **10x** execution speedup on the mobile device.

3. Approach

One design principle of ExtremeJS lies in the intuition that, as long as execution on the cloud is much faster (and more secure and more reliable) than that on mobile devices, paying the cost for sending the relevant data and code from the mobile device and back may be worth it. ExtremeJS performs partitioning at first class function level to keep flexibility on what to run where. Another design principle of ExtremeJS is that, when an application is loaded, ExtremeJS aims at automatically extracting the computation intensive

SPLASH'12,   October 19–26, 2012, Tucson, Arizona, USA.
ACM 978-1-4503-1563-0/12/10.

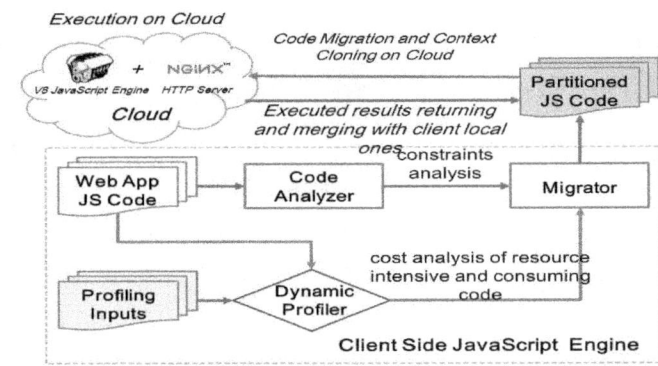

Figure 1. The ExtremeJS Framework

and resource consuming parts of the JavaScript code as well as the corresponding runtime contexts. By defining some partition constraints, the behavior of JavaScript code is preserved in the presence of first-class functions, prototype-based scope chains, et al. It promises the migration of codes and contexts can be consistent and safe.

In ExtremeJS, when the modified JavaScript application is running, the automatically chosen code fragments are migrated from the mobile device to a cloned context on a cloud, remaining the functionality of the un-migrated code on mobile devices. The application would suspend if it attempts to access the migrated state and objects that are dynamically modified. The migrated codes are executed in the cloned contexts on a cloud, possibly utilizing the features of hosting platform such as CPU, memory, hardware accelerators, enhanced software runtime, etc. Eventually, the execution results are returned to the client and merged with the original application context on mobile device. An optimizer is employed to optimize migration code fragment according to expected execution conditions. The whole architecture of ExtremeJS prototype is shown in Figure 1. For page limited, we briefly describe the main three components.

Profiling: To identify the computation-intensive and resource-consuming functions, we leverage a profiler to construct the cost model under execution settings. The profiler generates a set of executions, and for each execution a profile tree. With a tree-based analysis, a configuration file is generated to record the functions whose execution time cost exceeds the given time threshold.

Code Analysis: We then decide which functions can be migrated, from the profiling results. Since JavaScript is a dynamic language, we apply pointer analysis[2] to elaborate the functions that might rely on browser-specific native APIs and objects, or violate timer constraints. Nested migration and *eval* are forbidden in current prototype. Code analysis also extracts the context variables for the functions to be migrated.

Migrator: The migrator is responsible to send the migrated codes to cloud and synchronizes the application contexts. It

rewrites the migrated codes on device, by pointing to another instance without modification of original running one. We employ a mapping table to assist bi-directional synchronization of functions and corresponding contexts.

4. Current Implementation and Evaluation

We have a prototype implementation of our framework[1]. The framework is totally written in standard JavaScript language, whereby it can be simply loaded into most currently popular mobile Web browsers (including Safari, FireFox and Chrome). The cloud-side JavaScript engine employs Google Chrome V8. We take the Nginx[2] HTTP server as a proxy for the network connections.

We have also made series of experiments for evaluation. The test suites include two Mozilla JavaScript performance benchmarks[3]: Dromaeo and V8, and a typical computation-intensive application (the Gobang game), all of which are conducted over several combinations of various mobile devices platforms including Android smartphones/tablets and Apple iPhone/iPad[4]. The experimental analysis shows that our framework can achieve up to about **10x** speedup on average, which efficiently improves the performance for mobile applications.

Acknowledgments

This work is supported by the National Natural Science Foundation of China under Grant No. 61003010, the High-Tech Research and Development Program of China (Grant No. 2012AA010107) and the NCET.

References

[1] A. Feldthaus, T. D. Millstein, A. Møller, M. Schäfer, and F. Tip. Tool-supported refactoring for javascript. In C. V. Lopes and K. Fisher, editors, *Proceedings of the 26th Annual ACM SIGPLAN Conference on Object-Oriented Programming, Systems, Languages, and Applications, OOPSLA 2011, part of SPLASH 2011*, pages 119–138, Portland, OR, USA, 2011. ACM.

[2] G. Richards, A. Gal, B. Eich, and J. Vitek. Automated construction of javascript benchmarks. In *Proceedings of the 26th Annual ACM SIGPLAN Conference on Object-Oriented Programming, Systems, Languages, and Applications, OOPSLA 2011, part of SPLASH 2011*, pages 677–694, Portland, OR, USA, 2011. ACM.

[3] E. Tilevich and Y. Smaragdakis. J-orchestra: Automatic java application partitioning. In B. Magnusson, editor, *Proceedings of 16th European Conference on Object-Oriented Programming(ECOOP 2002)*, volume 2374 of *Lecture Notes in Computer Science*, pages 178–204. Springer, 2002.

---

[1] Available download at https://github.com/wangxd18/extremejs

[2] http://nginx.org

[3] http://www.dromaeo.com

[4] The experiment data analysis report can be found at https://github.com/wangxd18/extremejs

How to Achieve Scalable Fork/Join on Many-core Architectures?

Mattias De Wael *

Software Languages Laboratory
Department of Computer Science
Vrije Universiteit Brussel, Belgium
madewael@vub.ac.be

Tom Van Cutsem †

Software Languages Laboratory
Department of Computer Science
Vrije Universiteit Brussel, Belgium
tvcutsem@vub.ac.be

Abstract

Fork/Join is a parallel programming model that implicitly assumes uniform memory access. The transition from multi- to many-core architectures will render this assumption invalid, and consequently it is likely that Fork/Join in its current form will not scale. This research investigates implementations for Fork/Join to allow the transition to many-core.

Categories and Subject Descriptors D.1.3 [*Programming Techniques*]: Concurrent Programming, Parallel programming; D.3.3 [*Programming Languages*]: Language Constructs and Features Concurrent programming structures

Keywords Fork/Join, Work Stealing, Many-core

1. Introduction

Contemporary processors become ever more parallel, instead of faster as they used to. This new approach of increasing processor power has put a stop to the virtually free improvement of software performance with every newly released processor. Instead, if we want to continue the production of software that scales in performance with the new multicore processors, then the programs themselves need to become parallel as well. Simultaneous with the rise of parallel processors, the model of uniform memory access starts to break down, amplifying the bottleneck effect of memory latency on performance even more. Therefore, hardware architects do not only increase the number of cores on a chip, but also envision and implement new memory architectures. The latter is what is also referred to as the transition from multicore to many-core architectures. This research wants to prepare the convenient to use parallel programming model

---
* Supported by a doctoral scholarship of IWT-Vlaanderen, Belgium
† Postdoctoral Fellow of the Research Foundation - Flanders (FWO)

Fork/Join for this transition. This text presents the problems we foresee in this transition from multicore to many-core architectures, as well as some preliminary ideas to solve those problems.

2. Fork/Join and Work Stealing

Fork/Join is a convenient to use parallel programming model. Today we see a great variety of Fork/Join implementations. Either as library [9–11] or as language (extension) [3, 5]. The extra cognitive burden of Fork/Join for the programmer is limited to only 2 constructs: *fork* and *join*. Other concerns such as load balancing are taken care of by a scheduler. Fork/Join parallelism forces its users to focus on exposing parallelism by dividing a problem into potentially parallel tasks. These tasks, usually of recursive nature, form at run-time a directed acyclic graph of dependencies. The graph, usually referred to as the computation graph, forms a solid model to reason about the computation. At run-time, the generated tasks are assigned to processing cores without intervention of the programmer. Contemporary Fork/Join implementations all use some variation of work stealing, where idle processors steal work from busy procesors [2, 7].

3. The Shift from Multicore to Many-core

Today, multicore architectures with uniform memory access, up to cache hierarchies, are ubiquitous. However, with the rise of many-core architectures [4, 8, 12], uniform memory access becomes unfeasible. Hardware architects will have to shift to memory architectures with non-uniform access (NUMA). For instance, contemporary hardware exists where a shared memory is supported by an elaborate cache hierarchy, and, furthermore, these caches can be dynamically accessed by neighboring processing cores. Not only caches will play an important role, but also the idea of a network-on-chip that allows fast and direct inter-core communication can already be seen in contemporary hardware [13]. Now, data is not longer close by, or far away, but it can be anywhere in between.

4. Foreseen problems

All the Fork/Join implementations use a (slightly) different scheduling policy. Each flavor of Fork/Join (and its scheduler) behaves differently for different scenarios, and operates with different stack and memory bounds [7].

Today, Fork/Join and work stealing implicitly assume uniform memory access, in the sense that contemporary implementations do not allow access control. Therefore it is likely that in its current form Fork/Join programs will not scale into the many-core era. Since steals are randomized, and the number of potential victims for work stealing increases, the chance of counter productive steals increases due to bad data locality and other NUMA effects.

5. Ideas for possible solutions

To prepare Fork/Join and work stealing for the many-core era, we think changes are needed on three frontiers: at the level of *language* constructs, at the level of *algorithm* design, and at the level of the work stealing *scheduler*. We want to evaluate solutions proposed for multicore work stealing with improved data locality [1], as well as as solutions proposed for distributed work stealing and PGAS-like languages [5], and new solutions that emerge because of the potential of the upcoming hardware.

We will need a richer language to express new phenomena, such a data locality, without adding to much cognitive burden. Currently we think about expressing data locality similar as the efforts done for PGAS languages, such that data and/or tasks can express more elaborate on their data access patterns. On the other hand, we think about type annotations for tasks, added by the programmer or a compiler, to provide more information about the behavior of a task, e.g. tasks that synchronize by their very nature, require less synchronization at the scheduler level. At the algorithmic level, the use of cache oblivious algorithms and data structures [6], can aid programmers in creating scalable Fork/Join programs.

Finally, we want to improve upon the work stealing scheduler itself. We want to evaluate and adapt techniques such as locality guided work stealing [1], and adaptive work stealing [7] on the many-core architectures. A second idea on how to improve Fork/Join's work stealing scheduler is to anticipate on processors becoming idle before they actually do. For instance by sending non-blocking messages to nearby workers to ask for more work when they are about to become idle. Finally, with the extra information about the characteristics of a task (e.g. idempotent, self synchronizing), variants of the local deques can be implemented that require less syntonization and therefore induce less overhead.

6. Conclusion

Since the turn of the century, the need for parallel programs increases. Fork/Join proves to be a convenient to use model to express divide-and-conquer algorithms in a parallel fashion. The model is adopted and implemented by various industry strength vendors. However, with the rise of the many-core architectures this model is unlikely to scale on these new hardware. We propose to adapt Fork/Join on three frontiers to tackle the problems induced by the transition from multicore to many-core architectures.

References

[1] U. A. Acar, G. E. Blelloch, and R. D. Blumofe. The data locality of work stealing. In *Proceedings of the twelfth annual ACM symposium on Parallel algorithms and architectures*, 2000.

[2] R. D. Blumofe and C. E. Leiserson. Scheduling multithreaded computations by work stealing. *J. ACM*, September 1999.

[3] R. D. Blumofe, C. F. Joerg, B. C. Kuszmaul, C. E. Leiserson, K. H. Randall, and Y. Zhou. Cilk: An efficient multithreaded runtime system. In *Proceedings of the Fifth ACM SIGPLAN Symposium on Principles and Practice of Parallel Programming*, 1995.

[4] S. Borkar. Thousand core chips: a technology perspective. In *Proceedings of the 44th annual Design Automation Conference*, 2007.

[5] P. Charles, C. Grothoff, V. Saraswat, C. Donawa, A. Kielstra, K. Ebcioglu, C. von Praun, and V. Sarkar. X10: an object-oriented approach to non-uniform cluster computing. In *Proceedings of the 20th annual ACM SIGPLAN conference on Object-oriented programming, systems, languages, and applications*, 2005.

[6] M. Frigo, C. E. Leiserson, H. Prokop, and S. Ramachandran. Cache-oblivious algorithms. In *Proceedings of the 40th Annual Symposium on Foundations of Computer Science*, 1999.

[7] Y. Guo, J. Zhao, V. Cave, and V. Sarkar. SLAW: A scalable locality-aware adaptive work-stealing scheduler. *Parallel and Distributed Processing Symposium, International*, January 2010.

[8] J. Held, J. Bautista, and S. Koehl. From a Few Cores to Many: A Tera-scale Computing Research Overview. Technical report, Intel White Paper, 2006.

[9] Intel. Threading Building Blocks. http://threadingbuildingblocks.org/, September 2011.

[10] D. Lea. A java fork/join framework. In *Proceedings of the ACM 2000 conference on Java Grande*, 2000.

[11] D. Leijen, W. Schulte, and S. Burckhardt. The design of a task parallel library. *SIGPLAN Not.*, October 2009.

[12] Microsoft. The Manycore Shift. Technical report, Microsoft White Paper, November 2007.

[13] Tilera. TILE-Gx, TilePro, and Tile64 processors. http://www.tilera.com/products/processors, 2012.

Boa: Analyzing Ultra-Large-Scale Code Corpus

Robert Dyer   Hoan Nguyen   Hridesh Rajan   Tien Nguyen

Iowa State University
{rdyer,hoan,hridesh,tien}@iastate.edu

Abstract

Software repositories contain an enormous amount of information such as revisions and bugs. Analyzing this data requires knowledge in mining software repositories and a large amount of infrastructure. We present our infrastructure *Boa* to ease such analyses. Our results show writing analyses with our framework is simpler and executes faster.

Categories and Subject Descriptors D.1.3 [*Concurrent Programming*]: Distributed programming

General Terms Experimentation, Languages

Keywords MapReduce, software repository mining

1. Introduction

There are many very large software repositories, such as SourceForge (350k+ projects), GitHub (250k+ projects), and Google Code (250k+ projects). These repositories contain massive amounts of interesting data with potentially billions of lines of source code just waiting to be mined. Many researchers and engineers would like to ask questions about this data however doing so requires a large amount of previous expertise in software mining and a large amount of existing infrastructure to perform the mining task(s).

Consider for example a simple question such as "how many revisions exist on SourceForge for all Java projects that also use Subversion?" Answering such a question would require knowledge of (at a minimum): how to read/scrape the project metadata from the repository, how to mine the code repository locations, how to access those code repositories, additional filtering code, controller logic, etc. This assumes that the query is performed locally and runs on a single machine, which might take an extremely long time to complete depending on the task. Writing such a program in Java for example, would take upwards of 100 lines of code and require knowledge of at least 2 complex libraries.

```
1  total_revisions : output sum of int;
2  p: Project = input;
3  when (i: some int; match('^java$', p.programming_languages[i]))
4    when (j: each int; p.code_repositories[j].repository_type ==
       RepositoryType.SVN))
5      total_revisions << len(p.code_repositories[j].revisions);
```

Figure 1. Program in *Boa* answering "How many revisions in Java projects using Subversion?"

Instead, consider the example code written in *Boa* and shown in Figure 1. These 5 lines of code not only answer the question of interest, but run on a distributed cluster potentially saving hours of execution time. Note that writing this small program required no intimate knowledge of how to find/access the project metadata, how to access the repository information, or any mention of parallelization. All of these concepts are abstracted from the user providing simple primitives such as the `Project` type, which contains attributes related to software projects such as the name, programming languages used, repository locations, etc.

2. Related Work

There are a number of languages that provide efficient means for computing highly data-parallel tasks. These languages abstract as much of the parallelization details as possible from the user and scale to large numbers of machines.

Dean and Ghemawat describe a MapReduce system [2] where users write procedural code to take key-value paired input, filter it (via *mappers*), and then aggregate the results (via *reducers*). Languages like Sawzall [5] hide some of the map-reduce framework details from users, by requiring users to only write the map functions and then select from a set of pre-determined aggregators. Other languages like Dryad [3] and Pig Latin [4] provide SQL-like syntax and allow for more general computations. None of these languages however provide the software mining benefits of *Boa*.

3. Approach

Our language's syntax is inspired by the Sawzall programming language [5]. We also add additional domain-specific types for software mining. Our compiler is based on the Sizzle [6] open source implementation of Sawzall, which runs on the Hadoop [1] MapReduce [2] framework.

Boa abstracts the notion of map-reduce programs from the user. Users write only the map portion of a program and then select from a previously defined set of aggregation functions. Output in *Boa* is defined as tables, such as the table *total_revisions* (line 1). This table can have integers emitted to it (line 5) and proceeds to use the *sum* function to aggregate these integers into a final result, which is the sum of all values emitted to the table.

Input in *Boa* (line 2) is a domain-specific type provided by the language, the type `Project`. An overview of the provided types is given in Figure 2. These types provide attributes which can be used to filter the data. For example, this program uses the attributes to select only Java projects (line 3) that use Subversion (line 4) by using quantifiers and *when* statements.

Type	Attributes
Project	id, name, created_date, code_repositories, …
Repository	url, repository_type, revisions
Revision	id, log, committer, commit_date, files
Person	username, real_name, email

Figure 2. Domain-specific Types Available in *Boa*

In order to provide the capability to reproduce results and speed up execution of queries in our language, we cache the repository data locally on our cluster. First we download the data in its raw format and then proceed to translate it into a custom data format. This custom data format is described using Protocol Buffers, which is a data description format developed by Google with the goals of making it compact in binary form as well as extremely fast to parse.

4. Early Results

Early results are quite promising, as shown in Figure 3. This table lists 3 different mining tasks. The first counts the number of revisions for Java projects using Subversion (the code shown in Figure 1). The second counts the number of committers for Java projects using SVN. The third determines how many projects use more than one programming language. All tasks were implemented in both Java and in *Boa*.

	LOC		Time	
Task	Java	*Boa*	Java	*Boa*
Counting revisions	60	4	331m	<1m
Counting committers	69	6	1,596m	<1m
# Multi-lingual projects	32	4	10m	<1m

Figure 3. 3 mining tasks implemented in Java and *Boa*. Results for lines of code (LOC) and execution time given.

The results are given in terms of lines of code required to implement the mining task as well as the running time on an input size of over 620k projects. The Java versions all required over 8 times as many lines of code and made use of several libraries (for SVN and JSON parsing). The *Boa* versions however only required around 5 lines of code per

task. The execution times also show impressive results for *Boa*, taking less than one minute to run each task whereas the Java versions ran anywhere from 10 times slower to taking over a day to answer one single task.

We believe these early results show that our approach provides several benefits. First, programs are much smaller and simpler to write. They also require less knowledge about how you mine software. Second, program execution scales and thus even when querying extremely large datasets (such as all of SourceForge) the queries only take one minute.

5. Conclusions and Future Work

Despite having such a large wealth of information available in code repositories, mining that software is a difficult task requiring significant expertise not only in the mining technique used, but many additional libraries and approaches. There is a significant cognitive and infrastructure burden to overcome for anyone wishing to perform research in this area. Our language *Boa* and the associated framework helps users overcome this burden.

In the future we plan to extend our approach to additional repositories (GitHub, Google Code, etc) and additional version control systems (Git, CVS, Mercurial, etc). We also plan to investigate additional methods of abstraction to ease writing mining tasks and additional language constructs and data structures to provide further optimizations.

Acknowledgments

Dyer and Rajan are funded in part by NSF grant CCF-10-17334. Tien Nguyen and Hoan Nguyen are funded in part by NSF grant CCF-1018600.

References

[1] Apache Software Foundation. Hadoop: Open source implementation of MapReduce. http://hadoop.apache.org/.

[2] J. Dean and S. Ghemawat. MapReduce: simplified data processing on large clusters. In *Proceedings of the 6th Symposium on Opearting Systems Design & Implementation - Volume 6*, OSDI'04, 2004.

[3] M. Isard, M. Budiu, Y. Yu, A. Birrell, and D. Fetterly. Dryad: distributed data-parallel programs from sequential building blocks. In *Proceedings of the 2nd ACM SIGOPS/EuroSys European Conference on Computer Systems 2007*, pages 59–72, 2007.

[4] C. Olston, B. Reed, U. Srivastava, R. Kumar, and A. Tomkins. Pig latin: a not-so-foreign language for data processing. In *Proceedings of the 2008 ACM SIGMOD international conference on Management of data*, pages 1099–1110, 2008.

[5] R. Pike, S. Dorward, R. Griesemer, and S. Quinlan. Interpreting the data: Parallel analysis with Sawzall. *Sci. Program.*, 13(4): 277–298, 2005.

[6] A. Urso. Sizzle: A compiler and runtime for Sawzall, optimized for Hadoop. https://github.com/anthonyu/Sizzle.

Developing a Coding Scheme for the Analysis of Expert Pair Programming Sessions

Mark Zarb

School of Computing
University of Dundee
Dundee, UK
markzarb@computing.dundee.ac.uk

Abstract

Communication occurs constantly within pair programming, however, little is known about this communication, and how it changes according to skill or experience. This research presents the creation of a coding scheme, used for the analysis of expert intra-pair communication.

Categories and Subject Descriptors D.1.5 [**Programming Languages**]: Object-oriented Programming.

Keywords pair programming; XP; communication; video analysis; grounded theory; collaboration; analytic coding

1. Research Problem and Motivation

Pair programming is a method for software development "that favours both informal and immediate communication over [...] traditional design methods" [1]. It is primarily a coding activity during which two programmers collaborate continuously on the same program, usually at the same computer. The pair takes on different roles: one, the driver, has full control of the keyboard, whereas the other (the navigator) is in charge of reviewing the code and performing continuous analysis and design. It is common practice for partners to switch roles frequently. Pair programming encourages programmers to talk to each other – this 'pair pressure' results in greater enjoyment and increased knowledge distribution [2], as well as quality improvement.

Communication is an integral factor to pair programming [3]; however, it is also regarded as being one of the main factors leading to failure in pair programming [4]. Little is known about the nature of this communication, and how it impacts pair programming success. The goal of this research is to gain an understanding of the different communication topics that occur within the pair.

This approach and the results arising from the overall research project shall benefit novice pair programmers. The improved understanding in the way expert pairs communicate within successful projects could lead to the creation of communication patterns and guidelines. Novice pairs can be trained in these patterns to emulate expert methods of dealing with pair programming issues (e.g. how to break silence, regain focus, or recover from an interruption) in order to improve the way they aid each other whilst pairing.

2. Background and Related Work

Existing studies show that pairs who experienced a high rate of communication did not necessarily experience high satisfaction, nor a high level of confidence with the final outcome of their work [5]. Communication within the pair should stay on-topic to drive the work forward.

There are several studies that focus on analysing pair programming videos, however, many of them use both novices and experts to create their concepts [6, 7]. Furthermore, these studies focus on the *process* of pair programming, rather than on the types of communication. As such, there is no well-studied catalogue of communication techniques for pair programming. This initial investigation presents an analysis of several sessions from an expert pair of programmers, with the aim of creating a robust coding scheme for understanding pair programming success.

3. Approach

The coding scheme presented is a general coding scheme that can be applied to expert pairs, primarily to understand the various topics of communication that relate to software development, but also to gather data that will allow for the development of communication patterns.

An initial set of 60 videos (the *pairwith.us* project [8], with each video lasting approximately 30 minutes) showing the same pair of expert programmers working on an incremental software project have been acquired for the development of these codes. Twenty-nine videos were eliminated from the set due to problems which would hinder the investigation: most of the initial videos had bad audio-visual quality, several videos had no video feed, and some videos featured a distracting echo. The remaining 31 videos were re-watched and analysed using Grounded Theory.

During this analysis, the author observed various verbal and non-verbal (mouse pointing, gesturing, finger-drumming, grunting) instances of communication, as well as several notable behaviours (such as the programmers' constant awareness of their goals, and use of jokes to lighten the mood and regain focus). For every video watched, the author listed the key observations of these trends.

4.   Results and Contributions

The communication trends were continuously compared and condensed to create a list of ten common analytic codes (keywords that categorise segments of the audiovisual data) that could be seen to occur throughout all the videos: *talking about previous work; continuous review of the expected goal; explaining; silent instances; discussion; unrelated conversation; jokes; switching of roles; high 5; distraction.*

In order to verify the validity of the coding scheme, a sample of five videos from the original set of 31 was selected and fully transcribed. The videos were then re-watched, and the transcription was coded. The researcher noticed that certain codes were too vague. For example, a *Discussion* was difficult to pinpoint and thus was split up into *Explanation*, *Suggestion* and *General*. Furthermore, it was clear that there was a distinction between conventional 'quiet' silence, and muttering (e.g. whilst typing, or figuring out code logic). Thus, the codes were adapted with each viewing of the five videos, until a set of codes that could be applied to all instances was achieved.

The author ran inter-rater reliability tests to assess the new version of codes – increased to 11. The inter-rater reliability for the raters was found to be Kappa = 0.56 (p < 0.001), indicating a moderate agreement with the way the author coded the video. The data showed an overlap between certain codes, such as *Joke* and *Off-Topic*, as well as *Planning* and *Suggestion*, suggesting that raters were confused by similar codes.

To reduce the potential degree of error, and to ensure that the coding scheme could be used to analyse other pairs, it was decided to collapse the codes with the most variability. This resulted in a refined set of codes, ordered below by their frequency of occurrence across the sample videos:

- Suggestion
- Silence
- Off-Topic
- Explanation
- Review
- General
- Muttering
- Distraction
- Switch

The videos were re-coded, and preliminary inter-rater reliability tests resulted in Kappa = 0.71 (p < 0.001), indicating a higher agreement that was more substantial, with a closer match of the analytic codes. The data also indicates that the codes for *Distraction* and *Switch* are behaviour-led codes rather than communication-based – this shall be reviewed in later experiments. The author expects to test these codes on videos produced by other expert pairs. Future experiments shall also test the inter-rater reliability.

This paper presents a set of communication topics used within the pair. These codes can be used to gather data on the way expert pairs communicate between themselves: this is the first step towards discovering communication patterns that lead to success in pair programming.

Acknowledgements

The research work disclosed in this publication is funded by the Strategic Educational Pathways Scholarship (Malta). The scholarship is part-financed by the European Union – European Social Fund (ESF) under Operational Programme II - Cohesion Policy 2007-2013, "Empowering People for More Jobs and a Better Quality of Life".

The author would like to thank Dr Janet Hughes and Prof John Richards, for their attention and support.

References

[1]   Williams, L., et al., *Strengthening the Case for Pair Programming.* IEEE Software, 2000. 17(4): p. 19-25.

[2]   Bryant, S., P. Romero, and B. du Boulay, *The Collaborative Nature of Pair Programming*, in *Extreme Programming and Agile Processes in Software Engineering*, P. Abrahamsson, M. Marchesi, and G. Succi, Editors. 2006, Springer Berlin/Heidelberg. p. 53-64.

[3]   Cockburn, A. and L. Williams, *The costs and benefits of pair programming*, in *Extreme programming examined.* 2001, Addison-Wesley Longman Publishing Co., Inc. p. 223-243.

[4]   Sanders, D., *Student Perceptions of the Suitability of Extreme and Pair Programming*, in *Extreme Programming Perspectives*, M. Marchesi, et al., Editors. 2002, Addison-Wesley Professional. p. 168-174.

[5]   Choi, K.S., F.P. Deek, and I. Im, *Pair dynamics in team collaboration.* Computers in Human Behavior, 2009. 25(4): p. 844-852.

[6]   Cao, L. and P. Xu. *Activity patterns of pair programming.* 2005: IEEE.

[7]   Salinger, S. and L. Prechelt. *What happens during pair programming?* in *Proceedings of the 20th Annual Workshop of the Psychology of Programming Interest Group (PPIG '08).* 2008. Lancaster, England.

[8]   Marcano, A. and A. Palmer. *pairwith.us.* 2009 [cited 2012 31 July]; Available from: http://vimeo.com/channels/pairwithus.

Benchmarking Typestate-Oriented Programming Languages

Benjamin W. Chung

Carnegie Mellon University
bwchung@andrew.cmu.edu

Abstract

The performance of typestate-oriented programming languages is difficult to evaluate as existing benchmarks do not exercise the unique features of these languages. We address this by developing a new benchmark suite specifically designed to evaluate typestate-oriented functionality. These benchmarks model projected applications, providing overhead and memory loads similar to actual applications.

Categories and Subject Descriptors D.2.8 [*Software Engineering*]: Metrics; D.3.3 [*Programming Languages*]: Language Constructs and Features

General Terms Performance, Experimentation

Keywords Typestate, Protocols, Benchmarks, Performance, Dynamic Behavior

1. Introduction

Typestate-oriented programming languages raise the level of abstraction by directly expressing protocols, while maintaining a similar underlying structure to that of other dynamic languages. As dynamically modified interfaces are widely used in many applications, such as many Javascript applications and some virtual machines [2, 4], protocol alteration is a very important part of programming in dynamic languages. However, even in existing dynamic programming languages, interface alteration after object creation remains unexamined by many leading benchmark suites [5].

2. Plaid

Plaid is a new programming language being developed to support the idea of first-class state [6]. Each state can have fields and methods, and methods can transition the receiver. This enables several new design concepts that are little used in more traditional object-oriented languages.

SPLASH'12, October 19–26, 2012, Tucson, Arizona, USA.
ACM 978-1-4503-1563-0/12/10.

```
1   state Socket {
2     val identifier;
3   }
4   state ClosedSocket case of Socket {
5     method open() {
6       this <- OpenSocket;
7     }
8   }
9   state OpenSocket case of Socket {
10    method read() { ... }
11    method write() { ... }
12    method close() {
13      this <- ClosedSocket;
14    }
15  }
```

Figure 1. A basic Plaid program

An example of Plaid code can be found in Figure 1, which models a simple socket representation with two states, ClosedSocket and OpenSocket. Socket can transition between the two states via the open and close methods, and both expose custom functionality depending on the state they are in.

3. Existing Benchmarks

Existing benchmark suites are focused primarily on determining the speed of a system at performing certain algorithms, such as manipulating a splay tree[1]. It has been shown that these standard metrics are not representative of real-world application speed, and that optimizations targeting these benchmarks do not always improve speed of applications [1, 3]. In addition, little work has been done towards a benchmark suite for a typestate-oriented language such as Plaid. Two suites, DaCapo and V8, are particularly relevant for our project, as they represent commonly used benchmark suites for large programs and dynamic languages, respectively.

DaCapo DaCapo is a benchmark suite written to analyze the performance of Java Virtual Machines (JVMs) in actual use cases. It uses a selection of benchmarks that are common applications for the JVM, primarily based on large open-source software projects. This core causes the suite to represent the performance of a large number of Java applications,

---

[1] http://v8.googlecode.com/svn/data/benchmarks/v7/run.html

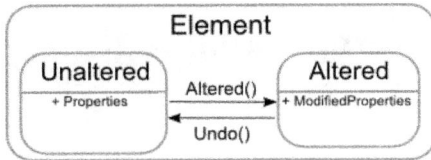

Figure 2. State diagram for implementation of the action pattern.

Benchmark	Plaid	Javascript	Java
Shell Sort	4.19	.131	.022
Binary Search Tree	1.09	.41	.0017
Splay Tree	18.26	.28	.11

Table 1. Preliminary comparison of execution times in seconds

as many applications either use the frameworks that make up DaCapo or use similar algorithms and memory structures to them [1]. However, this same functionality makes it difficult to apply the DaCapo suite to the typestate-oriented model, as it is highly Java specific.

V8 The V8 benchmark suite was written by the V8 team to act as a measure of the speed of the V8 Javascript engine. The V8 benchmark uses algorithmic benchmarks to arrive at a composite number, such as the DeltaBlue constraint solver[2]. Despite this popularity, V8 has significant disadvantages, focusing primarily on mathematical speed, rather than dynamic functionality.

4. Design Goals

Benchmarks that accurately represent the performance of a real application are hard to create by using small programs that a single algorithms. To mitigate this issue, we will create programs that perform tasks that are similar to those that a actual user might need. These programs should run algorithms that are reasonable use cases for the language, and should run in a reasonable amount of time. The use of a typestate-oriented language also imposes some requirements on the type of benchmarks used, so benchmarks should use state change regularly to evaluate the performance of protocol dynamism in Plaid.

5. Proposed Benchmarks

We have several benchmarks planned for the suite, that analyze several categories of application. We will be using a basic transactional database as well as heavily modified traditional benchmarks, such as sorting benchmarks and a subset of V8. These will benchmark different aspects of a potential real application.

Transactional Database A transactional database has features that can be modeled easily via typestate, such as the underlying tree data structure and the actions on the database. This benchmark will preform a large number of sequential operations on a B-tree data structure. Typestate can be used to implement the transaction system via a modification state, which tracks whether a particular node in the B-tree has been modified. This system can allow rollbacks of a transaction simply by changing the state of the affected nodes within the tree. A diagram of this model can be seen in Figure 2.

Algorithmic We also plan on porting traditional benchmarks from the V8 suite into Plaid, to analyze the speed of the Plaid runtime at executing standard algorithms, despite the limitations discussed above. In addition, we have created two more benchmarks to provide simpler, garbage collector intense operations. This reuse of traditional benchmarks also enables comparison of Plaid to the original language. In many cases, the more traditional benchmarks can be modified to take advantage of typestate oriented functionality. The Richards and BST benchmarks both use state change extensively. This is caused by the prevalence of state and state-like patterns in traditional object-oriented code.

6. Results

Current Benchmarks At the present time, we only have a small subset of the V8 suite, as well as our new algorithmic benchmarks. Javascript versions of all of our current benchmarks exist, allowing us to compare the existing performance of Plaid to V8.

Results Using our preliminary benchmarks, we have determined that Plaid is approximately 1 order of magnitude slower than the equivalent JavaScript program, and 2 orders slower than the equivalent Java program, as seen in table 1. All of the preliminary benchmarks were highly algorithmically centered, with large memory usage and extreme repetition and recursion. Results were gathered on a computer running the 1.6 JRE on Windows 7 with a Intel Core i7-2760QM CPU at 2.40GHz, and 8.00 GB DDR3 PC3-10600 RAM.

References

[1] S. M. Blackburn, R. Garner, B. Wiedermann, and et al. The DaCapo benchmarks: Java benchmarking development and analysis. In *OOPSLA '06*.

[2] A. Gal, B. Eich, M. Shaver, D. Anderson, and et al. Trace-based just-in-time type specialization for dynamic languages. In *ACM SIGPLAN 2009*, PLDI '09.

[3] M. Maass and I. Shafer. Instrumenting V8 to measure the efficacy of dynamic optimizations on production code. 2012.

[4] G. Richards, S. Lebresne, B. Burg, and J. Vitek. An analysis of the dynamic behavior of javascript programs. In *ACM SIGPLAN 2010*, PLDI '10, 2010.

[5] G. Richards, A. Gal, B. Eich, and J. Vitek. Automated construction of javascript benchmarks. *SIGPLAN Not.*, 2011.

[6] J. Sunshine, K. Naden, S. Stork, J. Aldrich, and E. Tanter. First-class state change in plaid. In *OOPSLA '11*.

---

[2] https://developers.google.com/v8/design

Mostly-Strongly-Timed Programming

Hiroki Nishino

NUS Graduate School for Integrative Sciences & Engineering, National University of Singapore
CeLS, #05-01, 28, Med. Drive, Singapore 117456
g0901876@nus.edu.sg

Abstract

Strongly-timed programming provides precise timing behaviours in logical time, which is crucial for audio programming. Yet, in the presence of time-consuming tasks, it
can easily fail in coordinating the advance of logical time
and the passage of real time. This can cause undesirable
results, such as unexpected noise in sound output. We propose mostly-strongly-timed programming, which integrates
asynchronous behaviours into strongly-timed programming
so that the underlying scheduler can suspend and resume
time-consuming tasks so as not to invalidate the synchrony
hypothesis. Such integration can enlarge the application
domain of the programming concept.

Categories and Subject Descriptors D.3.3 [**Programming Languages**]: Language Classifications– Specialized
application languages.

Keywords *computer music; programming concept*

1. Introduction

As Lee argues in [2], the lack of precise timing behaviors is
a significant problem in today's computer systems. In computer music applications, some sound synthesis techniques
such as granular synthesis require sample-rate accuracy in
scheduling to accurately render its sound output. Imprecise
timing behaviours can result in undesirable effects audible
to human ears [4]. Yet, many computer music languages
still exhibit this type of problem in timing behaviours and
are incapable of accurately rendering certain sound synthesis techniques without help from built-in objects [3].

Wang's *strongly-timed programming* [5] integrates logical
synchronous time within an imperative language and offers
a programming model that sufficiently matches the requirements for audio programming with sample-rate accurate precise timing behaviours in logical time. However, the
presence of time-consuming tasks can invalidate the *synchrony hypothesis*, on which the programming concept

relies, and a program may fail to meet the deadline for real-
time sound synthesis. Yet, such time-consuming tasks can
be often seen in computer music; such tasks may be better
described as asynchronous tasks rather than synchronous
ones.

We propose *mostly-strongly-timed programming*, which
integrates asynchronous behaviours that are not synchronized with logical time into strongly-timed programming.
Such an extension is helpful for solving the practical problems in audio programming and is potentially beneficial to
expand the application domains of the programming concept towards more general multimedia applications.

2. Related Work

Wang's *strongly-timed programming* is a variation of synchronous programming, which is based on *synchrony hypothesis* that assumes "*ideal systems produce their outputs
synchronously with their inputs*" and "*all computation and
communications are assumed to take zero time (that is, all
temporal scopes are executed instantaneously)*". During
implementation, this hypothesis is "*interpreted to imply the
system must execute fast enough for the effects of the synchronous hypothesis to hold*" [1, p.360].

```
#01 // synthesis patch
#02 SinOsc foo => dac;
#03
#04 // infinite time loop
#05 while( true )
#06 {
#07     // randomly choose a frequency
#08     Std.rand2f( 30, 1000 ) => foo.freq;
#09     // advance time
#10     100::ms => now;
#11 }
```

Figure 1. An example of *ChucK* program [5, p.43]

While many synchronous programming languages are
designed for *reactive systems*, strongly-timed programming
targets *interactive systems* with a significant focus on computer music systems. Because of such differences in the
target application, Wang's *ChucK* [5], a strongly-timed
computer music language is designed as an imperative

language that integrates explicit control of the advance of logical synchronous time.

Figure 1 shows an example in *ChucK* taken from [5, p.43]. Line #02 defines a simple sine wave sound module is built and the while loop between line 5-11 update the frequency with a random value (30-1000Hz). The core concept of strongly-time programming is the most explicit in line 10, where logical synchronous time is explicitly advanced. This causes the sine wave sound module defined in 2 to produce its output for 100ms. Since no progress of logical time can be made without such an explicit control and the program is executed completely at the same timing in logical synchronous time, the frequency in sound output changes exactly with 100ms period (in logical time). Thus, a strongly-timed program can achieve precise timing behaviours required for accurate sound rendering.

3. Mostly-Strongly-Timed Programming

Temporal semantics and timing precision in strongly-timed programming are favourable especially for live computer music systems. Yet, the presence of time-consuming tasks can invalidate the synchrony hypothesis, as the system fails to execute fast enough to hold the hypothesis; such time-consuming tasks can be often seen in computer music, e.g. loading and processing a large amount of sound data. This can suspend the real-time DSP and result in unexpected noise in the sound output. Such an issue is a significant obstacle in enlarging the application domain of strongly-timed programming towards more general audio programming. Hence, there is a necessity to extend the concept of strongly-timed programming so as not to let time-consuming tasks invalidate the synchrony hypothesis, while keeping its temporal semantics and timing precision.

We propose *mostly-strongly-timed programming* as an extension of strongly-timed programming to integrate asynchronous behaviours that do not have to be executed in a synchronous context and allow threads to switch freely between synchronous contexts and asynchronous contexts; when performing a time-consuming task that might invalidate the synchrony hypothesis, a thread can switch to an asynchronous context. The underlying scheduler can execute and if needed starve asynchronous threads at a lower priority than the synchronous threads while advancing its logical time, so as not to invalidate the synchrony hypothesis. In short, such asynchronous threads can be executed without synchronizing with logical synchronous time. After finishing time-consuming tasks, threads can switch back to a synchronous context as specified.

Figure 2 shows a design proposal for such a context switch between a synchronous context and an asynchronous context. As explained in the pseudo code, by explicitly switching to an asynchronous context, a program can avoid time-consuming tasks to invalidate the synchrony hypothesis and real-time DSP can be expected to continue without undesirable suspension; such explicit distinction of synchronous and asynchronous behaviours is necessary since some time-consuming task still must be finished before the progress of logical time. Furthermore, such a programming model would be more desirable to handle a time-consuming task more tersely than explicitly subdividing the task or writing some code to run in background and let synchronous tasks wait for the tasks to be finished.

```
//Switch to asynchronous context before performing a time-consuming
//task. The scheduler can advance the logical time, as the other
//synchronous tasks demand. Sound can be synthesized without being
//blocked by time-consuming tasks. Below async block will be
//executed asynchronously, regardless of the advance of logical time.
async {
  //loading sound files onto buffer no.0
  loadSndFileToBuffer(0, "largeSndFile.aif");
  while(true){
    //do some sound processing to the large sound file.
    //break when the whole sound data is processed.
  }
}
//switching back to synchronous context. Play the processed result
//with the interval of exactly 1 sec (in logical time).
while(true) {
  playBuffer(0);
  now += 1::sec;
}
```

Figure 2. A design proposal for mostly-strongly-timed programming

4. Conclusion

We proposed mostly-strongly-timed programming, which extends strongly-timed programming by integrating asynchronous behaviours. Such extension can avoid time-consuming tasks to invalidate the synchrony hypothesis, while keeping the benefit of its terse programming model and precise timing behaviours in logical time. Such a feature is beneficial to extend the application domain of the programming concept towards general audio programming.

References

[1] A. Burns and A. Wellings. *Real-Time Systems and Programming Languages: Ada 95, Real-Time Java and Real-Time POSIX (3rd Edition)*. Addison Wesley, 2001.

[2] E. Lee. Computing needs time. *Communications of the ACM,* 52(5):70–79, 2009.

[3] H. Nishino et al. LCSynth: A Strongly-Timed Synthesis Language that Integrates Objects and Manipulations for Microsounds. In *Proc. of Sound and Music Computing'12,* 2012

[4] C. Roads. *Microsounds*. The MIT Press, 2004.

[5] G. Wang. *The ChucK Audio Programming Language: A Strongly-Timed and On-the-Fly Environ/Mentality*. Ph.D thesis, Princeton University, 2008

Standard-based Strategy to Assure the Quality of the Mobile Software Product

Luis Corral

Free University of Bozen/Bolzano
Piazza Domenicani 3, 39100 Bolzano, Italy
Luis.Corral@stud-inf.unibz.it

Abstract

The high relevance gained by mobile software applications, the large number of users, and the growing development competition, trigger a need for a method to measure and track the quality of mobile software products from a domain-specific, quantitative point of view. We pursue the implementation of a strategy to extend software quality standards to supply mechanisms to measure the quality of mobile software products, for developers to have a well-founded understanding of whether their applications meet the market's demands and user expectations.

Categories and Subject Descriptors D.2.0 [**Software Engineering**]: General, Standards

Keywords ISO 9126; Markets; Metrics; Mobile; Process; Product; Quality; Standards

1. Motivation

The impact of the mobile software product grows every day, reaching a point in which mobile devices become one of the most important platforms for the distribution and utilization of user-oriented software. Mobile application stores are a primary channel for the dissemination of end-user software products, hosting thousands of *apps*, and reporting millions of downloads per day. Smartphones are driven by powerful operating systems that allow users to add and remove applications employing an architecture that is similar to a regular personal computer. However, these applications have to cope with several constraints inherent to the mobile ecosystem, not present in conventional desktop computing. In consequence, the quality of the mobile software product is driven by the conjunction of the traditional software quality characteristics with additional factors. The quality of mobile applications is usually regulated

by application market policies, and may also be communicated via customer's ratings and reviews. However, currently it has not been established a link between the quality goals posed on mobile applications, and specific characteristics that can be measured to determine the fulfillment of those quality goals quantitatively. Developers should have a solid understanding about whether their apps meet market demands and users' expectations, and they would benefit from knowing how a successful app was designed.

2. Research Problem

Mobile software engineers should put in practice a development strategy that considers several quality drivers: the mobile environment itself, the expectations of the end-user, and the restrictions set by application markets. After releasing a product, software developers may obtain an indirect quality appraisal from these drivers; for example, if their products are compliant with the market guidelines, they will be included in the application store; if their products satisfy customer expectations, they will receive positive reviews and high ratings. Several software development processes have been proposed to guide software engineers to produce high-quality mobile applications. These development processes are typically based on Agile methods, claiming that this approach is the most effective way to address the diverse and evolving requirements of the mobile environment [1-3]. Nevertheless, none of these lifecycles provide an appraisal model that delivers goals, methods and metrics to directly assess the software product in light of the conditions and constraints given by the mobile ecosystem. The main objective of this work is to accomplish the capability of associating market requirements and success factors of a mobile product with quality characteristics that can be measured and controlled. Our work hypothesis states that the mobile software product can be analyzed to relate measurable parameters of the software product with user expectations and market compliance criteria, delivering an accurate approximation of the product quality. To achieve these objectives, three main research questions were set: *RQ.1:* What are the most relevant quality requirements set upon a mobile application?; *RQ.2:* What is the impact given by the mobile environment on the quality of the software product?; and *RQ.3:* How can the quality of a mobile software product be measured?

3. Technical Approach

We organized our technical strategy in three stages that focus on providing answers for each question established in Section 2: First, to identify the most important quality requirements set on mobile apps, a comprehensive survey of the publishing guidelines of major application stores will be carried out: Publishing guidelines represent the minimum quality expectations for an application to be included in the distribution platform. Our first effort will concentrate on reviewing and comparing diverse publishing guidelines to extract commonalities and key quality attributes. The next step will be to conduct an analysis that allows us to relate mobile-specific characteristics with the corresponding measurable quality requirements. Such study will involve literature review and experimentation (e.g., performance analysis) to isolate additional needs and understand how the mobile environment by itself poses on mobile applications quality requirements that can be measured. Finally, with the information obtained from the previous stages, the Goal-Question-Metric (GQM) methodology [4] will be used for proposing a strategy for product quality measurement, including a formal statement of the goal and its description through questions and corresponding metrics. Our choice is to revisit ISO/IEC 9126, already suggested for similar domains [5, 6], and analyze its quality characteristics focusing in those applicable to the mobile software product in the given context. The essential software quality characteristics of ISO/IEC 9126 combined with those identified by us will be associated to metrics capable to deliver quantitative values to approximate the quality of the product in the required contexts, and also to provide information to feedback the development processes.

4. Evaluation Methodology

Following our work hypothesis, we pursue to know whether the mobile software product can be analyzed to relate measurable parameters of the software product (i.e., product metrics) with user expectations (e.g., ratings) and application market compliance criteria. To validate our approach, we will deploy an experiment consisting on the retrieval of a sample of assorted mobile applications from Google Play (Android OS market) and calculating from them the mobile software quality metrics defined the GQM. An automatic evaluation effort will be done using a non-invasive measurement framework able to analyze the source code and compute user-defined metrics [7, 8]. This will let us execute a multi-dimensional evaluation of the code without adding human-operator bias. The selected applications should focus on different purposes to cover a wider range of user and developer profiles; they must be distributed under Open Source licenses so that the access to the source code and code repositories can be guaranteed, to retrieve the code to perform the automatic analysis, and to study the behavior and evolution of the project [9, 10].

5. Future Work and Conclusions

In this paper, it is proposed a standard-based strategy for assessing the quality of mobile applications through metrics built upon the demands set by application stores and execution environments. Further work will concentrate on isolating the critical quality characteristics from markets and environments to later determine the metrics that will be used to approximate the quality of the mobile software product. The conduction of the experiment will supply the empirical data required to validate the accuracy of this approach, through the automatic calculation of the metrics and the correlation with product assessment parameters already existing in application stores and code repositories.

References

[1] Rahimian, V. Ramsin, R. 2008. Designing an Agile methodology for mobile software development: A Hybrid Method engineering approach. In *Proceedings of the 2nd Intl. Conf. on Research Challenges in Information Science.*

[2] Scharff, C., Verma, R. 2010. Scrum to support mobile application development projects in a just-in-time learning context. *In Proceedings of CHASE '10 (ICSE 2010)* pp. 25-31.

[3] Sillitti A., Succi G. 2005. Requirements engineering for Agile methods. *In Engineering and Managing Software Requirements.* Springer.

[4] Basili, V. 1993. Applying the goal question metric paradigm in the experience factory. *10th Conference of Software Metrics and Quality Assurance.*

[5] Spriestersbach, A., Springer, T. 2004. Quality attributes in mobile web application development. *In Proceedings of the 5th PROFES 2004.* LNCS vol. 3009, pp. 120-130.

[6] Mantoro, T. 2009. Metrics evaluation for context-aware computing. *In Proceedings of MoMM2009.* pp. 574-578.

[7] Scotto, M., Sillitti, a, Succi, G., Vernazza, T. 2006. A non-invasive approach to product metrics collection. *Journal of Systems Architecture, 52(11),* pp. 668-675.

[8] Sillitti, A., Succi, G., Vlasenko, J. 2011. Toward a better understanding of tool usage. *Proceedings of ICSE 2011(NIER).* pp. 832-835. IEEE.

[9] Sillitti, A., Succi, G., Vlasenko, J. 2012. Understanding the impact of pair programming on developer's attention: a case study on a large industrial experimentation. *Proceedings of ICSE 2012.* IEEE.

[10] Moser, R., Pedrycz, W., Sillitti, A., Succi, G. 2008. A model to identify refactoring effort during maintenance by mining source code repositories. *International Conference on Product Focused Software Improvement.*

Parallel Gesture Recognition with Soft Real-Time Guarantees

Thierry Renaux

Software Languages Lab
Vrije Universiteit Brussel, Belgium
trenaux@vub.ac.be

Abstract

When dealing with the complex task of extracting meaningful information from multiple continuous sensor streams, declarative rules can be employed to benefit from software engineering principles such as modularization and composition. We propose PARTE, a parallel scalable event processing engine proving predictable response times for a high-quality user experience.

Categories and Subject Descriptors D.1.3 [*Programming Techniques*]: Concurrent programming; D.3.4 [*Programming Techniques*]: Processors; I.5.5 [*Pattern Recognition*]: Implementation

General Terms Algorithms, Design, Performance

Keywords complex event processing, gesture recognition, actors, multimodal interaction, soft real-time guarantees, Rete, nonblocking

1. Introduction

To improve the quality of interactions between users and computers, interest in multi-touch input, gesture recognition, and speech processing on consumer hardware has recently emerged. To power natural user interfaces, primitive sensor readings, which are collected by devices for multimodal input, need to be correlated to create higher-level events. Since hard-coding these complex correlations in imperative programming languages is cumbersome, error-prone, and lacks flexibility, declarative techniques are the preferred solution. Multi-touch interaction frameworks such as Midas [6] and its multimodal successor Mudra [4], use an inference engine, which compares the events based on sensor readings with declarative rules describing the gestures.

2. Problem

To provide a high-quality user experience, the inference engine has to correlate events in a timely manner. When a user for instance interacts with a system through a multi-touch interface, changes should be reflected immediately and with a predictable delay to give the user a natural feedback. The same is true for multimodal interaction: When a user gives a series of speech and gesture commands, the right action should be performed without random delays that confuse the user about whether the command has been accepted or not.

Systems such as Midas embed inference engines which only tap the computational power of a single processing unit. However, the rise in sequential processing power offered by single processing units is stagnating, because efforts to increase clock-speed, instruction-pipeline depth, etc. offer diminishing returns. This severely limits the possible number of rules, their complexity, and the rate of events the system can handle. The only way to recognize more complex user interaction patterns without undermining the user experience by increased delays, is to embrace parallel processing power.

In addition to recognizing patterns in a timely manner, the system also needs to guarantee predictable responds times. This ensures that the system feels interactive and responsive. Akscyn et al. [1] show that long delays in interactive systems can distract users, and cause them to stop using the system. Consider for instance a user of a multi-touch gesture recognition system, who taps a certain location. If the user interface does not reflect this change within the timeframe the user has grown to expect, he will assume the command was not received, and may tap again. When the system then finishes processing the overdue gestures, the action will be executed twice. Users will rightfully blame the gesture detection system for this mistake. To prevent such errors, the detection of complex user interaction patterns should happen within a timeframe that can be predicted reliably up front.

However, the requirements of responsiveness and predictable runtime conflict: To offer the best performance on current hardware, the rule engine needs to use the available parallelism, and should provide real-time guarantees to ensure responsiveness. Current rule engines do not combine both requirements. They either are single-threaded in nature, or do not guarantee predictable worst-case execution times.

3. Approach

We propose the Parallel Actor-based ReTe Engine (PARTE), a complex event detection system, which address both the efficiency and the real-time requirement. The Rete algorithm [2] provides the desired efficiency, minimizing the asymptotic complexity.

The declarative rules defining gestures are transformed into a directed acyclic Rete network. In PARTE, each node of the Rete network corresponds to an actor. This enables both pipeline parallelism, as multiple stages of the Rete network can be processed simultaneously, and branch parallelism, as multiple branches in the Rete network can be processed simultaneously. Synchronization between the nodes happens in the form of inter-actor message-passing, where nodes only send messages to their successors in the Rete graph. The structure of the Rete graph in combination with the temporal properties of the events are exploited to guarantee synchronization between the branches, and with that, correctness. The actors' inboxes are represented by nonblocking queues using Michael's Safe Memory Reclamation technique [5].

By using nonblocking queues as the only concurrently accessed shared data structures, and by formalizing the execution steps, PARTE allows the reliable prediction of an upper bound on the execution time of the pattern matching. Our system is designed in such a way that every stage of the processing requires a bounded amount of time, which can be predicted given a set of gesture definitions and an upper bound on the rate of incoming events. Similarly, the number of stages required to process a series of events is bounded and constant for a given set of gesture definitions. To achieve this, we impose the requirement on rulesets that they must be *tiered*, a property that ensures that the rulesets do not express cycles. This approach enables us to guarantee soft real-time detection of gestures, given a set of rules defining gestures and an upper bound on the rate of incoming events.

Our preliminary performance evaluation used a number of microbenchmarks and a set of gesture definitions. The results showed that PARTE in its current unoptimized state is on average about three times slower than the highly optimized implementation of CLIPS [3] for the single threaded case. In the multithreaded case, PARTE was able to scale linearly up to 16 cores on our test machine, as such outperforming the sequential implementation.

4. Contributions and Future Work

The contributions of our work are:

Design and implementation of a parallel Rete engine tailored towards recognition of user interaction patterns with soft real-time guarantees.

Validation of real-time guarantees by evaluating the execution properties of the implemented algorithm, ensuring freedom of unbounded loops, and of blocking concurrent interactions.

Validation of practicality by showing the scalability of the parallel implementation and demonstrating that the overhead compared to CLIPS, a highly optimized sequential implementation, is acceptable.

Some limitations exist in the current version of PARTE. First, since test-expressions are separated from the nodes that join two branches, the full expressiveness of negation-as-failure is not supported in PARTE. Gesture recognition systems can work without a notion of negation, but the addition of it would be worthwhile nevertheless. Second, the coarseness of parallelization can further be tuned, as in some situations, the actor-based approach does not expose all options for parallelism. Inversely, in some situations, the actor-based approach imposes too high an overhead compared to the useful work. Finally, PARTE's current scheduler for the actors focusses only on correctness and real-time properties, but does not do any effort to prevent scheduling actors who do not have any message waiting in their inbox.

PARTE is compatible with existing single threaded inference engines such as CLIPS from NASA [3]. It can be used as a replacement of the core infrastructure of the multimodal Mudra framework [6], but can also be applied in a broader context where responsive and predictable complex event processing is needed. It can for instance be embedded in software monitoring network security, in algorithmic stock trading systems, etc. To conclude, PARTE is a parallel, actor-based variant for the Rete algorithm, offering soft real-time guarantees on the time it requires to process information from various sensor streams.

References

[1] R. M. Akscyn, D. L. McCracken, and E. A. Yoder. KMS: a distributed hypermedia system for managing knowledge in organizations. *Communications of the ACM*, 31(7):820–835, July 1988. ISSN 00010782.

[2] C. L. Forgy. Rete: A fast algorithm for the many pattern/many object pattern match problem. *Artificial Intelligence*, 19(1):17–37, Sept. 1982. ISSN 00043702.

[3] J. Giarratano. *CLIPS User's Guide, Version 6.0.* NASA - Lyndon B. Johnson Space Center, 1993.

[4] L. Hoste, B. Dumas, and B. Signer. Mudra: A Unified Multimodal Interaction Framework. In *Proceedings of ICMI 2011, 13th International Conference on Multimodal Interaction*, Alicante, Spain, November 2011.

[5] M. M. Michael. Safe memory reclamation for dynamic lock-free objects using atomic reads and writes. In *Proceedings of the twenty-first annual symposium on Principles of distributed computing - PODC '02*, page 21, New York, New York, USA, 2002. ACM Press. ISBN 1581134851.

[6] C. Scholliers, L. Hoste, B. Signer, and W. D. Meuter. Midas: A Declarative Multi-Touch Interaction Framework. In *Proceedings of TEI 2011, 5th International Conference on Tangible, Embedded, and Embodied Interaction*, Funchal, Portugal, Jan 2011.

Declarative Access Policies
based on Objects, Relationships, and States

Simin Chen

University of Texas at Austin, Carnegie Mellon University

simin.chen@utexas.edu

Abstract

Access policies are hard to express in existing programming languages. However, their accurate expression is a prerequisite for many of today's applications. We propose a new language that uses classes, first-class relationships, and first-class states to express access policies in a more declarative and fine-grained way than existing solutions allow.

Categories and Subject Descriptors D.2.10 [*Software Engineering*]: Design – Representation; D.3.2 [*Programming Languages*]: Language Classifications – Object-oriented languages

Keywords State, Relationship, Protocol, Access policies

1. Introduction

Access control is vital to create secure mobile web applications. A dominant model for access control is Fischer et al.'s Object-sensitive Role-Based Access Control (ORBAC) [3]. ORBAC is an extension of role-based access control [5] and allows for more fine-grained access. Fine-grained access policies restrict access to shared data accurately and thus increase the security of applications. For example, when a professor sets the grade of a student in a university grading system, we may want to ensure that the professor can only set of the grade of students in the professor's class. With ORBAC, this would be achieved by assigning unique id fields to each student. The professor would be allowed to set the grade of a student if the professor has a role *ProfessorOf* with the student's id number. However, if we also wished to guarantee that grades can only be set during the grading period of a college, id fields would not be enough; we would need information about the state [6] of the grade as well.

```
1    class Student {...}
2    class Class {...}
3    class Professor {...}
4    class College {...}
5    class Dean {...}
6    relationship Attends<Student stu, Class cl> {
7        char grade;   }
8    relationship Teaches<Professor prof, Class cl> {...}
9    relationship Employed<Professor prof, College col>
10       {...}
```

Figure 1. Classes and Relationships

In order to come up with general model of ORBAC, we first compiled a requirements document for a real-world university grading and evaluation system of a mobile web application. This document demonstrated that understanding the *entities* in the system, the *relationships* between them, and the *states* of the system is necessary to express access policies in a fine-grained and precise way.

Our language uses classes to represent entities and supports first-class relationships and first-class states. We propose a language that integrates classes, relationships, and states into a single language to express access policies *declaratively* and *accurately*. By integrating the concepts of classes, relationships, and states, fined grained access control similar to ORBAC can be achieved, and the concept of state allows further refinement for access control. By using these concepts, access polices can be expressed at a high level of abstraction, facilitating reasoning about access policies by the programmer. These declarative access policies can work towards building safer mobile web applications

2. Language Proposal

Our language introduces the following abstractions: *class*, *relationship*, and *protocol*, which contains states. The following sections elaborate on these abstractions.

2.1 Class

Like classes in an object-oriented language, classes in our language are used to represent an entity, such as a Student or a Professor. Classes can be instantiated, and can contain fields and methods. In Figure 1, classes Student, Class, Professor, College, and Dean are declared.

SPLASH'12, October 19–26, 2012, Tucson, Arizona, USA.
ACM 978-1-4503-1563-0/12/10.

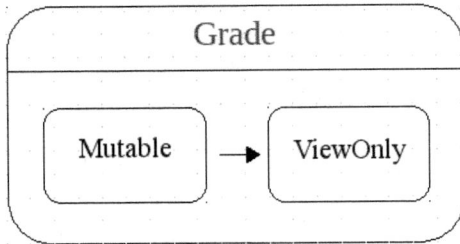

```
1   protocol Grade <College co> {
2       states: Mutable, ViewOnly;
3       transitions: end(): Mutable -> ViewOnly;
4       Mutable {
5           void setGrade(Attends at, char ch) {...}
6           char viewGrade(Attends at) {...} }
7       ViewOnly {
8           char viewGrade(Attends at) {...}
9       } }
```

Figure 2. Grade state diagram and resulting Grade protocol

In addition, a class can be a *principal*. A principal represents the current user of the system.

2.2 Relationship

Our language uses first-class relationships [1, 2]. Like classes, relationships can be instantiated. In Figure 1, relationships Attends, Teaches, and Employed are declared. Relationships take in two arguments and associate them. Since a relationship exists between a Class and a Student, the Class would not need to keep references to the Student instances in the Class. We can use relationships to infer these references. With relationships, we would not need to have an id field for the Student class as in the ORBAC model to ensure that a Professor is teaching a particular Student. The existence of relationships also allows us to have relationship-specific fields; grade, for example, is a field of the Attends relationship.

2.3 Protocols

Protocols define states and the transitions between states. States define state-specific methods. Protocols allow us to express state machines in the code. Figure 2 shows a Grade state chart and the resulting Grade protocol. The Grade protocol declares two states, Mutable and ViewOnly (line 2), and one transition from Mutable to ViewOnly (line 3). A call to end() will trigger the transition from Mutable to ViewOnly. Methods defined in a state are accessible only in that state. The method viewGrade() is redundant, but the principal that is allowed to access the method differs depending on the state. As development of the language continues, ways to eliminate this redundancy will be explored.

The argument that a protocol takes in, in this case a College instance, signifies the instance that is affected by the state changes. The grade for each Attends relationship in a particular College can be in a Mutable or ViewOnly state.

```
1   policy writeStudentGradeByProf(Attends a,
2       Teaches t, Employed e):
3       write of a.grade
4       if principal == t.prof && t.class == a.class &&
5           t.prof == e.prof && Grade<e.col> in Mutable
```

Figure 3. Access policy for setting a grade

To facilitate re-usability, protocols can be composed with other protocols. Composition can be done in the state declaration (line 2) of a protocol.

3. Access Policies

Access policies leverage relationships, states, and the *principal*. Figure 3 shows an access policy in our language. Line 3 declares the action being permitted. Lines 4 - 5 state the requirements that need to be met to perform the action. Our policy writeStudentGradeByProf states that the field a.grade can only be written if the principal is the prof in the Teaches relationship instance t and if cl in the Teaches relationship instance t is the same as the cl in the Attends relationship instance a and if the prof in the Teaches relationship instance t is the same as the prof in the Employed relationship instance e and if the Grade protocol with argument e.col is in the Mutable state.

In ORBAC, access permissions are declared as annotations on the methods that use the field or call. In our language, access policies are declared separately from the methods and have a global effect. This ensures that different methods do not have contradicting access policies.

4. Preliminary and Expected Results

This paper describes an ongoing work. At this time, we have identified the concepts needed for our language and the constructs needed to express these concepts. We have finished a parser and will work on an interpreter and dynamic checker.

References

[1] Stephanie Balzer and Thomas R. Gross. Verifying multi-object invariants with relationships. In *ECOOP*, pages 358–382, 2011.

[2] Gavin M. Bierman and Alisdair Wren. First-class relationships in an object-oriented language. In *ECOOP*, pages 262–286, 2005.

[3] Jeffrey Fischer, Daniel Marino, Rupak Majumdar, and Todd D. Millstein. Fine-grained access control with object-sensitive roles. In *ECOOP*, pages 173–194, 2009.

[4] David Harel. Statecharts: A visual formalism for complex systems. *Sci. Comput. Program.*, 8(3):231–274, 1987.

[5] Ravi S. Sandhu, Edward J. Coyne, Hal L. Feinstein, and Charles E. Youman. Role-based access control models. *IEEE Computer*, 29(2):38–47, 1996.

[6] Joshua Sunshine, Karl Naden, Sven Stork, Jonathan Aldrich, and Éric Tanter. First-class state change in plaid. In *OOPSLA*, pages 713–732, 2011.

Blended Analysis for JavaScript

a Practical Framework to Analyze Dynamic Features

Shiyi Wei

Department of Computer Science, Virginia Tech
wei@cs.vt.edu

Abstract

The inherent dynamism of JavaScript (e.g., runtime code generation, prototyping, and function variadicity) renders static analyses inadequate. To address this shortcoming, we analyze JavaScript programs by means of blended analysis, a technique combining dynamic and static analyses. Our empirical findings indicate that blended analysis can effectively analyze realistic JavaScript applications.

Categories and Subject Descriptors   D.2.11 [*Software Engineering*]: Software Architectures

Keywords   Program analysis, JavaScript

1. Introduction

JavaScript has become the *lingua franca* of client-side applications. Web browsers act as virtual machines for JavaScript programs that provide flexible functionality through their dynamic features. Unfortunately, the dynamism and flexibility of JavaScript is a *double-edged sword*. The dynamic constructs enable programmers to easily create client-side functionalities at the cost of rendering static analysis ineffective in their presence.

Recent study [1] reveals that JavaScript programs are full of dynamic features. Executable code can be generated at runtime via *eval*. A function can be called without respecting the declared number of arguments (i.e., functions may have any degree of variadicity). Object properties can be added/deleted at runtime. All of these dynamic features make it hard to precisely reason about JavaScript programs.

We have designed a blend of static and dynamic analyses to better handle the dynamism of JavaScript. The JavaScript Blended Analysis Framework captures rich information about dynamic language features. The framework is instantiated for points-to analysis, in order to show time cost and precision differences comparing to a pure static analysis.

2. JavaScript Blended Analysis

Figure 1 illustrates the three components of the JavaScript Blended Analysis Framework: the *Dynamic Analyzer* collects run-time information about an application; the *Selector* is an optional component designed to keep the analysis cost practical; the *Static Analyzer* analyzes the program representation that incorporates information obtained from the *Dynamic Analyzer*.

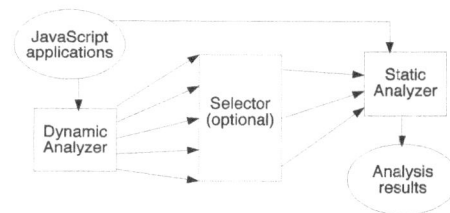

Figure 1. JavaScript Blended Analysis Framework

In our framework, JavaScript applications are instrumented and dynamic analysis produces run-time information for each execution. This information is used to construct a dynamic calling structure for the execution to serve as a program representation for inter-procedural static analysis. In addition, other dynamic information helps to improve static analysis accuracy. As shown in Figure 1, the *Dynamic Analyzer* outputs data for multiple executions. The *Dynamic Analyzer* used for blended points-to analysis instruments function calls (and captures their number of arguments), object allocations, and dynamically generated/loaded source code by modifying *TracingSafari* [1].

Optional use of the *Selector* may reduce the number of executions used as inputs to the *Static Analyzer*. Although each execution represents a different path in a JavaScript application, multiple executions can overlap in their methods. The *Selector* chooses executions that may have significant impact on the results of JavaScript blended analysis to lower the overall analysis cost, while maximizing code coverage.

The *Static Analyzer* consists of a pure static analysis algorithm that uses dynamic information about the executions as well as the application source code for the methods executed.

SPLASH'12,   October 19–26, 2012, Tucson, Arizona, USA.
ACM 978-1-4503-1563-0/12/10.

Because our JavaScript blended analysis aims to handle the dynamism of the language, this includes dynamic information that would be very hard for a pure static analysis to approximate well. The *Static Analyzer* analyzes each execution separately, preserving more context, and then combines the results of these analyses into a solution. We built our static infrastructure for analyzing JavaScript on the *IBM T.J. Watson Libraries for Analysis (WALA)* open-source framework.

3. Experimental Results

Our blended points-to analysis for JavaScript has been tested with JavaScript code from eight of the most popular web sites in *http://www.alexa.com*. In our experiment, we measured the difference between the points-to pairs produced by blended analysis versus those produced by a pure static analysis. For more detailed information, please refer to our technical report [2] which also includes related work.

Site	Blended coverage of static results(%)	Additional blended results(%)
google	89.7	5.9
facebook	85.3	7.5
youtube	89.1	9.9
yahoo	78.0	9.8
baidu	93.0	6.7
wikipedia	92.1	-
live	81.8	7.5
blogger	83.8	1.4
geom. mean	**86.6**	**7.0**

Table 1. blended points-to analysis results

Table 1 shows how well blended points-to solution compares to a pure static points-to analysis of the JavaScript code on a webpage, averaged across the pages explored at each website. The column labelled *blended coverage* presents the blended solution coverage of the static analysis solution as a percentage. The coverage of the static solution achieved by blended analysis (column 2) varies from 78.0% to 93.0%. The overall average (i.e., 86.6%) indicates that a large number of the programs are modeled well by blended analyses.

Column 3 in Table 1 illustrates the effect of dynamically loaded code on the points-to solution. The data present the average per webpage of the number of additional points-to pairs reported by blended analysis for each website, as a percentage of the entire program solution (i.e., pure static plus blended results). Blended analysis finds on average 7.0% additional points-to pairs per website.

4. Study of Object Dynamism

Our current JavaScript Blended Analysis Framework facilitates the challenges of analyzing JavaScript applications such as dynamic code generation and function variadicity; however, other dynamic features (e.g., prototyping, run-time property updates, and constructor polymorphism) have not yet been handled. A JavaScript object identity (i.e., the set of properties accessible by the object at a program point) can change at runtime because of these dynamic features.

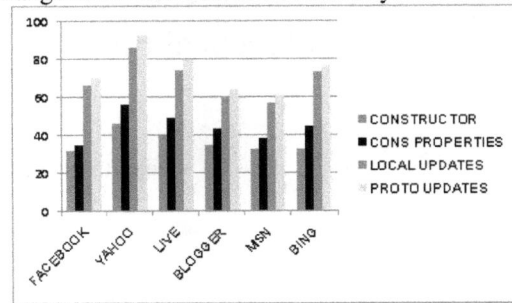

Figure 2. Study of dynamic object identities

We have performed a study to answer the question: How dynamic are JavaScript object identities? The study was executed on 17 websites and 30 traces were analyzed for each website. Figure 2 shows the results for 6 websites. In the study, we provide four ways to define dynamic object identities. *CONSTRUCTOR* bars show the number of unique constructor names observed at runtime. A JavaScript function acting as a constructor can create objects with different sets of properties, known as *constructor variadicity*. In addition to constructor names, *CONS PROPERTIES* bars exhibit the number of dynamic object identities with different sets of local properties in the constructors. As mentioned above, property addition/deletion can happen at runtime and change an object's identity. *LOCAL UPDATES* bars show the number of object identities with different sets of local properties during execution (i.e., we count a property addition/deletion as creating a new dynamic object identity). If an object acting as a prototype gets updated, it can affect the behavior of an other object that has the updated object in its prototype chain. The *PROTO UPDATES* bars reflect this transitive update of object properties via prototyping.

In Figure 2, the differences between *CONSTRUCTOR* and *CONS PROPERTIES* show that JavaScript constructors are quite variadic. The large increase when property updates are counted suggests property addition/deletion happens often in these websites. However, prototype objects do not change much because the *PROTO UPDATES* bars are almost the same height as the *LOCAL UPDATES* bars.

Based on the study, we believe constructor variadicity and runtime object property updates need better modeling to analyze JavaScript applications well. For future work, we would like to adapt JavaScript Blended Analysis Framework to handle these features.

Acknowledgments

This research is supported by NSF-0811518.

References

[1] G. Richards, S. Lebresne, B. Burg, and J. Vitek. An analysis of the dynamic behavior of javascript programs. PLDI '10.

[2] S. Wei and B. G. Ryder. A practical blended analysis for dynamic features in javascript. Technical report, Virginia Tech, 2012.

Security-oriented Program Transformations to Cure Integer Overflow Vulnerabilities

Zack Coker

Auburn University
zfc0001@tigermail.auburn.edu

Categories and Subject Descriptors: D.2.3[Software Engineering]: Coding Tools and Techniques; D.2.7 [Software Engineering]: Distribution, Maintenance, and Enhancement

General Terms: Security.

Keywords: Program Transformation, Integer Overflow.

1. Introduction

When integer operations in C mix the type of operands, the result may be unexpected. There are three possible vulnerabilities [1]: 1) a *signedness bug* occurs when an unsigned type is interpreted as signed, or vice versa; 2) an *arithmetic overflow* occurs when integer operations such as addition or multiplication produce a result that overflows the allocated storage; 3) a *widthness bug* is the loss of information when a larger integer type is assigned to a smaller type, e.g., int to short.

We describe three program transformations that cure the three types of integer overflow vulnerabilities. We implemented these program transformations on top of OpenRefactory/C [4]: our Eclipse-based infrastructure to develop program transformations for C programs. Our program transformations successfully removed all integer overflow vulnerabilities from 7,147 benchmark programs of NIST's SAMATE reference dataset [5]. They also remove real vulnerabilities from real programs. For space issues, we describe here the experience of applying them on one software—libpng.

2. Three Program Transformations

2.1 Add Integer Cast (AIC)

Context: Add Integer Cast transformation removes signedness bugs by explicitly adding type casts. Consider the program from the NIST's SAMATE reference dataset [5].

```
short data;
...
data = -1;
char dest[100] = "";
if (data < 100) {
    ...
    memcpy(dest, src, data);
```

A negative number for the variable `data` wrongly bypasses the conditional test. In the memcpy function, the value of `data` will be converted to a very large unsigned integer value. This will cause the program to write past the bounds of the char array `dest`.

Mechanism: A user selects an integer variable and invokes the AIC transformation. The program transformation determines the type of a variable (signed short in the example), checks if it is used in an unsafe context (signed short compared with an unsigned integer in the comparison expression), and explicitly add type casts.

```
short data;
...
data = -1;
char dest[100] = "";
if ((unsigned int) data < 100) {
    ...
    memcpy(dest, src, data);
```

2.2 Remove Artithmetic Operator (RAO)

Context: One of the most common vulnerabilities in C code are arithmetic overflows. Consider the vulnerability in rdesktop 1.5.0 [6]. In iso.c file, function iso_recv_msg contains:

```
s = tcp_recv(s, length - 4)
```

If length is less than 4, the subtraction silently wraps around producing an invalid/unexpected value.

Mechanism: A user selects an arithmetic operation, involving +, -, *, /, ++, –, +=, -=, *=, or /= operators, and invokes the transformation. The RAO transformation determines if the integer operation is unsafe and replaces it with safe functions from CERT's IntegerLib library [8]. The safe functions introduce callbacks that are explicitly invoked when an overflow occurs.

```
s = tcp_recv(s, ui2us(subui(length , 4)))
```

SPLASH'12,   October 19–26, 2012, Tucson, Arizona, USA.
ACM 978-1-4503-1563-0/12/10.

2.3 Integer Type Change (ITC)

Context: ITC corrects a variable's declared type. Consider this recent vulnerability in libpng v1.4.9 [7].

```
int copy = output_size - count;
if (avail < copy) copy = avail;
png_memcpy(output + count, png_ptr->zbuf, copy);
```

copy is declared a signed integer but png_memcpy requires an unsigned integer as its third argument. A negative value of copy will cause a buffer overflow in png_memcpy.

Mechanism: A user selects an integer variable and invokes ITC transformation. The program transformation determines the type of the variable, checks if it is used as another type in important contexts (e.g., when a variable is an lvalue or when a variable is used in a function call, etc.), and modifies the type to the appropriate type.

```
unsigned int copy = output_size - count;
if (avail < copy) copy = avail;
png_memcpy(output + count, png_ptr->zbuf, copy);
```

3. Evaluation

We implemented the transformations as Eclipse plugins. We did not use CDT, since CDT lacks sophisticated analyses. The transformations were developed on OpenRefactory/C [4], an in-house framework for building program transformations for C programs. OpenRefactory/C handles C preprocessor issues that complicate program transformations, and provides sophisticated analyses such as name binding analysis, type analysis, control flow analysis, and most importantly data flow analysis.

The transformations were validated in two ways. To validate that they successfully cure vulnerabilities, we applied them on NIST's SAMATE reference dataset. To validate that they do not break existing code, we applied them on real software—we describe the experience from libpng here.

3.1 SAMATE

SAMATE [5] is a joint project of NIST and DoHS. It has a suite of test bench programs in C, C++, and Java to demonstrate common security problems. For C\C++ code, the test suite version 1.0 provides 45,324 test programs for 116 different Common Weakness Enumerations (CWE). The transformations were applied on the relevant CWE-s. AIC was tested on CWE 194 (1296 programs) and CWE 195 (1296 programs), RAO on CWE 190 (2430 programs), CWE 191 (810 progams), and CWE 680 (324 programs), and ITC on CWE 196 (19 programs) and CWE 197 (972 programs). Our transformations successfully removed all vulnerabilities.

3.2 libpng

libpng, a graphics library, had a recent vulnerability in version 1.4.9 [7] that was fixed by ITC (section 2.3).

We ran the transformations repeatedly on libpng v1.4.9. The transformations were applied to preprocessed programs: in total 16 programs with 50,758 LOC.

AIC was applied on all local variables, all formal parameters, all array access expressions and all structure element access expressions—1830 in total. It changed 490 expressions that used unsafe local variables, 240 expressions that used an unsafe parameter, 83 expressions with an unsafe array access, and 547 expressions with an unsafe structure element access. In total, 1360 explicit cast were added.

RAO applied to all binary expressions, prefix expressions, postfix expressions, and arithmetic assignment expressions (e.g., +=)—11,849 in total. It changed 1,452 expressions: 1,310 binary expressions, 2 prefix expressions, 62 postfix expressions, and 78 arithmetic assignment expressions.

ITC was applied on all local variables. It checked 474 local variable declarations and changed 135.

To check that the program transformations do not break the code, we compiled the three resultant programs, one each from all invocations of AIC, RAO and ITC. The resultant programs passed libpng's test suite. While this is not a formal proof, correct test results even after a large volume of changes suggest that the transformations are robust.

4. Related Works

Most of the existing works on integer overflow vulnerability concentrate on detecting the vulnerability. Many sophisticated program analysis tools [2] [9] are available for automatically detecting these vulnerabilities in the source code. There are compiler based detection tools, such as gcc with -ftrapv option, which forces gcc compiler to insert additional calls (e.g., _addvsi3) before signed addition operations to catch overflow errors.

Our approach provides power tools for developers to remove integer vulnerabilities. They are similar to refactorings [3], but they do not intend to preserve behavior. They improve the security of systems, which means they preserve expected behavior, but remove the unintended vulnerability.

References

[1] blexim. Basic integer overflows. *Phrack*, 60, 2002.

[2] X. L. David Molnar and D. A. Wagner. Dynamic test generation to find integer bugs in x86 binary Linux programs. In *Proceedings of the 18th USENIX Security Symposium*, 2009.

[3] M. Fowler. *Refactoring: Improving The Design of Existing Code*. Addison-Wesley, Jun 1999.

[4] M. Hafiz and J. Overbey. OpenRefactory/C: An infrastructure for developing program transformations for C programs. In *Companion to OOPSLA 2012*. ACM.

[5] National Institute of Standards and Technology (NIST). SAMATE - Software Assurance Metrics and Tool Evaluation.

[6] National Vulnerability Database. CVE-2008-1801, 2008.

[7] National Vulnerability Database. CVE-2011-3026, 2012.

[8] R. Seacord. *CERT C Secure Coding Standard*. Addison-Wesley, 2008.

[9] T. Wang, T. Wei, Z. Lin, and W. Zou. Intscope: Automatically detecting integer overflow vulnerability in x86 binary using symbolic execution. In *NDSS*, 2009.

Automated Behavioral Testing of Refactoring Engines

Gustavo Soares

Federal University of Campina Grande, Campina Grande, PB, Brazil

gsoares@dsc.ufcg.edu.br

Abstract

Defining and implementing preconditions are non-trivial tasks. As a result, even mainstream refactoring engines contain critical bugs. We propose an automated approach for testing of Java refactoring engines. It has been useful for identifying more than 100 bugs in state-of-the-art industrial and academic refactoring engines.

Categories and Subject Descriptors D.1.5 [*Programming Techniques*]: Object-oriented Programming; D.2.5 [*Software Engineering*]: Testing and Debugging

Keywords Refactoring, Testing, Program Generation

1. Problem and Motivation

Refactorings may contain a number of preconditions needed to guarantee behavioral preservation. For instance, to pull up a method m to a superclass, we must check whether m conflicts with the signature of other methods in that superclass. In practice, testing refactoring preconditions involves manually creating an input program to be refactored and specifying a refactoring precondition failure as expected output.

However, developers choose input programs for checking just the preconditions they are aware of. Since specifying preconditions is a non-trivial task, developers may be unaware of preconditions needed to guarantee behavioral preservation. When the implemented preconditions are insufficient to guarantee behavioral preservation, we call it as *overly weak preconditions*. For instance, take class A and its subclass B as illustrated in Listing 1. The B.test() method yields 1. If we use Eclipse 3.7 to perform the Pull Up Method refactoring on m(), the tool will move method m from B to A, and update super to this. A behavioral change was introduced: test yields 2 instead of 1. Since m is invoked on an instance of B, the call to k using this is dispatched on to the implementation of k in B.

Schäfer and Moor [5] specified refactorings for Java, and proposed a tool called JastAdd Refactoring Tools (JRRT) [5]. However, the same problem occurs when we apply the previous transformation by using JRRTv1[1].

Listing 1. Pulling up B.k() by using Eclipse 3.7 or JRRTv1 changes program behavior.

```
public class A {
    int k() {return 1;}
}
public class B extends A {
    int k() {return 2;}
    int m() {return super.k();}
    public int test() {return m();}
}
```

Additionally, refactoring engine developers may also implement *overly strong preconditions*. In this case, the engine may refuse to apply refactorings.

2. Approach

We propose an approach for testing of Java refactoring engines. It performs four major steps. First, a program generator automatically yields programs as test inputs for a refactoring. Second, the refactoring under test is automatically applied to each generated program. The transformation is evaluated by test oracles in terms of overly weak and overly strong preconditions. In the end, we may have detected a number of failures, which are categorized in Step 4.

Test input generation. To perform the test input generation, we propose a Java program generator (JDOLLY [8]). It contains a subset of the Java metamodel specified in Alloy, a formal specification language. It employs the Alloy Analyzer, a tool for the analysis of Alloy models, to generate solutions for this metamodel. Each solution is translated into a Java program. In JDOLLY, the user can specify the maximum number (*scope*) of packages, classes, fields, and methods for the generated programs. The tool exhaustively generates programs for a given scope. In this way, it may generate input programs capable of revealing bugs that developers were unaware of.

Test oracle. We propose SAFEREFACTOR [7], a tool for checking behavioral changes, as oracle for weak preconditions. First, SAFEREFACTOR checks for compilation errors

SPLASH'12, October 19–26, 2012, Tucson, Arizona, USA.
ACM 978-1-4503-1563-0/12/10.

---

[1] The JRRT version from May 18th, 2010

in the resulting program, and reports those errors; if no errors are found, it analyzes the results and generates a number of tests suited for detecting behavioral changes. SAFEREFACTOR identifies the methods with matching signature before and after the transformation. Next, it applies Randoop, a random Java unit test generator, to produce a test suite for those methods. Finally, it runs the tests before and after the transformation, and evaluates the results. If results are divergent, it reports a behavioral change.

We also propose an oracle to detect overly strong preconditions based on differential testing. When a refactoring implementation rejects a transformation, we apply the same transformation by using one or more other implementations. If one implementation applies it, and SAFEREFACTOR does not find behavioral changes, we establish that the implementation under test contains an overly strong condition since it rejected a behavior-preserving transformation.

Test clustering. Our technique may produce a large number of failures, and some of them may be related to the same fault. Jagannath et al. [3] propose an approach to split failures based on oracle messages (Oracle-based Test Clustering - OTC). We adopt this approach to classify failures that introduce compilation errors in the output program. The failures are grouped by the template of the compiler error message, so that each group contains a distinct fault. We also use OTC to categorize the overly strong precondition failures based on the template of the warning message.

However, we cannot use this approach for classifying failures related to behavioral changes since there is no information from our oracle (SAFEREFACTOR) that could be used to split the failures. Instead, we propose an approach to classify them based on *filters* that check for structural pattern in each pair of input and output programs. For example, there are filters for transformations that enable or disable overloading/overriding of a method in the output program, relatively to the input program.

3. Evaluation

We evaluated our approach by testing refactoring engines from Eclipse JDT 3.7, NetBeans 7.0.1, and JRRT [8]. We evaluated two versions of JRRT. First, we tested the refactorings implemented by JRRTv1, and reported the bugs we found. Later, a new version was released with improvements and bug fixing (which we call JRRTv2); this new version was also subject to our analysis. We evaluated a total of 27 refactoring implementations.

Our technique identified 34 overly weak preconditions in Eclipse. Although all of them were accepted by the Eclipse developers, 16 of them were labeled as duplicated. So far, they have fixed just two of them. In NetBeans, our technique identified 51 overly weak preconditions. NetBeans team has already accepted 30 of them and fixed 7 bugs. Meanwhile, we reported 24 overly weak preconditions to JRRTv1, from which 20 were accepted and fixed (4 of the bugs were not

considered bugs due to a closed-world assumption of JRRT developers). We reported more 11 bugs to JRRTv2, from which 6 were accepted and fixed. JRRT team also incorporated our test cases into their test suite. Our technique did not find overly strong preconditions in NetBeans, but identified 17 ones in Eclipse. We have not received feedback about them from Eclipse developers prior to this submission. Moreover, It identified 7 overly strong preconditions in JRRTv1, from which 3 were fixed in JRRTv2.

4. Related Work

Proving refactoring correctness for the entire language is still a challenge [6]. Daniel et al. [1] proposed an approach for automated testing of refactoring engines. They used a program generator (ASTGen) to generate programs as test inputs, and implemented oracles to evaluate engine outputs. Their oracles try to detect behavioral changes by applying static analysis (e.g. they apply the inverse refactoring to the output program and expect that the result be equal to the input program). ASTGen allows users to directly implement how the Java constructs will be combined to generate programs. Later, Gligoric et al. [2] proposed (UDITA), a Java-like language that extends ASTGen allowing users to specify what is to be generated (instead of how to generate).

In a complementary work, Murphy-Hill and Black [4] characterize problems related to the process to apply automated refactorings. They propose principles that refactoring engine developers can use to turn these tools more popular.

Acknowledgments

I gratefully thank Rohit Gheyi, Max Schäfer and the anonymous referees for useful suggestions. This work was partially supported by the National Institute of Science and Technology for Software Engineering (INES).

References

[1] B. Daniel, D. Dig, K. Garcia, and D. Marinov. Automated testing of refactoring engines. In *ESEC/FSE '07*. ACM, 2007.

[2] M. Gligoric, T. Gvero, V. Jagannath, S. Khurshid, V. Kuncak, and D. Marinov. Test generation through programming in udita. In *ICSE '10*, pages 225–234, New York, NY, USA, 2010. ACM.

[3] V. Jagannath, Y. Y. Lee, B. Daniel, and D. Marinov. Reducing the costs of bounded-exhaustive testing. In *FASE '09*, pages 171–185, Berlin, Heidelberg, 2009. Springer-Verlag.

[4] E. Murphy-Hill and A. P. Black. Refactoring tools: Fitness for purpose. *IEEE Software*, 25(5):38–44, 2008. ISSN 0740-7459.

[5] M. Schäfer and O. de Moor. Specifying and implementing refactorings. In *OOPSLA '10*, pages 286–301. ACM, 2010.

[6] M. Schäfer, T. Ekman, and O. de Moor. Challenge proposal: verification of refactorings. In *PLPV '09*, pages 67–72. ACM.

[7] G. Soares, R. Gheyi, D. Serey, and T. Massoni. Making program refactoring safer. *IEEE Software*, 27:52–57, 2010.

[8] G. Soares, R. Gheyi, and T. Massoni. Automated behavioral testing of refactoring engines. *IEEE TSE*, 99(PrePrints), 2012.

Security Through Extensible Type Systems

Nathan Fulton

Carthage College, Carnegie Mellon University

nfulton@carthage.edu

Abstract

Researchers interested in security often wish to introduce new primitives into a language. Extensible languages hold promise in such scenarios, but only if the extension mechanism is sufficiently safe and expressive. This paper describes several modifications to an extensible language motivated by end-to-end security concerns.

Categories and Subject Descriptors   D.3.2 [*Programming Languages*]: Language Classifiers - Extensible languages

Keywords   Extensibility, Security

1. Introduction

Researchers involved in security research use language primitives to address software verification problems. However, many high-profile vulnerabilities have still not been addressed in popular languages. For example, although improperly sanitized user input is the top cause of vulnerabilities in mobile and web applications [3], popular languages have not incorporated language primitives that guarantee that input has been sanitized. Extensibility mechanisms capable of modularly expressing and verifying such primitives could help decrease the gap between research and practice.

Contributions   Ace is an extensible language being developed by our group. This paper describes an extension within Ace capable of statically verifying that a string is in a specified language. Implementing this extension required adding support for subtyping and type-casting to the Ace extension mechanism itself. We use the idea of type-directed compilation [5] to enforce a specified correspondence between the source and target type systems.

These contributions demonstrate the efficacy of using an extensible type system to verify mission critical portions of a program.

2. Constrained Strings in Ace

Although existing frameworks and libraries provide sanitation mechanisms, empirical studies show that developers misuse these tools [4]. This misuse suggests the need for a simple, universal language primitive that enforces best practices for string sanitation.

We address this need by providing a type system extension capable of statically checking that that a string is in a regular language. The inputs to insecure functions are constrained using a statically specified constrained string type. Our type system (see Figure 1, described later) provides a statically checked mechanism for converting strings into appropriately typed constrained strings. Values that have the type String must be cast to the specified type before use. Our type system provides a statically checked mechanism for achieving this conversion and updating the language a string belongs to when operations are performed on it.

Ace   Ace[1] compiles programs from a typed source language to a typed target language based on specifications associated directly with type definitions, written in a "type-level language". This approach is called "active compilation" [2].

Listing 1 is an Ace program demonstrating the constrained string extension. Ace functions are declared generically, then specialized with a `backend` (specifying the target language) and input types. Functions are compiled and specialized, one function at a time, on lines 4 and 9. Return types are inferred from input types. When `sanitize_query` is compiled, our typechecker ensures that the argument to `run_query` matches the input type specified on line 2.

```
1  CS = ConstrainedString
2  @ace.fn
3  def run_query(input):
4      return execute_query(input)
5  run_query = run_query.compile(backend,
6                  CS("(a-z0-9)+"))
7  @ace.fn
8  def sanitize_query(string):
9      return run_query(
10          `remove("^(a-z)+")`(string))
11  sanitize_query = sanitize_query.compile(
        backend, Str, run_query.type)
```

Listing 1. An Ace program using constrained strings.

SPLASH'12,   October 19–26, 2012, Tucson, Arizona, USA.
ACM 978-1-4503-1563-0/12/10.

[1] https://github.com/cyrus-/ace

Figure 1 area

$$\frac{t : Str}{t : L_*}\text{CS-INTRO} \qquad \frac{r \text{ is a regular language (RL)}}{L_r <: Str}\text{CS-LANG} \qquad \frac{r_1 \in r_2}{L_{r_1} <: L_{r_2}}\text{CS-SUBTYPE}$$

$$\frac{t_1 : L_{r_1} \qquad t_2 : L_{r_2}}{t_1 + t_2 : L_{r_1 r_2}}\text{CS-CONCAT} \qquad \frac{t_1 : L_{r_1} \qquad r_2 \text{ is an RL}}{\text{remove } \langle r_2 \rangle\, t_1 : L_{r_1 \setminus r_2}}\text{CS-REMOVE}$$

$$\frac{t : L_{r_1} \qquad r_2 \text{ is an RL} \qquad r_1 \in r_2}{\text{scast } t, L_{r_2} : L_{r_2}}\text{CS-SCAST} \qquad \frac{t : L_{r_1} \qquad r_2 \text{ is an RL} \qquad r_2 \notin r_2}{\text{dyncast } t, L_{r_2} : L_{r_2}}\text{CS-DYNCAST}$$

Figure 1. Some of the type checking rules relevant to the `ConstrainedString` extension.

The rest of Listing 1 is an application of the typechecking rules for constrained strings, as described in Figure 1. The expression surrounded by back-ticks on Line 7 uses static evaluation to parameterize the remove function with a regular expression. Calling the resulting function removes all substrings matching the constrained string type with the static string (see `CS-LANG` in Figure 1.) In this case, the value returned by `sanitary_query` has type `CS("(a-z)+")`. Subtyping between constrained strings permits this expression to be used where the larger type, `CS("(a-z0-9)+")`, is specified.

Constrained Strings Constrained strings are a family of types parameterized by the regular languages. We believe the checking rules provided in figure 1 describe a sufficiently expressing relation for addressing these needs:

- The `CS-LANG` rule establishes a correspondence between each regular language r and its constrained string type L_r.

- The `CS-SUBTYPE` defines subtyping as language inclusion: if the strings in one language are a subset of the strings in another language, then the smaller language is a subtype of the larger.

- The `CS-INTRO` rule admits arbitrary strings into the typing relation for constrained strings.

- The `CS-REMOVE` rule removes all substrings of t_1 matching r_2. Most sanitation algorithms have this form. The `CS-CONCAT` rule can be used to convert between constrained string types.

- The type casting rules are straight forward, but the evaluation rule for `CS-DYNCAST` inserts a runtime check.

Subtyping and Casting We modified Ace's extensibility mechanism so that backends and extensions may define subtyping and checked downcasts.

3. Checking Extensions to Ace

To have confidence in the security guarantees offered by an extension, we must check that the extension itself is correct. As an example, if Ace is compiling to C, then the constrained string type must enforce the typing relation given in Figure 1 and also generate code of type `char*`. The strategy for mechanizing this test follows from the design of Ace. Each expression generated by the compiler is tagged with an expected type, specified by the extension writer. The Ace type checker ensures that each generated expression has the expected type.

4. Related Work

Several languages provide mechanisms for extensibility. Ace uses a novel extension mechanism with type-directed specifications called Active Type Checking and Translation.

Regular expression types are used in several languages. Our subtyping extension is motivated by XDuce [1]. We are unaware of a predecessor to `CS-REMOVE`.

5. Future Work

Only portions of the Ace type system used by a program get checked during compilation. We plan to statically check these extensions be using a dependently-typed type-level language.

Acknowledgments

The author is advised by Cyrus Omar and Jonathan Aldrich and supported by a grant from the Army Research Office under Award No. W911NF-09-1-0273.

References

[1] Hosoya and Pierce. XDuce: A Statically Typed XML Processing Language. ACM Transactions on Internet Technology, 3(2):117-148, May 2003.

[2] Omar, Cyrus. Active Type Checking and Translation. SPLASH SRC 2012.

[3] OWASP. Top Ten Project. 2010.

[4] Scholte, Balzarotti, Kirda. Quo vadis? A study of the evolution of input validation vulnerabilities in Web applications. FCDS 2011.

[5] Tarditi, Morrisett, Cheng, Stone, Harper, Lee. Til: a type-directed optimizing compiler for ML. PLDI '96.

JavaScript: The Used Parts

Sharath Chowdary Gude

Auburn University

szg0033@tigermail.auburn.edu

Categories and Subject Descriptors   D.2.8 [*Software Engineering*]: Metrics; D.3.3 [*Programming features*]: Language constructs and features

General Terms   Languages, Measurement

Keywords   JavaScript, Empirical Study, Variable Scope

Abstract

1. Introduction

JavaScript(JS) is a language that is evolving. Some features proposed for JS arguably made it more complex and had to be abandoned (features in ECMAScript 4). Other efforts to evolve the language defined a subset of language that provides rigorous error checking and avoid error-prone constructs (ECMAScript 5). However, most of these attempts to include or exclude JS features were done without a scientific study of how the language features are used by developers.

Advances in JavaScript have not been backed by large-scale empirical studies on how people use JS features and how people react to the changes in JavaScript standards. Without this information, it is hard to determine how to evolve the language, which IDE features and refactorings to develop, how to optimize programs, how to teach developers good programming practices, etc.

We perform an empirical study on a huge corpus of JS programs. The test corpus consists of more than a million scripts from well-known and not-so-well-known webpages, and from Firefox Addons. We studied various JS features. This paper describes two JS features: the way JS variables are declared in block scope and function scope, and the way `for..in` statements are used in programs.

2. Research design

JavaScript is the most widely wide used language in the Internet and its in our best interest to collect JS programs coded by diverse group of programmers. Programs in the test corpus were collected from 3 sources.

(1) To collect JS programs from the wild, we used a web spider to crawl through the Internet and generate a unique list of 78644 URLs. These URLs reflect webpages from relatively remote websites. We loaded the URLs on an instrumented Google Chromium browser [2], that extracted the JavaScript programs from the URLs. In total, 1,064,793 separate JS programs were extracted.

(2) To collect JS programs that probably have better coding standards, we extracted JS programs from the top 100 websites (as per Alexa [1]). We visited and browsed these websites meaningfully to extract ubiquitously used JS functions in the web.

(3) The Mozilla Firefox Addons constitute the third source of corpus which include JS programs with most recent improvements in the languages. The top 40 Firefox Addons based on popularity are chosen for our research.

The test programs are then analyzed using an instrumented V8 engine. V8 is Google's open source JavaScript engine. It is written in C++ and is used in Google Chrome. We implemented visitors [4] that visited abstract syntax trees generated from JS programs. When V8 loads a JS program, the corresponding visitors were invoked and they stored the results in files. The individual results were aggregated later.

3. Results

The poster will describe several empirical study results. This document describes the results regarding two JS features: how variables are declared in JS, and how `for..in` statements are used to enumerate through an object's properties.

3.1 Variable Declaration in JS

We studied the scope of variable declarations inside functions. JavaScript does not have block scopes: Anything declared within a code block inside a function applies throughout the function. Crockford [3] considers this a bad feature of JS, and suggests that variables declared in block scope should be hoisted to the top of a function, so that they are in function scope. But do people follow the advice of experts? Are variables typically used outside their declaration scopes? Our study not only demonstrates the way people declare variables, but also justifies the need for a construct (`let` construct proposed in ES 6) for variables with local scope.

Of the 1,064,793 scripts in the corpus from spidered websites, 407,123 have a variable declaration. In total, 1,271,664 variables were declared: 1,241,344 were declared in functional scope, while the rest, i.e., 40,320, were in block scope. Of the 1,24,1344 variables in function scope, 787,502 were used in the function scope, 117,161 were declared within a function scope but used only within a block scope, and 346,781 were declared within a function scope but used both within block scope and function scope. Among the variables declared in block scope, 40,028 were limited within the block scope, but 282 escaped the block scope and were used within the function scope.

The scripts from Alexa top 100 websites shared similar pattern. 63,671 variable declarations were identified with declarations—61,236 in function scope and 2,345 in block scope. Of the function-scoped variables, 4,329 were used only within block scope, 15,564 were used within the function scope and 41,433 in both scopes. Among the block-scoped variables, only 15 escaped the scope.

Mozilla supports the `let` construct to declare block-scoped variables. 7 out of 40 Mozilla Addons from our corpus uses `let`—there were 1,800 variable declarations with `let`. As for regular variable declarations, there were 12,918—4,279 in block scope and 8,639 in function scope. Interestingly, all block-scoped variables were used within the scope. Among function-scoped variables, 1,034 were used only in block scope, 435 only in function scope, and the rest in both scopes.

Discussion A significant portion of the variables are declared in function scope and used in function scope. The most important observation is that the use of variables declared in block scope is limited to block scope. This implies that web programmers do follow Crockfordian ideas [3] about variable scope.

3.2 Property Enumeration with `for..in`

`for..in` is used for iterating through the properties of generic objects. `for..in` loops will not only enumerate every non-shadowed, user-defined properties, but also will enumerate the properties inherited from objects in the prototype chain. The `hasOwnProperty` construct can be used to distinguish an object's own and inherited properties. Our research focuses on the usage of `for..in` construct and whether they are used with `hasOwnProperty`.

There were 1,064,793 scripts extracted from the spidered websites. Among them 16725 instances of `for..in` were identified. Surprisingly, only 296 of them were refined with `hasOwnProperty` construct. The second source of repository are the scripts from Alexa top 100 sites which totaled 70,377 scripts. 777 of these functions contained `for..in` property and in those 17 instances were filtered with `hasOwnProperty`. The Firefox addons followed a similar pattern with 436 `for..in` functions and only 29 featuring `hasOwnproperty`.

Discussion The results indicate that the `hasOwnProperty` is seldom used with `for..in`. The above results evoked conjectures that the objects are stand-alone with no parents; it was verified to be true. Since most objects are created with null parents, it is not necessary to use `hasOwnProperty`.

Another interesting conclusion that can be drawn is that inheritance does not seem to be favored by web programmers with most of the objects being stand-alone. However, the addons have a higher percentage of `for..in`-s with `hasOwnProperty` because of the lengthier functions which often necessitate the need for inheritance.

4. Related Work

Empirical data on real-world usage of language features are available for popular languages, e.g., a study about preprocessor usage in C programs, but there has only been a few studies on JavaScript. JavaScript studies have focused on various dynamic features [6] [7], or the memory behavior [5], or security problems in JavaScript programs [8]. However, these studies do not target the language itself and how its features are used by developers. The test corpus that they use do not represent JS usage in the wild. Such studies are important for an evolving language to distinguish the used parts and focus on their evolution.

Acknowledgement

Allen Wirfs-Brock and Brendan Eich for their guidance.

References

[1] alexa.com/Topsites.

[2] chromium.org.

[3] D. Crockford. *JavaScript: the good parts*. O'Reilly Media, Inc., 2008.

[4] E. Gamma, R. Helm, R. Johnson, and J. Vlissides. *Design Patterns*. Addison Wesley, 1995.

[5] P. Ratanaworabhan, B. Livshits, and B. G. Zorn. Jsmeter: comparing the behavior of javascript benchmarks with real web applications. In *Proceedings of the 2010 USENIX conference on Web application development*, WebApps'10, Berkeley, CA, USA, 2010. USENIX Association.

[6] G. Richards, S. Lebresne, B. Burg, and J. Vitek. An analysis of the dynamic behavior of javascript programs. In *Proceedings of the 2010 ACM SIGPLAN Conference on Programming Language Design and Implementation, PLDI 2010, Toronto, Ontario, Canada, June 5-10, 2010*, pages 1–12. ACM, 2010.

[7] G. Richards, C. Hammer, B. Burg, and J. Vitek. The eval that men do - A large-scale study of the use of eval in javascript applications. In *ECOOP 2011 - Object-Oriented Programming - 25th European Conference, Lancaster, UK, July 25-29, 2011 Proceedings*, volume 6813, pages 52–78. Springer, 2011.

[8] C. Yue and H. Wang. Characterizing insecure javascript practices on the web. In *Proceedings of the 18th International Conference on World Wide Web, WWW 2009, Madrid, Spain, April 20-24, 2009*, pages 961–970. ACM, 2009.

CnC-Python: Multicore Programming with High Productivity

Shams Imam

Rice University

shams@rice.edu

Abstract

We present CnC-Python (CP), an approach to implicit multicore parallelism based on Intel's Concurrent Collections model. CP enables programmers to achieve task, data and pipeline parallelism in a declarative fashion while only being required to describe the program as a coordination graph with serial Python code for individual nodes.

Categories and Subject Descriptors   D.1.3 [*Programming Techniques*]: Concurrent Programming—Parallel programming

Keywords   Parallel Programming, Concurrent Collections, Python, CnC-Python

1. The Research Problem

In recent times, there is a higher emphasis being placed on programmer productivity, especially in the scientific community. Languages like Python and Matlab provide a high productivity development language for many domain experts due to their expressive yet simple syntax and semantics. Such programmers have limited experience with advanced parallel programming concepts such as threads and locks. With the advent of the multi-core era, it is clear that improvements in application performance will primarily come from increased parallelism [8]. The domain experts, who are not trained to write parallel programs, are faced with the unappealing task of extracting parallelism from their applications. The challenge then is how to make parallel programming more accessible to such programmers.

2. Background and related work

Python's [1] emphasis on code readability and a comprehensive standard library make it a highly productive language. It has support for extension modules that wrap external C libraries to deliver performance by running compiled native code without compromising productivity. However, the default implementation of Python uses a global interpreter lock (GIL) that ensures only one bytecode is executed by the interpreter at a time, thereby serializing multithreaded computations [7].

An approach to gain multithreaded performance in Python is by using SEJITS [3] which provides a AST wrapper (called *specializer*) and compiles the application Python code into efficient native code, at runtime. However, this approach is applicable only to existing specializers and not to general Python code. Another solution to obtaining parallel performance is to launch multiple Python processes and manage communication between them using the multiprocessing module from the standard Python distribution. An open source module, Parallel Python [11], provides an abstraction over the multiprocessing module. However, both these modules are comparatively low-level; parallelizing simple operations requires explicitly launching processes/jobs and managing synchronization of processes/jobs and data.

Concurrent Collections (CnC) [2] is a declarative and implicitly parallel coordination model that builds on previous work, notably TStreams [6] and Linda [5]. CnC was developed with the intention of making parallel programming accessible to non-expert programmers who provide serial code for computation called steps and a declarative description of data and control dependences. CnC supports combinations of task, data, and pipeline parallelism while retaining determinism. CnC-Python is an implementation of the CnC model which allows domain experts to express their application logic in simple terms using sequential Python code called *steps*. It is the responsibility of the compiler and a runtime to extract parallelism and performance from the application.

3. Approach and uniqueness

Our implementation of CnC-Python is currently targeted to shared-memory multiprocessors. The motivation for the current design is to allow the CnC runtime to behave as a coordination layer, and to enable (in the future) the user to express computation steps in any combination of languages such as Python, Matlab, Java, Scala, C, C++, and Fortran. The main components of the implementation are a layer to handle concurrency in Habanero-Java (HJ) [4], a language interoperability layer using Babel [10], and a layer in Python to actually execute the computation steps in parallel.

Core CnC Runtime The HJ task manager supervises the scheduling and execution of tasks in an internal thread pool. This allows us to avoid serializing of concurrent operations by the Python interpreter. Our runtime uses Data-Driven Tasks (DDTs) [9] to wrap execution of prescribed step instances inside lightweight tasks. Thus, DDTs enforce control synchronization and coordination in CP applications by delaying execution of steps by the Python interpreter.

Language Interoperability We require a language interoperability layer to invoke steps written in Python from the core CnC runtime implemented in HJ. We decided to use Babel because it focuses on high-performance in-process language interoperability within a single address space and is already widely-used by the scientific community [10].

Python Layer Babel manages the initialization of a single Python interpreter when the application starts and correctly handles parallel invocations into the interpreter. As the standard implementation of Python prefers spawning processes over use of threads to achieve true parallelism, the user steps execute in *child* processes spawned by our runtime. We maintain a one-to-one mapping between the main process threads and the spawned child processes. Executing the user steps in a separate address space prohibits the step computation from mutating its input data thus making our implementation of CnC capable of ensuring determinism with respect to shared data accesses.

We plan to extend our implementation to add support for productive languages such as Matlab allowing the user to write steps in any (supported) language of their choice. We are also exploring minimizing the cost of data serialization by introducing extensions that allow the programmer to express data locality hints in CnC programs.

4. Preliminary Results

We evaluate our runtime overhead by comparing with Parallel Python (PP) [11] v1.6.1. The applications were run on two quad-core Intel Xeon processors running at 2.83 GHz. Each processor can access up to 16 GB of RAM. It also included a Sun Hotspot JDK 1.7, HJ 1.2.0, Python 2.7.2, and Babel version 2.0.0-rc7437M. Each configuration of each application was run five times and the minimum execution time of each configuration is reported.

# of Workers	2	4	6	8
Parallel Python	125.63	63.61	42.24	32.19
CnC-Python	33.86	11.54	6.88	5.41
Speedup Factor	3.71	5.51	6.14	5.95

Table 1: Comparing the SumPrimes application using inputs of 101K, 102K, ..., 299K. Execution times are reported in seconds.

In PP, the user has to explicitly manage the data dependences for the computations and handle coordination of executing computations. In CP such dependencies are handled transparently as they can be deduced from the CnC graph description. Both PP and CP spawn processes to act as workers and manage serializing/deserializing the data and results. Table 1 shows that the CP implementation is much faster than PP on an application called SumPrimes (from the PP distribution). PP is considerably slower since the data synchronization is implemented using Python locks and the runtime is effectively single threaded (due to the GIL). The CP runtime overcomes this limitation by handling concurrency issues at the HJ layer where concurrent multithreaded execution is possible.

References

[1] Python Programming Language. URL http://python.org/.

[2] Z. Budimlić, M. Burke, V. Cavé, K. Knobe, G. Lowney, R. Newton, J. Palsberg, D. Peixotto, V. Sarkar, F. Schlimbach, and S. Taşırlar. Concurrent Collections. *Scientific Programming*, 18:203–217, August 2010. ISSN 1058-9244.

[3] Catanzaro, Bryan and Kamil, Shoaib Ashraf and Lee, Yunsup and Asanovi, Krste and Demmel, James and Keutzer, Kurt and Shalf, John and Yelick, Katherine A. and Fox, Armando. SEJITS: Getting Productivity and Performance With Selective Embedded JIT Specialization. Technical Report UCB/EECS-2010-23, EECS Department, University of California, Berkeley, March 2010.

[4] V. Cavè, J. Zhao, Y. Guo, and V. Sarkar. Habanero-Java: the New Adventures of Old X10. *9th International Conference on the Principles and Practice of Programming in Java (PPPJ)*, August 2011.

[5] Gelernter, David. Generative communication in Linda. *ACM Trans. Program. Lang. Syst.*, 7:80–112, January 1985. ISSN 0164-0925.

[6] Knobe, Kathleen and Offner, Carl D. Tstreams: A model of parallel computation (preliminary report). Technical Report HPL-2004-78R1, HP Labs, July 2005.

[7] PythonInfo Wiki. Global Interpreter Lock. URL http://wiki.python.org/moin/GlobalInterpreterLock.

[8] H. Sutter and J. Larus. Software and the Concurrency Revolution. *Queue*, 3(7):54–62, September 2005. ISSN 1542-7730. doi: 10.1145/1095408.1095421.

[9] S. Taşırlar and V. Sarkar. Data-Driven Tasks and their Implementation. In *Proceedings of the International Conference on Parallel Processing (ICPP) 2011*, September 2011.

[10] Thomas G. W. Epperly and Gary Kumfert and Tamara Dahlgren and Dietmar Ebner and Jim Leek and Adrian Prantl and Scott Kohn. High-performance language interoperability for scientific computing through Babel. *IJHPCA*, (1094342011414036), 2011.

[11] Vitalii Vanovschi. Parallel Python. URL http://www.parallelpython.com/.

Active Type-Checking and Translation

Cyrus Omar

School of Computer Science
Carnegie Mellon University
comar@cs.cmu.edu

Abstract

We introduce a statically-typed language extensibility mechanism called active type-checking and translation (AT&T) that aims toward expressiveness, safety and composability. This mechanism allows users to equip type definitions with type-level functions that control the compilation process directly, at points that are relevant to that type's semantics.

Categories and Subject Descriptors D.3.2 [*Programming Languages*]: Language Classifications—Extensible Languages; D.3.4 [*Programming Languages*]: Processors—Compilers; F.3.1 [*Logics & Meanings of Programs*]: Specifying and Verifying and Reasoning about Programs—Specification Techniques

Keywords extensible languages, type-level computation, typed compilation, specification languages

1. Extended Abstract

Programming languages have historically been specified and implemented monolithically. To introduce new primitive constructs, researchers or domain experts have developed a new language or a dialect of an existing language, with the help of tools like domain-specific language frameworks and compiler generators [1]. Unfortunately, taking a so-called *language-oriented approach* [3], where different languages are used for different components of an application, can lead to problems at language boundaries: a library's external interface must only rely on constructs that can be expressed in all possible calling languages. This means that specialized invariants cannot be checked statically, decreasing reliability and performance. It also often requires that developers generate verbose and unnatural "glue" code, defeating a primary purpose of specialized languages: hiding these low-level details from end-user developers.

Extensible programming languages promise to decrease the need for new standalone languages by providing more granular, language-based support for introducing new primitive constructs (that is, constructs that cannot be adequately expressed in terms of existing syntactic forms and primitive operations.) Developers would gain the freedom to choose those constructs that are most appropriate for their application domain and development discipline. Researchers would gain the ability to distribute new constructs for evaluation by a broader development community without requiring the approval of maintainers of mainstream languages, who are naturally risk-averse and uninterested in niche domains and still-emerging techniques.

A major example motivating our work is in the area of parallel programming abstractions. Many implemented abstractions require adding new type-checking and compilation logic to a language. Unfortunately, this has led to the development of new languages. An example for data parallel programming on accelerators and GPUs is the OpenCL language. Although OpenCL is largely based on C99, it is a distinct language and requires a separate set of tools. We would like a language that allows us to express the novel all of the novel aspects of OpenCL directly, so that it can be imported as easily as a library is today.

A significant challenge that faces language extensibility mechanisms is in maintaining the overall safety properties of the language and compilation process in the presence of arbitrary combinations of user extensions. The mechanism must ensure that basic metatheoretic and global safety guarantees of the language cannot be weakened, that extensions are safely composable, and that type checking and compilation remains decidable. The correctness of an extension itself should be modularly verifiable, so that its users can rely on it for verifying and compiling their own code. These are the issues that we seek to address in this work.

The approach we describe, *active type-checking and compilation* (AT&T), makes use of type-level computation in a novel way. To review, in languages supporting type-level computation, the syntactic class of types is not simply declarative. Instead, it forms a programming language itself (the *type-level language*). Types themselves are one kind of value in this language, but there can be many others.

SPLASH'12, October 19–26, 2012, Tucson, Arizona, USA.
ACM 978-1-4503-1563-0/12/10.

To ensure the safety of type-level computations, *kinds* classify type-level terms, just as types classify expression-level terms. A growing number of implemented languages now feature more sophisticated type-level languages, including Haskell. Type-level computation occurs during compilation, rather than at run-time, because type-level terms that are used where types would normally be expected must be reduced to normal form before type-checking can proceed. In this work, we wish to allow extensions to strengthen the static semantics of our language. Naturally, extension specifications will also need to be evaluated during compilation and manipulate representations of types. This observation suggests that the type-level language may be able to serve directly as a specification language. In this work, we show that this is indeed the case.

By introducing some new constructs at the type-level, developers are able to specify the semantics of the primitive operators associated with newly-introduced families of primitive types using type-level functions. The compiler front-end invokes these functions to synthesize types for and assign meanings to expressions, by translation into a *typed internal language*. Unlike conventional metaprogramming systems, these *type-level specifications* do not directly manipulate or rewrite expressions. Instead, they examine and manipulate the types of these expressions. By using a sufficiently constraining kind system and incorporating techniques from typed compilation into the type-level language directly, the global safety properties of the language and compilation process can be guaranteed. In other words, users can only *increase* the safety of the language.

We focus on extending the static semantics of a language with a fixed, though flexible, grammar. Techniques for extensible parsing have been proposed in the past, but we do not discuss this further here. We also focus on extending implementations, rather than declarative specifications, of language constructs. Extracting a compiler from a declarative language specification (e.g. one written in Twelf) has not yet been shown practical, but we note that a future mechanism of this sort could target a language implementing AT&T.

The organization and key contributions of this work are:

- We develop a core calculus, λ_A, and give examples of language features that can be expressed with it. We judgmentally specify the front-end compilation process and state several lemmas that lead to useful safety theorems for the compiler and language as a whole. We show how AT&T requires that the language provide a solution to a type-level variant of Wadler's expression problem [2].

- We introduce the Ace programming language, which is based fundamentally on an elaboration of AT&T that supports a richer set of syntactic forms and a variant of type inference. It uses object-oriented inheritance to solve the type-level expression problem. A number of practical extensions have been written using Ace, including a complete implementation of the OpenCL type system (based

```
import ace.OpenCL as OpenCL
T = OpenCL.int.global_ptr

@OpenCL.fn(T, T, T)
def sum(a, b, dest):
    gid = get_global_id(0)
    dest[gid] = a[gid] + b[gid]
```

Figure 1. An Ace function that uses the OpenCL extension.

```
typedef __global int* T;

__kernel void sum(T a, T b, T c) {
    size_t gid = get_global_id(0);
    dest[gid] = a[gid] + b[gid];
}
```

Figure 2. The corresponding OpenCL function.

on C99) as a library. Figure 1 shows how such an extension could be used. OpenCL's types are represented as objects in the type-level language (in Ace, this is Python). Here, `OpenCL.int.global_ptr` is the object representing the `__global int*` type. This object is an instance of a class extending `ace.Type`, and specifies methods for verifying and translating operations, such as indexing (`a[gid]`), into target language code. Compiling this code produces a function exactly equivalent to the OpenCL function in Figure 2.

- We briefly describe another point in the design space, a language design we call Birdie. Birdie lifts an extension of the Gallina language, used by the Coq proof assistant, into the type level (leading to a language with dependent kinds). This additional complexity allows for full proofs of correctness for type-level specifications, and can allow proofs soundness of functional specifications against conventional inductive specifications. The expression problem is solved using a constrained formulation of open data types, rather than using object-oriented inheritance. Birdie is ongoing work.

Acknowledgments

The author is grateful to Jonathan Aldrich. This work was funded by the DOE Computational Science Graduate Fellowship under grant number DE-FG02-97ER25308.

References

[1] M. Fowler and R. Parsons. *Domain-Specific Languages*. Addison-Wesley Professional, 2010.

[2] P. Wadler. The expression problem. *java-genericity Mailing List*, 1998.

[3] M. P. Ward. Language-oriented programming. *Software - Concepts and Tools*, 15(4):147–161, 1994.

Wavefront Chair's Welcome

SPLASH

As Wavefront enters its second year, we continue to strive to bring reports on innovative work that falls between the academic computer science research and the software currently being developed in the industry. Wavefront is about how industry applies the lessons learned from the software development community in deploying today's software and systems, as well as, how the community can learn from what is happening in the trenches of software engineering.

Part of Wavefront's ongoing goal is to provide a venue for practicing professionals to contribute to the software development community and also to create a process that allows them to participate even if they are unfamiliar with producing a conference paper. To enable this, we accepted proposal submissions of both full papers and extended abstracts. Program committee members were available to shepherd the authors of accepted papers as they worked toward final revisions.

All proposals were evaluated on the following criteria:

- Novelty: The paper presents new applications, system architectures, software designs, user interfaces, development tools, or implementation techniques.
- Interest: The paper addresses a significant and immediate problem or opportunity. The results in the paper have potential for immediate impact on state-of-the art software development projects.
- Evidence: The paper presents implemented designs, system case studies, or intriguing observations. Preference will be given to papers based upon deployed systems.
- Clarity: The paper is clearly written and understandable by practicing software developers. However, shepherding will be available for papers that present good ideas but need help in their presentation.

I would like to thank all of the authors and committee members for the time they put in to making Wavefront happen. I look forward to seeing this program grow and flourish as time goes on.

Christopher P. O'Connor
University of Michigan –
Institute for Social Research

A Methodology for Managing Database and Code Changes in a Regression Testing Framework

Roberto Salama, James McGuire, Michael K. Rosenberg

Morgan Stanley

{Roberto.Salama,James.McGuire,Mike.Rosenberg}@morganstanley.com

Abstract

Large system development typically involves changes to code and database components. In these environments, testing continues to be the biggest challenge. Since release cycles include both database and code changes, thorough testing of existing schemas and code base is paramount. Code needs to be tested with a static database, database changes need to be tested on a static code base, and finally, both changes need to be tested together.

In this paper we present the testing framework built during the development of Morgan Stanley's enterprise-wide time-series database, *Horizon*. The database, built using Kx's KDB+/Q, holds both tick-by-tick data originating from real-time feeds as well as periodic data received at regular intervals from vendors. The plant consists of several hundred cooperating processes which connect to real-time feeds, create in-memory databases, persist in-memory databases to disk on a regular basis, manage data set locations, and service client connections. At present, the database plant's size is approximately 1PB with an anticipated growth of .5PB/year.

Categories and Subject Descriptors D.2.4 [**Software/Program Verification**]: Validation. D.2.9 [**Testing and Debugging**]: Software Quality Assurance.

General Terms Database, Reliability, Verification.

Keywords Test Driven Development, Financial Time-Series Databases. KDB+/Q,

1. Introduction

A time-series is essentially a table where its primary key consists of a date and at least one other identifier (i.e. a stock ticker) along with observations (cells in the row) corresponding to events that happened at the same time (for example, bid and ask, or open, high, low, close, and volume). Moreover, financial time-series, once stored, are typically not modified. Corrections made to already recorded data are handled by storing the correction records as new

events and linking the correction event with the corrected event in a manner that we can query *as-of* a particular date. Our implementation is a fairly standard bi-temporal database similar to the ones in [1] and [2].

Time series databases are typically very large and grow very fast. At present, our database is approximately 1PB with an anticipated growth of 0.5 PB/year. With this footprint and growth profile, the existing containers, both relational, row-oriented databases were unable to keep up with the current volume let alone with projected volumes. In order to achieve this type of scalability it was necessary to switch to a column-oriented database. Refer to [3] for a comparison of both approaches.

As an enterprise-wide time series database, we need to store both tick-by-tick data and end-of-day data. Tick-by-tick data originates from exchanges where typically only the information that changes is sent over the wire, for example bid/ask prices where one record can contain only the bid, and the next, the ask. End-of-day data is sent by vendors at the end of the day; the data contains full records reflecting the end of day pricing (open, high, low, close, volume) of financial instruments. Corrections to full records can be sent during the day as either full or partial records. Thus, we needed to handle these different types of data sources within the plant.

We chose the Kdb+ database from Kx. Kdb+ is a column-oriented database with a single data format for real-time and historical formats providing a unified environment for handling all types of time-series data. It is programmed through its scripting language Q, a vector-based functional language, provides users with a powerful environment for querying data and applying transformations through anonymous functions, lambdas. Kdb+ is able to handle millions of records per second, billions per day accumulated in in-memory databases, and, trillions of historical records stored in databases on disk. [3]. Q is a vector processing language which is well suited for performing complex calculations quickly on large volumes of data [5].

2. The KDB+ Database

Kdb+ is a single architecture for both real-time and historical data [3]. On a real-time basis, Kdb+ stores incoming data in in-memory database tables. These tables are optimized for updates, adding rows to the end of the table. Dur-

ing the day, as data comes into the system, it is appended to these in-memory tables. At the end of the day, the in-memory databases are persisted to disk. Each day, a new partition on disk is created. Kdb+ stores its columnar data as memory-mapped files in the file system. Different persistence configurations of Kdb+ enable it to effectively use disk space by spreading data onto multiple disks
. The simplest, *serialized table* can be thought of as a *zero-dimensional* persisted form [5]. Data is stored in a single file and has not been split apart in any way:

file
table ▪

Where the symbol, ▪, represents a file.

In the next level, a *splayed table* can be thought of as *one-dimensional* persisted form [5] since it is cut vertically by splitting along columns and storing each column as a file[1].

column1 column2 column3 ...
table ▪ ▪ ▪ ...

In this configuration, a table consists of multiple files, one for each column of the table.

In the next level, a *partitioned table* can be thought of as *two-dimensional* persisted form [5]. The table is cut in two dimensions: vertically by splaying along columns and horizontally by slicing into partitions. In this configuration, the data for a column is spread across multiple files.

	column1	column2	column3	...
partition1	▪	▪	▪	...
partition2	▪	▪	▪	...
...	...	...	...	...

In the last level, a segmented table can be thought of as a *three-dimensional* persisted form [5]. The table is cut vertically by splaying, sliced horizontally by partitions and is additionally spread across physical locations in segments. The primary purpose of the third dimension is to allow operations against the tables to take advantage of parallel I/O and concurrent processing.

Kdb+ IPC enable a set of cooperating Kdb+ processes to communicate via Q data structures.

Segment 1

	column1	column2	column3	...
partition*	▪	▪	▪	...
partition*	▪	▪	▪	...
...	...	...	...	...

Segment 2

	column1	column2	column3	...
partition*	▪	▪	▪	...
partition*	▪	▪	▪	...
...	...	...	...	...

Where * denotes a (partial) column of a partion slice.[1]

3. Horizon Database Plant

The Horizon database plant relies on several hundred single-threaded Kdb+ processes interconnected via an asynchronous messaging system. The plant is capable of running these processes spread across multiple data centers. Figure 1 shows a typical set of processes used for ingesting data into the plant.

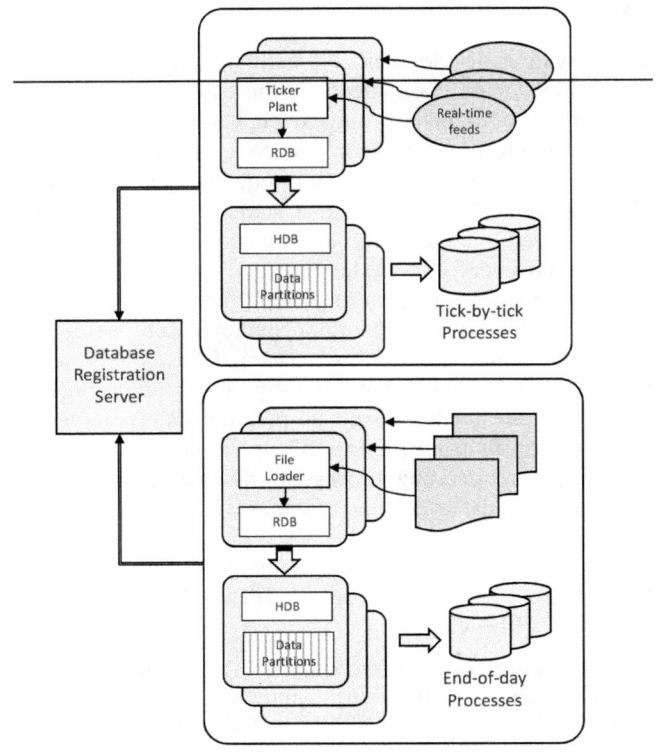

Figure 1. Plant Processes.

Processes shown in the tick-by-tick box are publish/subscribe processes which ingest data from real-time feeds. The *ticker plant* process manages data flow into the in-memory database and handles failover. Real-time data flows into in-memory databases (RDB's), which are also accessible for querying. At the end of the day and on a daily basis, the tick data accumulated in the RDB is persisted into a new partition on disk. Similarly, the processes shown in the end-of-day box handle the end-of-day data feeds which Horizon receives from a number of vendors. Data from either RDB's or HDB's can be queried and typically are queried together.

In Figure 2, the processes depicted on the left access the data exposed by HDB's and RDB's. A user typically connects into the plant via a dedicated *gateway* Q process. This dedicated process routes queries to the processes in the plant that contain the data that can service the query.

Other processes in the user space manage entitlements, serve as proxies, and help ease the load through load balancers.

3.1 Tick-by-tick processes

The tick-by-tick set of processes consist of a real-time feed connected to a publisher. As real-time data streams into the system, the *Ticker Plant process* creates a binary log of the incoming data. This binary log is used as a backup. If any of the processes in the subsystem fail, data can be played back from the binary log. The ticker plant also performs basic consistency checks before sending data to the RDB process. RDB's house the incoming data in in-memory tables allowing users to directly query them via Q. At present, Horizon subscribes to over 100 tick-by-tick data sources

3.2 End-of-day processes

The end-of-day set of processes operate in much the same way as the tick-by-tick processes; however, rather than reacting to real-time events, vendor-specific data loaders directly load feed files into their respective RDB's. Furthermore, as vendors publish corrections, these correction files are also loaded into RDB's and persisted along the same lines as with the tick-by-tick RDB. Since corrections can occur for events at any time in history, the end-of-day RDB to HDB process persist data into different date partitions.

3.3 Data Access processes

As shown in Figure 2, executing on the same machines as data collection processes, a set of processes called *workers* (**W**) handle all database queries. These processes have direct access to the underlying data, either RDB or HDB data partitions. Depending on the type of worker, the process is configured so as to maximize memory usage and I/O throughput. For instance, RDB's are typically run on machines with large RAM configuration (500Gb). HDB's are run on machines with a large number of I/O channels and

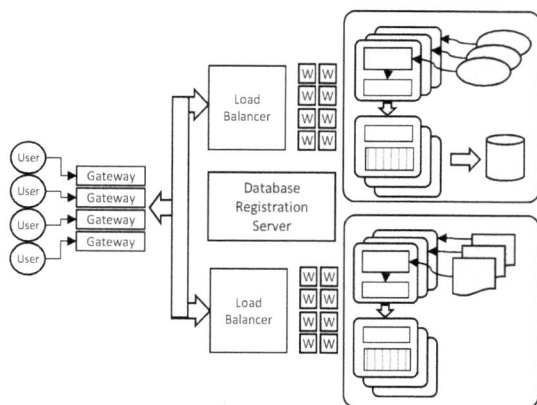

Figure 2. Data Access Processes.

configured with large and fast disks. *Load balancers* manage traffic to and from workers so as to maximize throughput.

3.4 Database registration service

As the respective data collection process clusters come online, they asynchronously publish their *identifier* (hostname and port) and the data sets they handle onto the *Database Registration Server*. This server maintains a table of (*host, port, dataset*) tuples for all the known resources in the plant. If the cluster of processes for a dataset were to become unreachable (as determined by the monitoring process), its (*host, port, dataset*) tuple is removed from the Database registration service until the cluster publishes its availability when it is ready to service requests. The plant maintains redundant clusters in separate data centers ensuring that there is always one side that can service queries.

3.5 User access processes

Users connecting into the plant are assigned a *gateway* process (Figure 2). Gateways are seeded with the available data sets filtered by the datasets the user is entitled to access. The *gateway* analyzes a user query, routes portions of the query to the cluster (or clusters) that contains the data (map). *Load balancers* schedule the query to be executed by an available *worker* on each of the clusters. When the data becomes available, it is routed back to the gateway which then assembles the data (reduce) before routing the result set back to the client.

3.6 Process managers

Lastly, there are a set of redundant processes on each machine in the data center responsible for ensuring that the processes running on a particular machine are indeed running. If a process dies or is unresponsive, the monitoring process creates a new one. As with other processes in the plant, new processes register themselves onto the Database Registration server.

4. Plant configuration

With such a diverse set of processes, configuration becomes an essential component of the Horizon plant. The configuration subsystem consists of a collection of configuration files which are read by each of the monitoring processes. They in turn start the requisite processes. Information in the configuration file consists of the following:

- Name of machine process is to run on
- Port on which the process accepts connections
- Type of process (HDB, RDB, Load Balancer)
- Set of Q scripts to be loaded, configures the process
- Path to physical database

5. Mini Plants and Regression Testing

With such a diverse set of processes, data sets, and machines, it is critical that developers be able to create a small portion of the plant, load it with canned data, and execute unit and regression tests on that portion of the plant. To this end, we use reduced configuration sets which configure and create the portion of the plant relevant to the test set. Figure 3 shows a subset of a plant used to test a real-time feed using canned data. In this configuration, we create a couple of gateway processes that will be used by the regression framework mocking a user connecting to the plant. A ticker plant and RDB processes are set up such that data can be played back played into a dummy real-time feed which then populates the RDB. Since the data contents are known a priori, the resulting RDB will always be the same and therefore immutable. We then connect this mini database plant to our regression framework, run all the regression tests performing actual vs. expected comparisons.

With this configuration, we can also execute real user queries to verify correctness. Most queries for tick-by-tick data involve window operations such as *moving average* and *volume weighted average price* (vwap). Leveraging the ability to query canned data played into existing user queries, we can also test algorithms that directly use these queries.

In this configuration, we also test the RDB to HDB path by running the end-of-day process that persists the in-memory database to disk. Since the RDB is immutable, the HDB is also immutable and again, we can run regression tests against the HDB data and verify correctness.

Another typical use case *stitches* data by querying from both the RDB and HDB. In its simplest form, this is a query that spans several days including the current day. With immutable RDB and HDB components mini-plants enable us to test these combined queries as well.

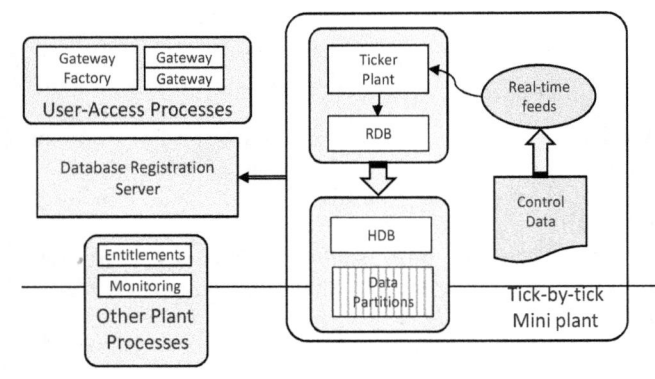

Figure 3. A typical mini-plant.

This plant configuration flexibility enables us to offer the regression testing framework to clients by allowing them to capture and can a dataset and then play it back into a mini plant. In this manner clients can also run regression tests against their queries during development and QA cycles.

6. Conclusion

In a system where both database and its underlying code can change, it is critical that we have a system where code changes are tested while holding the database constant. To this end, Horizon's flexible configuration system allows us to create a fully functional slice of the entire database plant complete with canned data and use it to test all the code changes slated for a release. The reverse is also possible, hold the code constant while changing the database. In this manner we have been successful at introducing testing much earlier in the development process. Typically developers work on a slice of the plant by configuring their environments to look like a reduced plant. This flexibility also enables us to test with our clients early on in the development process.

References

[1] Bela Stantic, Sankalp. Khanna, and John Thornton (2004), An Efficient Method for Indexing Now-relative Bitemporal Data, in Proceeding of the 15th Australasian Database conference (ADC2004), Denidin, New Zealand

[2] Christian S. Jensen, Richard T. Snodgrass (1999), Temporal Data Management, IEEE Transactions on Knowledge and Data Engineering

[3] Daniel J. Abadi, Samuel R. Madden, and Nabil Hachem [2008], Column-Stores vs. Row-Stores: How Different Are They Really? Proceedings of SIGMOD.

[4] Kx Systems White Paper, http://kx.com/papers/Kdb+_Whitepaper-2010-1005.pdf

[5] Jeffrey Borror (2008), Q for Mortals – A tutorial in Q Programming. ISBN 1434829014

[6] Kdb+ Database and Language Primer, Dennis Shasha (2005), http://kx.com/q/d/primer.htm

[7] FitNesse : http://fitnesse.org

[8] Roberto Salama (2012), A Regression Testing Framework for Financial Time-Series Databases, in Splash 2011, Portland Oregon

mbeddr: an Extensible C-based Programming Language and IDE for Embedded Systems

Markus Voelter

independent/itemis

voelter@acm.org

Daniel Ratiu
Bernhard Schaetz

Fortiss

{ratiu|schaetz}@fortiss.org

Bernd Kolb

itemis

kolb@itemis.de

Abstract

While the C programming language provides good support for writing efficient, low-level code, it is not adequate for defining higher-level abstractions relevant to embedded software. In this paper we present the mbeddr technology stack that supports extension of C with constructs adequate for embedded systems. In mbeddr, efficient low-level programs can be written using the well-known concepts from C. Higher-level domain-specific abstractions can be seamlessly integrated into C by means of modular language extension regarding syntax, type system, semantics and IDE. In the paper we show how language extension can address the challenges of embedded software development and report on our experience in building these extensions. We show that language workbenches deliver on the promise of significantly reducing the effort of language engineering and the construction of corresponding IDEs. mbeddr is built on top of the JetBrains MPS language workbench. Both MPS and mbeddr are open source software.

Categories and Subject Descriptors D.2.6 [*Software Engineering*]: Programming Environments - Programmer workbench

Keywords language extension, DSLs, development environments, embedded software, formal methods

1. Introduction

The amount of software embedded in devices is growing (see, for example, the German National Roadmap for Embedded Systems [9]). Embedded software development is challenging. In addition to functional requirements, strict operational requirements have to be fulfilled, including reliability (a device may not be accessible for maintenance after deployment), safety (a failure may endanger life or property), efficiency (the resources available to the system may be limited) or real-time constraints (a system may have to run on a strict schedule prescribed by the environment). Addressing these challenges requires any of the following: abstraction techniques should not lead to excessive runtime overhead; programs should be analyzable for faults before deployment; and various kinds of annotations, for example for describing and type checking physical units, must be integrated into the code. Process issues such as requirements traceability have to be addressed, and developers face a high degree of variability, since embedded systems are often developed in the context of product lines.

Current approaches for embedded software development can roughly be distinguished into programming and modeling. The *programming* approach mostly relies on C, sometimes C++ and Ada in rare cases. However, because of C's limited support for defining custom abstractions, this can lead to software that is hard to understand, maintain and extend. Furthermore, C's ability to work with very low-level abstractions such as pointers, makes C code very expensive to analyze statically. The alternative approach uses *modeling* tools with automatic code generation. The modeling tools provide predefined, higher-level abstractions such as state machines or data flow component diagrams. Example tools include ASCET-SD[1] or Simulink[2]. Using higher-level abstractions leads to more concise programs and simplified fault detection using static analysis and model checking (for example using the Simulink Design Verifier[3]). Increasingly, *domain specific* languages (DSLs) are used for embedded software [1, 17, 18]. Studies such

---

[1] http://www.etas.com/

[2] http://www.mathworks.com/products/simulink

[3] http://www.mathworks.com/products/sldesignverifier

as [7] and [?] show that domain-specific languages substantially increase productivity in embedded software development. However, most real-world systems cannot be described completely and adequately with a single modeling tool or DSL, and the integration effort between manually written C code and possibly several modeling tools and DSLs becomes significant.

A promising solution to this dilemma lies in a much tighter integration between low-level C code and higher-level abstractions specific to embedded software. We achieve this with an extensible C programming language. The advantages of C can be maintained: existing *legacy code* can be easily integrated, reused, and evolved, and the need for *efficient code* is immediately addressed by relying on C's low-level programming concepts. At the same time, domain-specific extensions such as state machines, components or data types with physical units can be made available as C extensions. This improves *productivity* via more concise programs, it helps improve *quality* in a constructive way by avoiding low-level implementation errors up-front, and leads to system implementations that are more amenable to *analysis*. By directly embedding the extensions into C, the mismatch and integration challenge between domain specific models and general purpose code can be removed. An industry-strength implementation of this approach must also include IDE support for C and the extensions: syntax highlighting, code completion, error checking, refactoring and debugging.

Developing such an extensible language and IDE is hard, but modern language engineering approaches promise to make it much simpler. The LW-ES research project, run by itemis AG, fortiss GmbH and Sick AG explores the benefits of language engineering in the context of embedded software development. The open source project is hosted at `http://mbeddr.com`. The code is available via this site.

Contribution In this paper we present mbeddr, an extensible C-based language and IDE for embedded software development. In particular, the paper makes the following contributions:

First, we present the design and implementation of mbeddr, which relies heavily on language engineering techniques. Extensions to C are *modular*, i.e. they can be developed without changing the C base language, and they are *incremental*, since they can be developed at any time and users can include extension modules into programs as the need arises. Extensions address syntax, type systems, semantics (by transformation to lower abstraction levels) as well as IDE support.

Second, the paper serves as a case study for the power and maturity of projectional language workbenches, and MPS in particular. We show how, with very limited ef-

fort, we were able to implement a significant set of languages that is ready to be used by embedded developers.

Third, we present a new approach to embedded software development located between programming and modeling. We illustrate a set of extensions to C that address important challenges in the embedded domain. Examples of such extensions include state machines, components and interfaces as well as the possibility of defining different restrictions of C in order to make programs conform to programming standards. We briefly illustrate how these extensions enable the use of advanced analyses such as model checking.

Even though the work presented here is centered on C and embedded software, the approach can be used with other domains and other base languages (we discuss this in Section 7). In this case, the first contribution would serve as a blueprint for identifying, motivating and designing language extensions. The second would serve as comparative reference for future (research) projects that use other language approaches or tools. The third would serve as a baseline for more specialized DSLs in specific subdomains of embedded software.

Outline In the next section we describe in more detail the challenges faced in embedded software development. In Section 3, we provide an overview over our solution approach and identify ways in which C must be extensible to allow the definition of adequate domain specific abstractions. Section 3.3 introduces a number of example extensions that address the challenges outlined in Section 2. We describe the implementation of these extensions, and with it, the design of the extensible C base language in Section 4. We discuss our experience in building mbeddr in Section 5. We wrap up the paper with related work (Section 6), a discussion (Section 7) and an outlook on future work in Section 8.

2. Challenges in Embedded Software

In this section we discuss a set of challenges we address with the mbeddr approach. We label the challenges C_n so we can refer to them from Section 3.3 where we show how they are addressed by mbeddr C. While these are certainly not *all* challenges embedded software developers face, based on our experience with embedded software and feedback from various domains (automotive, sensors, automation) and organizations (small, medium and large companies), these are among the most important ones.

C_1: **Abstraction without Runtime Cost** Domain-specific concepts provide more abstract descriptions of the system under development. Examples include data flow blocks, state machines, or data types with physical units. On the one hand, adequate abstractions have a higher expressive power that leads to shorter and easier to understand and maintain programs. On the other hand, by restricting the freedom of programmers, domain specific abstractions also enable constructive quality assurance. For embedded systems, where runtime efficiency is a prime concern, abstraction mechanisms are needed that can be resolved before or during compilation, and not at runtime.

C_2: **C considered Unsafe**   While C is efficient and flexible, several of C's features are often considered unsafe. For example, unconstrained casting via `void` pointers, using `int`s as Booleans or the weak typing implied by `union`s can result in runtime errors that are hard to track down. Consequently, the unsafe features of C are prohibited in many organizations. Standards for automotive software development such as MISRA [27] limit C to a *safer* language subset. However, most C IDEs are not aware of these and other, organization-specific restrictions, so they are enforced with separate checkers that are often not well integrated with the IDE. This makes it hard for developers to comply with these restrictions efficiently.

C_3: **Program annotations**   For reasons such as safety or efficiency, embedded systems often require additional data to be associated with program elements. Examples include physical units, coordinate systems, data encodings or value ranges for variables. These annotations are typically used by specific, often custom-built analysis or generation tools. Since C programs can only capture such data informally as comments or `pragma`s, the C type system and IDE cannot check their correct use in C programs. They may also be stored separately (for example, in XML files) and linked back to the program using names or other weak links. Even with tool support that checks the consistency of these links and helps navigate between code and this additional data, the separation of core functionality and the additional data leads to unnecessary complexity and maintainability problems.

C_4: **Static Checks and Verification**   Embedded systems often have to fulfil strict safety requirements. Industry standards for safety (such as ISO-26262, DO-178B or IEC-61508) demand that for high safety certification levels various forms of static analyses are performed on the software. These range from simple type checks to sophisticated property checks, for example by model checking [20]. Since C is a very flexible and relatively weakly-typed language, the more sophisticated analyses are very expensive. Using suitable domain-specific abstractions (for example, state machines) leads to programs that can be analyzed much more easily.

C_5: **Process Support**   There are at least two cross-cutting and process-related concerns relevant to embedded software development. First, many certification standards (such as those mentioned above) require that

code be explicitly linked to requirements such that full traceability is available. Today, requirements are often managed in external tools and maintaining traceability to the code is a burden to the developers and often done in an ad hoc way, for example via comments. Second, many embedded systems are developed as part of product lines with many distinct product variants, where each variant consists of a subset of the (parts of) artifacts that comprise the product line. This variability is usually captured in constraints expressed over program parts such as statements, functions or states. Most existing tools come with their own variation mechanism, if variability is supported at all. Integration between program parts, the constraints and the variant configuration (for example via feature models) is often done through weak links, and with little awareness of the semantics of the underlying language. For example, the C preprocessor, which is often used for this task, performs simple text replacement or removal controlled by the conditions in `#ifdef`s. As a consequence, variant management is a huge source of accidental complexity.

An additional concern is tool integration. The diverse requirements and limitations of C discussed so far often lead to the use of a wide variety of tools in a single development project. Most commercial off-the-shelf (COTS) tools are not open enough to facilitate seamless and semantically meaningful integration with other tools, leading to significant accidental tool integration complexity. COTS tools often also do not support meaningful language extension, severely limiting the ability to define and use custom domain-specific abstractions.

3. The mbeddr Approach

Language engineering provides a holistic approach to solve these challenges. In this section we illustrate how mbeddr addresses the challenges with an extensible version of the C programming language, growing a stack of languages extensions (see Fig. 1). The following section briefly discusses language extension in general and explores which ways W_m of extending C are necessary to address the challenges C_n. Section 3.3 then shows examples that address each of the challenges and ways of extending C.

3.1   Language Extension

In [35] we classify strategies for language modularization and composition. Traditionally, languages are composed by *referencing*: The partial programs expressed with different languages reside in their own files and refer to each other via references, often using qualified names. There is no *syntactic* integration, where a single program file contains language constructs defined in different languages. While referencing is sometimes useful, syntactic integration is required in many cases,

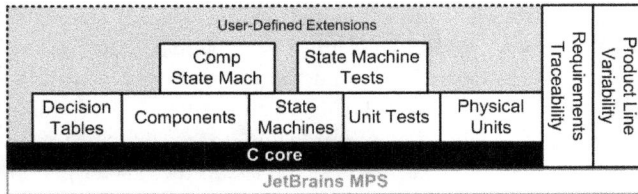

Figure 1. Based on MPS, mbeddr comes with an implementation of the C programming language. On top of C mbeddr defines a set of default extensions (white boxes) stacked on top of each other. Users can use them in their programs, but they don't have to. Support for requirements traceability and product line variability is cross-cutting. Users build their own extensions on top of C or on top of the default extensions. (Note: component/state machine integration and state machine tests are not discussed in this paper.)

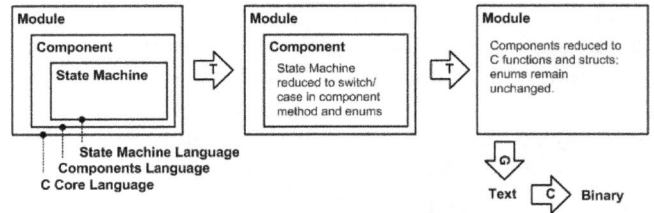

Figure 2. Higher-level abstractions such as state machines or components are reduced incrementally to their lower-level equivalent, reusing the transformations built for lower-level extensions. Eventually, C text is generated which is subsequently compiled with a C compiler suitable for the target platform.

as we will see in the examples provided in Section 3.3. In [35] we identify two strategies that support syntactic integration: language *embedding* refers to the syntactic composition of two independent languages. The embedded language has no dependency on the host language. Both have been developed independently, and the act of embedding does not require changes to either language. In language *extension*, a dependency from the extending language to the base language is allowed, for example, by inheriting from language concepts defined in the base language. The mbeddr system relies primarily on language extension.

To make language extension useful, it must provide deep syntactic and semantic integration, as well as an IDE that is aware of the language extensions. It is much more than a macro system or an open compiler (cf. Related Work in Section 6). Our implementation technology, the JetBrains MPS open source language workbench, supports the flexible definition, extension, composition and use of multiple languages. A language extension defines new structure, syntax, type system rules and semantics, as well, as optionally, support for refactoring, quick fixes and debugging. The semantics of an extension are typically defined by a transformation back to the base language, an approach also called assimilation [6]. For example, in an extension that provides state machines, these may be transformed to a `switch/case`-based implementation in C. Extensions can be stacked (Fig. 1), where a higher-level extension extends (and transforms back to) a lower-level extension instead of C. At the bottom of this stack resides plain C in textual form and a suitable compiler. Fig. 2 shows an example where a module containing a component containing a state machine is transformed to C, and then compiled.

A set of organizations, such as the departments in a large company, will likely not agree on a *single* set of extensions to C since they typically work in slightly different areas. Also, a language that contains *all* relevant abstractions would become big and unwieldy. Thus, extensions have to be *modular*. They have to be defined independent of each other, without modifying the base language, and unintended interactions between independently created extensions must be avoided (a discussion of automatic detection of interactions is beyond the scope of this paper). Also, users must be able to include *incrementally* only those extensions into any given program they actually need. Ideally, they should be able to do this without requiring the definition of a "combined language" for each combination of used extensions: for example, a user should be able to include an extension providing state machines and an extension providing physical units *in the same program* without first defining a combined language statemachine-with-units.

3.2 Ways to extend C

In this section we discuss in which particular ways C needs to be extensible to support addressing the challenges discussed above. Section 3.3 shows examples for each of the ways.

W_1: **Top Level Constructs** Top level constructs (on the level of functions or `struct` declarations) are necessary. This enables the integration of test cases or new programming paradigms relevant in particular domains such as state machines, or interfaces and components.

W_2: **Statements** New statements, such as `assert` or `fail` statements in test cases, must be supported. If statements introduce new blocks, then variable visibility and shadowing must be handled correctly, just as in regular C. Statements may have to be restricted to a specific context; for example the `assert` or `fail` statements must *only* be used in test cases and not in any other statement list.

W_3: **Expressions** New kinds of expressions must be supported. An example is a decision table expression that represents a two-level decision tree as a two dimensional table (Fig. 5).

W_4: **Types and Literals** New types, e.g. for matrices, complex numbers or quantities with physical units must be supported. This also requires defining new operators and overriding the typing rules for existing ones. New literals may also be required: for example, physical units could be attached to number literals (as in `10kg`).

W_5: **Transformation** Alternative transformations for existing language concepts must be possible. For example, in a module marked as `safe`, `x + y` may have to be translated to `addWithBoundsCheck(x, y)`, a call to an `inline` function that performs bounds-checking besides the addition.

W_6: **Meta Data Decoration** It should be possible to add meta data such as trace links to requirements or product line variability constraints to arbitrary program nodes, without changing the concept of the node.

W_7: **Restriction** It should be possible to define contexts that restrict the use of certain language concepts. Like any other extension, such contexts must be definable *after* the original language has been implemented, without invasive change. For example, the use of pointer arithmetic should be prohibited in modules marked as *safe* or the use of real numbers should be prohibited in state machines that are intended to be model checked (model checkers do not support real numbers).

Challenge	Example Extensions
C_1 (Low-Overhead Abstraction)	State machines (W_1, W_2) Components (W_1) Decision Tables (W_3)
C_2 (Safer C)	Cleaned up C (W_7) Safe Modules (W_5, W_7)
C_3 (Annotations)	Physical Units (W_4)
C_4 (Static Checks, Verification)	Unit Tests (W_1, W_2) State Machines (W_1, W_2) Safe Modules (W_2, W_5, W_7)
C_5 (Process Support)	Requirements Traceability (W_6) Product Line Variability (W_6)

Figure 3. Embedded software development challenges, example extensions in this section, and the ways of extending C each example makes use of.

3.3 Extensions addressing the Challenges

In this section we present example extensions that illustrate how we address the challenges discussed in Section 2. We show at least one example for each challenge. How such extensions are built will be discussed in the

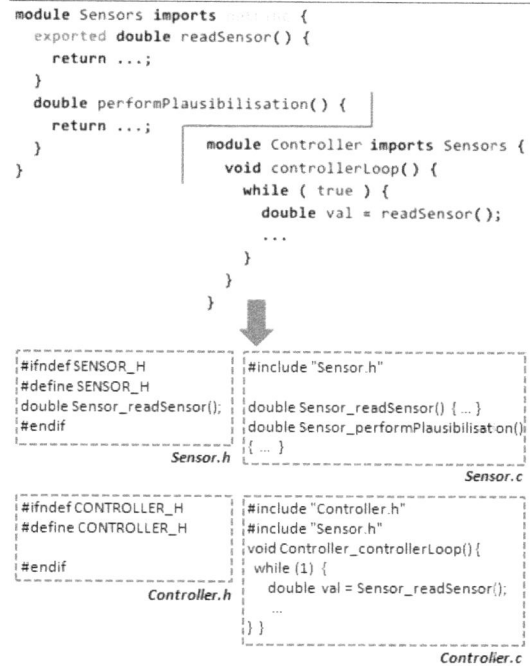

Figure 4. Modules are the top-level container in mbeddr C. They can import other modules, whose exported contents they can then use. Exported contents are put into the header files generated from modules.

next section, Section 4. Our aim in this paper is to showcase the extensibility of the mbeddr system, and, by this, language engineering using language workbenches. We will not discuss in detail any particular extension. The table in Fig. 3 shows an overview over the challenges, the examples in this section, and the ways of extension each example makes use of.

A cleaned up C (addresses C_2, uses W_7) To make C extensible, we first had to implement C in MPS. This entails the definition of the language structure, syntax and type system[4]. In the process we changed some aspects of C. Some of these changes are a first step in providing a safer C (C_2). Others changes were implemented because it is more convenient to the user or because it simplified the implementation of the language in MPS. Out of eight changes total, four are for reasons of improved robustness and analyzability, two are for end user convenience and three are to simplify the implementation in MPS. We discuss some of them below.

mbeddr C provides *modules* (Fig. 4). A module contains the top level C constructs (such as `structs`, functions or global variables). These module contents can be `exported`. Modules can *import* other modules, in which

---

[4] A generator to C text is also required, so the code can be fed into an existing compiler. However, since this generator merely renders the tree as text, with no structural differences, this generator is trivial. We do not discuss it any further

case they can access the exported contents of the imported modules. While header files are generated, we do not expose them to the user: modules provide a more convenient means of controlling modularizing programs and limiting which elements are visible globally.

mbeddr C does not support the *preprocessor*. Empirical studies such as [16] show that it is often used to emulate missing features of C in ad-hoc way, leading to problems regarding maintenance and analyzability. Instead, mbeddr C provides first class support for the most important use cases of the preprocessor. Examples include the modules mentioned above (replacing `#include`) as well as the support for variability discussed below (replacing `#ifdefs`). Instead of defining macros, users can create first-class language extensions including type checks and IDE support. Removing the preprocessor and providing specific support for its important use cases goes a long way in creating more maintainable and more analyzable programs. The same is true for introducing a separate `boolean` type and not interpreting integers as Booleans by default. An explicit cast operator is available.

Type decorations, such as array brackets or the pointer asterisk must be specified on the type, not on the identifier (`int[] a;` instead of `int a[];`). This has been done for reasons of consistency and to simplify the implementation in MPS: it is the property of a type to be an array type or a pointer type, not the property of an identifier. Identifiers are just names.

Decision Tables (addressing C_1, uses W_3) are a new kind of expression, i.e. they can be evaluated. An example is shown in Fig. 5. A decision table represents nested `if` statements. It is evaluated to the value of the first cell whose column and row headers are `true` (the evaluation order is left to right, top to bottom). A default value (`FAIL`) is specified to handle the case where none of the column/row header combinations is `true`. Since the compiler and IDE have to compute a type for expressions, the decision table specifies the type of its result values explicitly (`int8_t`).

Unit Tests (addresses C_4, uses W_1, W_2) are new top-level constructs (Fig. 6) introduced in a separate *unittest* language that extends the C core. They are like `void` functions without arguments. The *unittest* language also introduces `assert` and `fail` statements, which can only be used inside test cases. Testing embedded software can be a challenge, and the *unittest* extension is a first step at providing comprehensive support for testing. mbeddr also provides support for platform-independent logging as well as for specifying stubs and mocks. We do not discuss this in this paper.

Components (addresses C_1, uses W_1) are new top level constructs that support modularization, encapsulation and the separation between specification and im-

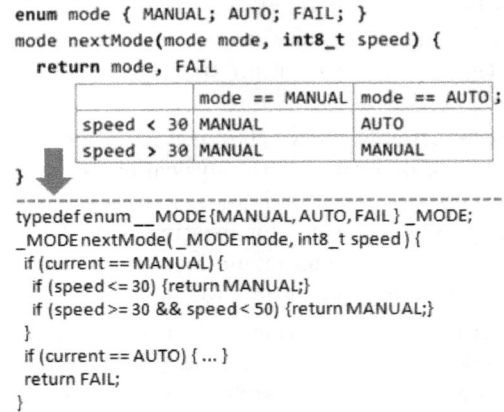

```
enum mode { MANUAL; AUTO; FAIL; }
mode nextMode(mode mode, int8_t speed) {
  return mode, FAIL
```

	mode == MANUAL	mode == AUTO
speed < 30	MANUAL	AUTO
speed > 30	MANUAL	MANUAL

```
}
```
```
typedef enum __MODE {MANUAL, AUTO, FAIL } _MODE;
_MODE nextMode( _MODE mode, int8_t speed ) {
  if (current == MANUAL) {
    if (speed <= 30) {return MANUAL;}
    if (speed >= 30 && speed < 50) {return MANUAL;}
  }
  if (current == AUTO) { ... }
  return FAIL;
}
```

Figure 5. A decision table evaluates to the value in the cell for which the row and column headers are `true`, a default value otherwise (`FAIL` in the example). By default, a decision table is translated to nested `ifs` in a separate function. The figure shows the translation for the common case where a decision table is used in a `return`. This case is optimized to not use the indirection of an extra function.

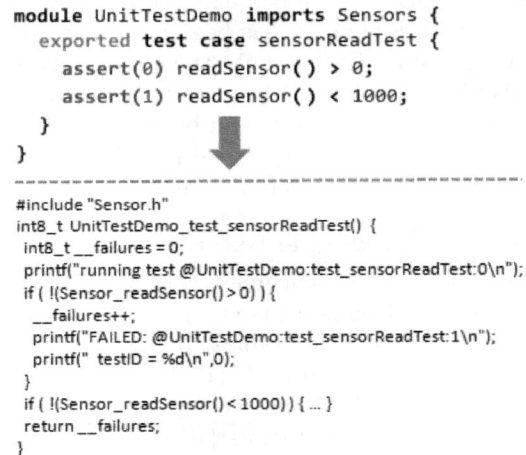

```
module UnitTestDemo imports Sensors {
  exported test case sensorReadTest {
    assert(0) readSensor() > 0;
    assert(1) readSensor() < 1000;
  }
}
```
```
#include "Sensor.h"
int8_t UnitTestDemo_test_sensorReadTest() {
  int8_t __failures = 0;
  printf("running test @UnitTestDemo:test_sensorReadTest:0\n");
  if ( !(Sensor_readSensor() > 0) ) {
    __failures++;
    printf("FAILED: @UnitTestDemo:test_sensorReadTest:1\n");
    printf(" testID = %d\n",0);
  }
  if ( !(Sensor_readSensor() < 1000) ) { ... }
  return __failures;
}
```

Figure 6. The *unittest* language introduces test cases as well as `assert` and `fail` statements which can only be used inside of a test case. Test cases are transformed to functions, and the `assert` statements become `if` statements with a negated condition. The generated code also counts the number of failures so it can be reported to the user via a binary's exit value.

plementation (Fig. 7). In contrast to modules, a component uses interfaces and ports to declare the contract it obeys. Interfaces define operation signatures and optional pre and post conditions (not shown in the example). Provided ports declare the interfaces offered by a component, required ports specify the interfaces a component expects to use. Different components can implement the same interface differently. Components can be

```
module SensorComp imports Sensors , LoggingService {
  exported c/s interface SensorAccess {
    double readValue()
  }
  exported component SimpleSensor extends nothing {
    ports:
      provides SensorAccess sensor
    contents:
      double read() ⟵ op sensor.readValue {
        return readSensor();
  } }
  exported component PlausiSensor extends nothing {
    ports:
      provides SensorAccess sensor
      requires LoggingService log
    contents:
      double read() ⟵ op sensor.readValue {
        double val = readSensor();
        if ( val > 100 ) {
          log.info("Sensor value unexpected big");
          return 100;
        }
        return val;
} } }
```

```
                                               Sensors.h
struct Sensors_compdata_SimpleSensor {};
double Sensors_SimpleSensor_read(void* inst_data);

struct Sensors_data_PlausiSensor {
  void* port_log;
  void (*op_log_info)(char*, void*);
}
double Sensors_PlausiSensor_read(void* inst_data);
                                               Sensors.c
#include "Sensors.h"
#include "Sensor.h"
#include "LoggingService.h"

double Sensors_SimpleSensor_read(void* inst_data) {
  return Sensor_readSensor();
}

double Sensors_PlausiSensor_read(void* inst_data) {
  double val = Sensor_readSensor();
  if (val > 100) {
    (*((struct Sensors_data_PlausiSensor*)inst_data)->op_log_info)
      ("Sensor value unexpected big",
      ((struct Sensors_data_PlausiSensor*)inst_data)->port_log);
    return 100;
  }
  return val;
}
```

Figure 7. Two components providing the same interface. The arrow maps operations from provided ports to implementations. An indirection through function pointers enables different implementations for a single interface, enabling OO-like polymorphic invocations.

instantiated (also in contrast to modules), and each instance's required ports have to be connected to compatible provided ports provided by other component instances. Polymorhphic invocations (different components "behind" the same interface) are supported.

State Machines (addresses C_1, C_4, uses W_1, W_2) provide a new top level construct (the state machine itself) as well as a **trigger** statement to send events into state machines (see Fig. 8). State machines are transformed into a **switch/case**-based implementation in the C program. Entry, exit and transition actions may only access variables defined locally in state machines and fire out events. Out events may optionally be mapped to func-

tions in the surrounding C program, where arbitrary behaviour can be implemented. This way, state machines are semantically isolated from the rest of the code, enabling them to be model checked: if a state machine is marked as **verifiable**, we also generate a representation of the state machine in the input language of the NuSMV model checker[5], including a set of property specifications that are verified by default. Examples include dead state detection, dead transition detection, non-determinism and variable bounds checks. In addition, users can specify additional high-level properties based on the well-established catalog of temporal logic properties patterns in [12]. We discuss the integration of formal verification into mbeddr in more detail in [?].

```
derived unit mps = m s⁻¹ for speed
convertible unit kmh for speed
conversion kmh -> mps = val * 0.27

int8_t/mps/ calculateSpeed(int8_t/m/ length, int8_t/s/ time) {
  int8_t/mps/ s = length / time;
  if ( s > 100 mps ) { s = [100 kmh ⟶ mps]; }
  return s;
}
```

Figure 9. The *units* extension ships with the SI base units. Users can define derived units (such as the mps in the example) as well as convertible units that require a numeric conversion for mapping back to SI units. Type checks ensure that the values associated with unit literals use the correct unit and perform unit computations (as in speed equals length divided by time). Errors are reported if incompatible units are used together (e.g. if we were to add length and time). To support this feature, the typing rules for the existing operators (such as + or /) have to be overridden.

Physical Units (addresses C_3, uses W_4) are new types that also specify a physical unit in addition to their actual data type (see Fig. 9). New literals are introduced to support specifying values for these types that include the physical unit. The typing rules for the existing operators (+, * or >) are overridden to perform the correct type checks for types with units. The type system also performs unit computations to deal correctly with speed = length/time, for example.

Requirements Traces (addresses C_5, uses W_6) are meta data annotations that link a program element to requirements, essentially elements in other models imported from requirements management tools. Requirements traces can be attached to any program element without that element's definition having to be aware of this (see green highlights in Fig. 10 and in Fig. 23).

Presence Conditions (addresses C_5 and W_6) A presence condition determines whether the program element

---
[5] http://nusmv.fbk.eu

```
module Counter imports Sensors {
  statemachine Counter {
    in count()
    out tick(int[0..100] val) ⇒ tickHandler
    local int[0..100] current = 0
    states ( initial = Init )
      state Init {
        on count [ ] → Counting
      }
      state Counting {
        on count [current < 100] → Counting {
          send tick(current);
          current++;
        }
        on count [current == 100] → Init
    } }
  void tickHandler(int8_t counterVal) { ... }
  void mainLoop(Counter counter1) {
    while ( true ) {
      if ( readSensor() > 100 ) {
        trigger(counter1, count);
} } } }
```

```
#include "Counter.h"
#include "Sensor.h"
void Counter_sm_execute_Counter(struct Counter_sm_data_Counter* instance,
        Counter_sm_events_Counter event, void** arguments) {
  switch (instance->__curState) {
    case Counter__state_Init: { ... }
    case Counter__state_Counting: {
      switch (event) {
        case Counter__event_count: {
          if ( instance->current < 100 ) {
            Counter_tickHandler(instance->current);
            instance->__curState = Counter__state_Counting;
            instance->current++;
            return ;
          }
          if ( instance->current == 100 ) { ... }
      }
  }
  void Counter_tickHandler(int8_t counterVal) { ... }
  void Counter_mainLoop(struct Counter_sm_data_Counter counter1) {
    while (1) {
      if ( Sensor_readSensor() > 100 ) {
        void* ___args[] = {};
        Counter_sm_execute_Counter(&counter1, Counter__event_count, &___args);
}}}
```
Counter.c

```
typedef enum _sm_events_Counter{
  Counter__event_count
} Counter_sm_events_Counter;

typedef enum _sm_states_Counter{
  Counter__state_Init,
  Counter__state_Counting
} Counter_sm_states_Counter;

struct_sm_data_Counter {
  Counter_sm_states_Counter __curState;
  int8_t current;
};
```
Counter.h

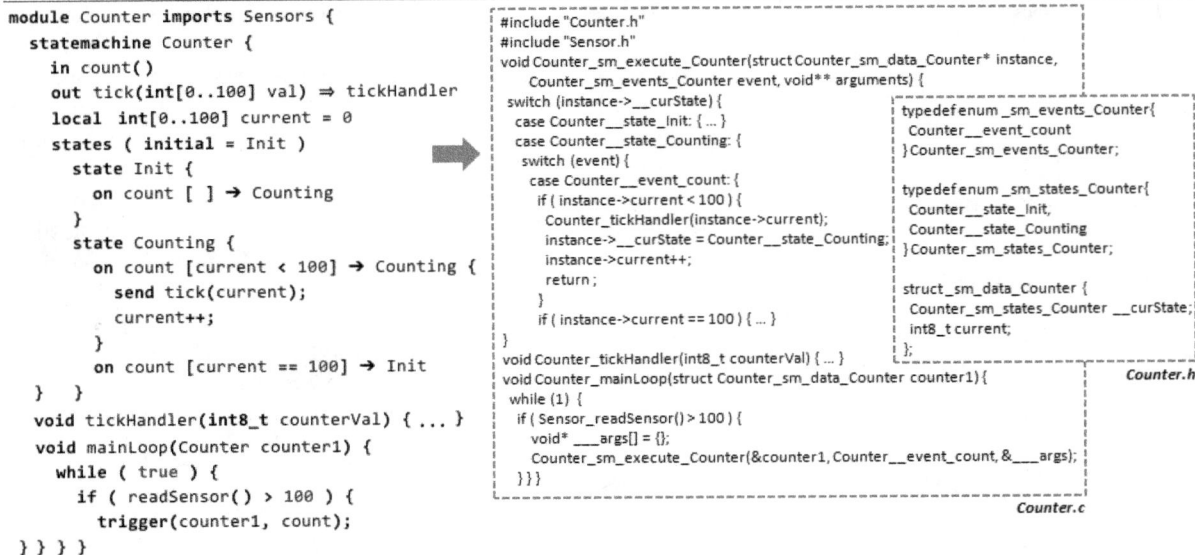

Figure 8. A state machine is embedded in a C module as a top level construct. It declares `in` and `out events` as well as local variables, states and transitions. Transitions react to `in events`, and `out events` can be fired in actions. Through bindings (e.g. `tickHandler`), state machines interact with C code. State machines can be instantiated. They are transformed to `enums` for states and events, and a function that executed the state machine using `switch` statements. The `trigger` statement injects events into a state machine instance by calling the state machine function.

to which it is attached is part of a product in the product line. A product is configured by specifying a set of configuration flags and the presence condition specifies a Boolean expression over these configuration switches[6]. Like requirements traces, presence conditions can be attached to any program element. For example, in Fig. 10, the `resetted` out event and the `on start...` transition in the second state have the `resettable` presence condition, where `resettable` is a reference to a configuration flag. Upon transformation, program elements whose presence condition evaluates to `false` for a particular product configuration are simply removed from the program (and hence will not end up in the generated binary). This program customization can also be performed by the editor, effectively supporting variant-specific editing.

Safe Modules (addresses C_2, uses W_5, W_7) Safe modules help prevent writing risky code. For example, runtime range checking is performed for arithmetic expressions and assignments. To enable this, arithmetic expressions are replaced by function calls that perform range checking and report errors if an overflow is detected. As another example, safe modules also provide the `safeheap` statement that automatically frees dynamic variables allocated inside its body (see Fig. 14).

---

[6] We use feature models to express product configurations, and the presence conditions are expressions over features. But this aspect is not essential to the discussion here.

3.4 Addressing the Tool Integration Challenge

We have not highlighted tool integration as an explicit challenge, because it is a cross-cutting issue that affects all of the challenges above. Nonetheless, in a project intended to be used by practitioners, this needs to be addressed. We do that by providing an *integrated environment* that provides state-of-the-art IDE support for C and all of its extensions. While we are still working on a debugger (see Section 8), all the other IDE support is available. This includes syntax highlighting, code completion, static error checking and annotation, quick fixes and refactorings. Fig. 10 shows a screenshot of the tool, as we edit a module with a decision table, a state machine, requirements traces and presence conditions.

4. Design and Implementation

This section discusses the implementation of mbeddr language extensions. For obvious reasons, this section cannot be a comprehensive tutorial of MPS. We refer to the MPS documentation[7]. However, the section provides a good overview of what it takes to build these extensions. We start by explaining in some detail how MPS works (Section 4.1). We then briefly discuss the structure of the C core language (Section 4.2). The major part of this chapter discusses each of the ways W_m of extending C (Section 4.3 through Section 4.9) based on the extensions discussed in the previous section.

---

[7] http://www.jetbrains.com/mps/documentation/index.html

```
module ADemoModule                          imports                 {

  enum MODE { FAIL; AUTO; MANUAL; }

  statemachine Counter {
    in start() <no binding>
         step(int[0..10] size) <no binding>  trace R2
    out started() <no binding>
         resetted() <no binding> resettable
         incremented(int[0..10] newVal) <no binding>
    vars int[0..10] currentVal = 0
         int[0..10] LIMIT = 10
    states (initial = start)
      state start {
        on start [ ] -> countState { send started(); }
      }
      state  step   ^inEvents (cdesignpaper.screenshot.ADemoModule)
             step   ^inEvents (cdesignpaper.screenshot.ADemoModule)
        on step [currentVal + size > LIMIT] -> start { send resetted(); }
        on step [currentVal + size <= LIMIT] -> countState {
    Error: wrong number of arguments + size;
             send incremented();
        }
        on start [ ] -> start { send resetted(); } resettable
      }
  }

  MODE nextMode(MODE mode, int8_t speed) {
    return  MODE, FAIL                                          trace R1;
```

	mode == AUTO	mode == MANUAL
speed < 50	AUTO	MANUAL
speed >= 50	MANUAL	MANUAL

Figure 10. A somewhat overloaded example program in the mbeddr IDE (an instance of MPS). The module contains an `enum`, a decision table and a state machine. Requirements traces are attached to the table and the `step` in event, and a presence condition is attached to an out event and a transitions

4.1 MPS Basics

MPS is a language workbench, a comprehensive tool for defining, extending, composing and using sets of integrated languages. As we will see, it supports the definition of various language aspects with highly expressive DSLs. MPS' most important characteristic is that it is a projectional editor. In parser-based approaches, users use text editors to enter character sequences that represent programs. A parser then checks the text for syntactic correctness and constructs an abstract syntax tree from the character sequence. The AST contains all the semantic information expressed by the program.

Projectional editors such as MPS do not use parsers. In projectional editors, the process happens the other way round: as a user edits the program, the AST is modified directly. A projection engine then creates a representation of the AST that reflects the changes. The user interacts with this representation. This approach is well-known from graphical editors: when editing a UML diagram, users don't draw pixels onto a canvas, and a "pixel parser" then creates the AST. Rather, the editor creates and instance of `uml.Class` as you drag a class from the palette to the canvas. A projection engine renders the diagram, in this case drawing a rectangle for the class. This approach can be generalized to work with any notation, including textual.

In projectional editors, every program element is stored as a node with a unique ID (UID) in the AST. References between program elements are based on actual pointers (references to UIDs). The AST is actually an ASG, an abstract syntax graph, from the start because cross-references are first-class rather than being resolved after parsing. The program is stored using a generic tree persistence mechanism, often XML.

The projectional approach can deal with arbitrary syntactic forms such as text, tables, symbols and graphics (graphics expected to be supported by MPS in 2013). Since no grammar is used, grammar classes are not relevant, and no syntactic ambiguities can result from the combination of independently developed languages. If two concepts (possibly defined by different language extensions) with the same syntax are valid in the same location, the user is forced to decide which one to instantiate as she enters the program. In principle, projectional editing is simpler than parsing, since there is no need to "extract" the program structure from a flat textual source. However, the challenge in projectional editing is making the editing experience convenient and productive. Traditionally, projectional editors have had a bad reputation because the user experience in editing programs was unacceptable. MPS has solved this problem, the editing experience is comparable to traditional text editors. Among others, MPS uses the following strategies to achieve this: aliases are used to instantiate language concepts from the code completion menu (e.g. you can just type `for` to instantiate a `ForStatement`); side transformations support entering trees linearly (e.g. you can just type + and 3 on the right side of a 2 to get 2+3); and the code completion menu shows targets of references directly instead requiring users to first instantiate the reference concept (e.g. when pressing Ctrl-Space after the + in 2+3, you will directly see all visible variables and arguments in the code completion menu).

4.2 The mbeddr Core Languages

C can be partitioned into expressions, statements, functions, etc. We have factored these parts into separate language modules to make each of them reusable without pulling in all of C. The `expressions` language is the most fundamental language. It depends on no other language and defines the primitive types, the corresponding literals and the basic operators. Support for pointers and user defined data types (`enum, struct, union`) is factored into the `pointers` and `udt` languages, respectively. `statements` contains the procedural part of C, and the `modules` language covers modularization. Fig. 11 shows an overview over some of the languages and constructs.

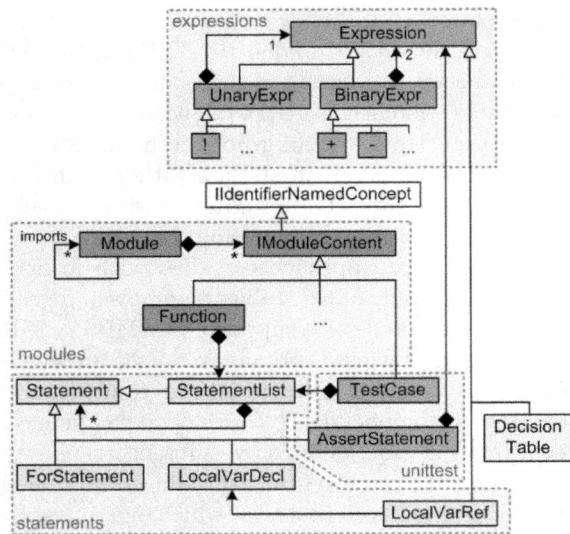

Figure 11. Anatomy of the mbeddr language stack: the diagram shows some of the language concepts, their relationships and the languages that contain them.

4.3 Addressing W_1 (Top-Level Constructs): Test Cases

In this section we illustrate the implementation of the `test case` construct as well as of the `assert` and `fail` statements available inside test cases.

Structure Modules own a collection of `IModuleContents`, an interface that defines the properties of everything that can reside directly in a module. All top-level constructs such as `Functions` implement `IModuleContent`. `IModuleContent` extends MPS' `IIdentifierNamedConcept` interface, which provides a `name` property. `IModuleContent` also defines a Boolean property `exported` that determines whether the respective module content is visible to modules that import this module. This property is queried by the scoping rules that determine which elements can be referenced. Since the `IModuleContent` interface can also be implemented by concepts in other languages, new top level constructs such as the `TestCase` in the `unittest` language can implement this interface, as long as the respective language has a dependency on the `modules` language, which defines `IModuleContent`. Fig. 11 shows some of the relevant concepts and languages.

Constraints A test case contains a `StatementList`, so any C statement can be used in a test case. `StatementList` becomes available to the unit test language through its dependency on the `statements` language. `unittest` also defines new statements: `assert` and `fail`. They extend the abstract `Statement` concept defined in the `statements` language. This makes them valid in *any* statement list, for example in a function body. This is

undesirable, since the transformation of `asserts` into C depends on them being used in a `TestCase`. To enforce this, a *can be child* constraint is defined (Fig. 12).

```
concepts constraints AssertStatement {
  can be child
    (context, scope, parentNode, link, childConcept)->boolean {
      parentNode.ancestor<TestCase>.isNotNull;
} }
```

Figure 12. This constraint restricts an `AssertStatement` to be used only inside a `TestCase` by checking that at least one of its ancestors is a `TestCase`.

```
test case exTest {        void test_exTest {        void test_exTest {
  int x = add(2, 2);        int x = add(2, 2);        int x = add(2, 2);
  assert(0) x == 4;         report                     if (!(x == 4)) {
}                              test.FAIL(0)                 printf("fail:0");
                               on !(x == 4);}           } }
```

Figure 13. Two-stage transformation of `TestCases`. The `TestCase` is transformed into a C function using the logging framework to output error messages. The `report` statement is in turn transformed into a `printf` statement *if* we generate for the Windows/Mac environment. It would be transformed to something else if we generated for the actual target device (configured by the user in the build configuration).

Transformation The new language concepts in `unittest` are reduced to C concepts: the `TestCase` is transformed to a `void` function without arguments and the `assert` statement is transformed into a `report` statement defined in the logging language. The `report` statement, in turn, it is transformed into a platform-specific way of reporting an error (console, serial line or error memory). Fig. 13 shows an example of this two-step process.

4.4 Addressing W_2 (Statements): Safeheap Statement

We have seen the basics of integrating new statements in the previous section where `assert` and `fail` extended the `Statement` concept inherited from the C core languages. In this section we focus on statements that require handling local variable scopes and visibilities. We implement the `safeheap` statement mentioned earlier (see Fig. 14), which automatically frees dynamically allocated memory. The variables introduced by the `safeheap` statement must only be visible inside its body and they have to shadow variables of the same name declared in outer scopes (such as the `a` declared in the second line of the `measure` function in Fig. 14).

Structure The `safeheap` statement extends `Statement`. It contains a `StatementList` as its body, as well as a list of `SafeHeapVars`. These extend `LocalVarDecl`,

```
int8_t measure() {
  int8_t result = 0;
  int8_t* a = malloc(sizeof int8_t);
  safeheap(int8_t* a = malloc(10 * sizeof int8_t)) {
    for (int8_t i = 0; i < 10; i++) { (a[i]) = readSensor(); }
    // the ⌈Error: cannot pass a safe heap var to a function⌉ss a heap var to function
    result = calcAverage(a);
  }
  // accessing a here would the one declare outside the safeheap
  return result;
}
```

Figure 14. A `safeheap` statement declares heap variables which can only be used inside the body of the statement. When the body is left, the memory is automatically freed. Notice also how we report an error in case the variable tries to escape.

so they fit with the existing mechanism for handling variable shadowing (explained below).

Behaviour `LocalVarRefs` are expressions that reference `LocalVarDecl`. A scope constraint, a mechanism provided by MPS, determines the set of visible variables for a given `LocalVarRef`. We implement this constraint by plugging into mbeddr's generic local variable scoping mechanism using the following approach. The constraint ascends the containment tree until it finds a node which implements `ILocalVarScopeProvider` and calls its `getLocalVarScope` method. A `LocalVarScope` has a reference to an outer scope, which is set by finding *its* `ILocalVarScopeProvider` ancestor, effectively building a hierarchy of `LocalVarScopes`. To get at the list of the visible variables, the `LocalVarRef` scope constraint calls the `getVisibleLocalVars` method on the innermost `LocalVarScope` object. This method returns a flat list of `LocalVarDecls`, taking into account that variables owned by a `LocalVarScope` that is *lower* in the hierarchy shadow variables of the same name from a *higher* level in the hierarchy. So, to plug the `SafeHeapStatement` into this mechanism, it has to implement `ILocalVarScopeProvider` and implement the two methods shown in Fig. 15.

Type System To make the `safeheap` statement work correctly, we have to ensure that the variables declared and allocated in the *safeheap* statement do not escape from its scope. To prevent this, an error is reported if a reference to a `safeheap` variable is passed to a function. Fig. 16 shows the code.

4.5 Addressing W_3 (Expressions): Decision Tables

Expressions are different from statements in that they can be evaluated to a *value* as the program executes. During editing and compilation, the *type* of an expression is relevant for the static correctness of the program. So extending a language regarding expressions requires extending the type system rules as well.

```
public LocalVarScope getLocalVarScope(node<> ctx, int stmtIdx) {
  LocalVarScope scope =
      new LocalVarScope(getContainedLocalVariables());
  node<ILocalVarScopeProvider> outerScopeProvider =
      this.ancestor<ILocalVarScopeProvider>;
  if (outerScopeProvider != null)
    scope.setOuterScope(outerScopeProvider.
                  getLocalVarScope(this, this.index));
  return scope;
}
public sequence<node<LocalVariableDecl>> getContainedLocalVars() {
  this.vars;
}
```

Figure 15. A `safeheap` statement implements the two methods declared by the `ILocalVarScopeProvider` interface. `getContainedLocalVariables` returns the `LocalVarDecls` that are declared between the parentheses (see Fig. 14). `getLocalVarScope` constructs a scope that contains these variables and then builds the hierarchy of outer scopes by relying on its ancestors that also implement `ILocalVarScopeProvider`. The index of the statement that contains the reference is passed in to make sure that only variables declared *before* the reference site can be referenced.

```
checking rule check_safeVarRef for concept = LocalVarRef as lvr {
    boolean isInSafeHeap =
      lvr.ancestor<SafeHeapStatement>.isNotNull;
    boolean isInFunctionCall =
      lvr.ancestor<FunctionCall>.isNotNull;
    boolean referencesSafeHeapVar =
      lvr.var.parent.isInstanceOf(SafeHeapStatement);
    if (isInSafeHeap && isInFunctionCall && referencesSafeHeapVar)
        error "cannot pass a safe heap var to a function" -> lvr;
}
```

Figure 16. This type system rule reports an error if a reference to a local variable declared and allocated by the `safeheap` statement is used in a function call.

Fig. 5 shows the decision table expression. It is evaluated to the expression in a cell c if the column header of c and the row header of c are `true`[8]. If none of the condition pairs is `true`, then the default value, `FAIL` in the example, is used as the resulting value. A decision table also specifies the type of the value it will evaluate to, and all the expression in content cells have to be compatible with that type. The type of the header cells has to be Boolean.

Structure The decision table extends the `Expression` concept defined in the `expressions` language. Decision tables contain a list of expressions for the column headers, one for the row headers and another one for the result values. It also contains a child of type `Type` to declare the type of the result expressions, as well as a default value expression. The concept defines an alias

---

[8] Strictly speaking, it is the *first* of the cells for which the headers are `true`. It is optionally possible to use static verification based on an SMT solver to ensure that only one of them will be `true` for any given set of input values

dectab to allow users to instantiate a decision table in the editor. Obviously, for non-textual notations such as the table, the alias will be different than the concrete syntax (in textual notations, the alias is typically made to be the same as the "leading keyword", e.g. `assert`).

Editor Defining a tabular editor is straight forward: the editor definition contains a `table` cell, which delegates to a Java class that implements `ITableModel`. This is similar to the approach to the approach used by Java Swing. It provides methods such as `getValueAt( int row, int col)` or `deleteRow(int row)`, which have to be implemented for any specific table-based editor. To embed another node in a table cell (such as the expression in the decision table), the implementation of `getValueAt` simply returns this node.

Type System As mentioned above, MPS uses unification in the type system. Language concepts specify type equations that contain type literals (such as `boolean`) as well as type variables (such as `typeof(dectab)`). The unification engine then tries to assign values to the type variables so that all applicable type equations become `true`. New language concepts contribute additional type equations. Fig. 17 shows those for decision tables. New equations are solved along with those for existing concepts. For example, the typing rules for a `ReturnStatement` ensure that the type of the returned expression is the same or a subtype of the type of the surrounding function. If a `ReturnStatement` uses a decision table as the returned expression, the type calculated for the decision table must be compatible with the return type of the surrounding function.

```
// the type of the whole decision table expression
// is the type specified in the type field
typeof(dectab) :==: typeof(dectabc.type);
// for each of the expressions in
// the column headers, the type must be boolean
foreach expr in dectab.colHeaders {
  typeof(expr) :==: <boolean>;
}
// ... same for the row headers
foreach expr in dectabc.rowHeaders {
  typeof(expr) :==: <boolean>;
}
// the type of each of the result values must
// be the same or a subtype of the table itself
foreach expr in dectab.resultValues {
  infer typeof(expr) :<=: typeof(dcectab);
}
// ... same for the default
typeof(dc.def) :<=: typeof(dectab);
```

Figure 17. The type equations for the decision table (see the comments for details).

4.6 Addressing W_4 (Types and Literals): Physical Units

To illustrate adding new types and literals we use physical units. We had already shown example code earlier in Fig. 9.

Structure Derived and convertible `UnitDeclarations` are `IModuleContents`. Derived unit declarations specify a name (`mps`, `kmh`) and the corresponding SI base units (`m`, `s`) plus an exponent; a convertible unit declaration specifies a name and a conversion formula. The backbone of the extension is the `UnitType` which is a composite type that has another type (`int`, `float`) in its `valueType` slot, plus a unit (either an SI base unit or a reference to a `UnitDeclaration`). It is represented in programs as `baseType/unit/`. We also provide `LiteralWithUnits`, which are expressions that contain a `valueLiteral` and, like the `UnitType`, a unit (so we can write `100 kmh`).

Scoping `LiteralWithUnits` and `UnitTypes` refer to a `UnitDeclaration`, which is a module content. According to the visibility rules, valid targets for the reference are the `UnitDeclarations` in the same module, and the *exported* ones in all imported modules. This rule applies to *any* reference to *any* module contents, and is implemented generically in mbeddr. Fig. 18 shows the code for the scope of the reference to the `UnitDeclaration`. We use an interface `IVisibleNodeProvider`, (implemented by `Modules`) to find all instances of a given type. The implementation of `visibleContentsOfType` simply searches through the contents of the current and imported modules and collects instances of the specified concept. The result is used as the scope for the reference.

```
link {unit} search scope:
    (model, scope, refNode, enclosingNode, operationContext)
                        ->sequence<node<UnitDeclaration>> {
    enclosingNode.ancestor<IVisibleNodeProvider>.
        visibleContentsOfType(concept/UnitDeclaration/); }
```

Figure 18. The `visibleContentsOfType` operation returns all instances of the concept argument in the current module, as well as all exported instances in modules imported by the current module.

Type System We have seen how MPS uses equations and unification to specify type system rules. However, there is special support for binary operators that makes overloading for new types easy: overloaded operations containers essentially specify 3-tuples of *(leftArgType, rightArgType, resultType)* plus applicability conditions to match type patterns and decide on the resulting type. Typing rules for new (combinations of) types can be added by specifying additional 3-tuples. Fig. 19 shows the overloaded rules for C's `MultiExpression` (the language concept the implements the multiplication operator `*`) when applied to two `UnitTypes`: the result type will be a `UnitType` as well, where the exponents of the SI units are added.

While any two units can legally be used with `*` and `/` (as long as we compute the resulting unit exponents

```
operation concepts: MultiExpression
  left operand type: new node<UnitType>()
  right operand type: new node<UnitType>()
is applicable:
  (operation, leftOpType, rightOpType)->boolean {
    node<> resultingValueType = operation type(operation,
              leftOpType.valueType , rightOpType.valueType );
    resultingValueType != null; }
operation type:
  (operation, leftOpType, rightOpType)->node<> {
    node<> resultingValueType = operation type(operation,
            leftOpType.valueType,  rightOpType.valueType );
    UnitType.create(resultingValueType,
                leftOpType.unit.toSIBase().add(
                  rightOpType.unit.toSIBase(),
                  1 ) );
  }
```

Figure 19. This code overloads the `MultiExpression`
to work for `UnitTypes`. In the `is applicable` section
we check whether there is a typing rule for the two value
types (e.g. `int * float`). This is achieved by trying to
compute the resulting value type. If none is found, the
types cannot be multiplied. In the computation of the
`operation type` we create a new `UnitType` that uses
the `resultingValueType` as the value type and then
computes the resulting unit by adding up the exponents
of component SI units of the two operand types.

correctly), this is not true for + and -. There, the two
operand types must be the same (in terms of their representation in SI base units). We express this by using
the following expression in the `is applicable` section:
`leftOpType.unit.isSameAs(rightOpType.unit)`.

The typing rule for the `LocalVariableDeclaration`
requires that the type of the `init` expression must be
the same or a subtype of the `type` of the variable.
To make this work correctly, we have to define a type
hierarchy for `UnitTypes`. We achieve this by defining
the supertypes for each `UnitType`: the supertypes are
those `UnitTypes` whose unit is the same, and whose
`valueType` is a supertype of the current `UnitType`'s
value type. Fig. 20 shows the rule.

```
subtyping rule supertypeOf_UnitType
          for concept = UnitType as ut {
  nlist<> res = new nlist<>;
  foreach st in immediateSupertypes(ut.valueType) {
    res.add(UnitType.create(st, ut.unit.copy));
  }
  return res;
}
```

Figure 20. This typing rule computes the direct supertypes of a `UnitType`. It iterates over all immediate supertypes of the current `UnitType`'s value type, wrapped
into a `UnitType` with the same unit as the original one.

4.7 Addressing W_5 (Alternative Transformations): Range Checking

The `safemodules` language defines an *annotation* to
mark `Modules` as safe (we will discuss annotations in

```
concept     PlusExpression
condition   (node, genContext, operationContext)->boolean {
              node.ancestor<ImplementationModule>.@safeAnnotation != null;
            }
  -->
module dummy imports arithmeticOps {
  void dummy() {
    <TF addWithRangeCheck($COPY_SRC$ 1 , $COPY_SRC$ 2 ) TF>;
} }
```

Figure 21. This *reduction rule* transforms instances
of `PlusExpression` into a call to a library function
`addWithRangeChecks`, passing in the left and right argument of the + using the two `COPY_SRC` macros. The
`condition` ensures that the transformation is only executed if the containing `Module` has a `safeAnnotation`
attached to it. A transformation priority defined in the
properties of the transformation makes sure it runs before the C-to-text transformation.

the next subsection). If a module is safe, the binary
operators such as + or * are replaced with calls to
functions that, in addition to performing the addition
or multiplication, perform a range check.

Transformation   The transformation that replaces
the binary operators with function calls is triggered by
the presence of this annotation on the `Module` which
contains the operator. Fig. 21 shows the code. The
`@safeAnnotation != null` checks for the presence of
the annotation. MPS uses priorities to specify relative
orderings of transformations, and MPS then calculates
a global transformation order for any given model. We
use a priority to express that this transformation runs
before the final transformation that maps the C tree to
C text for compilation.

4.8 Addressing W_6 (Meta Data): Requirements Traces

Annotations are concepts whose instances can be added
as children to a node N without this being specified in
the definition of N's concept. While structurally the annotations are children of the annotated node, the editor
is defined the other way round: the annotation editor
delegates to the editor of the annotated element. This
allows the annotation editor to add additional syntax
around the annotated element. Optionally, it is possible to explicitly restrict the concepts to which a particular annotation can be attached. We use annotations in
several places: the `safe` annotation discussed in the previous section, the requirements traces and the product
line variability presence conditions.

Structure   We illustrate the annotation mechanism
based on the requirements traces. Fig. 22 shows the
structure. Notice how it extends the MPS-predefined
concept `NodeAttribute` (it sould be named `Node-`
`Annotation`). It also specifies a `role`, which is the name

of the property that is used to store `TraceAnnotations` under the annotated node.

```
concept TraceAnnotation extends NodeAttribute implements <none>
  children:
    TraceKind        tracekind    1
    TraceTargetRef   refs         0..n
  concept properties:
    role = trace
  concept links:
    attributed = BaseConcept
```

Figure 22. Annotations have to extend the MPS-predefined concept `NodeAttribute`. They can have an arbitrary child structure (`tracekind`, `refs`), but they have to specify the `role` (the name of the property that holds the annotated child under its parent) as well as the `attributed` concept: the annotations can only be attached to instances of this concept (or subconcepts).

Editor As mentioned above, in the editor, annotations look as if they *surrounded* their parent node (although they are in fact children). Fig. 23 shows the definition of the editor of the requirements trace annotation (and an example is shown in Fig. 10): it puts the trace to the right of the annotated node. Since MPS is a projectional editor, there is base-language grammar that needs to be made aware of the additional syntax in the program. This is key to enabling arbitrary annotations on arbitrary program nodes.

Annotations are typically attached to a program node via an intention. Intentions are an MPS editor mechanism: a user selects the target element, presses `Alt-Enter` and selects `Add Trace` from the popup menu. Fig. 24 shows the code for the intention that attaches a requirements trace.

4.9 Addressing W_7 (Restriction): Preventing Use of Reals Numbers

We have already seen in Section 4.3 how constraints can prevent the use of specific concepts in certain contexts. We use the same approach for preventing the use of real number types inside model-checkable state machines: a `can be ancestor` constraint in the state machine prevents instances of `float` in the state machine if the `verifiable` flag is set.

5. Experiences

This paper is about the design and rationale of an extensible C language for embedded development, based on language engineering techniques. In Section 5.1 we provide a brief overview over our experiences in implementing mbeddr, including the size of the project and the efforts spent. Section 5.2 discusses to what degree this approach leads to improvements in embedded software development.

```
editor for concept  TraceAnnotation
  node cell layout:
    [> [> attributed node <] ?[> % tracekind % F(> % refs % <) <] <] <]
```

Figure 23. The editor definition for the `ReqTrace` annotation (an example trace annotation is shown in Fig. 10). It consists of a vertical list [/ .. /] with two lines. The first line contains the reference to the requirement. The second line uses the `attributed node` construct to embed to the editor of the program node to which this annotation is attached. So the annotation is always rendered right on top of whatever syntax the original node uses.

```
intention addTrace for BaseConcept {
  description(node)->string {
    "Add Trace"; }
  isApplicable(node)->boolean {
    node.@trace == null; }
  execute(editorContext, node)->void {
    node.@trace = new node<TraceAnnotation>(); }
}
```

Figure 24. An intention definition consists of three parts. The `description` returns the string that is shown in the intentions popup menu. The `isApplicable` section determines under which conditions the intention is avavailable in the menu — in our case, we can only add a trace if there is no trace yet on the target node. Finally, the `execute` section performs the action associated with the intention. In our case we simply put an instance of `TraceAnnotation` into the `@trace` property of the target node.

5.1 Language Extension

Size Typically, lines of code are used to describe the size of a software system. In MPS, a "line" is not necessarily meaningful. Instead we count important elements of the implementation and then estimate a corresponding number of lines of code. Fig. 25 shows the respective numbers for the core, i.e. C itself plus unit test support, decision tables and build/make integration (the table also shows how many LOC equivalent we assume for each language definition element, and the caption explains to some extent the rationale for these factors). According to our metric the C core is implemented with less than 10,000 lines of code.

Let us look at an incremental extension of C. The components extension (interfaces, components, pre and post conditions, support for mock components in testing and a generator back to plain C) is ca. 3,000 LOC equivalent. The state machines extension is ca. 1,000. Considering the fact that these LOC equivalents represent the language definition (incl. type systems and generators) and the IDE (incl. code completion, syntax

Element	Count	LOC-Factor
Language Concepts	260	3
Property Declarations	47	1
Link Declarations	156	1
Editor Cells	841	0.25
Reference Constraints	21	2
Property Constraints	26	2
Behavior Methods	299	1
Type System Rules	148	1
Generation Rules	57	10
Statements	4919	1.2
Intentions	47	3
Text Generators	103	2
Total LOC		**8,640**

Figure 25. We count various language definition elements and then use a factor to translate them into lines of code. The reasons why many factors are so low (e.g. reference constraints or behavior methods) is that the implementation of these elements is made up of statements, which are counted separately. In case of editor cells, typically several of them are on the same line, hence the fraction. Finally, the MPS implementation language supports higher order functions, so some statements are rather long and stretch over more than one line: this explains the 1.2 in the factor for statements.

coloring, some quick fixes and refactorings), this clearly speaks to the efficiency of MPS for language development and extension.

Effort In terms of effort, the core C implementation has been ca. 4 person months divided between three people. This results in roughly 2,500 lines of code per person month. Extrapolated to a year, this would be 7,500 lines of code per developer. According to McConnell[9], in a project up to 10,000 LOC, a developer can typically do between 2,000 and 25,000 LOC. The fact that we are at the low end of this range can be explained by the fact that MPS provides very expressive languages for DSL development: you don't have to write a lot of code to express a lot about a DSL. Instead, MPS code is relatively dense and requires quite a bit of thought. Pair programming is very valuable in language development.

Once a developer has mastered the learning curve, language extension can be very productive. The state machines and components extension have both been developed in about a month. The unit testing extension or the support for decision tables can be implemented in a few days.

Language Modularity, Reuse and Growth Modularity and composition is central to mbeddr.

Building a language extension should not require changes to the base languages. This requires that the extended languages are built with extension in mind. Just like in object-oriented programming, where the only methods can be overridden, only specific parts of a language definition can be extended or overwritten. The implementation of the default extensions served as a test case to confirm that the C core language is in fact extensible. We found a few problems, especially in the type system and fixed them. None of these fixes were "hacks" to enable a specific extension — they were all genuine mistakes in the design of the C core. Due to the broad spectrum covered by our extensions, we are confident that the current core language provides a high degree of extensibility.

Independently developed extensions should not interact with each other in unexpected ways. While MPS provides no automated way of ensuring this, we have not seen such interactions so far. The following steps can be taken to minimize the risk of unexpected interactions. Generated names should be qualified to make sure that no symbol name clashes occur in the generated C code. An extension should never consume "scarce resources": for example, it is a bad idea for a new `Statement` to require a particular return type of the containing function, or change that return type during transformation. Two such badly designed statements cannot be used together because they will likely require *different* return types. Note that unintended *syntactic* integration problems between independently developed extensions (known from traditional parser-based systems) can *never* happen in MPS. This was one of the reasons to use MPS for mbeddr.

Modularity should also support reuse in contexts not anticipated during the design of a language module. Just as in the case of language extension (discussed above), the to-be-reused languages have to be written in a suitable way so that the right parts can be reused separately. We have shown this with the state machines language. State machines can be used as top level concepts in modules (binding out events to C functions) and also inside components (binding out events to component methods). Parts of the transformation of a state machine have to be different in these two cases, and these differences were successfully isolated to make them exchangeable. Also, we reuse the C expression language inside the guard conditions in a state machine's transitions. We use constraints to prevent the use of those C expression that are not allowed inside transitions (for example, references to global variables). Finally, we have successfully used physical units in components and interfaces.

[9] http://www.codinghorror.com/ blog/2006/07/diseconomies-of-scale-and-lines-of-code.html

Summing up, these facilities allow different user groups to develop independent extensions, growing the mbeddr stack even closer towards their particular domain.

Who can create Extensions? mbeddr is built to be extended. The question is by whom. This question can be addressed in two ways: who is *able* to extend it from a skills perspective, and who *should* extend it?

Let us address the *skills* question first. We find that it takes about a month for a developer with solid object-oriented programming experience to become proficient with MPS and the structures of the mbeddr core languages. This may be reduced by better documentation, but a steep learning curve will remain. Also, *designing* good languages, independent of their implementation, is a skill that requires practice and experience. So, from this perspective we assume that in any given organization there should be a select group of language developers who build the extensions for the end users. Notice that such an organizational structure is common today for frameworks and other reusable artifacts.

There is also the question of who *should* create extensions. One could argue that, as language development becomes simpler, an uncontrolled growth in languages could occur, ultimately resulting in chaos. This concern should be addressed with governance structures that guide the development of languages. The bigger the organization is, the more important such governance becomes. The modular nature of the mbeddr language extensions makes this problem much easier to tackle. In an large organization we assume that a few language extensions will be strategic: aligned with the needs of the whole organization, well-designed, well tested and documented, implemented by a central group, and used by many developers. In addition, small teams my decide to develop their own, smaller extensions. Their focus is much more local, and the development requires much less coordination. These could be developed by the smaller units themselves.

5.2   Improvements in Embedded Development

Productivity and Quality   At this point we have not yet conducted large-scale industry projects with the mbeddr stack. We are currently in the process of setting up two real-world projects. However, two preliminary end-user experiments have been performed. The mbeddr development team itself has created a non-trivial case study based on the OSEK operating system and Lego Mindstorms. Second, a group of students from the University of Augsburg has developed a set of language extensions for controlling a quadcopter. Both cases resulted in much less code, a clearer implementation and fewer bugs compared to what we expected from traditional embedded software development. Both projects also developed extensions of the existing stack:

the OSEK/Mindstorms project extended the build language to integrate with the NXT OSEK build system and the quadcopter project has developed languages for controlling and planning the routing for the quadcopter.

The fact that formal verification is directly integrated into mbeddr, and the fact the requirements traceability and product line variability are directly supported promises to improve the overall quality of systems built with mbeddr.

Size and Practicability   We have run scalability tests to ensure that the environment scales to at least the equivalent of 100.000 lines of C code. A significant share of embedded software is below this limit and can confidently be addressed with mbeddr. We do not have any data which indicates significant performance degradation for larger systems, and we believe that by structuring systems into separate partitions that are transformed, compiled and linked separately, larger systems are feasible as well. However, to be sure, this requires further scalability testing.

Suitability of the Currently Available Extensions   Based on years of experience in embedded software development and dozens of conversations with practitioners in the field we are confident that the extensions we chose provide useful benefits in real-world embedded software development projects. In particular, state machines, interfaces and components as well as traceability and product line support are relevant for almost every developer we talked to and available in several established modeling tools.

However, while we are confident that the default extensions are useful in practice, they mainly serve as a proof-of-concept for the idea of incremental, modular language extension, where end-user organizations build their own custom extensions that fit their domain.

6.   Related Work

mbeddr touches several areas of research, so we we have structured the this section accordingly, one paragraph for each area: DSLs in embedded development, specific extensions of C, language and IDE extension and static analysis and formal verification.

DSLs in Embedded Development   In addition to the general-purpose embedded software modeling tools mentioned before (Simulink and ASCET), much more specific languages have been developed. Examples include Feldspar [1], a DSL embedded in Haskell for digital signal processing; Hume [18], a DSL for real-time embedded systems as well as the approach described in [17], which use DSLs for addressing quality of service concerns in middleware for distributed real-time systems. Our approach is different because our DSLs are directly integrated into C, whereas the examples mentioned in this paragraph are standalone DSLs that generate C code. As part of our future work we will investigate if and how some of these languages could benefit from a tighter integration with C based on mbeddr.

Specific Extensions of C Extending C to adapt it to a particular problem domain is not new. For example, Palopoli et al. present an extension of C for real time applications [28], Boussinot proposes an extension for reactive systems [3] and Yosi Ben-Asher et al. present an extension for shared memory parallel systems [2]. These are all *specific* extensions of C, typically created by invasively changing the C grammar. These extensions do not include IDE support, and the approach does not provide a framework for modular, incremental extension. However, these are all good examples of extensions that could be implemented as language extensions in mbeddr, if the need arises.

In contrast to these specific extensions of C, the Xoc extensible C compiler described by Cox [8] support arbitrary extensions. It uses a parser-based approach and uses source-to-source translation to transform modular C extensions into regular C code. In contrast to mbeddr, Cox' approach is limited by the fact that is uses a traditional parser based approach and that it does not address IDE extension.

There are also safer dialects of C, basically restricted sub-languages. Examples include Cyclone [21] and the Misra C standard [27]. We are actively working on implementing checks and restrictions to implement the Misra C standard as a language extension using restriction (W_7).

Language and IDE Extension mbeddr itself is not a language engineering tool — we rely on the MPS language workbench. Therefore the discussion of language engineering approaches and tools as part of related work will look at how these tools and approaches address language engineering, and how this differs from the MPS-based approach used in mbeddr.

Language extension is not a new idea. The Lisp community has always considered language extension essential to using Lisp effectively. Guy Steele's OOPSLA 1998 keynote *Growing a Language* (and a related journal article [22]) is maybe the most well-known expression of the idea, and Thrift's extension of Lisp with constructs for logic programming [34] is a concrete example. Obviously, Lisp extension could not have been used as a basis for mbeddr, since it is based on C.

The landmark work of Hudak [19] introduces embedded DSLs as language extensions of Haskell. While Haskell provides advanced concepts that enable such extensions, the new DSLs are essentially just libraries built with the host language and are not first class language entities: they do not define their own syntax, compiler errors are expressed in terms of the host language, no

custom semantic analyses are supported and no specific IDE-support is provided. Essentially all internal DSLs expressed with dynamic languages such as Ruby or Groovy, but also those embedded in static languages such as Scala suffer from these limitations.

Several works avoid these limitations by making language definition and extension first class. Early examples include the Synthesizer Generator [31] as well as the Meta Environment [24]. Both generate editors and other IDE aspects from a language definition. The topic is still actively researched. For example, Bravenboer et al. [5] and Dinkelacker [11] provide custom concrete syntax, Bracha [4] provides pluggable type systems and Erweg et al. [15] discuss modular IDE extensions. Eisenberg and Kiczales propose explicit programming [13] which supports semantic extension as well as editing extensions (concrete syntax) for a given base language.

Our approach is similar in that we provide extensions of syntax, type systems, semantics and IDE support for a base language. mbeddr is different in that it extends C, in that we use a projectional editor and in that we address IDE extension including advanced features such as type systems, refactorings and the debugger. The use of a projectional editor is especially significant, since this enables the use of non-textual notations and annotation of cross-cutting meta data.

A particularly interesting comparison can be made with the Helvetia system by Renggli et al. [30]. It supports language embedding and extension of Smalltalk using *homogeneous* extension, which means that the host language (Smalltalk) is also used for *defining* the extensions (in contrast to some of the embedded DSLs discussed above, Helvetia can work with custom grammars for the DSLs). The authors argue that the approach is independent of the host language and could be used with other host languages as well. While this is true in principle, the implementation strategy heavily relies on some aspects of the Smalltalk system that are not present for other languages, and in particular, not in C. Also, since extensions are defined in the host language, the complete implementation would have to be redone if the approach were used with another language. This is particularly true for IDE support, where the Smalltalk IDE is extended using this IDE's APIs. mbeddr uses a *heterogeneous* approach which does not have these limitations: MPS provides a language-agnostic framework for language and IDE extension that can be used with any language, once the language is implemented in MPS.

In the same paper, Renggli and his colleagues introduce three different flavors of language extension. A *pidgin* creatively bends the existing syntax of the host language to to extend its semantics. A *creole* introduces completely new syntax and custom transformations back to the host language. An *argot* reinterprets the semantics of valid host language code. mbeddr does not use any pidgins, because C's syntax is not very flexible, and because we have the language workbench at our disposal, so it is easier to implement creoles. W_1 - W_4 are creoles. In contrast, W_5 is an argot. It provides different semantics for existing constructs. W_6 is yet different. New syntax is introduced, but it can be attached to any language concept. The semantics is only relevant to additional tools, not to the core C program — no translation back to C takes place. W_7 *removes* concepts in new contexts and hence also does not fit with the categorization.

Cedalion [10] is a host language for defining internal DSLs. It uses a projectional editor and semantics based on logic programming. Both Cedalion and language workbenches such as MPS aim at combining the best of both worlds from internal DSLs (combination and extension of languages, integration with a host language) and external DSLs (static validation, IDE support, flexible syntax). Cedalion starts out from internal DSLs and adds static validation and projectional editing, the latter avoiding ambiguities resulting from combined syntaxes. Language workbenches start from external DSLs and add modularization, and, as a consequence of implementing base languages with the same tool, optional tight integration with general purpose host languages. We could not have used Cedalion as the platform for mbeddr tough, since we implemented our own base language (C), and the logic-based semantics would not have been a good fit.

Our work relates to macro systems such as Open Java [33] in that mbeddr customizes the translation of language extensions. However, mbeddr uses non-local transformations as well; those are not easily expressible with macros. Also, traditionally, macros have not addressed IDE extension.

Finally, open compilers such as Jastadd [14] are related in that they support language extension and custom transformation. However, while open compilers can typically be extended with independent modules, the input language often requires invasive adaptation. Also, open compilers do not address IDE extension.

Static Analysis and Formal Verification Static analysis of C programs is an active research area (as exemplified by [23, 26, 29]), and several commercial tools are available, such as the Escher C Verifier[10] or Klocwork[11]. We believe that we can simplify some of the analyses provided by these tools by providing extensions to C which embody relevant semantics directly, avoiding the need to reverse engineer the semantics for static analysis. For example, by expressing state-based behavior directly using state machines instead of a low level C implementation, the state space relevant to a model checker can be reduced significantly, making model checking less costly.

Another class of tools (such as Frama-C[12]) requires users to annotate C code with "semantic hints" to reduce the state space and enable meaningful verification. We plan to integrate Frama-C into mbeddr, expecting the following benefits: first, we will provide a language extension for the hints, so users don't have to use comments to specify them. IDE support will be provided. Second, we will provide C extensions on a higher level of abstraction with semantics that can be used to generate the verification hints. This way, users don't have to deal with the hints explicitly.

7. Discussion

Why MPS? A central pillar to our work is MPS. Our choice of MPS is due to its support for all aspects of language development (structure, syntax, type systems, IDE, transformations), its support for flexible syntax as a consequence of projectional editing and its support for advanced modularization and composition of languages. The ability to attach annotations to arbitrary program elements without a change to that element's definition is another strong advantage of MPS (we we use this for presence conditions and trace links, for example). No other freely available tool provides support for all those aspects, but some are supported by other tools. For example, Eclipse Xtext[13] and its accompanying tool stack supports abstract and concrete syntax definition, IDE support and transformations, but it is weak regarding non-textual syntax and modularization and composition of languages. TU Delft's Spoofax[14] concise type system definition. Intentional Software[15] supports extremely flexible syntax [32] and language composition (it is a projectional editor) but is not easily available.

Another important reason for our choice is the maturity and stability of MPS and the fact that it is backed by a major development tool vendor (JetBrains).

While the learning curve for MPS is significant (a developer who wants to become proficient in MPS language development has to invest at least a month), we found that is scales extremely well for larger and more sophisticated languages. This is in sharp contrast to some of the other tools the authors worked with, where implementing simple languages is quick and easy, and larger and more sophisticated languages are disproportionately more complex to build. This is illustrated

---

[10] http://www.eschertech.com/products/ecv.php
[11] http://www.klocwork.com/

[12] http://frama-c.com/
[13] http://eclipse.org/xtext
[14] http://spoofax.org
[15] http://intentsoft.com

by very reasonable effort necessary for implementing mbeddr (see Section 5.1).

Projectional Editing Projectional editing is often considered a drawback because the editors feel somewhat different and the programs are not stored as text, but as a tree (XML). We already highlighted that MPS does a good job regarding the editor experience, and we feel that the advantages of projectional editors regarding syntactic freedom far outweigh the drawback of requiring some initial familiarization. Our experience so far with about ten users (pilot users from industry, students) shows that after a short guided introduction (ca. 30 minutes) and an initial accomodation period (ca. 1-2 days), users can work productively with the projectional editor. Regarding storage, the situation is not any worse than with current modeling tools that store models in a non-textual format, and MPS does provide good support for diff and merge using the projected syntax.

Other Base Languages The technology described in this paper can be applied to other base languages. JetBrains, for example, is extending Java for building web applications. The advantage of using a heterogeneous approach (see the Helvetia discussion in Related Work) is that the tools built for language engineering are independent of the extended languages. No new frameworks or tools have to be developed or learned. Of course the to-be extended language has to be implemented in the tool stack first. We have discussed the effort for doing this in the case of C in Section 5.

Other Application Domains mbeddr's domain is embedded systems. However, the same approach can be used in other domains as well. As mentioned in the previous paragraph, JetBrains are developing Java extensions for web application development. These extensions include support for object-relational mapping, web page templating, and portability of application logic between the client and server by translating the same code into Java and Javascript. In internal communications with the authors, JetBrains have reported significant improvements in productivity and significantly reduced time (days and weeks instead of months) for getting new developers up to speed in web application development. JetBrains use this approach to develop the Youtrack bug tracking software, among others.

8. Conclusion and Future Work

In this paper we presented the mbeddr system, a large scale use of language engineering technologies in general and language workbenches in particular. We show how domain-specific extensions of C language can be used to address important challenges in embedded software development. To illustrate these ways of extension we provide a set of concrete examples and their implementation in the mbeddr system. The feedback on mbeddr received from practitioners so far convinces us that language engineering approaches have great potential to dramatically improve the development of embedded software. The mbeddr project also serves as a strong validation of the power and maturity of projectional language workbenches, in particular, MPS. The effort for building the C language and IDE and especially the incremental effort of building extensions is significantly lower than we expected when we started the project.

To realize the full potential of the mbeddr approach, more research is required in the following two major directions:

Extension of the Approach We are almost finised with a debugger that can be extended together with language extensions. While there is existing research (such as [25, 36]), there are still open questions such as how to calculate custom watches and how to avoid generating debug-specific code into the resulting C. We will also work more on formal analyses, including mapping higher-level DSLs to state machines and reinterpreting the verification results in the context of the higher-level DSL, exploring the relationship between general program analysis and language extensions as well as using SAT solvers to verify the structural integrity of variant-aware programs. In addition, we will add support for graphical notations for state machines and data flow block diagrams once MPS' support for graphical editors becomes available in the MPS 3.0 version.

Real-World Feasibility Since mbeddr is intended to be used for real-world software development, a major part of our future work is the validation of the approach in real-world embedded development projects. We are currently building a set of extensions specific to our application partner Sick AG who use mbeddr to build systems in the sensors domain. We are also setting up a project to develop a smart metering device. We will measure the increase in productivity and maintainability in order to provide solid data about the full potential of this approach. This line of future work will also include an automatic importer for functions, `structs`, constants, `enums` and `typdef`s defined in existing header files to simplify working with legacy code. We are also considering an importer for C implementation code (as long as it does not contain preprocessor statements). This will not be fully automatic, since some of the changes to mbeddr C require user decisions.

Acknowledgements We thank Marcel Matzat and Bernhard Merkle for their work on mbeddr. Supported by the German BMBF, FKZ 01/S11014.

References

[1] E. Axelsson, K. Claessen, G. Devai, Z. Horvath, K. Keijzer, B. Lyckegard, A. Persson, M. Sheeran, J. Sven-

ningsson, and A. Vajda. Feldspar: A domain specific language for digital signal processing algorithms. In *MEMOCODE 2010*.

[2] Y. Ben-Asher, D. G. Feitelson, and L. Rudolph. ParC - An Extension of C for Shared Memory Parallel Processing. *Software: Practice and Experience*, 26(5), 1996.

[3] F. Boussinot. Reactive C: An Extension of C to Program Reactive Systems. *Software: Practice and Experience*, 21(4), 1991.

[4] G. Bracha. Pluggable Type Systems. In *OOPSLA'04 Workshop on Revival of Dynamic Languages.*, 2004.

[5] M. Bravenboer and E. Visser. Concrete syntax for objects: DSL embedding and assimilation without restrictions. *SIGPLAN Not.*, 39, October 2004.

[6] M. Bravenboer and E. Visser. Designing Syntax Embeddings and Assimilations for Language Libraries. In *MoDELS 2007*, volume 5002 of *LNCS*. Springer, 2007.

[7] M. Broy, S. Kirstan, H. Krcmar, and B. Schätz. What is the Benefit of a Model-Based Design of Embedded Software Systems in the Car Industry? In *Emerging Technologies for the Evolution and Maintenance of Software Models*. ICI, 2011.

[8] R. Cox, T. Bergan, A. T. Clements, M. F. Kaashoek, and E. Kohler. Xoc, an extension-oriented compiler for systems programming. In *ASPLOS 2008*.

[9] W. Damm, R. Achatz, K. Beetz, M. Broy, H. Dämbkes, K. Grimm, and P. Liggesmeyer. *Nationale Roadmap Embedded Systems*. Springer, Mar. 2010.

[10] David H. Lorenz, Boaz Rosenan. Cedalion: A Language for Language Oriented Programming. In *Proceedings of OOPSLA/SPLASH 2011*, 2011.

[11] T. Dinkelaker, M. Eichberg, and M. Mezini. Incremental concrete syntax for embedded languages. In *Proceeding of the Symposium for Applied Computing 2011*.

[12] M. Dwyer, G. Avrunin, and J. Corbett. Patterns in property specifications for finite-state verification. In *ICSE 1999*.

[13] A. D. Eisenberg and G. Kiczales. Expressive programs through presentation extension. In *Proceedings of AOSD 2007*.

[14] T. Ekman and G. Hedin. The Jastadd extensible Java compiler. In *Proceedings of OOPSLA 2007*.

[15] S. Erdweg, L. C. Kats, T. Rendel, C. Kästner, K. Ostermann, and E. Visser. In *GPCE'11*, 2011.

[16] M. D. Ernst, G. J. Badros, and D. Notkin. An Empirical Analysis of C Preprocessor Use. *IEEE Trans. Softw. Eng.*, 28, December 2002.

[17] A. S. Gokhale, K. Balasubramanian, A. S. Krishna, J. Balasubramanian, G. Edwards, G. Deng, E. Turkay, J. Parsons, and D. C. Schmidt. Model driven middleware: A new paradigm for developing distributed real-time and embedded systems. *Science of Computer Programming*, 73(1), 2008.

[18] K. Hammond and G. Michaelson. Hume: a domain-specific language for real-time embedded systems. In *GPCE 03*, GPCE '03.

[19] P. Hudak. Modular Domain Specific Languages and Tools. In *ICSR '98*, jun 1998.

[20] F. Ivanicic, I. Shlyakhter, A. Gupta, and M. K. Ganai. Model Checking C Programs Using F-SOFT. In *ICCD'05*.

[21] T. Jim, J. G. Morrisett, D. Grossman, M. W. Hicks, J. Cheney, and Y. Wang. Cyclone: A Safe Dialect of C. In *USENIX 2002*. USENIX Association.

[22] G. L. S. Jr. Growing a Language. *Higher-Order and Symbolic Computation*, 12(3), 1999.

[23] S. Karthik and H. G. Jayakumar. Static Analysis: C Code Error Checking for Reliable and Secure Programming. In *International Enformatika Conference '05*.

[24] P. Klint. A Meta-Environment for Generating Programming Environments. *ACM Transactions on Software Engineering Methodology*, 2(2), 1993.

[25] R. T. Lindeman, L. C. L. Kats, and E. Visser. Declaratively Defining Domain-Specific Language Debuggers. In *GPCE 2011*, 2011.

[26] A. Mine. Static Analysis of Run-Time Errors in Embedded Critical Parallel C Programs. In *ESOP 2011*, volume 6602 of *LNCS*. Springer, 2011.

[27] MISRA. Guidelines for the Use of the C Language in Critical Systems.

[28] L. Palopoli, P. Ancilotti, and G. C. Buttazzo. A C Language Extension for Programming Real-Time Applications. In *6th International Workshop on Real-Time Computing and Applications (RTCSA 99)*. IEEE CS.

[29] A. Puccetti. Static Analysis of the XEN Kernel using Frama-C. *J. UCS*, 16(4), 2010.

[30] L. Renggli, T. Girba, and O. Nierstrasz. Embedding Languages Without Breaking Tools. In *ECOOP'10*.

[31] T. W. Reps and T. Teitelbaum. The Synthesizer Generator. In *First ACM SIGSOFT/SIGPLAN software engineering symposium on Practical software development environments*. ACM, 1984.

[32] C. Simonyi, M. Christerson, and S. Clifford. Intentional Software. In *OOPSLA 2006*. ACM, 2006.

[33] M. Tatsubori, S. Chiba, K. Itano, and M.-O. Killijian. OpenJava: A Class-Based Macro System for Java. In *1st Workshop on Reflection and Software Engineering, OOPSLA '99*, volume 1826 of *LNCS*.

[34] P. R. Thrift. Common Lisp relations: an extension of Lisp for logic programming. In *1988 Internation Conference on Computer Languages*. IEEE.

[35] M. Voelter. Language and IDE Development, Modularization and Composition with MPS. In *GTTSE 2011*, LNCS. Springer, 2011.

[36] H. Wu, J. G. Gray, S. Roychoudhury, and M. Mernik. Weaving a debugging aspect into domain-specific language grammars. In H. Haddad, L. M. Liebrock, A. Omicini, and R. L. Wainwright, editors, *SAC 2005*.

The CloudBrowser Web Application Framework

Brian McDaniel   Godmar Back

Department of Computer Science
Virginia Tech
brianmcd@vt.edu   gback@cs.vt.edu

CloudBrowser is a web application framework that supports the development of rich Internet applications whose entire user interface and application logic resides on the server, while all client/server communication is provided by the framework. CloudBrowser thus hides the distributed nature of these applications from the developer, creating an environment similar to that provided by a desktop user interface library. CloudBrowser preserves the user interface state in a server-side virtual browser that is maintained across visits. Unlike other server-centric frameworks, CloudBrowser's exclusive use of the HTML document model and associated JavaScript execution environment allows it to exploit existing client-side user interface libraries and toolkits while transparently providing access to other application tiers. We have implemented a prototype of CloudBrowser as well as several example applications to demonstrate the benefits of its server-centric design.

Categories and Subject Descriptors   D.2.2 [*Software Engineering*]: Design Tools and Techniques User Interfaces; H.5.3 [*Information Interfaces and Presentation*]: Group and Organization Interfaces Web-based Interaction

Keywords   web application framework, AJAX, server-centric, remote display, PaaS, cloud applications

1. Introduction

More and more applications are moving from the desktop to the web. Web applications can be accessed from any web browser, regardless of underlying platform, allowing them to be deployed and updated instantly. Users have begun to expect rich and expressive user interfaces whose single-page design mirrors that of desktop applications. At the same time, users assume that the data on which these applications operate resides "in the cloud," which stores any changes immediately and persistently. Increasingly, users expect that the state of the user interface is retained across page navigation and sessions so they can pick up where they leave off.

The creation of such rich Internet applications within the context of the current web infrastructure is difficult for multiple reasons. Application developers and framework designers must decide how to split the application's user interface code and its business logic between client-side JavaScript code and server-side code, and how to structure the communication between the client and the server on top of the stateless HTTP protocol.

Traditional AJAX [18] applications, which are developed using a mix of client- and server-side programming, fully expose developers to the underlying infrastructure's distributed nature. Developers must write view logic to produce an initial rendering of the user interface, then implement client-side controller logic to track the user interface state using JavaScript, use some variation of AJAX to inform the server of relevant changes to the application data, and incorporate any server responses into the HTML document that is rendered for the user. If the user refreshes the page, or makes use of the browser's navigation buttons, the ephemeral client state must be restored from scratch, often using hints stored on the server, because there is no automatic way of preserving user interface state.

To address these problems, server-centric AJAX frameworks [11, 27] move all application logic to the server, hiding most or all client-side programming from the developer. Such frameworks maintain the view state for each visit in a server-side representation, such as a document in a framework-specific, higher-level markup language that provides elements that represent user interface components. These components encapsulate the initial rendering into HTML, manage the forwarding of client-side events to server-side controller logic, and handle the propagation of any resulting updates to the client-side document with which the user interacts.

Existing server-centric frameworks suffer from multiple shortcomings. First, since they instantiate components for each visit, they also do not automatically preserve user interface state across visits. Second, they still require the programmer to synchronize updates to the application's model state across visits. Third, in practice they can make styling difficult, since the specifics of the rendering strategy used by these high-level components is encapsulated in their implementation. Fourth, the necessary computation of incremental client-side document updates after mutating the server-side view is tedious and error prone. Fifth, these server-centric frameworks often do not leverage the numerous JavaScript libraries that have been developed to facilitate the interaction with HTML documents, and thus cannot leverage the substantial skill sets developers have acquired.

This paper presents CloudBrowser, a web application framework that addresses these concerns. CloudBrowser maintains an application's user interface state server-side, as a document in a headless, virtual browser. The application logic interacts with the server-side representation in a manner similar to how a desktop application interacts with a graphical user interface (GUI) library, by creating and manipulating components and listening for events fired in response to user interactions. This design hides the distributed nature of the web from the application developer, because all client-server communication is encapsulated inside our framework. Clients connecting to application instances mirror the user interface state using a synchronization/update protocol we have developed. CloudBrowser automatically interposes on any changes to the server-side document, removing the need to manually compute updates. For efficiency, the actual layout and rendering of user interface elements is performed inside the actual browser by the client, rather than the virtual browser on the server.

CloudBrowser uses exclusively HTML, CSS, and JavaScript to express the user interface and its interaction with the application, allowing us to leverage existing libraries and developer skill sets, and avoiding any semantic overhead associated with a translation from high-level components to low-level components. Since CloudBrowser application instances persist across visits, this design naturally handles page navigation and refresh. It also provides a natural co-browsing ability since it can support simultaneous display to multiple clients.

CloudBrowser is targeted at developing web applications in which most user interactions trigger persistent changes to the application data that is stored on the server, and which do not require read access to the computed layout from the controller logic. Where necessary, CloudBrowser can be extended using traditional client-side components represented by proxy objects on the server.

We have developed a prototype of our framework and implemented several example applications, including some that use sophisticated JavaScript libraries. We have found that our framework greatly simplifies the development of the web applications we target and that it imposes acceptable latency overhead and bandwidth costs. We are currently creating a Platform-as-a-Service (PaaS) infrastructure based on Cloud-Browser.

2. Motivation

We motivate our approach using several example application scenarios. First, consider an example application such as the popular meeting scheduling service 'Doodle' (doodle.com). A user may initiate event scheduling by entering a set of possible meeting times, which are displayed to potential participants on a specially crafted webpage. Participants then enter their name, check boxes indicating their preferences when to meet, and hit a submit button, which navigates to a new page that displays their preferences along with the preferences of all other participants who have entered their preferences so far.

The user experience of Doodle, as well as many other currently available similar services, could in our opinion be significantly improved. For instance, a user does not see what other participants have entered until they submit their own, and subsequently only when they refresh or revisit the page, even when the potential meeting participants visit the page at around the same time. In addition, if the process of entering their name and checking appropriate times is interrupted, perhaps because the user clicked an ad and navigated to another page and returned to the page, the user will need to start over. Lastly, if the user overlooks the submit button before closing the page, their submission will not reach the server at all, which frequently happens to users accustomed to the single-click style used in their native OS (i.e., Mac OSX).

Second, consider a social forum application such as Piazza (piazza.com), which provides an interactive Q & A forum for instructional settings in which students can post questions to other students and to instructors. From an instructor's perspective, the Piazza user interface presents a constantly changing dashboard - new questions are being posted, questions are withdrawn, marked as answered by other instructors or students, or archived (hidden from view) after being answered. If the Piazza application is used from multiple computers (say, the instructor's work PC, work laptop, home PC, and perhaps a mobile device), the dashboard views are not kept in sync: already answered questions appear as unanswered when the instructor revisits the class site after returning home from work, forcing a manual refresh of the page. When such a refresh happens, some user interface state is lost - for instance, a different course may be selected, a homepage displayed instead of a student posting, displayed toolbars may disappear and have to be reenabled, or selected elements in an accordion-style display are not remembered, requiring the instructor to find the point in the application at which to resume responding to student questions.

Similar weaknesses apply to applications such as Google's Email service GMail. Although it is able to remember coarse information about which emails the user has read, it generally does not remember fine-grained state such as which emails in a thread the user looks at are shown in collapsed view and which are not, often requiring manual search to find the relevant email in a given thread. If a user was working on a draft, they will have to navigate to a "Draft" folder, find the draft, and continue, which sometimes results in duplicated edits or even duplicated emails.

Third, consider online tax preparation programs such as TaxACT (taxact.com). To prepare a tax return under the United States tax code, taxpayers have to enter income and expense information, and answer numerous questions to determine their tax burden. Many people visit the tax site multiple times as documents arrive from their employers or financial institutions and need to be entered, or if answering a question requires off-line inquiries. If the user revisits the site, they expect to be able to continue at exactly the question where they left off. In currently available implementations, users are instead led to a top-level navigation point from which they must find out where to continue, and often have to repeat answering questions they already answered. Similar considerations apply to configuration management applications that are web-based and which may involve many tabs, dialogs, input fields, checkboxes or radio buttons, which are often conditionally displayed or hidden based on a user's history of navigating through the application.

These motivating applications share the following common characteristics.

- The user interface of these applications is rich, resembling that of a desktop application. Users prefer a single-page application style that gives them free reign in how to use the application. The navigation space is typically large.

- There appears to be little potential for offloading any application logic, or keeping application state in the client's browser, which is used purely as a display device to display a view of a model's state that is kept server-side. In applications involving multiple users, a lack of immediate and tight synchronization between the displayed view of the user interface and the application's model state may result in a degraded user experience.

- Users expect, or would prefer, if most or even all interactions with the user interface resulted in persistent effects independent of the device used to access the application, and independent of how often they navigate to the application.

- The number of users that access an instance of the application simultaneously is small when compared to the number of users a video distribution site such as YouTube would need to accommodate. This reduces the need for replication of an application's state and makes them "embarrassingly" horizontally scalable in the sense that any increase in the amount of dedicated resources yields a proportional increase in the number of application instances (with disjoint state) that can be supported.

- The frequency with which a user triggers relevant user interface events is limited by human processing speed and low when compared to, for instance, video game applications. For instance, such applications generally do not require tracking of mouse (move) events.

Current application frameworks make it difficult to maintain and synchronize an application's view on the server. The dominant model-view-controller (MVC) paradigm views the client-side user interface as the view component that is controlled by changes in a server-side model that is usually devoid of user interface state. Programmers must manually decide which, if any, user interface state they deem important enough to include in their models. When a user returns to a page, an initial view is constructed in response to the browser's HTTP request, which often involves constructing HTML using server-side templating. Any changes resulting from past interactions with the user interface must be incorporated manually into the templating logic, based on saved model state. Even when such state is kept, it is often associated with sessions, which are typically implemented using cookies that are not synchronized across different devices a user may use to access an application. Lastly, once a page displays to the user, programmers must decide which portions of the view they wish to keep in sync, using methods such as long polling or server push which typically take extra effort.

3. Developing CloudBrowser Applications

This section presents four examples that illustrate the paradigm in which CloudBrowser applications can be built. We start with an example that demonstrates the server-side execution and compatibility with existing HTML/JS applications, then discuss how to use observers, templating, and how to access shared data, and finally present a short example of how to implement the model-view-controller paradigm with a database-backed model.

3.1 Simple Document Example

Figure 1 shows an HTML document that contains a complete CloudBrowser application. This application contains two HTML text `<input>` elements and a `<span>` element whose text content depends on the input the user enters into the text input fields. This example uses exclusively the DOM Level 2 API [8] to manipulate DOM elements, and retrieve and set their attributes. It runs in any DOM-Level 2 compliant browser when fetched via a URL; in CloudBrowser, this code is run *server-side* in a virtual browser. This example demonstrates a key benefit: existing browsers can be used to test the user interface logic before deployment, because there is no user interface logic outside the HTML document describing an application!

Today, most JavaScript developers use higher-level libraries such as jQuery [30] rather than the DOM API directly. Figure 2 shows the JavaScript code of the same application, expressed more compactly using the appropriate jQuery selectors and event bindings. CloudBrowser executes

```
<html>
  <body style="font-family: Arial">
    First name: <input id='fname' type='text' />
    Last name: <input id='lname' type='text' />
    Hello <span id='output'></span>!
    <script>
      var fname = document.getElementById('fname'),
          lname = document.getElementById('lname'),
          output = document.getElementById('output');

      function onChange () {
        output.innerHTML = fname.value + ' '
                            + lname.value;
      }

      fname.addEventListener('change', onChange);
      lname.addEventListener('change', onChange);
    </script>
  </body>
</html>
```

Figure 1. A simple CloudBrowser application.

this application as well, *without* requiring any changes to the jQuery (v1.7.1) library.

```
$('#fname,#lname').change(function () {
  $('#output').text($('#fname').val()
            + ' ' + $('#lname').val());
});
```

Figure 2. CloudBrowser applications can use libraries such as jQuery for DOM manipulation like the ones used in Figure 1.

3.2 Meeting Times Example

As the next example, consider the collaborative meeting time application discussed in Section 2. We prototyped this application using CloudBrowser using a model-view-controller (MVC) approach [10]. Most MVC implementations use some kind of expression language to bind views to controller logic that draws from and updates an underlying model. CloudBrowser facilitates the MVC paradigm by using existing JavaScript libraries originally designed for client-side use. For example, the popular Knockout [31] client-side library gives a concise syntax for associating DOM elements with model data, provides for the automatic update of the UI when the model state changes through observers and observables [17], and provides templating facilities to generate DOM elements based on a model. Being designed for the client portion of traditional AJAX applications, Knockout uses the term Model-View-View Model (MVVM) to express the assumption that the client-side UI ("View") is synchronized with a collection of JavaScript observables ("View Model") which is separately synchronized with the actual model that is kept server-side. When running Knockout in CloudBrowser, the 'view model' and the actual 'model' be-

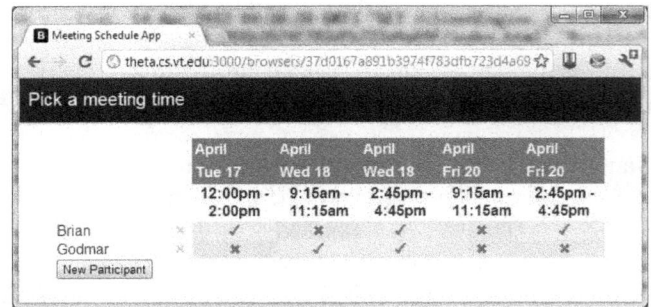

Figure 3. User interface of meeting time application.

```
<table>
  <thead>
    <tr><th width="25%"></th>
      <!-- ko foreach: times -->
      <th class="d-month container"
          data-bind="text: getMonth()"></th>
      <!-- /ko -->
    </tr>
    ...
  </thead>
  <tbody data-bind="foreach: participants">
    <tr class="participant-row">
      <td class="container">
        <a class="close" data-bind="
            visible: !editing(),
            click: $parent.removeParticipant">x</a>
        <span data-bind="
            visible: !editing(),
            click: function () {
              editing(true)
            },
            text: name"></span>
        <input data-bind="
            visible: editing,
            value: name,
            hasfocus: editing"></input>
      </td>
      <!-- ko foreach: available -->
      <td class="container" style="text-align: center"
          data-bind="
          text: $data.avail() ? '\u2714' : '\u2716',
          css: { 'alert-danger': !$data.avail(),
                 'alert-success': $data.avail()},
          click: function () {
            $data.avail(!$data.avail());
          }">
      </td>
      <!-- /ko -->
    </tr>
  </tbody>
</table>
<button data-bind="click: addParticipant">
    New Participant
</button>
```

Figure 4. Excerpts of the meeting time application.

```
function Participant(name, editing) {
  this.name = name;
  this.editing = ko.observable(editing);
  // ...
}

function Time(start, duration) {
  this.getMonth     = function ...
  // ...
}

var appModel = {
  times: ko.observableArray([
    // ...
  ]),
  participants: ko.observableArray(),
  addParticipant : function () {
    appModel.participants.push(
      new Participant('New Participant', true));
  },
  removeParticipant : function (participant) {
    appModel.participants.remove(participant);
  }
};
ko.applyBindings(appModel);
```

Figure 5. The view model for the meeting time application.

```
// if running in CloudBrowser, provide a
// JSON service to obtain current data
if (typeof require == "function") {
  var http  = require('http');
  http.createServer(function (req, res) {
    try {
      res.writeHead(200, {
              'Content-Type':
              'application/json'});
      res.end(ko.toJSON(appModel), 'utf-8');
    } catch (err) {
      res.writeHead(500);
      res.end('Server Error: ' + err);
    }
  }).listen(1337);
}
```

Figure 6. Exporting the view model as a JSON service.

come one and the same, eliminating the need for programming any client-server interaction.

Figure 4 shows relevant excerpts of the HTML describing this simple application, shown in Figure 3. An HTML table's headings are created from an array of possible meeting times, while its rows correspond to participants who have indicated their availability. Participants can toggle their availability, edit their names, or remove themselves from the schedule via mouse clicks. The set of participants and their availability is recorded in an underlying JavaScript object, which makes use of the observable pattern. For example,

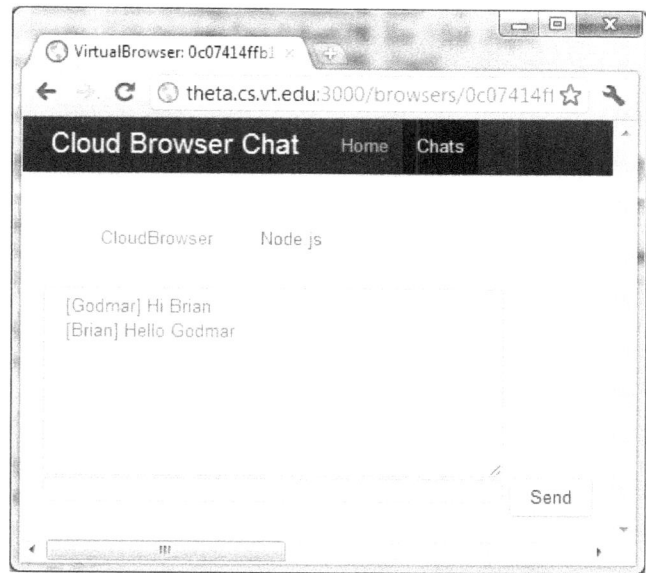

Figure 7. A screenshot of a simple chat room application.

clicking on a name trigger the corresponding 'click' data binding, which results in a transition to the editing state. In this state the `<input>` box is visible via the `visible` binding and its value is tied to the participant's name. The 'css' binding applies different styles (red vs. green) depending on the currently indicated availability.

Figure 5 displays excerpts of the associated JavaScript code. Knockout's `applyBindings` code ensures that any changes to the observable members of the `appModel` object are reflected in changes of the DOM. When run in Cloud-Browser, multiple users can use the URL at which the application is available. Any changes made by any user are displayed in real-time to all connected users. Moreover, if a user closes their browser and later reconnects, even from a different browser using a different session, they will be able to rejoin this meeting application.

Like the example shown in the previous section, we were able to program and test the entire logic offline using a web browser within the confines of a JavaScript sandbox. Figure 6 shows how to add interaction with the outside world. Using node.js's `http` package, a simple HTTP server can be created that provides a JSON [12] service that exports the current results.

3.3 Chatroom Example

We prototyped a simple chatroom application, shown in Figure 7, to highlight two additional features of CloudBrowser. Like the meeting time application, the chatroom keeps track of model state (in this case, chat messages) in a JavaScript object and updates observables when it changes. Unlike in the previous example, multiple virtual browsers are instantiated since each user may be at a different navigation point. For instance, users may have joined different chat-

```
<div id="chat-tabs" data-bind='foreach: myChats'>
  <div class='tab-pane'
      data-bind="visible:
                   $root.activeRoom() === $data">
    <textarea rows='20' data-bind='value: messages'>
    </textarea>
  </div>
</div>
<input type='text' size='160'
      data-bind='value: currentMessage'>
</input
<button data-bind='click: postMessage'>Send</button>
```

Figure 8. An excerpt of chat room application view responsible for displaying chat messages. The 'foreach' binding duplicates its contained DOM nodes for each chat room that the user has joined. The 'visible' data binding ensures that only the currently selected chat room is shown. The 'messages' binding displays the chat messages for a room.

rooms. CloudBrowser allows the sharing of state across virtual browser instances, thus allowing observers in all instances to be notified when a new message appears in a chat room. An excerpt of the view expressed using Knockout bindings is shown in Figure 8. For instance, the "data-bind='value: messages'" attribute inside the `<textarea>` element ties the textarea's content to the array of chat messages.

The second key feature demonstrated by this example is the possibility for reusing higher-level UI libraries designed for client-side use. For instance, the Bootstrap/JS library [1] is used to implement a set of tabs (one per chatroom), which are declared using HTML `<ul>` and `<li>` elements. When the document is loaded, additional DOM elements and styles to represent actual tabs will be produced. The number of tabs, and their labels, are thus tied directly to the number of chatrooms that are accessible. The ability to run such widgets is crucial for creating a rich user experience.

3.4 Phonebook Example

Whereas the preceding chatroom example used in-memory JavaScript variables to represent its model state, a more typical scenario is the use of a persistent store such as a relational database. We provide a simple example of a phone book application whose entries are backed by a database. We use the Sequelize [15] Object Relational Mapping package to map JavaScript objects to a MySQL [2] database.

Figure 9 shows the HTML template that lists phone book entries and renders them in a table using Knockout's `text` data bindings. The phone book entry objects whose properties (e.g., 'fname', 'lname') are referred to in these bindings are constructed directly from the database. Figure 10 shows a screenshot of the resulting application.

The view model for the application is shown in Figure 11. Here, some glue is necessary to construct a view model suitable for use in Knockout, which wraps the sequelized phone

```
<table>
  <thead>
    <tr>
      <th>First Name</th>
      <th>Last Name</th>
      <th>Phone Number</th>
    </tr>
  </thead>
  <tbody data-bind="foreach: entries">
    <tr data-bind="click: $parent.rowClick">
      <td data-bind="text: fname" /></td>
      <td data-bind="text: lname" /></td>
      <td data-bind="text: phoneNumber" /></td>
    </tr>
  </tbody>
</table>
```

Figure 9. The 'foreach' data binding is used to map database entries to table rows.

Figure 10. A simple database-backed phone book application.

book entries that are mapped to the database. The callback functions which are invoked for the 'Save' and 'Delete' actions directly affect the persistent storage using methods provided by the reconstituted objects. This example demonstrates how CloudBrowser applications can avoid separate client- and server-side representations of their data, creating the appearance of a non-distributed environment in which application objects can be mapped to database records.

4. Design and Implementation

We chose the open source Node.js [14] JavaScript execution environment for our prototype, for multiple reasons. First, Node.js is based on Google's V8 JavaScript en-

```
var vm = {
  entries     : ko.observableArray(entries),
  currentEntry : ko.observable(),
  rowClick    : function () {
    vm.currentEntry(this);
  },
  save : function () {
    this.save();   // persist to db
    vm.entries.remove(this);
    vm.entries.push(this);
    vm.currentEntry(null);
  },
  remove : function () {
    this.destroy(); // remove from db
    vm.entries.remove(this);
    vm.currentEntry(null);
  },
  create : function () {
    this.currentEntry(phoneBook.createEntry());
  }
};
```

Figure 11. View model used in phone book application.

gine, which represents the current state of the art with respect to execution performance. Second, Node.js's developer community provides many packages we use, such as the JSDOM JavaScript library [20] or the Sequelize [15] object-relational mapping, and many others which provide an environment that facilitates access to other application tiers. Third, Node.js provides a single-threaded environment whose semantics matches exactly the familiar execution semantics found in today's browser. Fourth, Node.js's event-based design provides for fast and efficient I/O, although it requires the programmer to rearrange (i.e., stack-rip [9]) their application to handle all I/O completion in asynchronously invoked callbacks.

Figure 12 shows an overview of CloudBrowser's design and components. The left half of the figure shows the client engine, which uses an update protocol to communicate with a virtual browser instance executing inside a server-side JavaScript virtual machine, shown on the right half of the figure. This section discusses the application life cycle, the client and server engine implementations, and the update protocol used by CloudBrowser applications.

4.1 Application Life Cycle

If a client sends an HTTP request to a configured application entry point (say /example/index.html), the Cloud-Browser server starts a new virtual browser instance, creates an entry point for it (such as /browsers/2e90b4b3/ index.html), and redirects the user's browser to that entry point. This browser URL is valid for the lifetime of the virtual browser instance. It may be shared among multiple users wishing to interact with the same application.

When a virtual browser accepts a new client, it sends a small amount of HTML along with JavaScript code to boot-

PageLoaded(records)
DOMNodeInsertedIntoDocument(records)
DOMNodeRemovedFromDocument(parent, target)
DOMAttrModified(target, name, value)
DOMPropertyModified(target, property, value)
DOMCharacterDataModified(target, value)
DOMStyleChanged(target, attribute, value)
AddEventListener(target, type)
PauseRendering()
ResumeRendering()

Table 1. Client Engine RPC Methods

strap the client engine. The client engine then requests the current state of the virtual browser's DOM, which is retrieved and sent by the virtual browser's server engine. Unlike in a traditional AJAX application, refreshing or navigating to the browser URL does not discard and re-initialize the virtual browser's document. Clients can disconnect and reconnect while the application instance's state is preserved in the context of the virtual browser document.

Virtual browsers pose a resource management problem. Our current implementation provides an administrative module to list, inspect and terminate instances. When used in connection with user authentication, it allows the implementation of such policies as limiting each authenticated user to at-most-one browser instance for a configured application so that the inadvertent creation of multiple, separate instances is prevented. Alternatively, users may maintain and select from multiple instances. Conversely, it is also possible to implement single-instance applications in which there is at most one virtual browser instance shared by all users.

If virtual browser instances are not terminated manually, CloudBrowser supports an idle timeout after which a browser is terminated if no clients interact with it, allowing for automatic garbage collection. If necessary, a callback allows an application to save any transient state before terminating.

4.2 Client Engine

The client engine is responsible for receiving and rendering the initial state of the virtual browser's document, as well as for handling events on the client and receiving and rendering any updates to the document. We use a remote procedure call (RPC) abstraction to structure this communication. This RPC layer is implemented on top of a bidirectional message-based transport provided by the Socket.io [6] JavaScript library, which in turn encapsulates a number of underlying transport mechanism (web sockets for browsers that support them, or other AJAX-based long polling mechanisms such as Vault [34]).

At initialization, the client engine creates a connection to the server engine and establishes an RPC endpoint. This endpoint provides the methods shown in Table 1. The server

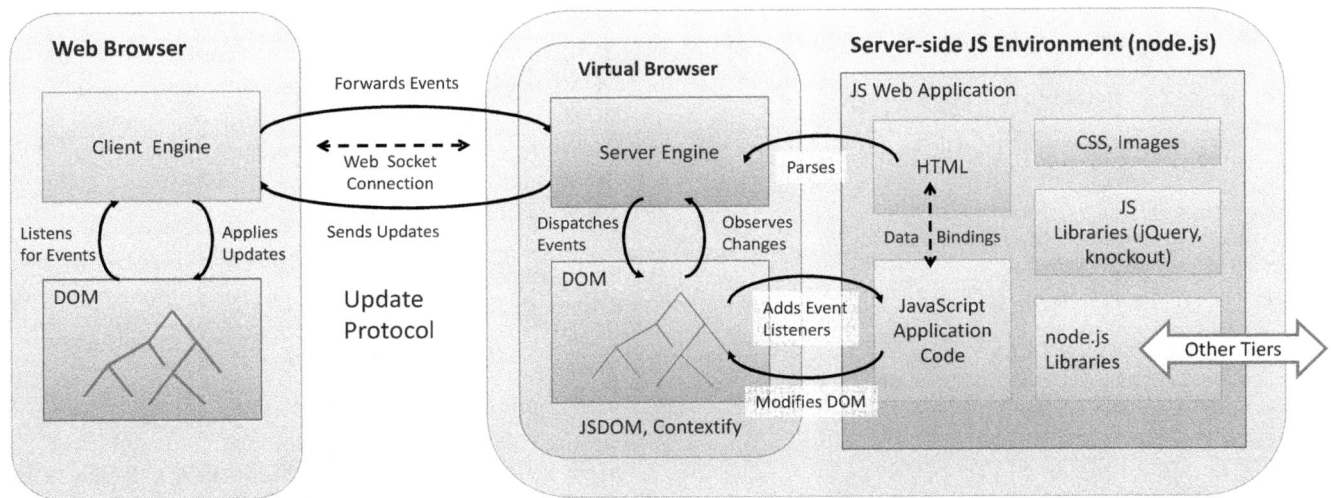

Figure 12. CloudBrowser Architecture Overview

processEvent(event)
setAttribute(target, attribute, value)

Table 2. Server Engine RPC Methods

Property	Type	Description
type	String	The type of node: 'text' or 'element' or 'comment'
id	String	The node's unique identifier.
owner-Document	String	The id of the document to which this node belongs
parent	String	The id of this node's parent node.
name	String	For element nodes, the type of element (e.g. 'div')
value	String	For comment and text nodes, the content of the node.
attributes	Object	The node's attributes, in with object properties as attribute names and property values as attribute values.

Table 3. DOM Node Record Format

engine then performs a pre-order traversal of the DOM tree, which results in a serialized representation of the DOM's nodes that is sent to the client engine in JSON format, using the 'PageLoaded' RPC method shown in Table 1. Each DOM node is assigned an id that can subsequently be used to refer to it. The client engine reconstructs the DOM by interpreting the received representation. Table 3 shows the record format used in this JSON representation.

The client engine must listen for and forward any client events to the server engine. The client engine does not keep track of which specific elements have event listeners asso-ciated with them in the virtual browser application. Instead, it exploits capturing event handlers as defined in the DOM Event specification. Any event that results from a user interaction is first dispatched to capturing event listeners associated with the event target's ancestors, starting with the document root. The client engine intercepts the event here, encodes the event in a message, and forwards it to the server engine. The event's 'stopPropagation' and 'preventDefault' methods are then invoked to prevent the browser from further processing the event. Preventing the default actions means that, for instance, clicks on links represented by `<a>` elements do not result in the user navigating away from the page. Instead, default actions are processed by the server engine and any resulting updates are propagated to the client.

Instead of having the client engine blindly listening for all possible event types, the server engine infers which events are actually being listened for in the server-side document by intercepting calls to the `addEventListener` API. When a server-side event listener is added, the `AddEventListener` RPC is invoked at the client, instructing it to add a capturing event listener for that event type. This optimization avoids excessive client-server traffic for high-frequency event types such as mouse movement events unless the application makes use of them. Certain types of events are always listened for on the client, such as mouse clicks, to avoid the inadvertent execution of client-side default actions.

4.3 Server Engine

The server engine is part of the implementation of each virtual browser instance. It comprises an HTML parser and a complete implementation of the DOM Level 2 and DOM Event APIs, based on the JSDOM library [20].

The server engine processes forwarded events sent by the client engine(s) with which it maintains connections. Table 2 shows the RPC methods exposed by the server engine's entry point. Besides the main `processEvent` method, which clients invoke when forwarding events, the server provides a `setAttribute` method that allows a client to set certain element attributes that might be accessed from within event handlers. For instance, when a 'change' event fires on a `<input>` field, the change event listener expects to be able to access the current 'value' attribute of the `<input>` element.

The `processEvent` method dispatches the received event to the server document according to the DOM Event specification, invoking registered event listeners and/or performing the default actions for certain events (e.g., navigation when a 'click' event is dispatched on a `<a>` anchor). These event listeners are typically part of the application's controller code, and may directly or indirectly result in changes to the server side document. The server engine uses aspect-oriented techniques [22] (e.g., advices associated with the DOM manipulation methods) to interpose on any changes to the server document. Consequently, unlike in server-centric frameworks such as ZK [11], neither the server document implementation nor the application code incur any additional implementation burden to ensure that server document changes are propagated to the client.

The interposed advice code invokes the client engine's `DOM*` methods shown in Table 1. To reduce the number of calls to the client, we do not send a DOM node until after it has been attached to the server document. Frequently, user interface libraries build complex structures of unattached DOM nodes before inserting them into the document. Sending these nodes to the client when they are inserted allows us to batch such updates by sending a serialized array of records representing a node and all its descendants.

An event listener will typically cause multiple updates to the server document. If these were sent to the client and immediately applied to the client's document, flicker would result since the browser will re-render the document after delivering each RPC request. To avoid these unnecessary rendering cycles and prevent the associated flicker, the server surrounds all DOM updates occurring during an event handler with `PauseRendering` and `ResumeRendering` calls. `PauseRendering` instructs the client engine to buffer any DOM updates it receives until it receives the `ResumeRendering` call, at which point all DOM changes are applied to the client document. Batching the execution of multiple RPC requests by the client engine, rather than the server engine, allows us to reduce latency by overlapping the transmission of requests with the computation of additional requests.

To reduce the bandwidth consumption associated with client/server RPC calls, we exploit two compaction methods that are applied transparently to reduce the size of each RPC request message. First, instead of using method names, we use a numbered encoding for each RPC method. Since we do not use an IDL compiler, the encoding table is built

dynamically by the server engine, and the method codes are broadcast to all connected clients as necessary.

Second, instead of sending full DOM records as JSON objects based on the format shown in Table 3, we use a positional encoding that avoids repeating the property names and omits those properties that are not used in a particular call. These encoding operations are implemented transparently in a separate layer whose code is shared between client and server and which is downloaded as part of the bootstrap library. Additional compression techniques such as GZip compression could be applied by the underlying transport, although web sockets currently do not support any.

In addition to dispatching client events and forwarding DOM modifications to the client, the server engine must provide a faithful implementation of the host environment in which the application code's can run. As discussed in Section 3, our goal is to provide an environment that is nearly indistinguishable from the environment familiar to web developers writing ordinary JavaScript code that operates on a client document. To achieve this goal, we implemented host methods such as 'setTimeout', 'setInterval', 'XMLHttpRequest' etc. using Node.js's and V8's facilities. We created a helper library, *Contextify*, which allows us to bind a JavaScript object whose properties contain the implementations of these methods to a V8 context such that these properties are visible in the global scope to JavaScript code executing in this context. This library ensures invariants upon which JavaScript libraries rely, such as the invariant that global variables appear as properties of the object to which `window` is bound, as well as corner cases such as the expression `window === this`, which must yield true within the global scope.

4.4 Styling and Layout

The server engine includes a resource proxy and translator for style sheets and other resources used by an application. We rewrite references to those resources so that they refer to the rewritten resource. We maintain application-defined CSS style classes, element ids, and element hierarchy, allowing us to send the style sheet mostly unchanged to the client, except where there are references to other resources (e.g. @import, or url() in background-image).

Unlike remote display systems such as Opera Mini [3] or SkyFire [5], CloudBrowser does not layout or render HTML components server side. We deemed it too expensive to re-compute the layout inside the server engine, and we also discarded the idea to send computed layout information from the client to the server for the simple reason that it is difficult to predict which properties the code might access. Moreover, when supporting multiple, simultaneous visitors to the same CloudBrowser instance, we cannot assume that they use identical screen sizes.

As a result, JavaScript code that accesses layout properties that are computed post layout, such as 'offsetWidth,' will not work. Some JavaScript libraries use such information to

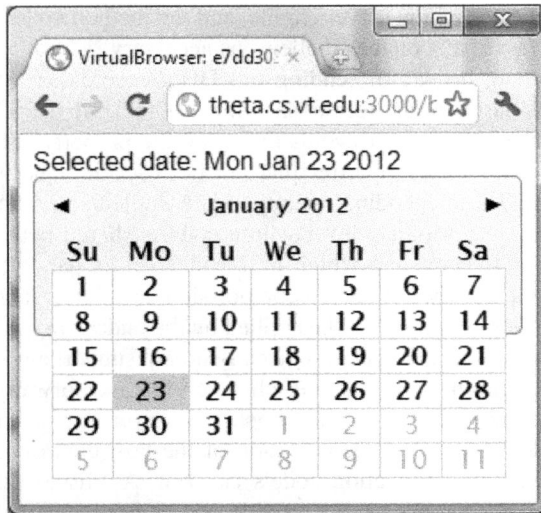

Figure 13. Encapsulating the YUI-3 DatePicker component in CloudBrowser

```
<script>
window.addEventListener('load', function () {
  var vm = { selectedDate : ko.observable() };
  ko.applyBindings(vm);

  var picker = cloudbrowser.createComponent(
      'calendar',
      document.getElementById('datePicker'),
      { // options
          height : '100px', width : '300px',
          showPrevMonth : true,
          showNextMonth : true
      });

  picker.addEventListener('Calendar:dateClick',
    function (e) {
      var date = new Date(e.info.date)
      vm.selectedDate(date.toDateString());
    });
});
</script>

<body style="font-family: Arial">
  <div>Selected date:
    <span data-bind='text: selectedDate'></span>
  </div>
  <div id='datePicker'></div>
</body>
```

Figure 14. Encapsulating the YUI-3 DatePicker component in CloudBrowser

position elements based on the actual size of content or the size of the viewport. Often, though not always, the desired effect of such computations can be expressed using style rules, particularly when targeting browsers that support the newer CSS3 standard. We note that CloudBrowser does support the manipulation of CSS styles via JavaScript, e.g., setting `elem.style.display = 'block'` or `$.addClass` works.

We have observed a trend in the web design community away from directly accessing layout properties and relying on CSS properties instead wherever possible. For instance, the Bootstrap CSS library used by Twitter.com and other major websites minimizes the use of JavaScript. For instance, many cases where JavaScript accesses and manipulates position information can be expresses via CSS's fixed and absolute positioning. JavaScript-based animations can be replaced via CSS3 transitions; in fact, modern JavaScript libraries default to their use when it is available.

4.5 Client-side Components

For applications whose user interface cannot be expressed using CSS style rules, we provide a mechanism to embed client-side components in a CloudBrowser application. This mechanism is based on the observation that well-designed user interface libraries, such as the Yahoo! User Interface Library, Version 3 (YUI-3) [7], are typically designed to coexist with other JavaScript code in the same page, and that they provide their functionality encapsulated in components that can be instantiated as JavaScript objects. We provide client-side and server-side glue code for these components that allows them to be included in server documents. The client-side code includes the original component library's JavaScript code, instantiates client-side components, inserts them into the client document, registers event handlers, and

provides way to set a component's properties. For instance, for a component such as a slider, the client glue code may set/get the slider's value, and register event handlers to listen for value changes. Like for ordinary events, the client-side glue forwards those events to the server engine.

The server-side glue code allows the application to instantiate components, which returns a server proxy object that the application code can use to interact with the component. For instance, the application can attach event listeners to this proxy object, which are fired when the client-side event listener fires and forwards the corresponding event to the server engine. We provide a cache to support direct access to properties. For instance, if application code accesses the 'value' property of a proxied slider component, it will obtain the last known snapshot of the component's 'value' property. All component-related events send a copy of a component's properties to the server engine, allowing it to update this cache before executing event handlers.

As a proof of concept, we have implemented the glue code for two components, YUI-3 Slider and DatePicker (calendar) components. Figures 13 and 14 show how such components can be integrated in a CloudBrowser application. The 'CloudBrowser.createComponent' API encapsulates access to the server-side glue for each supported components. We were able to encapsulate these components with rela-

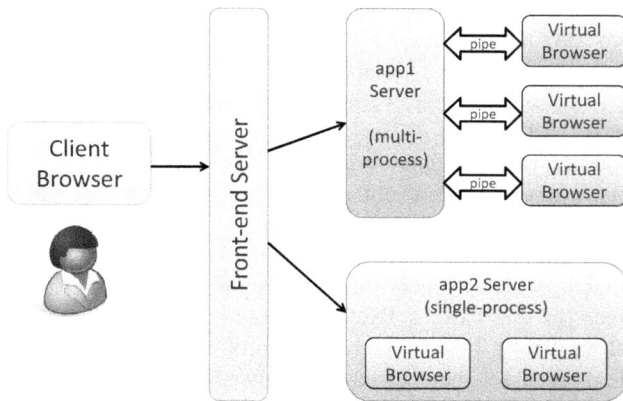

Figure 15. Load balancing across multiple CloudBrowser instances.

tively little effort; because of YUI-3's inheritance-based design, much of the code is reusable to support the inclusion of other components.

Providing support for components required changes to our DOM event capturing model in the client engine, as some events are now handled locally and must be passed through so the local browser can process them. In addition, the PageLoaded call was extended to instruct the client engine to load and instantiate the needed component libraries and instantiate the client-side glue.

4.6 Multiprocess Implementation

Single-threaded, event-based servers such as Node.js have the potential for high performance [28, 29, 37], but they cannot take advantage of multiple CPUs or cores. Moreover, long-running event handlers that involve such tasks as the parsing of large HTML documents delay the processing of subsequent events, increasing request latency. To overcome this problem, we defined a load balancing architecture that allows CloudBrowser instances to be distributed across multiple processes on a single machine or multiple machines, as shown in Figure 15.

Our architecture allows for flexible mappings of virtual browser instances to OS-level processes - each virtual browser may have its own dedicated process, or multiple virtual browser instances may share one process. Such colocation is required only if an application shares JavaScript state across instances.

A front-end server hands off requests to a server that manages instances for each application. Our current implementation uses client-side redirection (via a 301 HTTP response), but other mechanisms such as passing of sockets via sendmsg(3) could be used. For multi-process arrangements, the application server forwards requests and responses via an inter-process communication mechanism (i.e., Unix pipes). Since this arrangement leaves the application server involved

in each request/response, we are currently exploring how to extend the Socket.io library to support the handing off of an established web socket connection directly to the corresponding process.

5. Evaluation

We have evaluated our prototype in terms of memory usage, event-processing latency, bandwidth consumption, and the completeness of our server-side DOM implementation.

5.1 Memory Usage

We measured two aspects of memory usage: the cost of allocating a virtual browser and the additional cost of adding a client to an existing virtual browser when co-browsing. We created a benchmark application that spawns an instance of the CloudBrowser server and connects a configurable number of clients to it. The clients can connect to existing virtual browsers or force the creation of new ones. In between each connection, we force a full garbage collection cycle on the server and record memory usage as reported by Node.js process.memoryUsage() API, which reports the size of the live heap maintained by the V8 virtual machine.

The memory requirements of a virtual browser depend on the size of the HTML document describing the application, as well as the amount of CSS stylesheets and JavaScript code, which must be parsed and compiled by the V8 engine.

Using our x86_64 Node.js implementation, we found the base memory consumption for an empty browser (with just 3 DOM nodes for <html>, <head>, and <body>) to be 164 KB. Including the jQuery 1.7.2 library and the Knockout.js 2.0.0 libraries increases this consumption by 1.05 MB and 0.33 MB, respectively. The chat application discussed in Section 3.3, which in addition includes the Bootstrap CSS stylesheets, consumes about 2.6MB per browser instance. We see 2 opportunities for optimizations that have the potential to reduce this memory usage drastically. First, the V8 engine could recognize if the same JavaScript code is included in multiple browsers and transparently share the resulting intermediate representations and machine code, a technique commonly exploited in multitasking Java virtual machines such as MVM [13]. Second, the CSS implementation could similarly recognize when style sheets are included multiple times and share the immutable portions of their representation.

Adding additional clients to an existing virtual browser adds only minimal overhead of about 16KB per connection, independent of the memory consumed by the virtual browser.

5.2 Latency

To measure latency, we ran a single-process CloudBrowser server on a server machine with 2 AMD Opteron 2380 2.5GHz quad-core processors and 16GB of RAM. Our simulated clients run within multiple processes (100 clients per

```
<html>
  <head></head>
  <body>
    <div id='target'></div>
    <script>
      var count = 0;
      var div = document.getElementById('target');
      div.addEventListener('click', function () {
        div.innerHTML = ++count;
      });
    </script>
  </body>
</html>
```

Figure 16. The example application used in the latency tests.

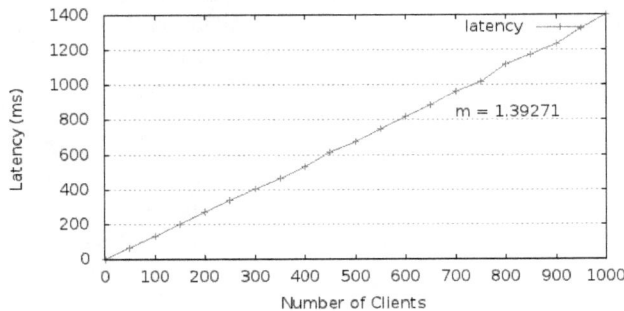

Figure 17. The average latency for all connected clients when running the application in Figure 16 with increasing numbers of clients. In this experiment, clients sent new requests immediately upon receiving a response to their previous request.

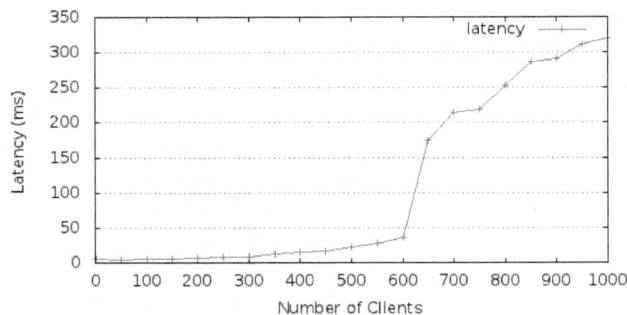

Figure 18. The average latency for all connected clients when running the application in Figure 16 with increasing numbers of clients. In this version of the experiment, clients paused for between 1 and 5 seconds using a uniformly random distribution before sending subsequent events.

process) on a separate machine with an Intel Q9650 quad-core 3.00GHz processor with 8GB of RAM. The 2 machines were connected via a Gigabit LAN.

The simulated clients each connect to the CloudBrowser server and request a new virtual browser instance. The CloudBrowser application used is shown in Figure 16. The clients send a click event object corresponding to a click on the DIV element, which triggers an event handler that modifies the DOM by setting the innerHTML property of an element, which triggers the necessary RPC requests to the client (in this case, a DOMNodeRemovedFromDocument followed by a DOMNodeInsertedIntoDocument call). The client measures the elapsed time between sending the event and receiving the resumeRendering RPC call, signifying the end of the DOM updates for that event. Once a client receives a response, it sends another event. This simulates a user that interacts with a page, waits to see the results of their action, and then interacts with the page again. To model a more realistic use case, we added a uniformly random delay between 1 and 5 seconds before the client submits the next request, modeling the frequency with which a human might interact with the application.

We measured the average latency for each client while increasing the number of connected clients (up to 1000, with a step size of 50). Each step was run with fresh CloudBrowser server and client processes. When clients are sending requests back-to-back, latency increases linearly by about 1.4ms per client for this particular interaction, which is shown in Figure 17. The different arrival process that results from a 1-5 second delay that models active human users results in the latency characteristics shown in Figure 18. These results show that for this benchmark, a single CPU can support up to 600 clients interacting with an equal number of virtual browser instances before the average delay exceeds 37 ms. These results were obtained over a LAN; a WAN deployment would incur added latency equal to the connection's TCP round-trip time, which primarily depends on the propagation delay introduced by geographical distance and the queuing delay due to network congestion. As a point of comparison, Keynote's Internet Health report considers latencies of less than 90ms between major US backbone providers "healthy" [21].

A well-known result from usability engineering research [25] holds that response times of less than 100ms feel instantaneous to the user, and that response times between 100ms and 1 second, while noticeable, allow uninterrupted workflows. Our results show that CloudBrowser is able to support an acceptable number of users economically for applications that benefit from the interaction style that motivates our approach. We expect that the use of multiple processes, as discussed in Section 4.6, could further increase the number of supported clients without adding significant latency, especially when connections are handed off to separate processes.

Client Engine	7.44KB
Socket.io Client	8.18KB
jQuery	29.09KB
Base HTML	771 bytes
Total	45.46KB

Table 4. Sizes of static bootstrap files.

Site	Snapshot Size	Raw HTML
twitter.github.com/bootstrap	276.03 KB	82.06 KB
news.ycombinator.com	54.60 KB	22.92 KB
ebay.com	123.87 KB	70.86 KB
reddit.com	169.57 KB	84.03 KB

Table 5. Comparing CloudBrowser snapshots with the equivalent HTML that would be sent to a regular browser.

5.3 Bandwidth Consumption

Although not as important as latency, bandwidth consumption is an important performance indicator, particularly in cloud environments. CloudBrowser consumes bandwidth during the bootstrapping process, to download an application's initial DOM snapshot, and for client and server engine RPCs. This section provides estimates for each of these components. We instrumented our server to count the number of bytes sent and received at the TCP level. We selected the web socket transport mode for the client/server communication and used Google Chrome (v16) as our client browser.

Table 4 shows the sizes of the bootstrap files sent to the client. The JavaScript code (our Client Engine, and the Socket.io Client and jQuery libraries we use) is minified and GZip-compressed. Their bandwidth consumption is small when compared to the amount of JavaScript code that is transferred to clients in contemporary AJAX applications, and they can be cached across different applications.

Table 5 compares the initial DOM snapshot sent to a CloudBrowser client compared to the equivalent HTML that would be sent to a regular browser when loading the same page for selected URLs. The record-based serialized representation of the DOM snapshot eliminates the need for a parser, but introduces an increase in size ranging from 1.7x to 3.4x when considering uncompressed sizes. As mentioned in Section 4.3, web sockets do not currently support GZip compression, although such an optimization is being considered [38]. GZip compression at the web socket layer would transparently reduce the required bandwidth.

The bandwidth consumed during server engine RPC calls is small, typically around 300 bytes for serialized events. A `setAttribute` call, if required, adds an additional 70-80 bytes. The bandwidth consumed for client engine calls depends on the number of DOM elements changed; we would

Test Suite	Pass	Total	% Passed
Core	1306	1309	99.77
Callbacks	418	418	100
Deferred	155	155	100
Support	28	38	73.68
Data	290	290	100
Queue	32	32	100
Attributes	453	473	95.77
Events	476	482	98.75
Selector (Sizzle)	310	314	98.72
Traversing	297	298	99.66
Manipulation	530	547	96.90
CSS	58	93	62.37
AJAX	329	349	94.26
Effects	367	452	81.19
Dimensions	61	83	74.49
Exports	1	1	100
Offset	N/A		
Selector (jQuery)	N/A		

Table 6. jQuery Test Suite Performance

expect a similar ratio when compared to the size of an equivalent HTML representation as for the initial DOM snapshot.

5.4 DOM Conformance

To measure the completeness of our virtual browser implementation, we have used the jQuery test suite (version 1.7.1), which includes 5828 tests that exercise all aspects of the jQuery JavaScript library. We run the tests in their unmodified QUnit test harness inside a virtual browser, which we visit to observe the results.

The results of running the jQuery test suite are shown in Table 6. The results show that our server document implementation is mature enough to pass a majority of the jQuery tests. This result, which reflects the implementation effort invested so far by us and the developer community supporting JSDOM, indicates that a complete server-side implementation of DOM specification is feasible with additional engineering effort. We use jQuery heavily for our administrative interface, which is written itself as a CloudBrowser application.

We also compared the time it took to run the jQuery test suite inside a virtual browser to the time it takes when run in the Google Chrome browser. We observed a slowdown of roughly 15x, indicating a tremendous potential for optimizations in the server document implementation.

6. Related Work

ZK [11] is a Java-based server-centric web framework that is in wide use. ZK applications are constructed using components, which are represented using the ZK User Interface Markup Language (ZUML). ZUML components are translated into HTML and CSS when a page is rendered. A client-side library handles synchronization between the client's view of and interaction with components, and their server-side representation. Our extensive experience deploying applications with ZK [16, 35] inspired the work on Cloud-Browser. Compared to CloudBrowser, ZK does not maintain a representation of the server document across HTTP requests. Every visit to a ZK page creates a new ZK desktop, at which point the developer must use session-state information to bring the UI back into the desired initial state, which may be far from the state it was in when the user last visited it. Unlike CloudBrowser, ZK aims to support layout attributes, but we have found that the complexity of its client engine leads to numerous layout and compatibility bugs developers must work around, particularly when the server-side document and the client-side document are not identical.

ItsNat [32] is a Java-based AJAX component framework similar to ZK, although it uses HTML instead of ZUML to express server documents, along with the Java W3C implementation. Unlike CloudBrowser, it also does not maintain the server document state across visits, and cannot make use of existing JavaScript libraries.

The Google Web Toolkit [19] allows the implementation of AJAX applications in Java that are compiled to JavaScript (or other targets). Like CloudBrowser, it provides an environment similar to that provided by desktop libraries, but focuses on the client-side only; communication with the server is outside its scope.

Fiz [26, 27] is a server-centric component-based AJAX framework that uses page properties to maintain component state on the server. Unlike in CloudBrowser, the server-side implementations of Fiz components can be balanced across multiple machines, allowing for horizontal scaling. Fiz does not present the abstraction of a server-side document to application developers, but it provides a way to build component-based web applications, and simplifies the development of additional components within its framework.

FlapJax [24] reduces the complexity of client-side JavaScript programming by introducing "event streams" and "behaviors" abstractions. Behaviors provide a data binding mechanism similar to Knockout.js's, and event streams provide a way to react to asynchronous events. The FlapJax primitives are intended to be used to simplify the client-side portion of an AJAX application, but the communication is still handled by the programmer. Since CloudBrowser applications can use existing client-side libraries, FlapJax could be used in conjunction with CloudBrowser to mitigate the error proneness of asynchronous programming; in fact, we were able to run a subset of the published Flapjax examples without changes.

Ripley [36] uses server-side browser emulation and event processing to ensure the integrity of client-side computation in AJAX applications. Ripley is integrated with Volta, a distributing compiler that partitions .NET applications be-

tween client and server. Similar to CloudBrowser, client-side events are sent to the browser where they are dispatched into a server-side DOM. Unlike CloudBrowser, the events are also dispatched into the client-side DOM. With Ripley, the resulting server-side DOM changes are used only to verify that the client has not sent malicious code or data to the server, and the client- and server-side DOMs are compared after event processing. For the example application studied, Ripley used around 1.3 MB of memory for each server-side DOM, which is similar to CloudBrowser's memory usage.

Crawljax [23] is web crawler that supports AJAX applications, which are commonly ignored by search engines due to their reliance on client-side computation. Crawljax explores AJAX applications using a programmatically controlled browser via the Selenium testing framework [4]. Unlike CloudBrowser, Selenium uses off-the-shelf browsers (IE, Chrome, Firefox) that render into a framebuffer display device that is not made visible to the user.

Opera Mini [3] is a mobile browser that optimizes the client experience by offloading browser rendering to a server. Compression algorithms are run on the rendered output from the server, reducing bandwidth requirements. While Opera Mini does use a server-side DOM representation, its goals are inherently different from CloudBrowser. Thus far, we have not tested CloudBrowser on mobile devices, but the popularity of Opera Mini shows that it may be possible to leverage server-side computation to provide a better mobile experience than traditional AJAX applications.

Our system shares ideas with traditional thin-client and remote display systems, going back to "dumb terminals" based on the X Window System [33]. Compared to these systems, CloudBrowser is unique in that it uses a markup document and differential update to it to describe the structure and evolution of the user interface that is rendered to the user.

7. Conclusion

This paper presented CloudBrowser, a server-centric web application framework for the development of rich Internet applications that keep both their application and their presentation state on the server. As a result, web application development is greatly simplified because both the stateless and the distributed nature of the web is hidden from the developer. By providing existing client-side programming environments such as HTML documents and JavaScript virtual machines on the server, existing libraries and skill sets can be reused, and translation overhead is minimized. We have developed a prototype environment and applications, which indicate that a server-centric approach is feasible and desirable for web applications in which users expect that most interactions with the user interface result in updates that are immediately stored "in the cloud," even across page visits.

8. Acknowledgements

This material is based upon work supported by the National Science Foundation under Grant No. CCF-0845830.

The source code for CloudBrowser is available at `https://github.com/brianmcd/cloudbrowser`. An application showcase is being created at `http://cloudbrowser.cs.vt.edu/`.

References

[1] Twitter Bootstrap JavaScript Demo. `http://twitter.github.com/bootstrap/javascript.html`.

[2] MySQL. `http://mysql.com`.

[3] Opera Mini Mobile Browser. `http://www.opera.com/mobile`.

[4] Selenium web browser automation. `http://seleniumhq.org`.

[5] SkyFire Mobile Browser. `http://www.skyfire.com/en/for-consumers/android/android`.

[6] Socket.io. `http://socket.io`.

[7] Yahoo! User Interface Library. `http://yuilibrary.com`.

[8] Document Object Model (DOM) Level 2 Events Specification. Technical report, Nov. 2000. URL `http://www.w3.org/TR/DOM-Level-2-Events/`.

[9] A. Adya, J. Howell, M. Theimer, W. J. Bolosky, and J. R. Douceur. Cooperative Task Management Without Manual Stack Management. In *Proceedings of the General Track of the annual conference on USENIX Annual Technical Conference*, pages 289–302, Berkeley, CA, USA, 2002. USENIX Association.

[10] S. Burbeck. Application Programming in Smalltalk-80: How to use Model-View-Controller (MVC). Technical report, University of Illinois in Urbana-Champaign (UIUC).

[11] H. Chen and R. Cheng. *ZK: Ajax without the Javascript Framework*. Apress, Berkely, CA, USA, 2007.

[12] D. Crockford. Json. `http://www.json.org`.

[13] G. Czajkowski and L. Daynès. Multitasking without compromise: a virtual machine evolution. *SIGPLAN Not.*, 36(11): 125–138, Oct. 2001. doi: 10.1145/504311.504292.

[14] R. Dahl. Node.js. `http://nodejs.org`.

[15] S. Depold. Sequelize. `http://sequelizejs.com`.

[16] S. H. Edwards and G. Back. Bringing creative web 2.0 programming into CS1: conference workshop. *J. Comput. Sci. Coll.*, 26(3):54–55, Jan. 2011.

[17] E. Gamma, R. Helm, R. Johnson, and J. Vlissides. *Design Patterns: Elements of Reusable Object-Oriented Software*. Addison-Wesley, 1994.

[18] J. Garrett. AJAX: A new approach to web applications. `http://www.adaptivepath.com/ideas/ajax-new-approach-web-applications`, 2005.

[19] Google, Inc. Google web toolkit (gwt). `http://code.google.com/webtoolkit/`.

[20] E. Insua. JSDOM. `http://jsdom.org`.

[21] Keynote Systems, Inc. Internet health report. `http://www.internetpulse.net/`.

[22] G. Kiczales, J. Lamping, A. Mendhekar, C. Maeda, C. Lopes, J.-M. Loingtier, and J. Irwin. Aspect-oriented programming. In *ECOOP'97 Object-Oriented Programming*, volume 1241, pages 220–242. Springer Berlin / Heidelberg, Berlin/Heidelberg, 1997. doi: 10.1007/BFb0053381.

[23] A. Mesbah, A. van Deursen, and S. Lenselink. Crawling Ajax-Based Web Applications through Dynamic Analysis of User Interface State Changes. *ACM Trans. Web*, 6(1), Mar. 2012. doi: 10.1145/2109205.2109208.

[24] L. A. Meyerovich, A. Guha, J. Baskin, G. H. Cooper, M. Greenberg, A. Bromfield, and S. Krishnamurthi. Flapjax: a programming language for Ajax applications. In *Proceedings of the 24th ACM SIGPLAN conference on Object oriented programming systems languages and applications*, OOPSLA '09, pages 1–20. ACM, 2009. doi: 10.1145/1640089.1640091.

[25] J. Nielsen. *Usability Engineering*. Morgan Kaufmann, 1st edition, Sept. 1993. ISBN 9780125184069.

[26] J. Ousterhout. Fiz: A component framework for web applications. Technical report, Dep. of CS, Stanford University, 2009.

[27] J. Ousterhout and E. Stratmann. Managing state for Ajax-driven web components. In *Proceedings of the 2010 USENIX conference on Web application development*, WebApps'10, page 7, Berkeley, CA, USA, 2010. USENIX Association.

[28] D. Pariag, T. Brecht, A. Harji, P. Buhr, A. Shukla, and D. R. Cheriton. Comparing the performance of web server architectures. *SIGOPS Oper. Syst. Rev.*, 41(3):231–243, Mar. 2007. doi: 10.1145/1272998.1273021.

[29] W. Reese. Nginx: the high-performance web server and reverse proxy. *Linux J.*, 2008(173), Sept. 2008.

[30] J. Resig. jQuery. `http://jquery.com`.

[31] S. Sanderson. Knockout. `http://knockoutjs.com`.

[32] J. M. A. Santamaria. ItsNat: Natural AJAX. component based Java web application framework. `http://itsnat.sourceforge.net`.

[33] R. W. Scheifler and J. Gettys. The X window system. *ACM Trans. Graph.*, 5(2):79–109, Apr. 1986. doi: 10.1145/22949.24053.

[34] E. Stratmann, J. Ousterhout, and S. Madan. Integrating long polling with an MVC framework. In *Proceedings of the 2nd USENIX conference on Web application development*, WebApps'11, page 10. USENIX Association, 2011.

[35] E. Tilevich and G. Back. "Program, enhance thyself!": demand-driven pattern-oriented program enhancement. In *Proceedings of the 7th international conference on Aspect-oriented software development*, AOSD '08, pages 13–24, New York, NY, USA, 2008. ACM. doi: 10.1145/1353482.1353485.

[36] K. Vikram, A. Prateek, and B. Livshits. Ripley: automatically securing web 2.0 applications through replicated execution. In *Proceedings of the 16th ACM conference on Computer and communications security*, CCS '09, pages 173–186, New York, NY, USA, 2009. ACM. doi: 10.1145/1653662.1653685.

[37] M. Welsh, D. Culler, and E. Brewer. SEDA: an architecture for well-conditioned, scalable internet services. In *Proceedings of the eighteenth ACM symposium on Operating systems principles*, volume 35 of *SOSP '01*, pages 230–243, New York, NY, USA, Dec. 2001. ACM. doi: 10.1145/502034.502057.

[38] T. Yoshino. WebSocket Per-frame DEFLATE Extension. Technical Report draft-tyoshino-hybi-websocket-perframe-deflate-04.txt, IETF Secretariat, Fremont, CA, USA, Aug. 2011. URL `http://www.rfc-editor.org/internet-drafts/ draft-tyoshino-hybi-websocket-perframe-deflate-04. txt`.

SPLASH 2012 Wavefront
Experience Papers

Welcome to the SPLASH 2012 Wavefront Experience track. SPLASH is a place to talk about software technology – and our Wavefront Experience presenters have a lot to talk about.

Wavefront Experience papers may not be as "academic" as some conference papers, but there is a lot to learn from practical experiences. Experience reports are a blend of science and engineering: some innovative ideas used in a practical setting. Each experience report is filled hard-won ideas, insights, and lessons. The experiences are built on some great ideas from the research world, and many of the ideas have been the subject of research papers in the OOPSLA and Onward tracks in previous years. For all of these technologies, we can honestly say "the future is now."

Our presenters are creative people from industry and academia who had a problem to solve, they want to share what they learned, and they hope to get you to think differently about your own problems. There are two sessions of experience papers in this year's conference. *Modeling and Estimation* is the theme of the first session, which highlights some useful practices and tools for data modeling, model driven engineering, and project planning. The second session, *Cloud Development and Cloud Deployment*, explores some of the challenges that many developers and data center managers are facing in a cloud-obsessed world.

We encourage you to participate: talk to the experience report authors, think about how you could apply some of their lessons, share some of your own thoughts with us, and think about submitting an experience report paper at a future SPLASH conference!

Dennis Mancl
Alcatel-Lucent

Is Text Search an Effective Approach for Fault Localization: A Practitioners Perspective

Vibha Singhal Sinha, Senthil Mani and Debdoot Mukherjee

IBM Research – New Delhi, India

{vibha.sinha, sentmani, debdomuk}@in.ibm.com

Abstract

There has been widespread interest in both academia and industry around techniques to help in fault localization. Much of this work leverages static or dynamic code analysis and hence is constrained by the programming language used or presence of test cases. In order to provide more generically applicable techniques, recent work has focused on devising text search based approaches that recommend source files which a developer can modify to fix a bug. Text search may be used for fault localization in either of the following ways. We can search a repository of past bugs with the bug description to find similar bugs and recommend the source files that were modified to fix those bugs. Alternately, we can directly search the code repository to find source files that share words with the bug report text. Few interesting questions come to mind when we consider applying these text-based search techniques in real projects. For example, would searching on past fixed bugs yield better results than searching on code? What is the accuracy one can expect? Would giving preference to code words in the bug report better the search results? In this paper, we apply variants of text-search on four open source projects and compare the impact of different design considerations on search efficacy.

Categories and Subject Descriptors   D.2.5 [*Testing and Debugging*]: [Debugging aids]

General Terms   Experimentation,Measurement

Keywords   Empirical Study, Bug-Solving

1. Introduction

Identifying buggy code fragments can be particularly time-consuming and tedious; statistics suggest that over half of the total time in any software project is spent in locating and fixing bugs [16, 19]. To address this problem, many automated fault-localization techniques based on static and dynamic program analyses have been developed. The most widely researched approach in the area is based on program slicing (e.g., [3], [4], [10], [14]); other approaches include statistical debugging (e.g., [7, 13, 15]) and delta debugging [23, 24].

A different class of debugging techniques, based on text analysis, uses the text in the bug report to recommend source files that potentially need to be fixed. Given the bug report for a new bug, one may search the project's bug repository for similar bugs resolved in the past to get a better understanding of the problem and a potential resolution of the bug-at-hand (e.g., [5, 8]). If source files were fixed to resolve similar bugs, then these may be recommended for the new bug as well. Yet another way to apply text-search is to directly search on the code repository with the text of the bug report taken as a query (e.g., [1, 11, 20]). The underlying principle here is that the bug report often contains references to code terms—class names, function names, variables etc. Also, comments in the code are written as free flowing text, so it is likely that we may find common words between bug reports and code comments.

The text-search based approaches can be applied more generically than the rigorous program analysis techniques since they are not restricted by the programming language used in the application or limited by the presence of test cases to reproduce the fault. However, they may suffer in case: (1) there is a low overlap between the vocabulary of the bug report used to query and that of the search repository. Enslen et. al. [2] suggest a way to increase vocabulary overlap between bug reports and code through *identifier splitting*, whereby all code terms are converted to their componentized words. For example, the code word *TextfieldTool* would be translated to three words: *text, field, tool*. (2) the bug repository does not record linkages to code fixes necessary to resolve bugs. However, increasingly project teams are realizing the benefits of preserving this linkage and adopting bug management systems such as Jira or Rational Team Concert, which allow linkage with version management repository. In these tools, the developer can link a bug with the code change set that was committed in the version management system to fix the bug.

Most of the existing work in applying text-search based techniques has been evaluated on small subjects only. In *DebugAdvisor* [5], the authors use a proprietary Microsoft application as their subject and search on a repository of past bugs. They evaluated the precision and recall of search for 50 bug queries. Rao and Kak [20] used the iBUGs dataset (291 bugs), which primarily has bugs from AspectJ and Rhino. They search on source code, which is pre-processed using identifier splitting. Others [1, 18] have reported results of searching on the code repositories of Mozilla, Eclipse, Rhino and JEdit. However, the number of bugs used in these evaluations are very low—5 to 15 bugs. Prior art [1, 11, 20] studies the search performance of different language models (e.g., Unigram, Vector Space Model, Latent Semantic Indexing) in great depth. In fact, Rao and Kak [20] empirically study (using a test suite of 291 bugs) that simple language models such as VSM provide equivalent to the more complex models such as LDA.

One of the biggest drawbacks of the existing works is that because of the small test suite size, it is difficult to make a judgment on general applicability of the technique. For example, in [1], the authors reported when they searched for 3 Eclipse bugs on the code repository they were able to find a correct file recommendation in top 2 search results. They used the LDA language model for search and claimed that it worked better than LSI, which returned the correct match for each of these three bugs in top 7 search results. However, when we applied VSM model on 815 bugs from a sub-project in Eclipse, we found a correct file returned only for 10% (80) bugs in the top 7 results. Considering [20] already showed that VSM provides equivalent efficacy to LDA, this makes us believe that the 3 eclipse bugs evaluated in [1] were not indicative of the general population of bugs. The aim of this paper, is to provide practitioners a truer picture of both lower and upper bound efficacies of text search, by doing an empirical study on large number of bugs from multiple subjects.

Another gap in the existing published literature is that none of the efforts perform a comparative study on the two variants of the search approach–*searching on past bugs* and *searching on code*. Also, no prior work discusses the effect of pre-processing techniques (e.g., identifier splitting) or bug characteristics (e.g. size of bug, number of files modified to fix the bug etc) on the effectiveness of the text search recommendations.

In this paper, we address these issues through an extensive empirical study of four large open-source projects - *BIRT, Eclipse-Datatools, Hadoop and Derby*. Overall, we have a test data-set comprising of 1177 bugs. Our goal is to establish statistically grounded empirical evidence about the impact of different design criteria (for the search approach) on the productiveness of search-based recommen-dations for bug solving. We believe that such a study is necessary to make the idea of using text-search for bug solving more widely acceptable. It also helps us better understand the available design options in terms of their benefits and tradeoffs. Our empirical study aims to study the following.

- We compare the efficacy of three techniques, each of which search over a different kind of search repository - (1) the collection of all bugs resolved in the past, (2) the code base, and (3) a version of the code base processed through identifier splitting. In all the three cases, the complete text of the bug report, comprising of the title and the description, is taken as a query. We determine whether the accuracies of these techniques are better than chance and whether they are similar or complementary in terms of their recommendations. We find that there is no clear winner between *searching on code* and *searching on past bugs*. When the search result set size is taken to be 5, the precision varies from 4% to 13% across our four subjects while searching over bug repository versus 4% to 5% while searching over code. For comparing different techniques, we introduce a new metric called *Bug Coverage* defined as the percentage of bugs where the approach returns at least one correct file match for a given search result size. The bug coverage varies from 30% to 54% across our subjects.

- We analyze the possibility of combining the results of the three techniques to make more effective recommendations, more consistently. Athough, the efficacy of an average search over past bug repositories is similar to that over code repositories, we find that the techniques are complementary because one technique may score over another for certain bugs, and the other may prove to be superior in certain other cases. We experiment with different ways to combine the search results from these techniques in order to form a better final result set (improvement in bug coverage varying between 1% and 46%).

- We study the impact of various query construction strategies (boost to title words, code terms etc.) on search performance. We find that giving a preference to words in the title improves the bug coverage from 1.6% to 7.8% across our subjects for a search result size of 5. Further, we note the correlation between coverage and other physical features of a bug report such as total number of words in a bug report, number of code words and title words.

The main contributions of the paper are: (1) An empirical evaluation of text-search based fault localization on four open source projects. We compare various search design criteria of index creation and query construction. (2) A novel way of combining *search-over-bug-history* and *search-over-code-base*, that achieves greater bug coverage than the individual techniques themselves. (3) An evaluation of whether different bug features correlate with search efficacy.

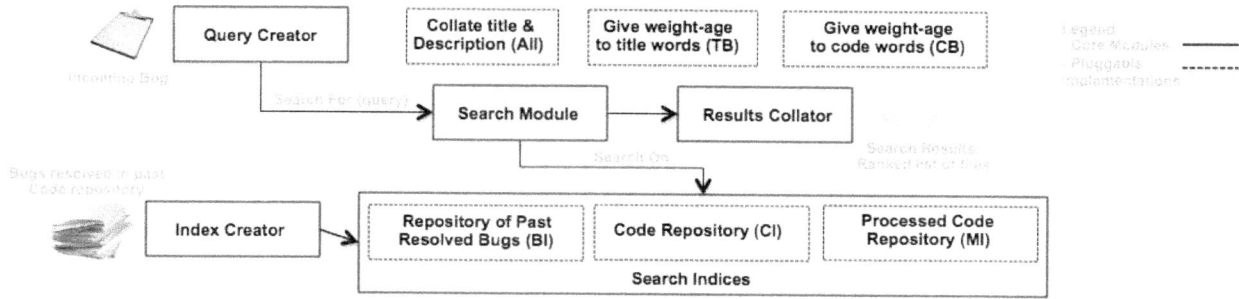

Figure 1. Search Approach. The framework contains four core modules: (1) Query Creator, (2) Index Creator, (3) Search Module, (4) Results Collator. The implementations of these modules is pluggable. A module can have more than one implementation depending on the choice of design considerations.

Rest of the paper is organized as follows. In the next section, we outline the search framework we developed for our experimentation. In Section 3, we present the results of empirical evaluation of the various search considerations on four open source projects. Section 4 outlines the related work in the area of debugging and fault localization. Finally, in Section 5 we summarize our findings.

2. Approach

Figure 1 outlines the search framework implemented for our evaluation of the different text-search methods that recommend relevant source files for an incoming bug. It is composed of: (1) an *index creator* with a pluggable search repository, which processes *documents* to create *indices* [17] that make searching easier[1]; (2) a *query creator*, which processes the text in the incoming bug report to form a query with pluggable design variant; (3) a *search module*, which fetches documents from the indices that are similar to the query. When searching over the code base, the source files returned in the set of search results can be the recommendations from our system. However, a search over the corpus of bug reports yields a set of bug reports and the recommendations are the source files associated with these bug reports. (4) a *result collator*, which combines the results returned from the different repositories to increase the relevance of recommendations. We choose the Vector Space Model (VSM) to design our search system. Rao and Kak [20] have shown that VSM works no worse than other models of information retrieval (e.g., Latent Semantic Indexing, Latent Dirichlet Allocation) that have greater sophistication.

Index Creation: We experiment with three kinds of indices: (1) *Bug Index (BI)* indexes terms extracted from past bug reports; (2) *Code Index (CI)* indexes the source code files (taken as-is); and (3) *Meta Index (MI)* indexes a processed version of the source files–making them closer to nat-

ural language text. In *MI*, we store documents created from the *code terms* and comments present in each source file. The *code terms* include names of packages, classes, class variables, methods, formal arguments and method variables. Further, *identifier splitting* [20] is applied to each code term in order to convert the *term* to its constituent words. For example, the code term *getName* is translated to *get* and *name*, and the code term *com.xxx.foo.TestClass* is translated to the words *com, xxx, foo, test* and *class*. The splitting is done by separating words based on camel case rules. Note that code terms might also occur as part of comment text and these are not split. The extracted code terms are also stored separately as the *code dictionary*, which is later used during the query creation phase.

Query Creation: We create a query vector from the terms present in the title and description of the bug report. As a pre-processing step, we remove the stops words such as *to, is, and* etc and *Java* keywords such as *java, package, class* etc. Then, we compute TF-IDF scores for all query terms and create the query-vector. This is our first querying strategy - *All (A)*. For fine tuning search performance, we employ two more querying strategies, *Code Boost (CB)* and *Title Boost (TB)*. In the *CB* querying technique, each term in the query is matched against the code dictionary. The weight of matching terms is given a boost relative to others. Similarly, in *TB*, we update the query vectors by increasing the weight of terms that come from the bug title.

Search : We use Apache Lucene's implementation of a VSM based full text search engine to host our index creation and query creation strategies. We search each of our indexed repositories *CI, MI* and *BI* separately by applying the querying strategies *A, CB* and *TB*. For a given query vector, Lucene returns a similarity score for every document in the chosen index. The scores indicate a relevance rank of the document with respect to the query. For each query that is run over *CI* and *MI*, the top *X* search results are returned as recommendations. However in case of *BI*, the search results

---

[1] A *document* is any text file in the repository being searched. In our case, the repository may be a code base (either as-is or processed) or a collection of past bugs. An index is a mapping of words (a.k.a terms) to the locations in the documents where they are present.

Subjects	Releases	Total # of Bugs	# of Bugs in test-set	# of Files in release	# of Bugs in repository
Birt	2.5.0	1777	815	6351	
	2.5.1			6524	
	2.5.2			6633	21064
Datatools	1.0	1130	93	1925	
	1.5			2379	
	1.6			2968	2698
Derby	10.5.3.0	242	136	1687	
	10.8.1.2			1742	3492
Hadoop	0.20.0	191	133	837	
	0.21.0			1328	3879

Table 1. Details of the subjects used for our experiments

are bug reports; so we return all the source files fixed for the top X similar bugs as our recommendations[2]

Result Collation : This module combines the results returned from searching different repositories. The objective is to combine the results optimally to increase the number of bugs for which we return at least one correct recommendation without increasing the size of the recommendation set. We present different heuristics to combine the recommendations in Section 3.3.2.

3. Experiments

We evaluate the different search indices and querying strategies described in Section 2 on four open source projects. In this section, we describe the experimental subjects and the method used in our study. Next, we present the empirical results and analyze them in order to answer the following research questions:

- **RQ1 (Effectiveness)**: How does searching on —Bug Index (BI), Code Index (CI) and Meta Index (MI), fare in terms of the effectiveness of the recommendations produced by them? Are they just as good as chance or any better? Also, how do they compare with one another?

- **RQ2 (Combination)**: How can we combine the sets of recommendations from the three search indexes to increase the bug coverage without sacrificing the accuracy of the resultant recommendation set (as measured by F1-score)?

- **RQ3 (Feature Impact)**: How do different aspects of the source code and the bugs available in a project impact the effectiveness of search?

3.1 Experimental Data & Setup

We select our experimental data-set from four open source projects, *Birt* [3] and *Datatools*[4] of Eclipse and *Derby*[5] and

---

[2] If the search results return a bug, which in turn has greater than 10 files modified, we do not include any files from that bug in our search results. This was done to remove any un-toward positive bias in calculating efficacy of BI.

[3] http://www.eclipse.org/birt/phoenix/

[4] http://www.eclipse.org/datatools/

[5] http://db.apache.org/derby/

Hadoop[6] of Apache. For each of these projects, we obtain the list of fixed bugs from its bug management system and code for those releases that record a high number of the bugs relative to the project.

To create the experiment oracle (or ground truth), we need to know the source files that were modified to fix the bugs. The Apache based projects use a bug management system called *JIRA*[7], which keeps a record of the files fixed to resolve a bug. For the Eclipse projects, we trace the linkages from bugs to the buggy source files by mining their version management systems. We study the version logs to define regex patterns that are able to detect bug identifiers mentioned as part of comments inserted during code commits (an approach followed in [8]); e.g, if the commit-comment contains "#234561" or "Bug-234561", then it indicates that the code change is related to the bug – 234561.

For each of the four subjects, we prepare a test-set such that it consists of only those bugs that are reported against one of our chosen releases and has at least one source file associated with them. Table 3 gives details for each subject—the selected code releases, the total number of bugs reported for those releases, the number of bugs selected from total numbers of bugs available to create the test set, the total number of *java* files available per release and the total number of fixed bugs in the project's bug repository. The total number of bugs in our test-set for our experiments across all four subjects is 1177 bugs. This is 35% of the total bugs available for the subjects across the 10 releases that we consider (column (2) of Table 3). We ignore the remaining 65% as either they were not associated with any changes to source (.java) files (for JIRA based bugs) or we were not able to infer the association (for Eclipse projects bugs). However, 1177 bugs can be considered to be a significantly large test data set in comparison to the same for prior work [1, 5, 18, 20]. For each subject, the size of the test-data is 3-4% of its corresponding bug repository.

Further, we index all bugs in the subject's bug repository to create three different search indices –BI, CI and MI (as explained in Section 2). For each bug in the test-set for the subject, we create three different queries following the strategies—A, CB and TB.

Depending on the research question to be answered, we execute different *search techniques*—combinations of an indexing technique and a querying strategy. For example, the search technique {MI:TB} means applying the querying strategy TB to search the index MI. The source files returned in the recommendation sets produced by a search technique are matched against the actual fixed files (ground truth) in order to compute the following measures:

- *Bug Coverage:* The percentage of bugs in the test set for which the search returns at least one file in the recom-

---

[6] http://hadoop.apache.org/

[7] http://www.atlassian.com/software/jira/

mendation (B_T) set matching the ground truth.

$$BC = \frac{B_T}{n} * 100 \qquad (1)$$

where n is number of bugs in the test data set.

This metric is same as the "Rank" metric used in [1, 20] which is defined as, the number of queries/bugs for which the relevant source files are retrieved with ranks rlow $<=$ R $<=$ rhigh where rlow $= 1$ and rhigh is configurable. We vary rhigh from 1 to 30, for the purposes of our experiments.

- *Average Precision, Recall and F1-Score:* For each bug in the test set, we calculate the traditional measures of precision, recall and F1-score.

As part of answering **RQ1** in Section 3.2.1 we discuss why the traditional measures of precision and recall are not good to compare the efficacy of the search techniques under investigation.

3.2 Effectiveness of the Indexing Techniques

In this study, we try to answer **RQ1** by evaluating the effectiveness of the three search techniques {MI:A}, {CI:A} and {BI:A}. First, we present and discuss the efficacy of the three search techniques through the metrics P_A, R_A, $F1-Score_A$ and BC. Then, we statistically test whether the techniques are any better than chance.

3.2.1 Efficacy of the Search Techniques

For each bug in the test-set we perform the search over the indices 10 times, varying the size of the search results from 1 through 30. Figure 2 plots the average precision (P_A), recall (R_A) and F1-Score ($F1 - Score_A$) as line graphs across search techniques MI:A, BI:A and CI:A. Graphs in each columns plot the metrics P_A, R_A and $F1 - Score_A$ while each row represents these metrics calculated for each search technique.

In Figure 2, we observe that, across all subjects and search techniques, the average precision decreases and recall increases with increase in the size of the search result set. In contrast, the F-Score graphs shows a slight increase early on and then a steady decline. Beyond the search result size of 3, the precision decreases drastically as we return more results and the increase in recall does not compensate enough for the drop in precision. Usually, there are not too many files fixed in a bug (the mean being around 3 files per bug), so a large number of results are necessarily spurious when the size of the search results increases beyond a point. Interestingly, precision and recall for *Hadoop* are the highest amongst all techniques upto a search result size of 5. The F1-Score increases slightly as we move from a search result size of 1 to 3 and then drops steadily for all subjects.

The scale of the graphs indicate that the maximum values for precision, recall and F1-Score, across all subjects and

techniques, are 0.3, 0.6 and 0.28 respectively. **The low increase in bug level recall indicates that text-search based techniques are not effective when the aim is to find all or most of the files to be modified for a bug.** Based on these observations about precision and recall, it seems that these are not good metrics to compare efficacy of various search techniques because all the numbers are very low. From an end user perspective, given a bug, text search should be used to find a file that can start the debugging investigation. So even if the search is able to return one correct result, it should be considered useful. Hence, we have chosen to use *Bug Coverage* as a comparison metric in rest of the paper.

Figure 3 plots the bug coverage as line graphs for each subject across the different sizes of search results and search techniques. We observe that, unlike F-Score, the values for bug coverage, across all subjects and techniques, increase with increase in the search result set size. For a maximum search result size of 30, at least one of the search techniques attains a minimum bug coverage of 55% for all the subjects. All the three techniques perform equally well for *Hadoop* with minimum bug coverage of 30% to a maximum of 70% across various search result sizes. In fact, *Hadoop* has similar bug coverage as an industrial project analyzed in [5], which reports a coverage of 68%. For *Birt*, searching over past bugs (*BI:A*) clearly outperformed the other two search techniques across all search result sizes. Interestingly, for *Datatools* the bug coverage remained constant beyond the search result size of 5 for the technique *BI:A*. A similar pattern is also observed in precision, recall and F1-Score for *Datatools* in Figure 2.

If we compare the different search techniques, *BI:A* and *CI:A* work better than *MI:A* across all our subjects. The extra effort in performing identifier splitting and other processing on actual code repository does not seem to yield any extra benefits as evident from the bug coverage observed for our subjects. Based on these results, for our subjects, none of the search techniques emerge as a clear winner (shown statistically in the later part of this section). However, the nature of the subject does impact the effectiveness of text-based search as observed for *Hadoop*.

3.2.2 Are the techniques any better than chance?

To objectively quantify that the search techniques are significantly better than chance, we compared their efficacy with that of a user who randomly selects source files from the code repository as the files to be fixed to resolve a bug. Suppose, there were n files in the repository when a bug was reported and f files were actually fixed to resolve the bug. Then, the hypergeometric distribution gives the probability, p, of getting at least x files that require a fix by choosing k files at random from the repository. [8]

---

[8] Think of the code repository as a bin of black and white balls, where the files that need fix for a bug resolution are considered to be white balls; rest

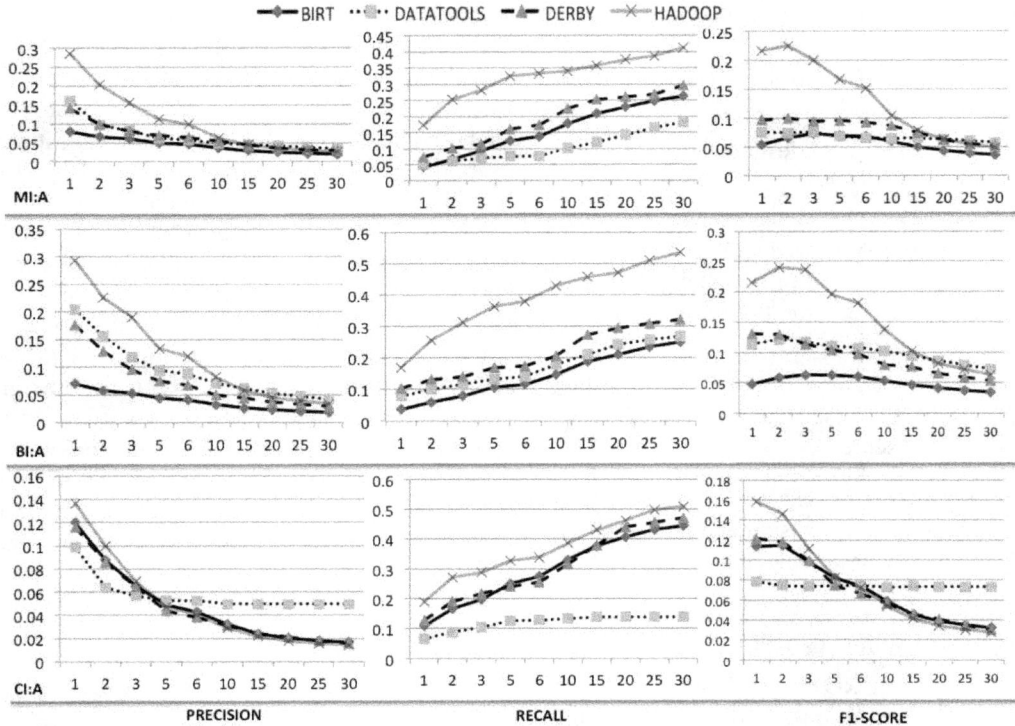

Figure 2. Average P_A (left), R_A (middle), and $F1 - Score_A$ (right) for MI:A, CI:A and BI:A across all subjects and search result sizes. X axis represents 10 iterations of the experiment with varying search result sizes. Y-axis represents the metrics value. Each line plots the scores across search result size for each subject.

$$p = 1 - \sum_{i=0}^{x-1} \frac{{}^{f}C_i \, {}^{n-f}C_{k-i}}{{}^{n}C_k}$$

Now, if a search technique returns x correct files in a set of k search results shown for a bug, then p gives the probability that one can get same or better results by drawing k files purely through chance. Thus, we use p (*p-value*) to test the null-hypothesis that a search technique is no better than chance. Further, we conduct the hypothesis test for all bugs (taken as queries) in our subject, which amounts to a case of multiple testing of hypotheses. To maintain an overall False Discovery Rate (FDR) of below 0.05, we lower the individual p-values during the testings by the Benjamini-Hochberg adjustment [6].

We tested the null-hypothesis for every bug in all our subjects separately for each of the three search techniques *BI:A*, *CI:A* and *MI:A*. Table 3.2.2 shows the percentage of bugs that recorded a p-value of less than 0.05 and that passed the FDR test for a search result size of 5. In general, the numbers look very close to that of bug coverage; indicating that even if one correct result is returned for a bug then the result is usually significant. Again, a high percentage of search results that are significant pass the FDR test too.

Datatools is an exception where many of adjusted p-values miss the cut-off—in case of *MI:A*, almost half the cases that pass the significance test at 0.05 end up failing the FDR test. We traced the reason behind higher p-values to the fact that bugs in *Datatools* have higher number of files (f) associated with them. In two bugs as many as 491 files were found to be fixed. On an average across the subjects *Birt*, *Datatools* and *Derby*, 32% of the bugs analyzed for *BI:A*, 25% for *CI:A* and 21% for *MI:A* passed the significance test with $p < 0.05$. However for *Hadoop*, an average of 60% of bug reports passed across all techniques. Also, we record the average number of files per subject that can make the significance test fail (p = 0.05), in other words the number of files in the repository when the techniques break even with chance. The numbers range from 66 in *Derby* (*MI:A*) to 158 in *Datatools* (*CI:A*); suggesting that the techniques may not be applicable when the repository contains any lesser files.

Summary for RQ1

- No single search technique emerges as a clear winner.

- Size of code repository should be taken into account when deciding whether to use text search for fault localization or not. Break even score should be calculated. If bug triaging is already happening at a module level, then number of files in module should be considered to calculate break even.

- None of the search variants returns search recommendations with high precision, recall or bug coverage numbers and hence text search need to be applied in projects with realistic expectations.

---

of the files are black balls. Now, the hypergeometric distribution gives the probability of choosing white balls without replacement.

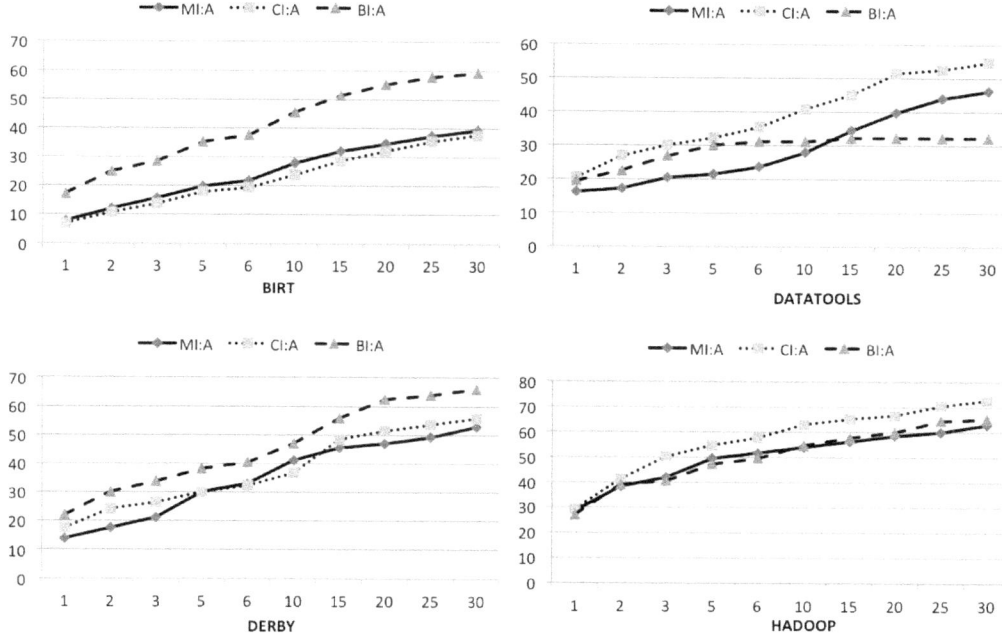

Figure 3. Bug Coverage for search techniques MI:A, BI:A and CI:A across the four subjects and search result sizes. X axis represents the various search result size. Y-axis represents BC (%). Each line plots the BC across search results for a given search technique.

Subject	BI:A		CI:A		MI:A	
	< 0.05	FDR	< 0.05	FDR	< 0.05	FDR
Birt	35.1	35	19.75	19.14	17.9	17.4
Datatools	30.1	23.6	31.18	20.43	20.43	9.67
Derby	37.5	34.5	30.1	28.6	29.4	26.5
Hadoop	47.4	41.4	54.9	51.1	41.6	41.4

Table 2. Percentage of Search Results that passed the significance test (p < 0.05) and the FDR test

Subjects	MI:A & CI:A	MI:A & BI:A	CI:A & BI:A	MI:A & CI:A & BI:A
Birt	0.67	0.17	0.14	0.30
Datatools	0.67	-0.01	0.09	0.25
Derby	0.70	0.26	0.12	0.35
Hadoop	0.83	0.36	0.34	0.51

Table 3. Kappa Numbers for Search Result Size - 5

3.3 Combining Search Techniques

In this study, we try to combine the results from the different search techniques evaluated in the previous subsection (what we call *base techniques* hereafter), in order to output more effective sets of recommendations; and hence answer **RQ2**. First, we check whether the results of the techniques are subsumed in one another. If so, then combining them may not be interesting at all. However, if the techniques turn out to be complementary, then we can design methods that synthesize a better set of recommendations by drawing from the results of the base techniques.

3.3.1 Kappa Analysis

For each subject, we perform Fleiss' Kappa [12] analysis to measure the degree of agreement (κ) amongst the three base techniques. Fleiss' κ is a statistical measure of inter-rater agreement or inter-annotator agreement for qualitative (categorical) items for any number of raters / annotators.

Each of our techniques map to an annotator (rater) and the categories are boolean–*Yes* indicates that the technique *cov-*

Subjects	Max (MI:A, CI:A, BI:A)	Combination			
		Rank Score	Norm Score	Aggregate Score	Sample Score
Birt	287	302	269	210	265
Datatools	30	44	40	32	42
Derby	52	58	57	47	60
Hadoop	73	74	78	70	76

Table 4. Comparison of Bug Coverage values between base and combination of techniques for search result size 5

ers the bug (i.e., there is atleast one correct result returned), and *No* indicates that the technique does not cover the bug. With such an analogy, we setup a rater problem, where a technique (rater) rates a bug as *Yes* or *No*. Next, we compute the Kappa measure, κ, as:

$$\kappa = \frac{\bar{P} - \bar{P}_e}{1 - \bar{P}_e} \tag{2}$$

where $\bar{P} - \bar{P}_e$ gives the degree of agreement actually achieved above chance and $1 - \bar{P}_e$ gives the degree of agreement that is attainable above chance. $\kappa = 1$ indicates complete agreement between the raters (techniques) and $\kappa <= 0$ points to no agreement. For further details on how these are calculated please refer to [12].

As per the Kappa statistics (listed in Table 3.3.1), *MI:A* and *CI:A* turn out to be quite similar with at least 60% agreement. This is intuitive as both their indices are created from code files. Also, code comments are common in both code based index and meta index. However, both these techniques exhibit a very low rate of agreement with *BI:A*; 36% in the best case and -0.01% in the worst.

This analysis shows that bug based techniques and code or meta based techniques are significantly different from each other in terms of bugs that they address effectively. Hence, there lies a possibility improving the overall effectiveness of text-search (bug coverage) based fault localization by suitably combining these distinct techniques.

3.3.2 Heuristics for Combining Search Techniques

The aim behind combining results from the different search techniques is to improve the bug coverage. We apply the following heuristics to synthesize stronger recommendation sets by choosing from the results of the base techniques. (We evaluated these heuristics for all search result set sizes, but we present the data only for a search result size of 5 as a similar trend is observed for all other sizes.)

- *Rank based synthesis on score (RankScore)*: We rank all the search results across the three base techniques on the basis of their search similarity scores and choose the top X search results from this ranked set.

- *Rank based synthesis on normalized score (*NormScore*)*: Same as the above heuristic, the only difference being that the search scores are normalized (as a fraction of the maximum score returned by its query) before they are used for ranking.

- *Rank based synthesis on aggregate score (*AggregateScore*)*: For each file returned by a query, we sum up the similarity scores assigned to it by the different techniques. Next, we return the top X results from a ranked list prepared on the basis of such an aggregate score.

- *Sampling (*Sample*)*: We sample X search results for every query by picking the top 2*(X/5) search results from the results of {*BI:A*} and {*CI:A*}, and the remaining X/5 results from {*BI:A*}. Since, {*BI:A*} and {*CI:A*} are the most complementary techniques (from Kappa Statistics), we sample a higher number of results from them–striving for greater diversity in the results.

Table 4 presents the average bug coverage of the recommendations when we apply the different heuristics to combine search results. *RankScore* technique works better than the best of the individual techniques for all four subjects. *NormScore* and *SampleScore* techniques work better in most cases except for *Birt*. *AggregateScore* is the worst performing heuristic across all subjects and search result size.

The improvement in bug coverage due to *RankScore* ranges from 1% (*Hadoop*) to 46% (*Datatools*).

Summary for RQ2

- *Search over code repository* and *Search over past bug repository* are complementary. So, they can be combined to increase the bug coverage.
- *RankScore* heuristic provides consistent improvement in bug coverage and is a feasible approach for combining search results stemming from different search techniques.

3.4 Impact of bug and code features on search techniques

In this study we explore the impact of different aspects of bug and code on our text-search system in order to answer **RQ3**. First, we evaluate whether biasing terms during query construction improves the efficacy of search. Then, we inspect how the search performance is impacted by different physical aspects of bug reports (size, number of code terms etc.) and source code (lines of code, length of comments etc.). Finally, we study the impact of external factors such as the vocabulary overlap between bug queries and search indices, and the number of files fixed per bug.

3.4.1 Biasing terms during query construction

The TF-IDF scheme assigns a weight to a term (or word) such that it indicates the relative importance of the term in a document or a query in the context of the search index. However, when the number of words in a query becomes large, it may so happen that certain key terms do not get adequately high weights in the query vector. In such a scenario, if we have a good idea about the words in the bug report that may be important from a search perspective, then we can adjust the default TF-IDF weights in a query vector to direct greater focus on those *keywords*.

Table 3.4.1 shows the size of queries created (in base techniques) for each of our subjects–*low*, *high*, and *mean*. It also lists the average number of words in the title—title-words, and the average number of code terms present in these queries—code-words. Note, that we remove the stop words and Java specific keywords before calculating the queries. The mean query sizes vary from 20 for *Hadoop* to 157 for *Birt*. The number of words in title and the number of code terms are very less (4 to 17). To counter the effect of large query size, we evaluate the two query construction strategies—giving boost to title words, (*TB*), and giving boost to code words, (*CB*); we compare their effectiveness with that of the simple–All (A) strategy.

Bug coverage results of the different search techniques formed with *TB* and *CB*, are compared with those of the base techniques in the Figure 4. The graph is plotted only for search result size of 5. X- axis represents the subjects and y - axis represents the bug coverage (%). Per subject there are 9 vertical bars. The first three bars corresponds to the *MI* index, the next three corresponds to *BI* index and the last three are for *CI* index. This segregation is indicated by a vertical line in the figure. Further within the bars corresponding to

Subject	Low	High	Mean	Title	Code
Birt	2	311	157	9	9
Datatools	18	94	56	4	17
Derby	9	234	67	6.5	19
Hadoop	3	130	20	5	7

Table 5. Query Size (number of words)

Subjects	Index	Query Construction					
		A		TB		CB	
		CW	TW	CW	TW	CW	TW
(1)	(2)	(3)	(4)	(5)	(6)	(7)	(8)
Birt	MI	75.2	28.7	78.7	41.8	80.6	31.1
	BI	62.6	22.7	64.2	29	66.7	24.3
	CI	73.2	27.9	74.8	40.3	79.2	29.5
Datatools	MI	65.7	20.8	71.7	34.7	77.0	24.7
	BI	47.6	13.8	54	26.0	55.7	17.6
	CI	64.6	20.2	70.2	31.7	73.6	20.5
Derby	MI	57.7	16.5	65.1	23.9	68.9	20.3
	BI	49.4	14.6	53.1	26.8	59.5	19.1
	CI	57.9	16.3	64.5	23.4	68.8	19.7
Hadoop	MI	65.5	57.8	65.4	66	69.3	59.3
	BI	58.2	59.9	59.0	75.2	67.1	64.0
	CI	63.1	57.6	63.3	65.2	67.9	59.1

Table 6. Percentage of significant Code Words (CW) and Title Words (TW)

these indices, the first one corresponds to base technique *A* (empty bar), the second corresponds to title boost *TB* (vertical line bar) and third one is code boost - *CB* (horizontal line bar).

As evident from the plot, between *TB* and *CB*, boosting the title words during the query construction (*TB*) had positive impact on bug coverage across all indices and subjects except for *Hadoop*. The maximum gain in coverage was observed for *Derby* (11%) for *BI* index. However, boosting code words (*CB*) showed more mixed results. It only provided an increased bug coverage for *Derby* over the base *BI* and *MI* techniques. It also improved the bug coverage for *Hadoop* over the *MI* technique. Overall *TB* technique seems to outperform *CB* techniques for the subjects and indices considered.

Now, we investigate the reason why title-boost proves to be beneficial and not code-boost. For every search query that is run, our Lucene-based search system returns the set of query terms that are significant in computing the search-similarity scores. Table 6 lists the percentage of title-words (TW) and code-words (CW) that feature in the set of significant query terms, across the subjects, when different search techniques are applied. The rows represent each indexing technique (across all subjects) and the columns represent the query construction strategies. Columns (3) and (4) correspond to All (*A*) , columns (5) and (6) to Title-Boost (*TB*), and columns (7) and (8) to Code-Boost(*CB*) strategies.

For *Hadoop*, the queries used in the base techniques contain more than 57% of the significant title words, while the queries of the other three subjects have less of such words (22% for *Birt*, 13% for Datatools, 14% for Derby). When title boost (*TB*) is applied the percentage of significant title

Subjects	Unique Terms			Intersect	
	MI	CI	Bugs	Bugs-MI	Bugs-CI
Birt	41621	148451	6460	2257 (35%)	2778 (43%)
Datatools	24634	70763	1818	1098 (60%)	1152 (63%)
Derby	28315	65913	65797	1940 (50%)	2021 (51%)
Hadoop	14070	55285	1610	1020 (63%)	1131 (70%)

Table 7. Size of Repository Index and Overlap with Bug Test Set

words in queries almost doubles for *Datatools* (from 13.8% in *MI:A* to 26%) resulting in a increase of bug-coverage. However for *Hadoop*, further boosting of title words does not actively contribute toward increases in bug coverage because most of the keywords in the title are already considered to be significant even in the base techniques. Unlike title words, the percentage of significant code words are much higher (47% - 75%) for all subjects in the base techniques— *MI:A*, *CI:A* and *BI:A*. Also, when *TB* is applied, the code words in the title also get a boost (column (5) > column(3)).

To summarize, **giving preference to title-words in the query helps to improve the effectiveness of the search**. On average when compared to the base techniques across all indices, title boost *TB* provided 1.6% increase in bug coverage for *Birt*, 3.9% for *Datatools* and 7.8% for *Derby*. For *Hadoop*, this did not work as already title words were well represented in the significant query terms.

For each bug report under analysis, we collect the following features: *Total number of words*, *Number of code words* and *Number of title words*. Further, we note the *Search-Similarity score* returned by the search engine as we execute queries. Next, we compute *Spearman's rank correlation coefficient* between the features and whether the search technique returns a correct or an incorrect match for that bug, i.e., coverage at the bug level. We find the *Search-Similarity score* to be positively correlated across almost all subjects (except Hadoop) and techniques. This confirms the intuition that the likelihood of suggesting a correct match is high if the Search-Similarity score is high. The number of code words is positively correlated with coverage in 5 of the 12 cases. So, there is some evidence that code words in bug description can improve search performance; however we cannot be conclusive about this result. The total number of words in a bug report is negatively correlated in some cases–perhaps indicating that the search techniques are not able to deal with too much noise in the bug descriptions.

3.4.2 Impact of Subject Level Features

The high efficacy of all search variants on *Hadoop* (Figure 3) made us investigate if there are specific subject level features that bias text-based search. We analyzed two factors:

- Do the techniques work well only when the number of files to be fixed associated with bug reports is large? Figure 5 plots the spread of number of files fixed for each bug in our test suite—per subject. Except for a

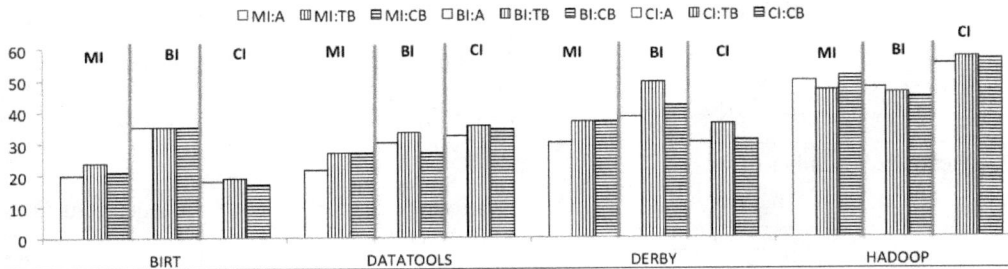

Figure 4. Bug coverage (BC %) across the base techniques and boost techniques are plotted for all subject for search result size of 5. X axis represents the subjects. Y axis represents the bug coverage.

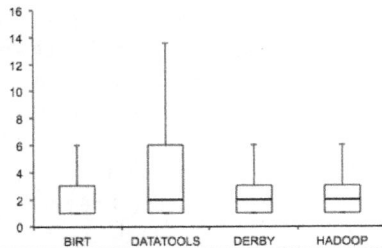

Figure 5. Spread of files modified per Bug per subject in the oracle. The red stars indicate outliers. The bottom and top whiskers show the low 25 and top 25 percentile. The box shows the spread for remaining 50 percentile.

few outliers (ranging from 4% for *Datatools* to 10% for *Hadoop*)), 75% of the bugs across subjects require 6 files or less to be modified and remaining 25% require 15 files or less . The wider spread of upto 15 files is due to *Datatools*, which also impacts the FDR significance test for this subject (as discussed in Section 3.2). The spread for *Hadoop* is very much similar to *Derby* or *Birt*, hence the measure of number of files fixed per bug does not seem to have any impact on the text based search.

- Do the code search techniques work well only when there is a high vocabulary overlap between the code index and the bugs analyzed? Table 7 lists the size of the two variants of code index *CI*, *MI*. Column 4 gives the number of unique terms in the bug queries created from the test suite. Column 6 and 7 gives the absolute and percentage of intersection between words in the test suite (bugs) and the two code indices. The overlap is highest in *Hadoop*— 63% for *CI* and 70% for *MI*. This validates the fact that these techniques work the best for *Hadoop* (as observed in Figure 3). The overlap is lowest for *Birt*—manifested in the fact that we note the lowest bug coverage for *Birt* when we search over the code index (*CI*). Thus, across subjects, **the vocabulary overlap between code index and bug reports impacts search efficacy.** Again, we note that identifier splitting does not lead to an increase in vocabulary match—note the percentage overlap across columns 5 and 6 in table 7. The bug to index vocabulary match is higher in the *CI* technique (where code is not processed) than the *MI* technique (where the code is pre-processed with identifier splitting).

Summary for RQ3

- Boosting the title words as part of query construction helps in increasing the bug covergae. Minimum of 1.65% in *Birt*, and maximum of 7.8% in *Derby*.

- Too many words in bug description can negatively impact search accuracy.

- There is some evidence that presence of code words can help search. However, we are still not conclusive.

- Search similarity score seems to be the only feature, which is almost always significantly correlated to a correct or incorrect search match.

---

4. Related Work

Traditionally, research on fault localization always meant application of some program analysis or debugging technique. Different variants of program slicing [4] have been tested on their efficiency of localizing faults. However, the *slicing criterion* (the point of interest in the program where analysis can start) may not be always clear from a description of a reported bug; thus slicing techniques cannot be immediately applied. Statistical debugging or spectra-based fault localization [13] evaluates various program spectra and pass/fail status of test cases in order to compute the risk of containing a fault for each program entity. Such techniques need a large number of passing test cases to be effective, which may not be always available in practice. Delta debugging [23] instruments the test environment such that it is possible to systematically make the input to a failing test case smaller. Mutation based approaches [21] modify the program state or control flow such that failing test cases can pass. However, they are not very scalable since the search space of program states can become really large and can only be applied to limited types of faults.

Hipikat [8] applies information retrieval to recommend existing software development artifacts (e.g., change tasks, design documents, source files) in context of a task being performed. *PROMESIR* [11] shows that Latent Semantic Indexing (LSI) and scenario based probablisitic ranking (SPR) methods can be effective to locate features (formulated from title and description of bugs) within source code. Lutkins et al. [1] show that querying a Latent Dirichlet Allocation (LDA) model built from the source code can outperform LSI-based methods. Rao and Kak [20] evaluate five generic text models—Unigram Model, Vector Space Model, Latent Semantic Analysis, LDA and Cluster Based Decision Making with respect to their effectiveness in localizing bugs of the iBUGS dataset [9]. *DebugAdvisor* [5] can launch fat semantic queries (comprising of bug description, debugger output, logs etc.) over software repositories that aggregate data from diverse systems such as version control systems, debugging sessions and bug databases.

To the best of our knowledge, there exist no prior work that compares and contrasts the approaches of searching over source code and past bug reports; and the benefits of combining them.

5. Conclusion

In this paper, we study the efficacy of different text-search approaches in bug localization through an empirical evaluation on four open source subjects. Specifically, we examine techniques that directly search the code repository and those that search over a historical collection of bug reports. Overall, no technique comes out as significantly better over the other; for a search result set size of 5, code repository search as well as bug repository search yielded a bug coverage varying from 20 to 60% across our study subjects. Doing any pre-processing of the code to split identifiers into words did not yield benefits. However, we find that these techniques are complementary; we measure an improvement in the bug coverage (1% - 46%) when the techniques are applied in tandem. Favoring words in title help in producing better recommendations in most cases. All experimental data (bugs, truth set, search results) are available here [9].

References

[1] S. K. Lukins, N. A. Kraft, and L. H. Etzkorn. Source Code Retrieval for Bug Localization Using Latent Dirichlet Allocation. In *Proceedings of the 2008 15th Working Conference on Reverse Engineering*, 2008.

[2] L. P. . Enslen, E. Hill and K. Vijay-Shanker. Mining Source Code to Automatically Split Identifiers for Software Analysis. In *Working Conference on Mining Software Repositories, MSR*, pages 71–80, 2009.

[3] H. Agrawal, R. Demillo, and E. Spafford. Debugging with dynamic slicing and backtracking. *Software: Practice and Experience*, 23(6):589–616, 1993.

[4] H. Agrawal, J. Horgan, S. London, and W. Wong. Fault localization using execution slices and dataflow tests. In *Software Reliability Engineering, 1995. Proceedings., Sixth International Symposium on*, pages 143–151. IEEE, 1995.

[5] B. Ashok, J. Joy, H. Liang, S. Rajamani, G. Srinivasa, and V. Vangala. DebugAdvisor: A Recommender System for Debugging. In *Proceedings of the the 7th joint meeting of the ESEC/FSE*, pages 373–382. ACM, 2009.

[6] Y. Benjamini and Y. Hochberg. Controlling the false discovery rate: a practical and powerful approach to multiple testing. *Journal of the Royal Statistical Society. Series B (Methodological)*, pages 289–300, 1995.

[7] T. M. Chilimbi, B. Liblit, K. Mehra, A. V. Nori, and K. Vaswani. Holmes: Effective statistical debugging via efficient path profiling. In *Proceedings of the 31st International Conference on Software Engineering*, pages 34–44, 2009.

[8] D. Cubranic, G. C. Murphy, J. Singer, and K. S. Booth. Hipikat: A project memory for software development. *IEEE Trans. Softw. Eng.*, 31:446–465, 2005.

[9] V. Dallmeier and T. Zimmermann. Extraction of bug localization benchmarks from history. In *Proceedings of the twenty-second IEEE/ACM international conference on Automated software engineering*, pages 433–436. ACM, 2007.

[10] R. A. DeMillo, H. Pan, and E. H. Spafford. Critical slicing for software fault localization. pages 121–134, Jan. 1996.

[11] Y. Denys Poshyvanyk et al. Feature location using probabilistic ranking of methods based on execution scenarios and information retrieval. *IEEE Transactions on Software Engineering*, pages 420–432, 2007.

[12] J. F. et al. Measuring nominal scale agreement among many raters. *Psychological Bulletin*, 76(5):378–382, 1971.

[13] J. Jones and M. Harrold. Empirical evaluation of the tarantula automatic fault-localization technique. In *Proceedings of the 20th IEEE/ACM international Conference on Automated software engineering*, pages 273–282. ACM, 2005.

[14] B. Korel and J. Rilling. Application of dynamic slicing in program debugging. In *Proceedings of the 3rd International Workshop on Automatic Debugging*, May 1997.

[15] B. Liblit, M. Naik, A. X. Zheng, A. Aiken, and M. I. Jordan. Scalable statistical bug isolation. In *Proceedings of the 2005 ACM SIGPLAN Conference on Programming Language Design and Implementation*, pages 15–26, 2005.

[16] B. Lientz, E. Swanson, and G. Tompkins. Characteristics of application software maintenance. *Communications of the ACM*, 21(6):466–471, 1978.

[17] C. Manning, P. Raghavan, and H. Schutze. Introduction to information retrieval. Cambridge University Press 2008.

[18] A. Marcus, A. Sergeyev, V. Rajlich, and J. Maletic. An information retrieval approach to concept location in source code. In *Reverse Engineering, 2004. Proceedings. 11th Working Conference on*, pages 214–223. IEEE, 2004.

[19] J. McKEE. Maintenance as a function of design. In *Proceedings of the National Computer Conference and Exposition*, pages 187–193. ACM, 1984.

[20] S. Rao and A. Kak. Retrieval from software libraries for bug localization: a comparative study of generic and composite text models. In *Proceeding of the 8th working conference on Mining software repositories*, pages 43–52. ACM, 2011.

[21] C. D. Sterling and R. A. Olsson. Automated bug isolation via program chipping. 37(10):1061–1086, Aug. 2007.

[22] F. Tip. A survey of program slicing techniques. *Journal of programming languages*, 3(3):121–189, 1995.

[23] A. Zeller. Isolating cause-effect chains from computer programs. *ACM SIGSOFT Software Engineering Notes*, 27(6): 1–10, 2002.

---

[9] https://sites.google.com/site/searchbugs/

[24] A. Zeller and R. Hildebrandt. Simplifying and isolating failure-inducing input. *IEEE Trans. Softw. Eng.*, 28(2):183–200, Feb. 2002.

Bring Your Own Device (BYOD) with Cloud 4 Education

Ruth Lennon

Computing Department, Letterkenny Institute
of Technology
Letterkenny, Co. Donegal, Ireland.
Ruth.Lennon@lyit.ie

Abstract

This paper presents an outline of the issues encountered in the progression from wired PCs to supporting Bring Your Own Device (BYOD) for learners. The paper also documents the simultaneous transition to cloud hosting of teaching resources. The paper describes the issues that Letterkenny Institute of Technology faced in the planning and evaluation phase during the move to BYOD. It is expected that the details provided here will be of benefit to other educational institutions considering such a move.

Categories and Subject Descriptors   C.0 [**General**]: Modeling of computer architecture, System architectures, Systems specification methodology. C.4 [**Performance of Systems**]: Reliability, availability, and serviceability H.1.1 [**Models and Principles**]: Systems and Information Theory - General systems theory. H.3.4 [**Information Storage and Retrieval**]: Systems and Software - Distributed systems. H.3.5 [**Information Storage and Retrieval**]: Commercial services.

General Terms   Management, Design, Reliability, Experimentation, Security, Human Factors, Standardization.

Keywords   Cloud, System Architecture, Data Governance.

1.   Introduction

This paper focuses on research carried out on the application of BYOD and Cloud support for learners in an Institute of Technology in a rural part of Ireland.

The well documented economic downturn in Europe has led to many countries seeking to refocus their human resources into new highly skilled areas. The Irish government, in particular, is looking to reduce the number of young skilled people emigrating by investing in new research programs. Funding is being focused on encouraging innovative technological companies to be established in Ireland, which enables new avenues for graduates and the unemployed. An investment of €1.2 million euro was just announced [1] in Ireland in an attempt to make Ireland a world leader in Cloud technologies.

In the Irish educational system, Institutes of Technology are higher educational institutions that are separate and distinct from universities. Institutes of Technology focus on applied research, and universities focus on the arts and theoretical scientific research. Institutes of Technology offer learners a choice of technical degree programs and certificate programs in a wide range of practical fields, and the learner body is very diverse in age, skills and prior education.

We have experimented with a combination of BYOD and Cloud support for learners in order to meet several educational challenges in our environment:

- Many of our learners are part-time learners;
- Commuting learners who live and work far from the Institute may find it more convenient to do class work remotely instead of in our on-campus laboratory facilities;
- Younger learners are comfortable using new high-tech computing and communications devices, but most older non-traditional learners are not so proficient with the latest technologies.

The design and deployment of a BYOD and Cloud environment must consider the following issues:

- The computing environment must conform to the data security and data privacy policies of the educational institution and all applicable laws and regulations on data privacy;

- Software licenses and digital media copy protection.

The BYOD and Cloud deployment needs to include the following elements:

- Secure network storage – both private password-protected network storage and shared network storage for a course or a research program;
- Security and privacy policies – the policies for how network storage is allocated and used must be defined and communicated to all users;
- Rapid setup of a "virtual lab" – a set of virtual machines for use by a group of learners for a defined time period (from one week to an entire semester).
- Software license management – there must be a simple process for users to set up the correct software licenses in a virtual lab;
- Hands-on-training for users on the use of cloud applications – especially for non-traditional learners who might be unfamiliar with web applications - especially for non-traditional learners who might be unfamiliar with web applications, smart phone apps, social networking, Dropbox;
- Hotline support for laptop and application configuration problems –occasionally problems will arise when connecting to the campus wireless network, attaching to a virtual lab, searching for on-line resources, or adding files to a shared repository.

2. The Modern Learner

Most young learners have some experience with popular devices and network tools: smart phones, e-book readers, web browsers, social networking sites, blogging tools, and web-based file sharing tools.

The current recession in Ireland has resulted in increased age diversity in the classroom. We now have many learners returning to education after years in employment. These people may have been employed on a factory line in business or management positions prior to returning to education. These learners have been away from formal education for a number of years, and they are often unfamiliar with modern teaching methods. Tools such as virtual learning environments, hosted resources and modern approaches to pedagogy might seem daunting to these learners.

We have other kinds of diversity, including learners from different countries. The standards of the European Higher Education Arena make it possible for learners to start a program of study in one country and continue it in another.

3. The Cloud Environment at LYIT

The private cloud at LYIT consists of 50 virtualized servers on a Storage Area Network (SAN) with 40 TB of local storage. This environment replaced a data center with 110 servers on the main campus. The new configuration uses less energy, and it also allows learners and staff to have individual virtual drives on the SAN.

Virtual learning environments are not new to LYIT, but the use of virtual learning services has been increasing. In the current environment, staff and learners use the Blackboard system, which is hosted in a public cloud. This system has been adopted by 55% of all academic staff in the past two years.

The cloud environment at LYIT is a "mixed model" – a private cloud that supports many applications, but with some use of computation and storage capabilities from public cloud systems. For example, the Blackboard system is hosted on a public cloud. Also, a public cloud is also used for some storage services: each learner has 25GB of storage on SkyDrive, thanks to an agreement negotiated for all of the third level educational institutes in Ireland.

Some classes are starting to define and use virtual Windows and Linux servers for course exercises and activities. There has been some exploration of the use of virtual machines to support specialized applications for various courses and departments. There are big differences in the complexity of the VMs depending on the department and course. VMs used by departments such as nursing and business studies are relatively basic. On the other hand, many engineering courses require modeling tools and analysis packages. VMs for these courses might require a machine with more memory and faster processor to have adequate performance.

The main impacts of cloud and virtualization services have been:

- Reduction in energy costs;
- Lower equipment costs;
- First-year learners like the new environment, which has improved retention;
- On-line resources have allowed classes to continue during bad winter weather;
- Discussion boards in Blackboard have encouraged work in teams.

On the other hand there have been some issues and problems:

- The current network configuration has made it more complicated for learners to get their virtual environment running;
- Learners should be using moderated forums for collaboration, but moderated forums take a lot of staff time; un-moderated forums are a risk because there is a potential for abuse of resources
- Licensing issues for deploying commercial software in a cloud environment;

- Data privacy issues – ensuring that personal data (such as learner identification numbers and grades) are protected from public disclosure.

4. Bring Your Own Device (BYOD)

In the initial investigation period the range of devices currently employed by staff were examined. Next, a number of devices were identified for suitability based on future need, basic software and hardware requirements. Finally, an initial security assessment was carried out. Four devices were purchased and were supplied to the heaviest wireless throughput users within the staff.

Testing of these devices is ongoing and at an early stage, however the issues surrounding how the BYOD system should work are described here. There is a large branch of a multi-national company in Letterkenny who is currently moving completely to laptop devices as opposed to desktop PCs. In a business where staff are fully employed and all devices belong to the company this is feasible.

An educational institution has a different set of usage scenarios than a business, and there are different data access and data security issues to consider. In an educational institution there are three categories of users with different needs: learners, administration staff, and teaching/lecturing staff. Administration staff has issues regarding data privacy but the data privacy constraints are not more stringent than for a bank, for example. For teaching staff, there is an issue with the types of materials they may place on their device. Teaching staff may place large amounts of raw research data onto their device, and this data may be irreplaceable if lost. The teaching staff often chose to install software or place personal data on their work device.

Learners will likely need grants or loans in order to purchase outright their own device conforming to the specification provided. In this way the learners will be able to get the best deal possible and the educational institution will ensure that all learners will be able to purchase an appropriate device.

Issues that might arise include:

- Learners might register for a course but refuse to purchase the specified device
- Learners might fail to bring their device to the scheduled class
- Learners might have problems replacing a device that fails or is damaged mid-term in sufficient time to complete the specified course

The strict application of rules and regulations may be considered an interim solution to some of these issues. On the other hand, it would be better to have a more flexible policy about which devices they are permitted to use, to allow learners to bring a different device if they already had one, or to borrow a device if they could not afford one, etc.

5. Using Cloud Computing and Teaching Cloud Computing

The importance of Cloud computing has been much documented and is therefore is not covered here. The ACM/IEEE-CS Science Curricula for 2013 [2] as outlined in the Strawman document is direct evidence of the importance of cloud computing in education. When describing the characteristics of graduates, topics to be covered in Core Tier1 Networking include cloud networking, scaling in the cloud and the social and legal aspects. Indeed, the document further requires learners to understand the impact of cloud computing on social interactions at a personal level.

Cloud Computing has become a part of many courses outside of computing science. For example, many courses make extensive use of cloud storage products such as Dropbox. Both staff and learners use these products extensively already, although they are not currently endorsed or supported in any way.

The first useful service that a local educational cloud ought to support is local cloud storage. This is just one step away from the current use of public drives and virtual private networks.

The next extension of the system to use the local cloud to support course resources such as software and other materials. This would improve learners' access to educational materials, and it might also provide avenues of revenue for the educational institutions. They could become online portals for a wider community of learners than the conventional learner community.

5.1 Using Cloud Computing.

Cloud computing has been provisioned to all courses in the form of the Virtual Learning Environment (VLE). The VLE utilized in the institute is Blackboard. When considering a new course such as the Bachelors of Engineering (Honours) in Fire Safety Engineering, it is not always easy to see how such a course could be supported via the cloud. The course has been developed as a four year *ab initio* course. There are many subjects on this course which lend themselves easily to cloud hosted VLE's such as: computer aided design, fire modeling and reliability and human behavior in fire. These subjects all include mathematical, statistical or computer aided modeling packages. However, practical subjects such as Fire Service Operation and Fire Dynamics require further consideration.

Fire Dynamics laboratory exercises include a number of pieces of laboratory equipment used for practical tests, such as a cone calorimeter and flame spread apparatus. The learners must test the flammability properties of various materials. The test data may include the rate of burn, the intensity of the flame, etc. In Figure 1, fire technology learners may burn a tray of kerosene in a scaled down version of a room. Each data item regarding the path of the flame can then be recorded on a data logger. This laboratory may be videoed and placed on the VLE for learners to watch. The raw data from the data logger may also be placed on the VLE. From the raw data the learners then perform their calculations to indicate the relative flammability of the materials. Instructions on how to carry-out the calculations may be placed in a pdf file hosted on the VLE. Podcasts of the relevant theory may also be hosted on the cloud through the VLE. In this way learners who might require a second look at the experiment have an additional opportunity to review the steps carried out.

Figure 1. Recording fire data for use in a course

5.2 General Impact of the Cloud on the Teaching Environment.

While most courses can be supported via the Cloud through resource sharing, some issues have become apparent. The choice of VLE has an impact on the quality of the materials delivered. Most VLEs provide useful tools for learners and instructors, such as on-line discussion groups and support for automated marking of test materials, but the system's capabilities vary with the provider.

The Blackboard system hosts all the materials on the cloud, which greatly reduces the number of servers required by the institute. Further it reduces the time spend by technical support staff in maintaining the service. However, Blackboard has some limitations: for example, it does not support a wide variety of web browsers. The lack of support for some combination of browsers, operating systems and file types can cause significant difficulties for lecturers when deciding on the most appropriate format for learning resources. The cost of developing and host a private cloud solution for a virtual learning environment is prohibitive.

5.3 Teaching Cloud Technology on the Cloud.

The learning resources for a course on cloud technology will need to include some type of cloud environment for learners to explore in class exercises. The environment they use must consider both the security of learner laptops and the security and performance of the institute's private cloud.

Teaching networking technologies through virtual learning environments also has highlighted interesting problems. When learners install a virtual network on a virtual server hosted on a windows machine the firewall and router grind to a halt. This may be the case with specific virtualization software or may be a more widespread problem. Further investigation of this problem is ongoing.

One potential security issue for learners: When they use their laptops to connect to a local cloud to run some cloud lab exercises, it might be necessary for them to temporarily disable their laptop's firewall software. Instructors and technical support staff need to maintain a higher standard of security for a cloud environment used for cloud lab exercises, and learners also need to remember to enable their local firewall again before resuming normal work.

6. Physical Access to Resources

The Institute is broken into a number of campuses. In the main campus of Letterkenny Institute of Technology there are approximately 800 PCs in offices and labs. At present there are also approximately 550 associated devices on the wireless network at any given time and of these currently only approximately 250 are authenticated devices. An authenticated device is a device that has been authorized and fully authenticated by the IT department. An associated device is any device that the wireless network can see, such as a laptop, iPod, xda, etc. Although the Letterkenny Institute of Technology currently only supports laptops, it can be seen that seen a significant number of mobile devices are attempting to access the network.

6.1 Remote Access to Resources.

Given the increasing number of unauthenticated devices connecting to the network it was deemed necessary to review the level of support for remote access to the network. Learners were surveyed to ascertain the level of broadband support each could access from their home. Seventy six percent of learners described their home location as a town with only 24% indicating that they lived in a village. Just over 70% of learners had a wireless router with the remainder using dongles. The prevalent line speed paid for by learners was 8GB. Not surprisingly 69.5% of learners indicated that they did not often get the line speed they paid for. When the 64% of learners who work from home for more than 20 hours per week, this is certainly a concern. The high number of hours worked at home was most often due to family constraints. Another concern was security: 94% indicated that their connection was secure, however when further investigated, this involved simple WEP security. The vast majority of learners did not update their virus protection software and had little or no knowledge of the security risks in using open networks.

Clearly an increased level of risk awareness is required. A course on the correct usage of BYOD devices and their security will be mandatory for all BYOD users. It is not anticipated that this will remove all risks. It should however in combination with enforced security such as mandatory virus updates and remote wiping provide a much more secure system.

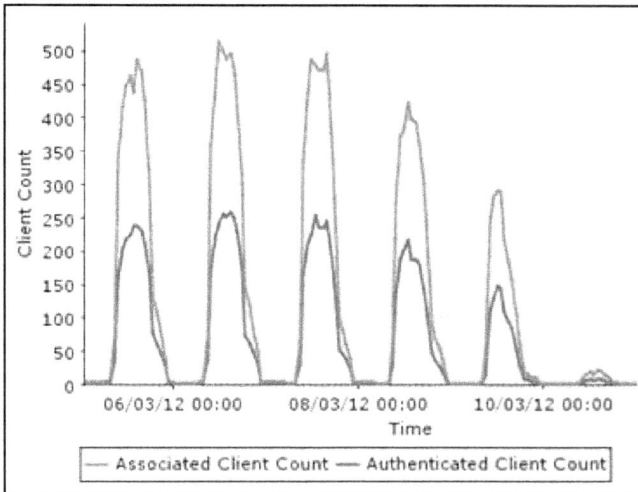

Figure 2. Port Road Campus Client Count.

6.2 Increased Classroom Capacity.

It was anticipated that the utilisation of BYOD would provide greater utilisation of teaching resources including classrooms. A survey of the utilisation of all teaching rooms is carried out at the end of each academic year. This survey provides an indication of the efficiency of the timetabling of courses to optimize resource usage. The percentage utilisation of each room by classification is provided in Figure. 3. From this it can be seen that there is significant underutilisation in classrooms while the computer laboratories are running at close to maximum efficiency.

The institute is located in a rural part of Ireland. This has a significant impact on the hours during which classes can be scheduled as the buses travelling to other parts of the country depart at lunch-time on Fridays. Thus learners returning home for the week-end will not attend classes on Friday evenings. In an effort to combat this, some of the most important classes were scheduled for Friday evenings to increase learner attendance. Unfortunately it simply resulted in a lower retention rate. Thus 13:30-17:30 on Friday are considered dead hours.

BYOD helps tackle the inefficient use of classrooms by enabling the re-designation of classrooms as computer laboratories. Each learner will have access to his/her own device with the appropriate software installed. If the 'dead-

hours' are not considered, then the application of BYOD has an impact of approximately 26%.

Utilisation of laboratories also increases as specialized software is no longer limited to a small number of laboratories. An increased number of courses can therefore be run within the 40-hour week. There is a move towards a 45 hour teaching week, 9:00-18:00, which would provide further efficiencies in room utilisation. These efficiencies are further extended via a greater distribution of incidental costs such as lighting/heating across a greater number of courses. Consequently the implementation of BYOD has a greater impact on overheads accumulated during courses than was first realized.

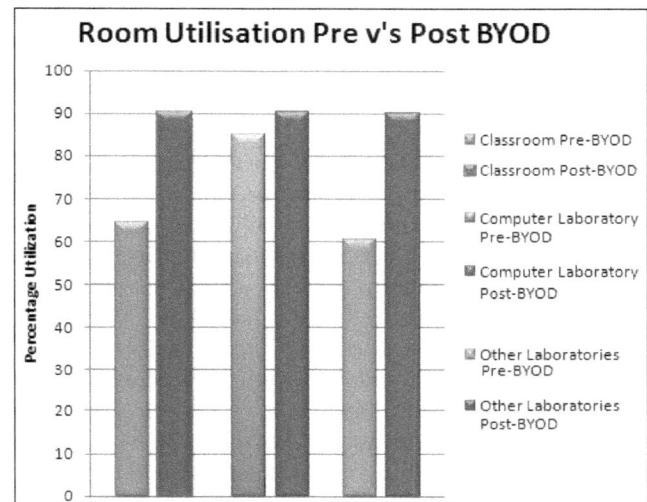

Figure 3. Port Road Campus Room Utilisation.

6.3 Power Consumption.

It is anticipated that there will be a significant increase in power consumption if not carefully reviewed prior to the final roll-out of BYOD. This increase in power consumption could not be absorbed by the educational institution. As such it would be necessary to apply new technologies to enable the BYOD clients to attach to power sockets on a pay-as-you-go system.

Companies such as ChargeBox (www.fleetconnect.ie) would enable the deployment of charging stations at a variety of locations throughout the campus. At present ChargeBox provide locations for secure charging of personal devices which can be plugged into and then locked in a secure cabinet. This has many advantages such as security of the device, 95% reduction in carbon emissions, PAT security, and a reduction of electrical costs to the institution. The ChargeBox for laptops will be available for general sale from the end of October. Based on implementations currently deployed in universities in England it has been calculated that between 150 and 200 units would be required to support 3,000 learners. With a unit cost of £3,000 stg. and a per unit electricity charge of £1.50 for 30 minutes use to the learner, the ROI is realized in approximately 1 year. An obvious disadvantage to these systems is that the device cannot be used during the charging period as the device is securely locked away.

Sony is currently developing hardware to use a touch-card platform, Felica, to enable a pay-per-use form of electricity at the socket. These types of systems could be adapted in a similar fashion to current photocopying facilities with each learner having a card which they would 'top-up' with credit. This would allow the BYOD user the flexibility of utilizing the system while charging. It is envisaged that a combination of both these types of technologies would be required for efficient BYOD adoption.

6.4   Learner Retention.

In the current economic depression, it is necessary to ensure that the maximum number of learners may be accommodated using the least number of resources. Many new learners have previously been in employment and are now returning to education to re-skill. Retention of traditional and new learners is essential to ensure that each of our client obtain the maximum benefit possible from their time in education. The application of BYOD enables learners to work from home and indeed access more of their learning resources while travelling or between items of personal obligation. The application of the cloud through the Virtual Learning Environment (VLE) has enabled the lecturers to develop teaching resources in bite-size portions often referred to as learning nuggets. These learning nuggets may be downloaded from the cloud onto the learner's personal device for on-the-go learning. This is particularly helpful also for those learners with shorter retention spans. It is the combination of BYOD with cloud resources that enables this form of learning.

The placement of learning resources such as podcasts, videocasts, lecture notes and laboratory instructions onto the cloud results in an increased time-frame during which learners may complete their work. Enabling learners to continue their learning when mitigating circumstances intervenes will have a knock-on effect of increasing retention.

7.   Software Licenses and Deployment

There are many legal issues to supporting the learner through their own devices many of which are discussed in the next section, however in this section mention is made of the complexities involved in supporting the variety of software licenses for products commonly used in Letterkenny Institute of Technology (LYIT). As far as possible the author has attempted to provide a general picture of the issues that educators face when supporting learners in such a fashion so as not to focus on issues that

may be specific to this campus. To ensure that there is no ambiguity here it is worth point out the variety of courses provided in LYIT. Courses include: Computer Science, Networking, Computer Forensics, Digital Media and Entertainment, Enterprise Applications, Fire Safety Engineering, Business Studies, Design, Nursing, Mechanical, Electrical, Culinary and Science Courses. This is simply a sample of the courses selected specifically due to the specialized software each require and the types of issues each bring about when planning the support of BYOD.

There are over 250 separate packages which technicians are responsible for in each 'phase' of each campus of the educational institute. In the example graph below from the Port Road, Main Building Phase 2B, it is clear that there is a wide variety of licensing applied to the various types of software.

Figure 4. Port Road Campus Client Count.

It is worth taking a closer look at the software that is utilized by learners during the academic year. To simplify the discussion, software from the east wing of the campus

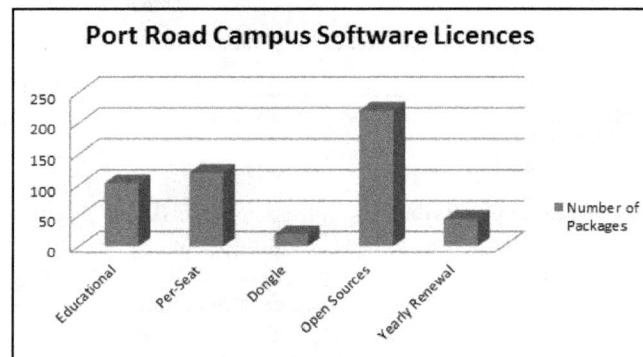

is discussed here. Figure 5 provides a breakdown of software by type of license. As 72% of the software is proprietary, it is necessary to establish the appropriate licenses for BYOD or cloud hosting. In some cases restrictions by the vendor will dictate whether or not the software can be hosted on the cloud. With some smaller companies producing specialist software, such as CFAST for fire modeling, negotiations on licensing agreements are possible. However with the majority of software vendors this is not possible.

Some of the computing courses use open source software, so these courses have few software licensing issues.   But the Fire Engineering course requires a commercial fire modeling software package with a license that uses dongle-based authentication. The simplest solution is to move to hosting of the software to a virtual server, accessible to the learners. However, as the software is a modeling package, it requires significant processing power and involves the transfer of large amounts of data across the network. The execution of the software on each learner's individual device would require a higher specification of device than would be necessary for the majority of learners.

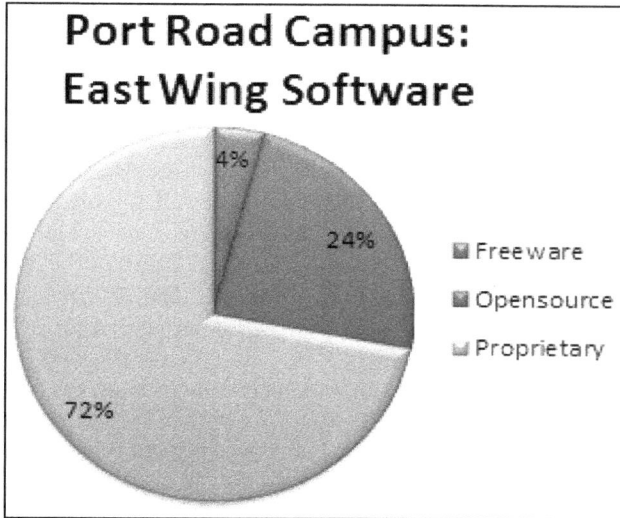

Figure 5. Port Road Campus: East Wing Software

As there are only a relatively small number of users of the specialized package, negotiations are underway with regard to licensing for hosting on the cloud. It is not anticipated that the new licenses will be available for the next academic year. However, as the licenses are renewed yearly on a per-seat basis, it is anticipated that this will be resolved for the final phase of roll-out of cloud hosted support for learners.

It is interesting to note that only 28% of the software packages are Microsoft and 24% of packages are Open-source. While there are obvious potential security risks with many open source packages, they have proved most helpful when deploying BYOD & Cloud. The remaining 48% of software packages are either freeware or limited license software.

It is also important to consider which software is necessary to all learners and which packages may be needed only by learners in a narrow specialty. This knowledge aids with selective deployment of software packages, which can reduce the cost of purchasing licenses for packages that have a per-seat or per-device charge. Further, the knowledge of which combination of specialized packages are needed for each specialty will enable a more precise definition of the minimal requirements of the BYOD devices to be purchased by the learner. It should be noted that the analysis here is of the software currently used in one wing of the main campus of the institute and does not cover the myriad of courses that the institute offers. It is presented as an overview as it houses a greater variety of courses than other wings. For example there is one wing of the college that is devoted to science and nursing science only.

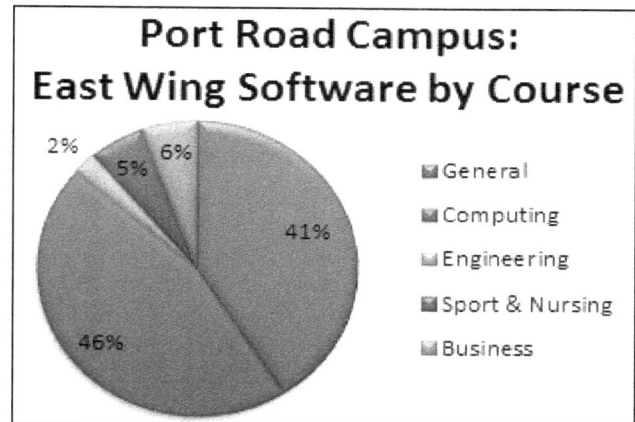

Figure 6. Port Road Campus Proportion of MS Software.

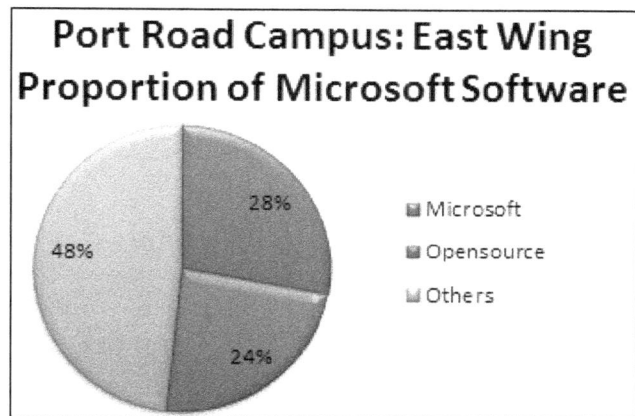

Figure 7. Port Road Campus: Classification of Software Packages by Specialty

Another difficulty that educational institutions face that is not as great a problem in other industry is the need to deploy 'bleeding edge' software to learners. Learners are provided with the background theory to legacy and modern technologies. While a great number of the software and hardware technologies in the institute are widely used and commercially accepted, it is also necessary for degree and postgraduate students to have experience with ground breaking technologies. As these technologies are constantly evolving, it not always possible to anticipate the impact of the installing a new software package on the end system. Problems can quickly be corrected on institute-owned PCs, but deployment to BYOD devices is a significantly more complex problem due to software/hardware constraints, access to the devices and legal implications.

8. The Law

The variation in laws from one country have caused significant concern in the application of cloud computing.

In Ireland the Data Protection Act 2003 is a cause of concern when transferring data between Ireland and the E.U. This is particularly important when the data being transferred is personal data [3]. Certainly the storage of learner's grades could be considered personal data. It is unclear however whether submitted continuous assessment, thesis, code segment or other items could be considered personal data. If this data is stored with a cloud provider with locations outside the E.U., that data may become transferred to a variety of locations. If the personal data is transferred out of Europe, it is no longer covered by E.U. laws and therefore becomes subject to the laws of the country where is resides. This is particularly important as the Data Protection Act labels a number of countries as prohibited for data transferal [4]. This means that if the educational institute does not religiously monitor the provision of the cloud, we might easily violate EU law.

The Act is written with the directive of protecting user privacy. The European Data Protection Regulation 2012 was created to standardize data protection throughout Europe. These rules may be seen as a significant impediment to cloud computing. As part of this regulation the Data Protection Commissioner may request the physical location of data storage. When data is stored in the cloud this information is not always readily available.

The educational institutes are audited regularly both by internal bodies and external bodies. This makes knowledge of what data is held, where it is held and in what form important. Neelie Kroes [5] in her vision for a European Cloud Partnership outlined the economic and security benefits of having these updated laws. There is however significant concern that requirements such as the disclosure of security breaches within 24 hours are unworkable. In the educational institute it may be seen that this provides little if any time to gather evidence of the breach. Consider an attack late on a Saturday evening after normal closing. The attack may not be discovered during limited coverage hours on a Sunday where limited staff levels are on duty. This simple example would leave the educational institution in breach of E.U. law.

The duration the personal data must be stored is also important. At present learners examination scripts and continuous assessment materials are kept for 18 months. If these materials are stored on the cloud, they may be required to be removed with a clear record of the removal process. It would be particularly difficult to establish the recording procedure and the location of all copies of the materials as well as all references to the materials such as the marks awarded for each element of the continuous assessment.

There may be operational issues that cause the data on the cloud to become corrupted or lost, and this might lead to the educational institution being placed in "Statutory Default" of the European Law, which has serious ramifications.

The Legal issues are such that the Irish Department of Finance has warned its own government departments and public sector bodies, of which the education sector is just one, that they should not purchase cloud computing services without first obtaining legal advice [6].

The use of external service providers through tenders is a measure often used by the education sector to obtain economies of scale. The Data Protection Act 2003 requires that appropriate security measures must be implemented to counter unauthorized access to data in addition to the unauthorized destruction of or leaking of data. Where staff and learners are supplying their own devices for access to the cloud it becomes increasingly difficult to regulate the security to an appropriate level. While it has been deemed appropriate to limit the variety of supported devices and to physically impose restrictions to ensure updates/patches are applied, there will always be a number of users that evade the regulations.

This Law is also significant as it has a greater impact when considering the throughput of learners within the educational institution. Is it required that the security system has to be applied to all learners own devices regardless of whether or not they remain within the education system? If so, then resources that will be spent on supporting the upgrade of their system, etc. as previously described might not be recuperated from learner fees. It is also difficult to regulate what the short term registered learner will do with the resources transferred to his/her device. While the obvious solution might be to add a hardware or software lock to resources once the learner deregisters, often the learners do not deregister or do so weeks after having left the course. This applies both to resources placed on learner devices and placed on the cloud with learner accounts.

The scenario does not arise as often with staff devices, it becomes an interesting issue with research learners who also occupying teaching positions.

9. Conclusions

The following is a rough outline of the conclusions that have been drawn to date from this research.

It is necessary to modernize the educational system to support learners not only through updated teaching pedagogy but also through modern devices.

The variety in technology skills, life skills, etc. of mixed ability classes makes it difficult to classify learners for ease of support.

Learners require support not only during any given course but also within the placement. Lifelong learning promotes the development of learning portfolios comprising of formal and informal learning.

The move to support learners through BYOD in Letterkenny Institute of Technology has thrown up a number of serious and some unexpected issues. The access to broadband facilities at home can be a significant difficulty which is outside of the control of the educational institution. Efficiencies in physical resources can be gained through careful timetabling of rooms when BYOD is applied.

Software licensing issues are not trivial and will not be resolved in the immediate future.

There are a number of legal issues which should be considered. The legal issues outlined in this paper focus on European law but similar issues exist in the U.S.

Acknowledgments

The author would like to thank the SPLASH Wavefront Experience technical panel and mentors for their helpful comments on earlier drafts of this paper. The author would especially like to Dennis Mancl for his invaluable advice. Finally the author would like to thank the LYIT technical staff and Liam McIntyre in particular for the in depth and inspiring technical discussions carried out over the past year.

References

[1] Breaking News, The Irish Times, 12 April 2012. www.irishtimes.com/newspaper/breaking/2012/0402/breaking21.html

[2] ACM/IEEE-CS Computer Science Curricula, SIGPLAN Education Board, CS2013 - Strawman Draft, http://ai.stanford.edu/users/sahami/CS2013/

[3] Philip Nolan, Cloud Computing: The Legal Issues, Irish Software Association – Breakfast Briefing, Mason, Hayes and Curran, www.mhc.ie/podcasts/download/4/. 22 February 12

[4] David Navetta, Legal Implications of Cloud Computing – Part One (The Basics and Framing the Issues), Law and Technology Resources for Legal Professionals, 12 September 2009, www.llrx.com/features/cloudcomputing.htm

[5] Neelie Kroes, Blogg of the Vice-President of the European Commission, 30 January 2012, blogs.ec.europa.eu/neelie-kroes/european-cloud-partnership/

[6] Warning over Cloud Computing Usage, The Irish Times, 2 February 2010.

Migration to Model Driven Engineering in the Development Process of Distributed Scientific Application Software

Raphael Gayno

IFP Energies nouvelles
Rueil-Malmaison
France
raphael.gayno@ifpen.fr

Jean Marc Gratien

IFP Energies nouvelles
Rueil-Malmaison
France
j-marc.gratien@ifpen.fr

Goulwen Le Fur

OBEO
Nantes
France
goulwen.lefur@obeo.fr

Daniel Rahon

IFP Energies nouvelles
Lyon site
France
daniel.rahon@ifpen.fr

Sébastien Schneider

IFP Energies nouvelles
Lyon site
France
sebastien.schneider@ifpen.fr

Abstract

For several years now the IFP Energies nouvelles (IFPEN) group has been developing the OpenFlowSuite, a software suite in the oil and gas domain based on Eclipse RCP, incorporating graphical components and parallel calculators. These calculators are themselves developed in Fortran or C/C++. The processing chain "data entry", "database persistence", "calculator input", "execution" and "result processing" entails mapping between models and requires the development and maintenance of complex communication code. The progress made in recent years in the field of model driven engineering, and the accompanying Eclipse tools, led us to consider introducing these solutions in management of the communication code. In this article we describe the introduction and use of Model Driven Engineering (MDE) Eclipse tools in this context of industrial development of distributed scientific applications.

Categories and Subject Descriptors D.2.11 [**Software Engineering**]: Software Architectures – data abstraction, domain-specific architectures

General Terms Performance, Design, Reliability.

Keywords Modeling; code generation; Eclipse; numerical simulation.

1. Introduction

The IFPEN group is a major actor in the software market of oil & gas reservoir simulation and characterization and basin modelling with its OpenFlowSuite software. The applications in OpenFlowSuite incorporate the results of scientific research in the form of complex and high performance computation models held in the OpenFlow platform in 3D graphical applications based on Eclipse [1].

OpenFlow is a platform composed of a business data model. It is used to create, import, modify and store the different models of reservoir and basins studied and all the information necessary for the simulation of physical phenomena via the calculators. The computations may be distributed on a local network and the results are available in real-time for analysis and post-processing by oil reservoir engineers or geologists. The integration and execution of Fortran or C/C++ scientific calculators requires the definition of protocols for communication and exchange with the OpenFlow platform. These exchanges are accompanied by model transformations to map the OpenFlow "user" oriented model to the calculators' "simulation" oriented structures. All this technical code, initially handled manually, is complex to implement, develop, optimize to avoid impacting computation performance and maintain, especially in terms of integrating any upgrades and modifications to the OpenFlow platform.

This situation led us to consider the introduction of solutions to automate - as far as possible - development of this technical code for mapping and communication. The sever-

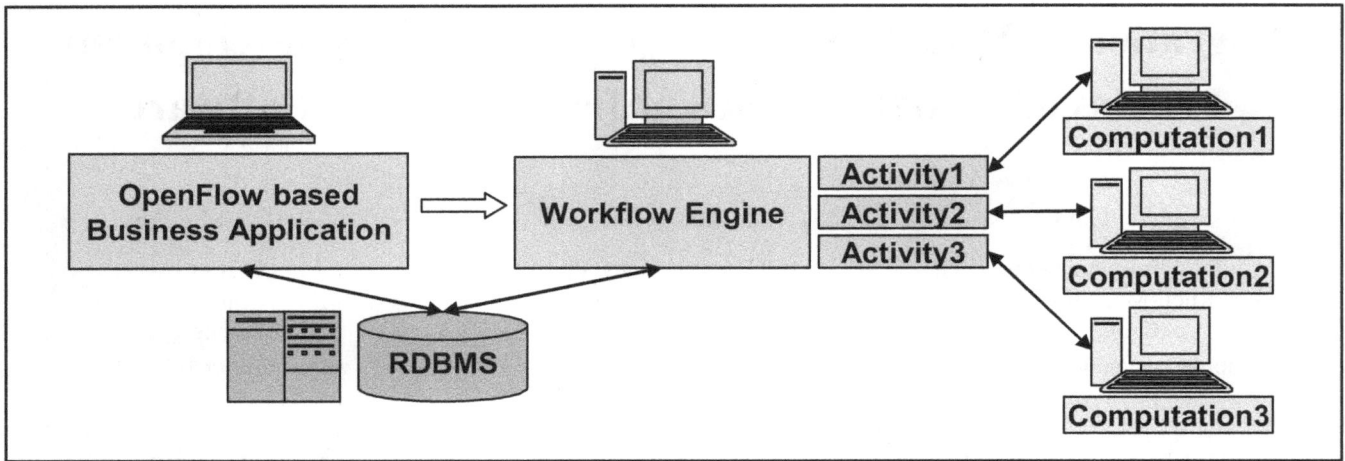

Figure 1. OFS outline diagram

al work produced in MDE [2, 3] implementation in the development of business application in the recent years [4, 5, 6, 7]. Our application case is complementary, since it involves a context of integration between a Java client application, where MDE most commonly applies, and Fortran/C/C++ calculators, for which this approach is more original.

In addition, to facilitate testing and calculator integration, data entry editor generation solutions have been studied and proposed. This article therefore describes a complete approach to the use of MDE and code generation, with the aim of simplifying the integration and use of calculators from a graphical client.

2. The Situation

2.1 OpenFlow/Calculators communication

OpenFlow consists of a graphical application based on Eclipse-RCP, with plugins for data management, data edition, multiple scientific plots and graphics, data analysis, etc. OpenFlow includes a concept of batch executable scientific business activities which can be grouped together to form workflows in the field of exploration and characterization of oil reservoir and basin modeling. These business activities may have an embedded simulator or scientific calculator which is executed when the workflow execution is requested by the user. Simulations are executed on a network of machines and integration takes place via the database, centralizing data, and the workflow engine chaining activities.

The **Figure 1** shows the main components of the OpenFlowSuite including the graphical client (Business Application) used to manage data, interactive treatments and workflows definition. The Workflow Engine handles activities execution on a local network.

Both data and activity management system are written in Java. The calculators are complex scientific components developed in Fortran or C/C++.

To input data to a calculator, manage its remote launch, retrieve its results and monitor its execution, the platform uses a dedicated component, OpenDataServer (ODS). As illustrated on **Figure 2** the ODS main tasks are to start the calculator, open a network communication channel with it and respond to its requests for transmission of data and reception of results.

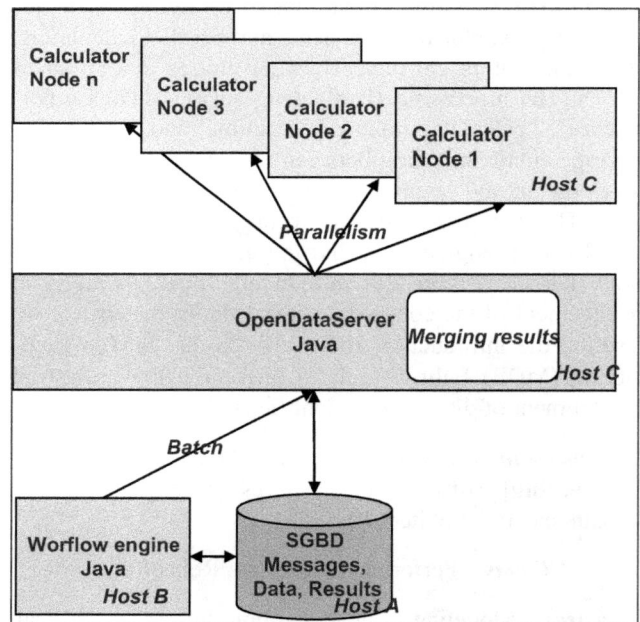

Figure 2. OpenDataServer component

In addition, ODS had to meet some design goals and constraints:

1. To provide an efficient communication solution to avoid creating a bottleneck for the calculator and keep network transfers to a minimum;

2. To process clients for parallel executions. This constraint entails the ability to adapt the data sent/received depending on the number of processors;

3. To monitor execution: computation client logs, errors and exceptions report accessible by the graphical client and the ability to stop, pause or restart the computation.

Finally the solution should be based on an open, standardized, scalable architecture to facilitate the connection of new calculators even if they use a different communication system.

This set of constraints led to the construction of a fairly complex technical component written in Java to manipulate the OpenFlow data model, using a low level communication socket to connect to Fortran or C/C++ tools. It is based on a XML dictionary defining the client/server communication protocol. Also, mapping between the OpenFlow model and the calculator models is sometimes performed by server side services, other times by client side services when processing messages are received.

2.2 A simple example

To better illustrate this problem of model transformation and system maintainability, we consider a simple example modeling the surface facilities used in reservoir simulation to compute properties of oil and gas phases at surface condition. This example is based on:

- The Java class *Separator* in the OpenFlow data model with two attributes modeling the temperature and pressure parameter of the business concept of separator;

```
public final class Separator {
    // Temperature in separator
    private double temperature = 0.0;
    // Pressure in separator
    private double pressure = 0.0;
}
```

- A C++ class *Process* that store in the reservoir calculator the number of separators and their parameters and a C++ function that load the Separator parameters to instantiate that class;

```
class Process {
 private:
    int m_nb_of_separator;
    double* m_temperature;
    double* m_pressure;
};

private void loadProcess() {
 // Get DataServer
```

```
ods = OpenDataServer::GetOpenDataServer();
// Send message to load data
ods->Write("LoadAllSeparatorData");
// Mapping starts here
int nbSep = 0;
ods->Read(&nbSep );
double* p = new double(nbSep);
double* t = new double(nbSep);
for(int i=0; i< nbSep ; i++){
  ods->Read(p);
  ods->Read(t);
  p++; t++;
}
Process proc = new Process(nbSep, p, t);
}
```

- The XML file that drives the services enabling the mapping between the *Separator* model in the database and the *Process* structure use in the calculator.

```
<services>
<!-- All methods in the internal section are
only used by the server side -->
  <internal>
    <method name="getTemperature"
     class="data.model.Separator"
     type="double">
    </method>
    <method name="getPressure"
     class="data.model.Separator"
     type="double">
    </method>
    <macroSequence id="SendSeparator" >
     <alias tar-
get="data.model.Separator.getTemperature "/>
     <alias tar-
get="data.model.Separator.getPressure"/>
    </macroSequence>
  </internal>

<!-- All this services can be directly called
by the client side -->
  <external>
    <macroSequence id="LoadAllSeparatorData"
     collection="GetAllSeparator">
     <alias target="SendSeparator"/>
    </macroSequence>
  </external>
</services>
```

This simple example illustrates the different components involved in the data transfer from the Java based persistent data model to the C++ calculators. C++ clients have only access to the <external> services declared in the XML dictionary. Internal mechanisms of the OpenDataServer transform external requests in access to the Java data model.

2.3 The current state

The ODS component is developed and maintained entirely manually, giving rise to problems. System complexity was a major difficulty, which has made fixing bugs harder. Maintenance of dictionaries has also been hard, especially because the data model has been changing frequently to satisfy new needs. It has also been difficult to transfer certain business knowledge from the calculators to the server services to facilitate mapping.

In our simple study case, if we enriched the surface facility model and added a new parameter maxRate we need to update manually:

- The *Separator* Java class to add the new attribute;

```java
public final class Separator {
    // Temperature in separator
    private double temperature = 0.0;
    // Pressure in separator
    private double pressure = 0.0;
    // Max allowed rate in separator
    private double maxRate = 0.0;
}
```

- The C++ *Process* class and the load function;

```cpp
class Process{
 private:
   int m_nb_of_separator ;
   double* m_temperature;
   double* m_pressure;
   double* m_max_rate;
};
private void loadProcess() {
 // Get DataServer
 ods = OpenDataServer::GetOpenDataServer();
 // Send message to load data
 ods->Write("LoadAllSeparatorData");
 // Mapping starts here
 int nbSep = 0;
 ods->Read(&nbSep );
 double* p = new double(nbSep);
 double* t = new double(nbSep);
 double* r = new double(nbSep);
 for(int i=0; i< nbSep ; i++){
   ods->Read(p);
   ods->Read(t);
   ods->Read(r);
   p++; t++; r++;
 }
 Process proc = new Process(nbSep, p, t, r);
}
```

- The XML dictionary file to ensure the mapping of the transformed model;

```xml
<services>
<!-- All methods in the internal section are
only used by the server side -->
  <internal>
      <method name="getTemperature"
    class="data.model.Separator"
    type="double">
    </method>
    <method name="getPressure"
    class="data.model.Separator"
    type="double">
    </method>
    <method name="getMaxRate"
    class="data.model.Separator"
    type="double">
    </method>
    <macroSequence id="SensSeparator" >
    <alias tar-
get="data.model.Separator.getTemperature "/>
    <alias tar-
get="data.model.Separator.getPressure"/>
    <alias tar-
get="data.model.Separator.getMaxRate"/>
    </macroSequence>
    </internal>
    .....
</services>
```

These observations and the development of MDE tools around the Eclipse platform led us to consider a code generation strategy for part of the server functions. The introduction of MDE is also accompanied by a stricter definition of the server role, particularly in terms of model transformation.

3. Tools

The tools used to introduce MDE in the development of OpenFlow elements are Eclipse project tools. Eclipse RCP is our application support platform and development tool. It is therefore logical for us to use tools integrated into our environment: Eclipse EMF, EcoreTools for modelling, Acceleo for code generation and EEF for SWT editor generation.

3.1 EMF

Eclipse Modeling Framework (EMF [8]) is a set of modeling tools used to simplify code generation for building tools based on data models. These tools are widely used to develop applications for developers and are now increasingly used in business applications (TopCased, for example [9]).

3.2 Ecore Tools

Use of the EMF project entails definition of the data model to be manipulated by business applications. This definition is based on the Ecore formalism provided by the EMF project.

Ecore Tools offers components for management of Ecore models: graphical construction, editing, maintenance and validation.

3.3 Acceleo

Acceleo [10] is an open source code generator from the Eclipse Foundation, used to implement the model driven approach for building applications from models. It is an implementation of the standard from the Object Management Group (OMG) [11]for model to text transformation.

The language used by Acceleo is an implementation of the standard MOF MTL (Model to Text Language). This code generation language uses a template based approach. With this approach, a template contains static and dynamic text fields to define the code to be generated. The dynamic text fields allow information to be extracted from the model by defining expressions navigating the entities and properties of this model. Within Acceleo, these expressions are based on OCL language.

Acceleo contains a code generation modules editor with syntax highlighting, completion, error detection and refactoring.

4. Integration of the New Solution

The main structural change is replacing part of the code produced and processed manually in OpenDataServer and client-side (**Figure 3**) by generated components based on a communication model. The **Figure 3** details in the internal square the different elements on both server and client side that compose the communication solution: the XML dictionaries expose available messages which are processed by OpenDataServer to access persistent data model. Then a first model transformation is done to send data as messages to the client where messages are decoded to recreate data structures used by the simulator. All bricks are manually developed and maintained.

The solution proposed for the new architecture is based on MDE EMF concepts and on the Eclipse tools used to implement them: EcoreTools and Acceleo.

The target architecture is therefore based on a model of communication between the data server and the client calculators. This model allows use of code generation tools and a much better separation between the communication layer and upgrades that may occur on the OpenFlow platform and its persistent model.

The principles applied in the target solution and illustrated **Figure 4** are as follows:

1. Definition of a communication data model and implementation as an Ecore model;

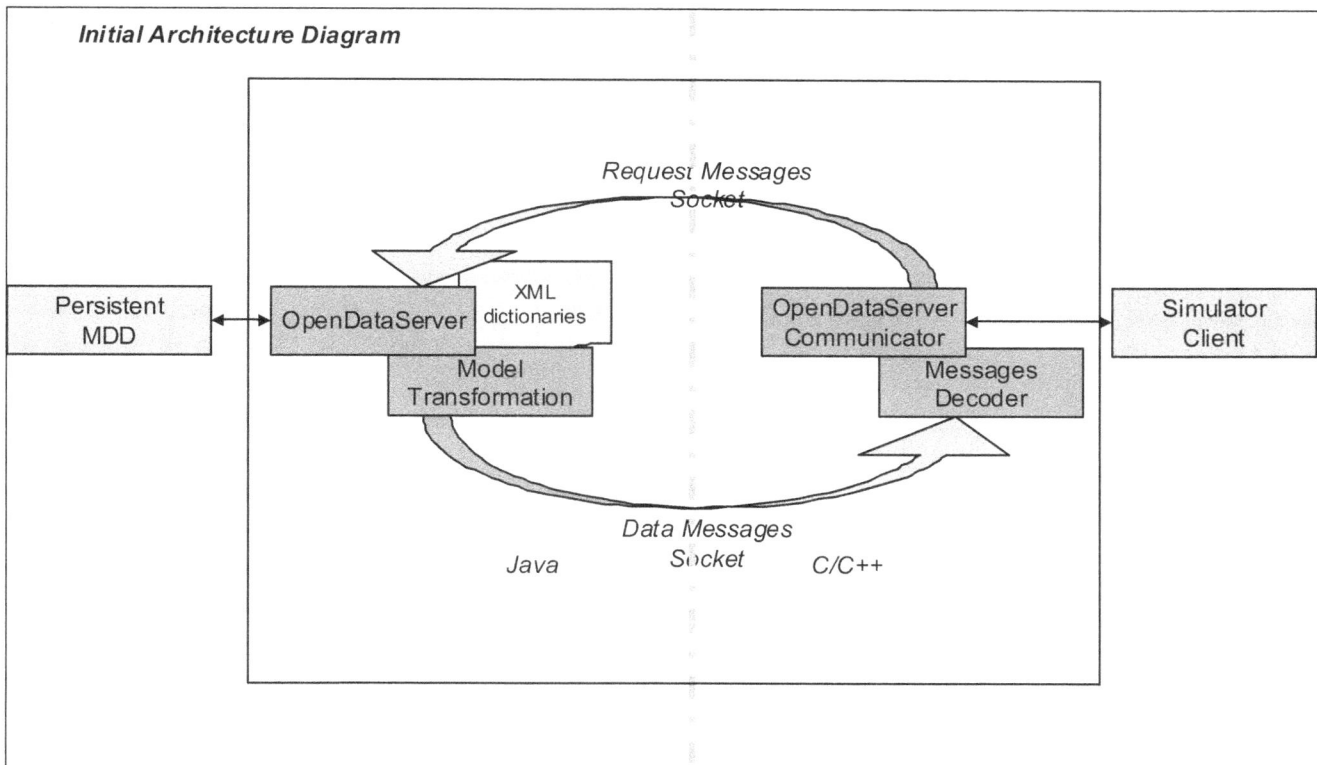

Figure 3. Existing architecture

185

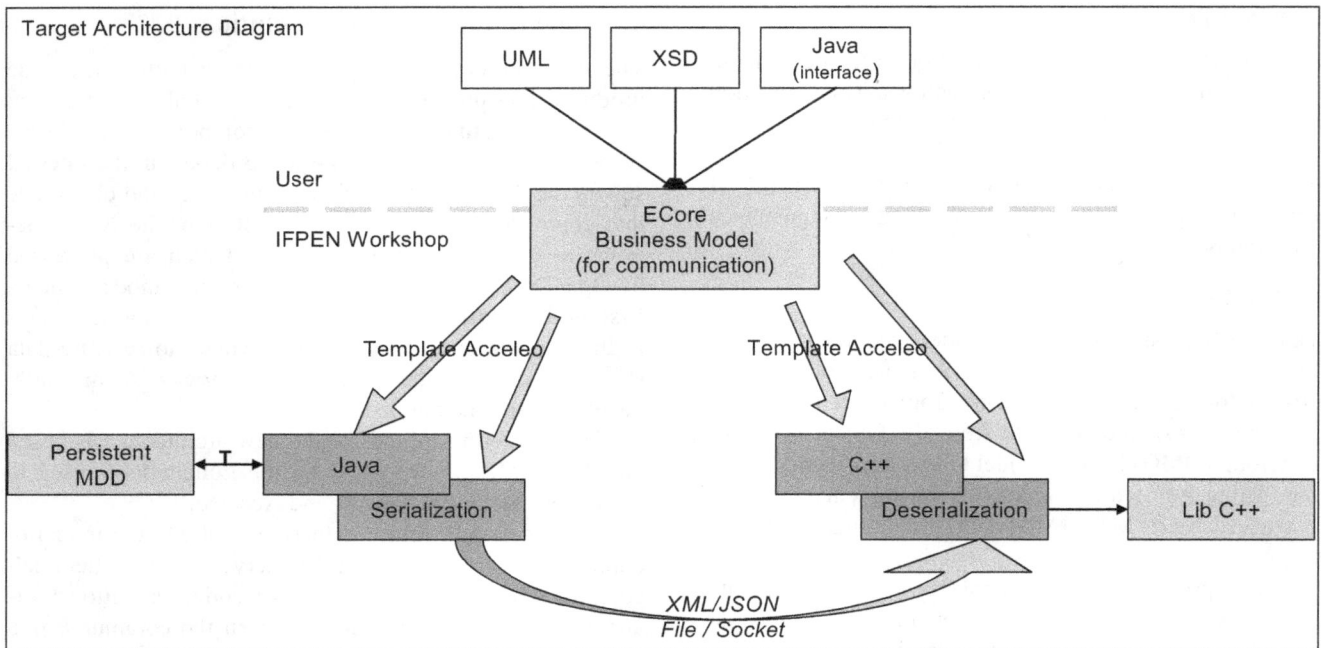

Figure 4. Target architecture

2. Generation of the Java code of this communication model with an Acceleo based generator;

3. Serialization of the communication model with a class also generated with Acceleo.
Deserialization of the communication into a C++ model. This is done by a C++ class generation with Acceleo;

4. From the calculator, access to data via the C++ model getters. The XML dictionary is no longer necessary;

5. No business knowledge will be put in the communication section. Optimization and transformation for adaptation to the calculator can be done via construction of an appropriate communication model.

For example, with our small case study, we work with a EMF model of *Separator*. With our new solution, the Java class is generated and there is no more XML dictionary. There is a new generated C++ *Separator* class used by the `loadProcess` function as in the following listing.

```
private void loadProcess() {
 // Get DataServer
 ods = OpenDataServer::GetOpenDataServer();
 // Send message to get data
 ods->Write("LoadAllSeparatorData");
 std::vector<Seperator*> separators;
 // Creates C++ objects
 ods->load(separators);
 // Do complete mapping in C++ on client side
Process proc = createProcessFromSepara-
tors(separators);
}
```

Any modification in the persistent data model leads to the generation of new version of the Java and C++ classes. At this stage, the only manual edition should be realized in the mapping function on the client side.

5. Implementation – validation

5.1 Organization in projects – plugins

Remember that the final goal is to provide the developers with an IFPEN work environment so that they can develop efficiently an OpenFlow – Calculators data exchange.

In order to have generation functions in the work environment we therefore need:

- An Eclipse version with environment for EMF modeling and Acceleo 3;

- An Eclipse plugin with Java code generation templates and serializer;

- An Eclipse plugin with C++ code generation templates and deserializer;

- An Eclipse plugin with the generation actions and wizard for selection of elements to be generated.

Based on this work environment, the actions to be performed by the developer to develop the OpenFlow - Calculators exchange are as follows:

- Define a new plugin project;

- Construct an Ecore communication model. This model corresponds to the data that will actually be communicated to the calculator;

- Apply Java, C++ generation;

186

- Integrate the Java plugin generated in OpenDataServer via the extension point;

- Link the C++ generated libraries including the model and the deserializer with the calculator;

- Complete the calculator code to request the data and perform mapping to its own model.

5.2 Implementation

This involves implementing the design elements listed above for an existing calculator operating on the initial architecture. This implementation applies to new business entities to be communicated to the calculator. It is therefore a matter of getting the two architectures to co-exist in order to gradually upgrade the initial solution to the target solution.

The following assumptions are made to ensure this co-existence:

- In the first steps, to validate operation, we assume that the communication model and the persistence model are similar. To manage the differences we semantically annotating the data model. Annotations are taken into account during the generation process;

- The co-existence in the data server of two modes "with dictionary" and "without dictionary" will be handled by a special branch. The idea is to configure the project with a key helping the server to choose which branch to use.

Based on these assumptions, the Acceleo templates for generation from the Ecore model are developed together with the GUI action for generation. Taking the assumptions into account, only the templates for generation of the Java serializer in XML, the C++ model and the C++ deserializer are developed. A Java-Json serializer is also tested for reasons of compactness. These plugins are deployed as an IFPEN toolkit and integrated in Eclipse for tests.

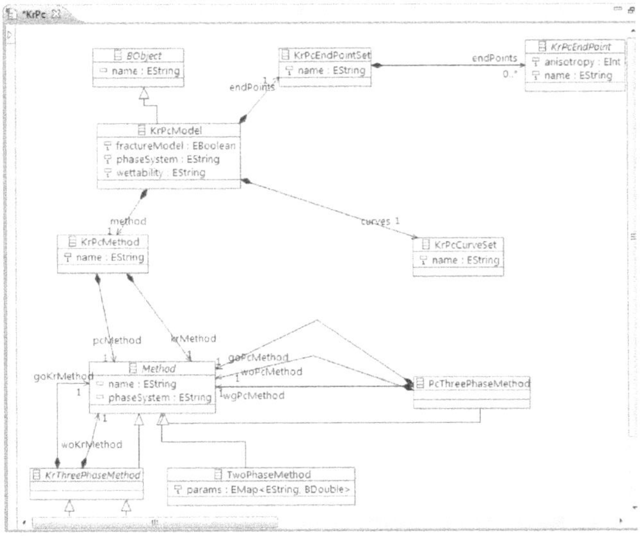

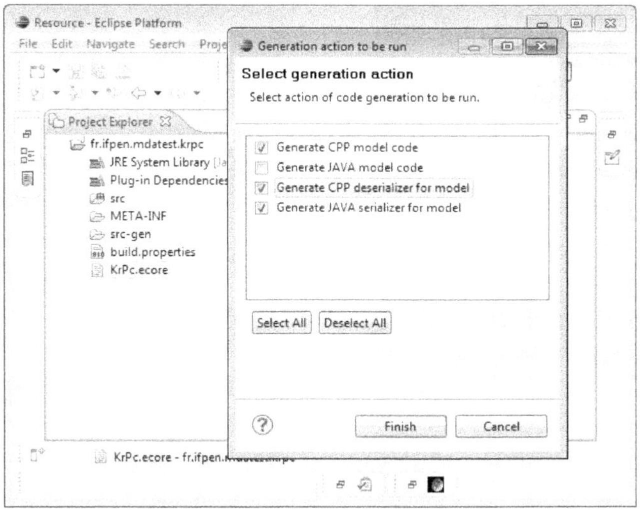

Figure 6. Code generation action

5.3 Test on an actual case

The elements developed are validated using an existing data model already processed with the old architecture in order to compare the results. The data model is based on the persistent model of KrPc (rock type, relative permeability and capillary pressure), some of which is reproduced in **Figure 5**.

The generation action for the different source codes is available on selection of the Ecore model (**Figure 6**). The output code is then compiled and integrated in OpenDataServer for Java and in the client for C++.

5.4 Execution

Once the elements have been generated and integrated in the different entities, the next step is the execution sequence (see **Figure 7**).

1. The C++ client sends a request for data to OpenDataServer. This operation is based on a protocol which is also generated with Acceleo templates;

2. The Java server ODS processes the request, loading the data via the persistent model;

3. The server then calls data adaptors if necessary;

4. The Java instances are serialized, then transferred to the client;

5. The client calls the deserialization tool and retrieves the C++ instances from the transferred data;

6. The client can then use the data.

As mentioned in paragraph 5.2 old and new architectures coexist in a validation version and therefore simulations can be run with both solutions. Results are compared to validate the new architecture. The simulated physical phenomena, oil and gas production at wells in our case, should be strictly identical and it is in this way that we can validate our architecture.

Figure 5. Ecore model for validation

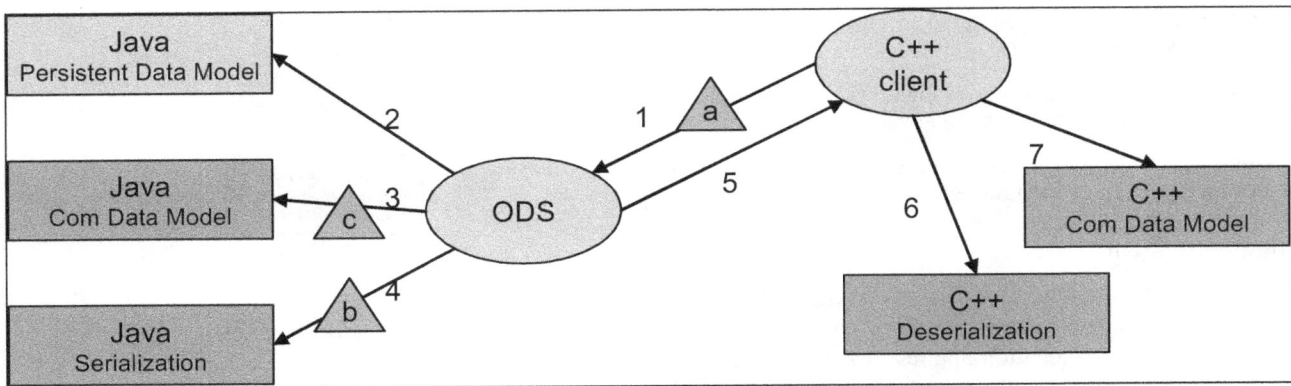

Figure 7. Runtime sequence

The meanings of the small triangles in the **Figure 7** are:

a. Requires a communication protocol between client and server;

b. Uses an Eclipse extension point to register communication data model and serialization tool;

c. Defines mapping between two data models and applies M2M transformation if communication data model and persistent data model differ.

6. Some Metrics

In order to better illustrate the impact of the introduction of MDE in the development process we can quantify the part of technical code that can be generated.

These two tables show the reduction of technical code to maintain when introducing the MDE based solution. The first table counts technical code written once and used as framework in each solution.

Table 1: Generic code metrics

What	Number of lines of code in initial solution	Replace by in IFPEN Workbench
XML for communication	10k	
Java for communication	30k	Acceleo Java template (<1k)
C++ for communication	30k	Acceleo C++ template (<1k)

The second table counts technical code written for each business model. Considering that we have at least 20 different business models to communicate between OpenFlow and a simulator and about 5 to 10 different simulators to manage, more or less 1 million lines of manually written and maintained code can be replaced by Ecore models and generated Java and C++.

Table 2: Per model metrics

What	Number of lines of code in initial solution for KrPc model	Replaced by in IFPEN Workbench
XML for communication	2k	An Ecore model (30 classes)
C++ for model	5k	

The key point is that Acceleo generator is written only once. Then only different data models evolve during the application lifecycle. The maintenance action is then reduced to the maintenance of the workbench (the Acceleo generator) and all generated technical lines of code are not modified any more.

7. Lesson Learned

The objective of this study was to propose a solution to simplify the global mechanism of data transfer from a Java application managing information structured with a data model to C++ or Fortran scientific simulators using this information but through different structures.

The analysis of our existing architecture allowed us in a first time to question the technical choices by returning in particular on the initial constraints, dating almost 10 years, which are not necessarily relevant today. In particular the notion of open services described in a dictionary, if it allows to connect simulators without intervention in the data server, turns out too heavy to maintain in our context. Actually we have the full control of the simulators to be connected and can intervene to manage evolutions of the services.

Besides, the dispersion of the mapping of the data models, partly in the data server, partly on client side turns out to be a source of permanent problems in a model in evolution.

All this analysis and the study of the solutions based on MDE and code generation brought to us to propose a more rigorous solution leaning on a unique reference: the data model. The first step was to build a persistent Java data model that use database. But in the future, the data model will evolve to be based on communication rather than persistence. The existence of the data model allows us to build an efficient and easy-to-use development environment based on the powerful EMF tools.

8. Conclusion

This study demonstrated the advantages of introducing MDE for implementation of a communication system between a graphical environment, a database and distributed numerical simulators.

The main advantage is, of course, to reduce the amount of technical code manually managed and therefore drastically decrease the development time required for the integration of new simulator and the update effort necessary for each evolution of the data model to be transferred.

Another significant advantage is the ability to regulate and harmonize operating modes. In particular, working on a pure communication model ensures that business processing always takes place in the same location and that the role of OpenDataServer is exclusively to send data to the calculators. Within the framework of manual management, it is tempting to perform business processing in this Java section before providing data to the simulators. But scattering business processing throughout OpenDataServer will create upgrade problems. For example, replacing one simulator with another will become more difficult.

The IFPEN workbench therefore also allows developers to work in a better defined framework, and to switch more easily from one simulator to another while concentrating on the connection aspects.

This solution also has limitations, particularly in terms of parallelism and high performance. In the context of a parallel simulator, it may be necessary to supply it with data corresponding to a partitioning. Within this framework the use of MDE can be very difficult. The solution implemented works well for a transfer of a cluster of objects with a parent node and a moderate total volume. In some cases the volume of data to be exchanged has to be finely tuned, and this can only be done manually.

The prospects for industrial implementation are however very interesting for a high number of information elements and simulators that require distribution but not necessarily parallelism. The aim is therefore to put the solution into practice for new data and future simulators every time the impact on performance is negligible.

References

[1] Eclipse Foundation: What is Eclipse and the Eclipse Foundation?, http://www.eclipse.org/org/ (2012)

[2] Schmidt, D.C.: Model-Driven Engineering, IEEE Computer (2006)

[3] Object Management Group: MDA Spécifications, http://www.omg.org/mda/specs.htm

[4] Steinberg, D., Budinsky, F., Paternostro, M., Merks, E.: EMF: Eclipse Modeling Framework, 2nd Edition, Addison-Wesley Professional, (2008)

[5] Baker, P., Loh, S., Weil, F.: Model-driven engineering in a large industrial context - Motorola case study. In: Briand, L.C., Williams, C. (eds.) MoDELS 2005. LNCS, vol. 3713, pp. 476–491. Springer, Heidelberg (2005)

[6] Staron, M.: Adopting model driven software development in industry - a case study at two companies. In: Nierstrasz, O., Whittle, J., Harel, D., Reggio, G. (eds.) MoDELS 2006. LNCS, vol. 4199, pp. 57–72. Springer, Heidelberg (2006)

[7] Fleurey, F. et al.: Model-Driven Engineering for Software Migration in a Large Industrial Context, MoDELS 2007, LNCS 4735, pp. 482–497. Springer, Heidelberg (2007)

[8] Eclipse Foundation: Eclipse Modeling Framework, http://www.eclipse.org/modeling/emf/ (2012)

[9] TOPCASED: The Open-Source Toolkit for Critical System, http://www.topcased.org/ (2011)

[10] Eclipse Foundation: Acceleo, http://www.eclipse.org/acceleo/ (2012)

[11] Object Management Group: Object Constraint Language Spécifications, http://www.omg.org/spec/OCL/ (2012)

MySQL to NoSQL

Data Modeling Challenges in Supporting Scalability

Aaron Schram

Department of Computer Science
University of Colorado
Boulder, Colorado, USA
aaron.schram@colorado.edu

Kenneth M. Anderson

Department of Computer Science
University of Colorado
Boulder, Colorado, USA
kena@cs.colorado.edu

Abstract

Software systems today seldom reside as isolated systems confined to generating and consuming their own data. Collecting, integrating and storing large amounts of data from disparate sources has become a need for many software engineers, as well as for scientists in research settings. This paper presents the lessons learned when transitioning a large-scale data collection infrastructure from a relational database to a hybrid persistence architecture that makes use of both relational and NoSQL technologies. Our examples are drawn from the software infrastructure we built to collect, store, and analyze vast numbers of status updates from the Twitter micro-blogging service in support of a large interdisciplinary group performing research in the area of crisis informatics. We present both the software architecture and data modeling challenges that we encountered during the transition as well as the benefits we gained having migrated to the hybrid persistence architecture.

Categories and Subject Descriptors D.2.11 [**Software Engineering**]: Software Architectures; D.2.13 [**Software Engineering**]: Reusable Software.

General Terms Design, Reliability.

Keywords *crisis informatics; NoSQL; data modeling; scalability; software architecture; software infrastructure*

1. Introduction

Collecting, integrating and storing large amounts of information is quickly becoming a necessity among software engineers in industry, as well as by scientists in research settings. Crisis informatics [8] is one research area in which this need has never been greater. Crisis informatics studies how information and communication technology are used in emergency and hazard response. An emerging branch of this discipline investigates how members of the public make use of social media and other forms of computer-mediated communication to aid one another during times of mass emergency [7]. The analysis of this type of data relies heavily on a robust and scalable data collection infrastructure. The ephemeral nature of the data (e.g. Twitter status updates) requires collection to be done in real-time and with uncompromising reliability. Since Fall 2009, we have been engaged in the design and development of this type of data collection infrastructure via our work in Project EPIC (Empowering the Public with Information in Crisis) [7].

We have designed and developed this infrastructure in an iterative fashion, implementing it initially using a standard, three-tier web architecture. We then expanded the system to expose layers of services that could be leveraged by other research groups—as well as within our own team—to isolate the complexities of interacting with our data model and permit reuse of our collection tools. We also exposed a layer of web services to allow geographically distributed mobile clients better access to our services and data. While these are modern software engineering practices, we were eventually faced with the challenge of scaling our persistence tier due to the enormous amounts of data produced by even a single mass emergency event [1], leading to the need for us to pursue additional techniques and technology.

We report here on the current state and future direction of the data collection infrastructure we are developing to support research in crisis informatics. Software engineering has begun to play an even more critical role than we could have initially imagined in this domain. The data collected and stored by our system are vital to the research of our colleagues in such areas as natural language processing (NLP), systems and security, internet policy, and human centered computing (HCC). For these groups to extract representative samples and to make statistically significant research claims they rely almost entirely on the accurate and timely collection of social media data by our system.

This dependence puts constraints of scalability and robustness at the forefront of system design, often receiving priority over simple feature requests involving our analysis tools. These constraints put a great deal of pressure on our software engineering research team because the work they do on the design and development of the infrastructure is often concealed from the rest of the research group. Having accurate and complete data sets are often thought of as a given by research colleagues, who have become accustomed to working with publicly available data sets such as the "Brown Corpus" [6]. Our goal is to meet this expectation and provide them with near real-time access to data sets of similar quality. In designing a system to support these highly demanding needs we are tasked with providing a system that is fault-tolerant in a number of areas involving highly distributed and scalable systems—characteristics not typically required when developing software prototypes in service of software engineering research.

2. Background

Project EPIC's data collection infrastructure is composed of multiple services that can be leveraged individually or in composition. These services abstract away the inherent complexities present in collecting, storing, and analyzing status messages from the Twitter micro-blogging platform. Each service exposes a well-defined set of interfaces that can be utilized as-is or extended to meet the varying needs of a particular client. Project EPIC shares these services across multiple web and command line applications running on separate machines and in separate Java virtual machines allowing each application to create, modify, and query entities in a consistent way on a shared data store [1].

Like many web architectures, our first choice for a storage solution was a traditional relational data store. For our purposes we chose the open source relational database management system, MySQL.[1] It offered the best set of features for our project's needs and is widely used amongst some of the biggest web companies in existence, including Facebook and Flickr. We also heavily relied upon the popular object relational mapping (ORM) framework, Hibernate, which is known to integrate well with MySQL. The focus at the time of the initial system design was on quickly providing our colleagues with a set of features that would be immediately useful in collecting the datasets they needed to conduct their own research. Scalability and reliability

---

[1] Note: All of the specific technologies mentioned in this paper are either well known or easily found via an Internet search.

were considered but, as with many initial projects, it was difficult to anticipate the scope of our storage needs.

Although it is well known that traditional relational databases can be made to scale through techniques such as the *sharding* of data amongst a set of machines or the acquisition of often-expensive hardware, we report here on our investigation into a class of technologies referred to as NoSQL. The requirements placed on our infrastructure by our research colleagues are those where current NoSQL technologies excel, such as high availability and scalability. In this paper, we report on the challenges facing our software engineering group as we transition from a MySQL-only persistence architecture to a hybrid model which makes use of both MySQL and NoSQL.

3. NoSQL

NoSQL is a term used to describe a broad class of technologies that provide an alternative approach to data storage compared with traditional relation database management systems. Often these technologies provide the user with low-cost solutions to the problems of high availability and scalability at the loss of a flexible query language, making ad hoc access of the data generally more difficult. The term NoSQL was initially meant to make this clear by standing for *"no SQL"* but the term has more recently been updated to mean *"not only SQL"* as very few production systems eliminate relational databases altogether.

The current offerings of these technologies are heavily influenced by Google's Bigtable [2] and Amazon's Dynamo [4] systems. Current NoSQL systems include: HBase, MongoDB, Riak, Voldemort, Cassandra, Memcached, Tokyo Cabinet, Redis, and CouchDB. Each has its own specialties and they are often differentiated by how they can scale to handle extremely large datasets.

In contrast to a relational database, a NoSQL datastore attempts to group similar data together on disk to limit the number of seeks required to manipulate data to improve access times. The data models provided by NoSQL systems often force the user to structure their data in easily distributable multidimensional maps (across a cluster of machines). Access to these key/value maps is provided by APIs that expose traditional, easily understood map operations (i.e. get, put, contains, and remove). This approach has the added benefit of allowing the segments of the data to be read and processed in parallel using a MapReduce [3] framework, such as Hadoop. Project EPIC has chosen to migrate the data collection aspect of its software architecture to the Apache open source project Cassandra [5]. This decision was driven in part due to the growing popularity and high development activity on the Cassandra project as well as the availability of a newly released product from DataStax, which bundles together Cassandra, Hadoop, and Hive. Hive offers a SQL-like syntax for analyzing data stored in Hadoop; it is an attempt to provide a query language to those projects that prefer the query functionality provided by relational storage technologies over the Bigtable-influenced, non-relational APIs of NoSQL.

3.1 Cassandra

Cassandra was originally a project developed at the popular social media site, Facebook, to serve data to hundreds of millions of users during peak usage levels [5]. Specifically, it was designed to fulfill the storage requirements of the Inbox Search feature, which allowed users to quickly search all the contents of their message inbox. It was released to the open source community in July 2008, later transitioning into an Apache Incubator project in March 2009. It is now in commercial use at a variety of companies, such as Digg, Reddit, and Twitter.

Cassandra is a mix of techniques taken from Bigtable and Dynamo, essentially running the Bigtable data model [2] on top of the Dynamo fully-distributed architecture [4]. It possesses the most favorable traits of both its predecessors resulting in a fault tolerant, decentralized system with rich data modeling capabilities. It is fully distributed and even allows for replication to take place between data centers. Cassandra was an ideal fit for the research goals of Project EPIC because it directly attacks the complex problems of data replication, scalability, and 100% uptime while allowing our existing data models to be represented (albeit not without significant work in making the transition—see Section 6).

4.   System Architecture

Project EPIC's existing architecture (see Fig. 1) is a production-ready system that includes multiple web and command line applications. In its two years of deployment it has collected over 2B disaster-related status messages covering numerous mass emergency events that occurred in 2010-2012 while maintaining 99% uptime. This reliability has been achieved through careful design of the infrastructure's service tier, which is responsible for abstracting the inherent complexities involved in data collection, persistence, and aggregation from disparate sources [1].

The service tier relies on the persistence tier to handle all interactions with the data store. Initially these interactions were limited to MySQL, taking responsibility for isolating and abstracting away the complexities of managing database create, read, update, and delete (CRUD) operations, transactions, and queries. These interactions are accomplished through the use of a callback that wraps logic defined in the service tier that will eventually be executed in the persistence tier, often within the context of a database transaction. The configuration of the persistence tier is done through the use of property files, allowing clients to specify, at run-time, such settings as database hosts, ports, and names. Indeed, it would even be possible for a particular client to configure services to communicate with com-

pletely separate data stores. This can be easily accomplished because all of Project EPIC services are *wired* at run-time through the use of the Spring dependency injection framework. This allows the service consumer to configure each service independently and, in some cases, even swap out configuration settings during program execution. The use of the Spring framework also enables a high degree of modularity, increasing testability through mock objects frameworks (e.g. JMock), and allowing our team to develop the infrastructure incrementally.

A strong advantage of using Project EPIC's service tier is the ability to work with a rich set of domain objects. These domain objects model many of the commonly encountered artifacts of crisis informatics research, providing getter and setter methods for each available property. An example domain object is the Tweet object, which exposes such attributes as the user that generated the tweet, the time the tweet was created, and the text of the tweet. If used in conjunction with the appropriate service, all fields are automatically populated for the consumer of the service regardless of the source of the tweet. Currently a tweet may be retrieved directly from Twitter over HTTP, or from any relational database, or a Lucene index. The client requires no specialized knowledge for how to retrieve a tweet matching their needs from each potential data source, which otherwise would require the knowledge of many different APIs; instead the client is simply returned a fully populated object graph that fulfills the constraints of the query issued by the client.

The flexibility of this architecture allows for the addition of a number of different persistent storage solutions without changing the client software. As long as the contract provided by the service to the client remains valid, how the persistence tier chooses to store the information should be irrelevant to the client. The Project EPIC architecture then allows for the addition of a high availability storage solution, in this case Cassandra, to be introduced incrementally into the system without breaking current clients. This transition would not have been possible if our clients had been interacting directly with our data stores rather than the abstract interfaces of our service and persistence tiers.

5.   Data Model

One of the key design changes that must be accomplished for a successful transition from relational technology to the use of NoSQL techniques and technology is the transformation of the system's existing data model. Indeed, this can be a challenging task. Software engineering students are taught to model the world as objects that interact with one another via messages and to think of relationships between objects in terms of one-to-one, one-to-many, many-to-one, and many-to-many. A single object is seldom valuable without well-defined relationships with other objects. This style of design is well suited for transferring an object

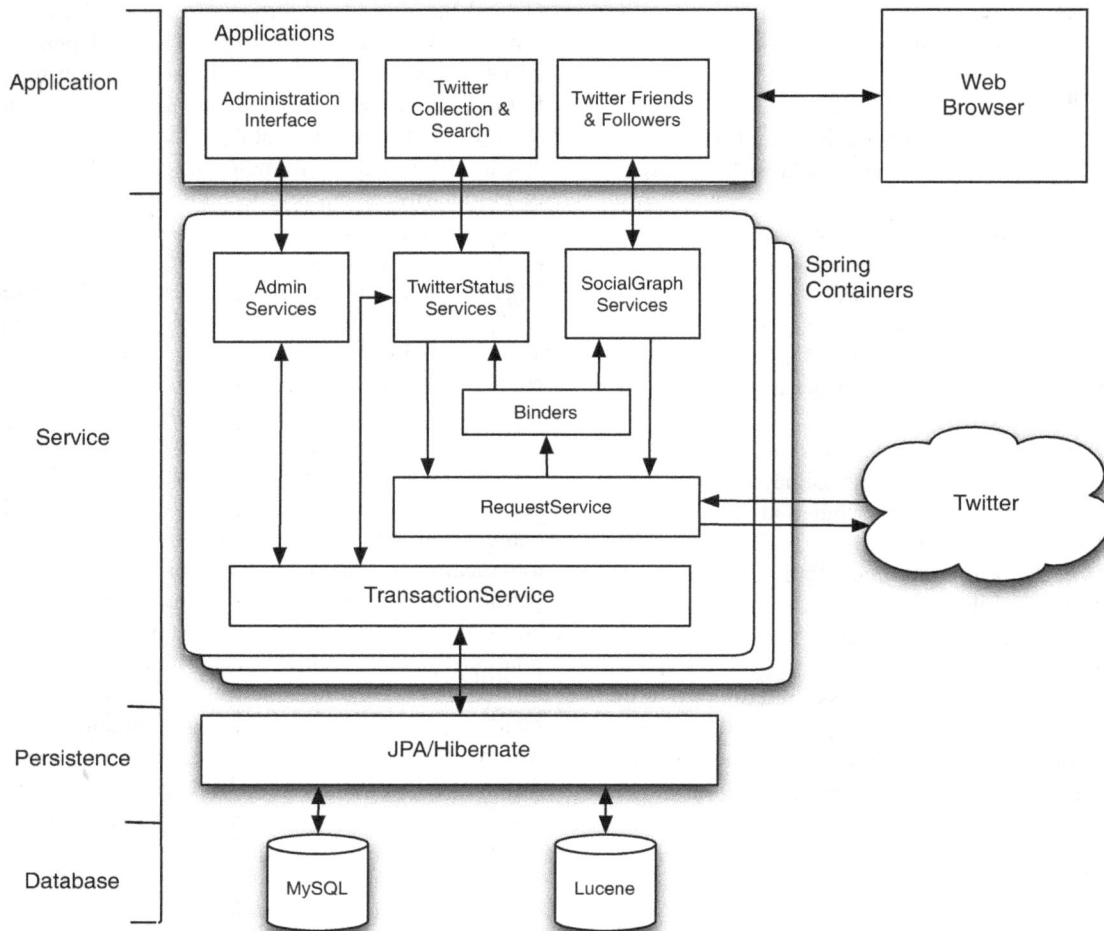

Figure 1. The Project EPIC software architecture before the addition of NoSQL technologies [1]. As a testament to its flexible, abstract design, the architecture remains largely the same after the transition. Existing services can continue to access data initially persisted in MySQL and Lucene. In the persistence layer, new infrastructure is added to manage access to a Casandra cluster (see Fig. 7). New services can then be created to access the new persistence infrastructure.

model into a relational database. The relational style allows a software engineer to model objects as database tables and the relationships between objects as primary and foreign keys that link the tables together. These relationships can then be exploited by issuing queries via SQL.

Today there is a direct, well-traveled path for software engineers to take requirements and develop complex models that are easily represented in traditional relational data stores. Requirements can be read and easily translated into UML, which is used to model complex relations and actions. Current UML tools can even generate the source code for classes from UML diagrams. That code can then be annotated using frameworks like Hibernate to automatically generate the necessary database tables to persist objects without requiring the developer to have any knowledge of the underlying relational database. The tasks

required to take an arbitrary data model from a set of requirements to a fully functioning persistence tier have been abstracted fantastically well. These are very valuable tools to have available to modern day software engineers as it allows a software engineer to focus on the application being built not on the complex details required to create and manage a database. It is now standard practice to rely on ORM frameworks for handling all interactions with the database, enabling the client to interact only with objects and their relationships. Indeed, Project EPIC's persistence and service tiers and the models they share are based on these same *best practices*.

Project EPIC's data model is a rich set of plain old Java objects (POJOs). POJOs are often referred to as Java beans, implying that they conform to the convention that each object exposes a set of properties that will have similarly

Event
name: String
start: Date
end: Date

Tweet
id: long
createdAt: Date
text: String
...

User
id: long
screen_name: String

*   *   *

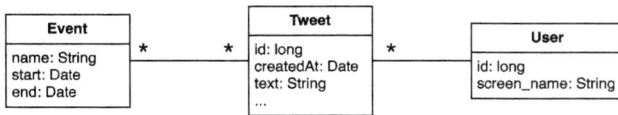

Figure 2. Project EPIC's simplified object model for collecting data from Twitter during a disaster event.

named getter and setter methods also available. As an example a Person object with a *name* property will, by convention, expose two methods: *getName()* and *setName()*. This allows other Java frameworks to make assumptions about how to interact with this object. Using run-time reflection it becomes possible to access or define the value of any object property easily using the Java bean convention. The Java Persistence API (JPA), which defines a specification for automatically persisting Java objects, makes use of these POJOs. All of Project EPIC's domain objects are marked with Java 5.0 annotations that allow them to be persisted using the JPA with little effort on behalf of the development team. This technology allowed our team to move from whiteboard to a fully functioning persistence system in a short amount of time simply by following JPA best practices. However—shortly after initial deployment—it became clear to the team that although we were able to develop and deploy a system quickly, we were ignorant of details that cause performance bottlenecks in these systems.

JPA provides the developer with a simple set of annotations to define how to persist object properties and object relationships. Objects are often automatically discovered via the *@Entity* annotation and database tables, column names, and column types are often created via reflection of the object's properties. Relationships between objects can be persisted through the use of the *@OneToOne, @OneToMany, @ManyToOne,* and *@ManyToMany* annotations. These annotations are extremely powerful as they enable a developer to model a variety of complex object relationships; incredibly, these annotations are able to automatically generate complex primary keys, foreign keys, and join tables that are needed to model these relationships in the underlying database. Although a great and necessary asset, these annotations can produce a variety of performance problems forcing the relational database into inefficient operations to support an arbitrary model being utilized in a separate tier of the application.

For example, in Fig. 2, we present a simplified version of the object model we use when collecting data from Twitter during a disaster event: *Users generate tweets; tweets can be associated with one or more Events.* Collecting data from Twitter during a mass emergency event is the primary focus of the Project EPIC data collection infrastructure. Collection must be done in real-time with little to no errors during the designated event window. Tweets collected during an event remain associated with that event. As an ex-

ample, during March of 2011, Project EPIC was monitoring several events including the Japan earthquake; the continuing conflicts of the "Arab Spring"; the Christchurch, New Zealand earthquake; and a local wildfire near Boulder, Colorado. Due to the constraints of the Twitter Streaming API, our infrastructure returned tweets that match any of up to 400 distinct search terms. The infrastructure must analyze each tweet returned by that API and associate it with its corresponding event(s). Once data collection for an event ends, the corresponding tweets can be exported to a variety of formats or moved from production to other machines to free up storage space for new events.

There is a many-to-many relationship between Event and Tweet and there is a one-to-many relationship between User and Tweet. If we annotated the Java objects that represent Event, Tweet and User with the @ManyToMany and the @OneToMany annotations, an object-relational manager such as Hibernate would automatically produce the join tables and foreign keys in a relational data store that would allow, e.g., a developer to traverse from an Event object to a collection containing all of that event's Tweet objects. The problem is that Hibernate will create that collection whether it contains 100 Tweets or 75 million (the size of our Haiti dataset). In the latter case, the client program will sit blocked as Hibernate pulls back the information needed to instantiate 75 million instances of the Tweet class and will eventually crash as the system runs out of memory.

There are other issues that can occur with the use of ORM technologies at scale but this example illustrates the essential problem: ORM frameworks can not scale to truly large datasets as the relationships between objects will cause the framework to pull information into memory unnecessarily. For instance, the simple act of collecting a new tweet from Twitter and adding it to an existing event can cause an object-relational manger to pull into memory all of the tweets associated with an event if the system is not engineered to guard against such automatic behavior. This automatic behavior is incredibly useful; it unfortunately just does not scale to large datasets.

Modeling relationships is the most difficult aspect of using ORM frameworks. As we have just seen, application-level logical abstractions often do not translate into efficient storage representations. This makes it very difficult to build a highly available and scalable application using these technologies, especially when following what are widely held as good software engineering principles such as object-oriented design heuristics and data normalization. What we have found is that in order to enable scalability many of these software engineering best practices must be employed *outside of the persistence tier*. In the world of high scalability, data is often replicated and distributed amongst hundreds or thousands of machines. *Normalized, relational data have no place here*, and this in turn leads to design choices that deal with the complexities associated

Row Key 1	Column Name 1	•••	Column Name N
	Value	•••	Value
•••			
Row Key N	Column Name 1	•••	Column Name N
	Value	•••	Value

Figure 3. Casandra's Column Family: Each row maps to a potentially different set of columns.

with highly scalable and distributed systems that do not mesh well with the classical software engineering view of the world. But, these tradeoffs typically enable true and easy horizontal scalability, something that is difficult to achieve with a traditional relational database system.

6. Making the Transition

The data collection aspect of Project EPIC's software infrastructure was identified as the first piece of the architecture to be transitioned to NoSQL technology. Now that we have billions of tweets to store and analyze, the benefits of making this transition are many. Data replication, horizontally-scalable storage, and high availability are characteristics that are difficult to achieve with our initial design based on relational databases but are straightforward to achieve with NoSQL. Additionally, our team was not made up of professional system administrators yet more and more of our daily tasks were moving from software engineering research to monitoring, maintaining, and scaling our existing storage solution. Moving our events and tweets into a NoSQL data store fulfills many of our storage needs and promises to reduce the maintenance tasks that were taking us away from our research. In addition, the transition presented several software engineering and data modeling challenges with implications for software architecture and the design of scalable software systems.

To make the transition, we needed to ensure that the existing services would not break simply because our data moved from a relational database to a NoSQL platform. The current service tier allows clients to retrieve all tweets collected during an event. An example would be a client asking for all tweets associated with the March 2011 Japan earthquake. The service tier also allows for the retrieval of a set of tweets by user regardless of event association. Finally, our research colleagues require the ability to retrieve tweets by specifying a date range, since it is often necessary to focus on a subset of the tweets collected during an event. We will address each one of these concerns individually and how these requests require a specific approach to object/data modeling within a NoSQL data store.

6.1 Events and Tweets

As mentioned above, Project EPIC has decided to adopt Cassandra, a NoSQL technology developed and maintained by the Apache Software Foundation. Cassandra directly addresses the need to have our data replicated across multiple machines to enable high availability; in addition, it provides a flexible mechanism for modeling the objects within our application domain. Cassandra makes use of a data model similar to that described in the work on Google's Bigtable [2]. In particular, Cassandra provides modeling concepts similar to Bigtable's *rows*, *columns*, and *column families*. Cassandra also exposes another type known as a *super column*; however super columns have been shown to impose a 10-15% performance penalty on reads and writes, so we have decided not to use them as our current object modeling tasks do not require their use.

The first step in transitioning our existing relational model is denormalizing our data. In a relational model, a many-to-many relationship would require a join table, tying events to tweets, allowing a single tweet to be associated with many events. Modeling the same type of relationship in Cassandra can be done in two ways. First, it is possible to maintain a join table representation as a column family (in essence maintaining the data in a relational form). Another option, more suited to our purposes, is to simply store the representation of the tweet in multiple places. Although this duplication may seem like a poor choice as it goes against the practices of normalizing (i.e. not duplicating) data in the relational style, in NoSQL the assumption is that "storage is cheap" and one should not shy away from storing duplicate copies of an artifact when necessary.

Cassandra makes use of *column families* to store its data (see Fig. 3). A column family consists of *rows* that point to many *columns*. Each *column* has a *column name* and a *column value*. This structure is essentially a hash table of hash tables. Note: there is no requirement that each row store the same columns. One row can have columns x, y, and z storing a string, an integer and a date while the next row has columns a, b, and c storing an integer, a float and a string.

We will be using the column family data structure to model the relationship between Events and Tweets. For our purposes we will create one column family called *Events*. This column family will use event data as its *row key* and tweet data for its columns. A *row key* in Cassandra is a unique key that allows the client to index into the column family and retrieve columns. Row keys can be of any number of types including—but not limited to—strings, dates, and numbers. With respect to Fig. 2, we would like to retrieve tweets based on event names. It would also be possible to generate unique event ids and maintain the mappings between the event names and the unique ids somewhere else. Indeed, this is something that we do in our production system but for the purposes of illustration we will simply use a unique event name as our row key. Cassandra can then use these keys to distribute and/or replicate our data across a cluster of machines.

Event Name 1	Tweet Id 1	•••	Tweet Id N
	JSON	•••	JSON
•••			
Event Name N	Tweet Id 1	•••	Tweet Id N
	JSON	•••	JSON

Figure 4. Events Column Family.

The next step in converting our existing relational model will be storing the tweets themselves. Each tweet is given a unique numeric identifier from Twitter. This unique id will be used as the column name for our event columns. This decision merits some explanation. Cassandra is a schema-less data store, which means that it enforces no requirements that the rows contain similar columns, as mentioned above. One example where this would occur would be in storing a set of users and their attributes. The unique username would serve as the row key and the associated columns would store the attributes allowing the retrieval of attribute values by attribute name. As such, a client could ask for a user's date of birth by specifying the row key, perhaps *jsmith*, and the attribute of interest, perhaps *date_of_birth*. This would return to the client the user's date of birth. Our storage of events and tweets will not work like this since tweets are delivered with a large set of metadata that changes over time (as Twitter evolves the services and information it provides to its developers). We take advantage of Cassandra's lack of schema enforcement to store a new tweet in every column of an event row, using the tweet's unique id as the column name. Thus, each row in our Events column family will contain a different number of columns based on the number of tweets collected for that event (which can number in the tens of millions or more). The value for each column will be the raw JSON object that Twitter delivered to us at the time of collection (see Fig. 4). A column value can be of any number of types. In this example JSON can simply be stored as a string or it may be advantageous to store the JSON as a series of bytes in a compressed format, requiring compression and expansion for all writes and reads. These operations could be isolated within the service or persistence tiers and may limit the amount of time spent on IO resulting in increased performance.

These data modeling choices allow us to map our existing object model into Cassandra while providing us with the most flexibility for analyzing the data at a later point in time. By storing the full JSON object, no information about the tweet is lost. However, since each tweet contains a complete copy of its user's metadata, this approach results in a large amount of data duplication since rather than storing the information about a user only once (as we would in a relational model) we now are storing the entire user object for each tweet that a user contributed to the event.

Despite this duplication, this approach to storing the data is in fact better than our current relational structure because, as mentioned above, the attributes of a tweet returned to us by Twitter are often subject to change without notice. With the relational model, you are either forced to store the tweet as a BLOB or CLOB (thus losing the very power that the relational approach was trying to provide) or you must spend time updating your schema to store the new metadata and then migrate your entire data store to the new schema. With NoSQL, the promise of relational functionality was never offered in the first place but in exchange it offers a data store that provides horizontal scalability ("need more data, just add another machine to your cluster") and high availability through replication across the cluster. However, this technique is not without its faults. Storing the raw JSON data of the tweet as the column value limits Cassandra's ability to provide useful results to queries against the column's values. These concerns are addressed in the next section.

6.2 Tweets and Attributes

In some situations, our collaborators on Project EPIC may need to run queries against the attributes of the tweets that our data collection infrastructure has captured during an event, across multiple events, or even independent of an event altogether. A common case—and one our infrastructure supported before this migration—is retrieving all tweets that have been collected for a given Twitter user. If a user then wanted to further limit the results to tweets only generated during a specific event, they could easily filter the results by date or some other attribute.

To support this functionality in Cassandra, our Events column family is not enough. It only implements traversal of our original many-to-many relationship from events to tweets; details concerning attributes—such as which user created a particular tweet—are hidden away in the JSON object stored as a column value in that column family, which is an opaque data type from Cassandra's point of view. In order to go the other direction—from tweets to events—or to search tweets directly we will need to define a new column family in Cassandra.

There are multiple ways to model this column family for this particular use case. One option would be to follow the event example set forth in the previous section using the screen_name of the user as the row key in place of the event name. Although this would work, it is not as versatile as we might like. It limits us to searching only on the screen_name and not via other attributes such as the text of the tweet, the day it was created, or its latitude and longitude (if it was a geocoded tweet).

To enable this type of search, we make use of the *secondary indexing* feature provided by Cassandra. Secondary indexes allow the client to execute very simple queries against column values that can be indexed by Cassandra.

Tweet Id 1	createdAt	text	screen_name	•••
	Date	String	String	•••
•••				
Tweet Id N	createdAt	text	screen_name	•••
	Date	String	String	•••

Figure 5. Tweets Column Family.

This feature makes it worth our while to model each tweet as a row (using its unique tweet id as the row key) in which each column corresponds to an attribute of the tweet that we care about. We can then ask Cassandra to create a secondary index on any of the columns that we know will be used to locate tweets independent of an event; for this use case, we will index the *screen_name* column of each row. The resulting column family can be seen in Fig. 5.

Using this representation a tweet and its attributes can now be retrieved via a lookup on the tweet's unique id or by looking up all tweets that match a given value for a column that carries a secondary index. Indexing the screen_name attribute will allow a client to request all tweets for a given user. As an example all the tweets for a user with a known screen_name *jsmith* could be retrieved by asking for all tweets where *"screen_name = 'jsmith'"*. In addition, in order to implement the other direction of our many-to-many relationship between Events and Tweets, we could simply add one (or more) columns that store the event names (or event ids) of the events each tweet is associated with. Then, it would not matter what query brought us to a particular tweet, since pulling the event information from the appropriate column(s) will allow us to access information about that tweet's events from other column families. However, performance may suffer slightly in this case because the read operations of the disk may not be sequential like they will be for the Events column family.

6.3 Time Slicing Events

An important aspect of data collected by Project EPIC is the matter of temporality: When was a tweet collected? When did an event start? How active was a particular user on this day? Many of our research colleagues base their analysis techniques on time windows and timelines. As such our data model must support the ability to partition data by time. The fidelity of these time windows can range from one day to the full duration of an event. To support that functionality using NoSQL technology, we will store the data in the smallest increment required, one day, and "roll-up" to a desired duration. Doing so will enable a high degree of flexibility for use by our existing services.

To support time slicing of tweets across events we will need to segment our data by the day the tweet was collected

from Twitter. To accomplish this we will need a mapping of days to tweets collected on those days. This could be done via the addition of a new column family. That approach, however, would require the service tier to join together the data from the new column family and the Events column family, which is not ideal for our purposes. Until now we have omitted discussing a common "gotcha" in NoSQL data modeling. Indeed, it is a problem present even in our previous discussion of the Events column family.

A single event in the Events column family may contain an extremely large number of tweets (in the 10s of millions). This results in a single row key with an extremely large number of columns. Generally this is considered a bad practice. When Cassandra attempts to replicate keys and their associated data (columns) around a cluster of machines all of the key's data is replicated as a unit. This can result in long delays or timeouts when adding additional nodes to the cluster. Our Events column family, as shown in Fig. 4, could encounter scalability problems during events of long duration. Adding the requirement of supporting the partitioning of the data by time actually enables and ensures linear scalability. By decreasing the number of columns stored with each key the amount of data that must be moved with each key when it is replicated across the cluster is also decreased, resulting in faster key replication. In fact, data reads may also be more efficient because the client may now specify the exact data they are interested in receiving instead of requesting all the data available. To enable this new approach, we must slightly modify our Events column family via the use of a *composite row key*.

Our initial row key for our Events column family was simply a unique event name. This key mapped a single event to all the tweets associated with the event. Since the row key for our Events column family is simply a string, we will make a small modification to the string to support the time partitioning requirements. The new row key will be a composite string starting with the unique event name and ending with the day the tweets in this row were collected; the two elements of a composite key are separated—by convention—with a colon (":").

Given a date range and an event name, we can now construct the required composite keys in our service tier to retrieve the desired set of tweets. This change can be seen in Fig. 6. This simple change now allows for the full range of time slicing operations required by our research colleagues and also greatly enhances scalability by preventing the rows of the Events column family from becoming too large to efficiently replicate across a cluster. In addition, this scheme is easily extended to handle time windows of finer granularity by splitting existing rows into smaller rows and extending the key to also include a timestamp.

7. After the Transition

The previous section discussed various data modeling challenges that software engineers will encounter when their scalability needs force a transition away from relational technology and towards NoSQL technology. However, this transition is not one of completely replacing the former with the latter—hence the "not only SQL" expansion for the NoSQL term—but rather adding NoSQL technologies into an existing software infrastructure providing it with a hybrid persistence architecture.

After the addition, of NoSQL technologies to Project EPIC's data collection infrastructure, its software architecture now takes the form shown in Fig. 7. The existing persistence-related components—our transaction service, Hibernate, MySQL, and Lucene—are all still present and all services and applications that previously made use of them still function with their previous levels of scalability and reliability [1]. Now, however, an additional API called Hector exists within the persistence tier and is now available to any service within our service tier. Hector is a Java wrapper for Cassandra's native API, which makes use of the Apache project Thrift. Thrift handles interactions with the services of a Cassandra cluster and Hector provides access to Thrift via a Java API.

Project EPIC's software architecture was well-suited for a transition from a relational-only persistence architecture to a hybrid persistence architecture due to its use of the Spring dependency injection framework. In Fig. 1, all of the services shown in the service tier have abstract interfaces that get implemented by particular concrete classes. All interactions between services occur via the abstract interfaces and rely on Spring to plug-in concrete implementations at run-time to achieve desired functionality.

So, while it was not made explicit in Fig. 1, it is *not* the TwitterStatusService that talks to the TransactionService but the MySQLTwitterStatusService that talks to the ProjectEPICTransactionService at run-time. These latter two classes are concrete implementations of the previous two abstract interfaces. MySQLTwitterStatusService knows how to make use of the transaction service and Hibernate to store and access tweets in MySQL. Meanwhile the Twitter Collection & Search application that lives within the application tier knows only about the abstract TwitterStatusService interface and knows nothing about MySQL and has no dependence on it.

As a result of this carefully designed software architecture, the transition to Cassandra within the infrastructure is easily accommodated. We simply needed to create a concrete implementation of the TwitterStatusService called CassandraTwitterStatusService that encapsulates the knowledge of how to create the appropriate column families in Cassandra (via Hector) to store events, tweets and twitter users after they have been retrieved from Twitter by the RequestService (also an abstract interface with multiple concrete implementations) shown in Fig. 1. Since CassandraTwitterStatusService is hidden behind the abstract TwitterStatusService interface, the existing Twitter Collection & Search application runs *unmodified* on top of this new implementation and now has the ability to collect and search over significantly larger datasets than before. The difficult part in making this transition was the data modeling challenges discussed in the previous section; the actual transition due to the abstract and flexible nature of our software architecture was straightforward.

Of course, in making this transition there exists the need to create and configure a Cassandra cluster, and that is a non-trivial task. However, developers who are in contexts that have acquired datasets sufficient in size to require the use of NoSQL technologies are often in settings that have access to the system administration expertise and resources needed to acquire the hardware, configure the cluster and install the relevant software. While our software infrastructure can be run on a single machine, the advantages of NoSQL technologies cannot be truly realized until they are running on a sizeable cluster of machines.

For instance, for popular queries, Twitter can deliver 50-60 tweets per second, twenty-four hours per day, via its Streaming API. That translates to ~5M tweets per day. With our old infrastructure, that rate would cause our memory-based queues to fill with 1000s of unprocessed tweets as Hibernate Search struggled to keep pace. Now, on our cluster, Cassandra's ability to provide sub-millisecond inserts allows us to process 50-60 tweets per second with no need to store tweets in a queue waiting for our persistence mechanism to update its records. We are now confident that we can handle the 100+ tweets per second rate (~8.6M tweets per day) that we experienced while collecting data during the 2011 Japan Earthquake.

Event Name 1: Day W	Tweet Id 1	•••	Tweet Id N
	JSON	•••	JSON
•••			
Event Name 1: Day X	Tweet Id 1	•••	Tweet Id N
	JSON	•••	JSON
•••			
Event Name N: Day Y	Tweet Id 1	•••	Tweet Id N
	JSON	•••	JSON
•••			
Event Name N: Day Z	Tweet Id 1	•••	Tweet Id N
	JSON	•••	JSON

Figure 6. Events Column Family partitioned by day.

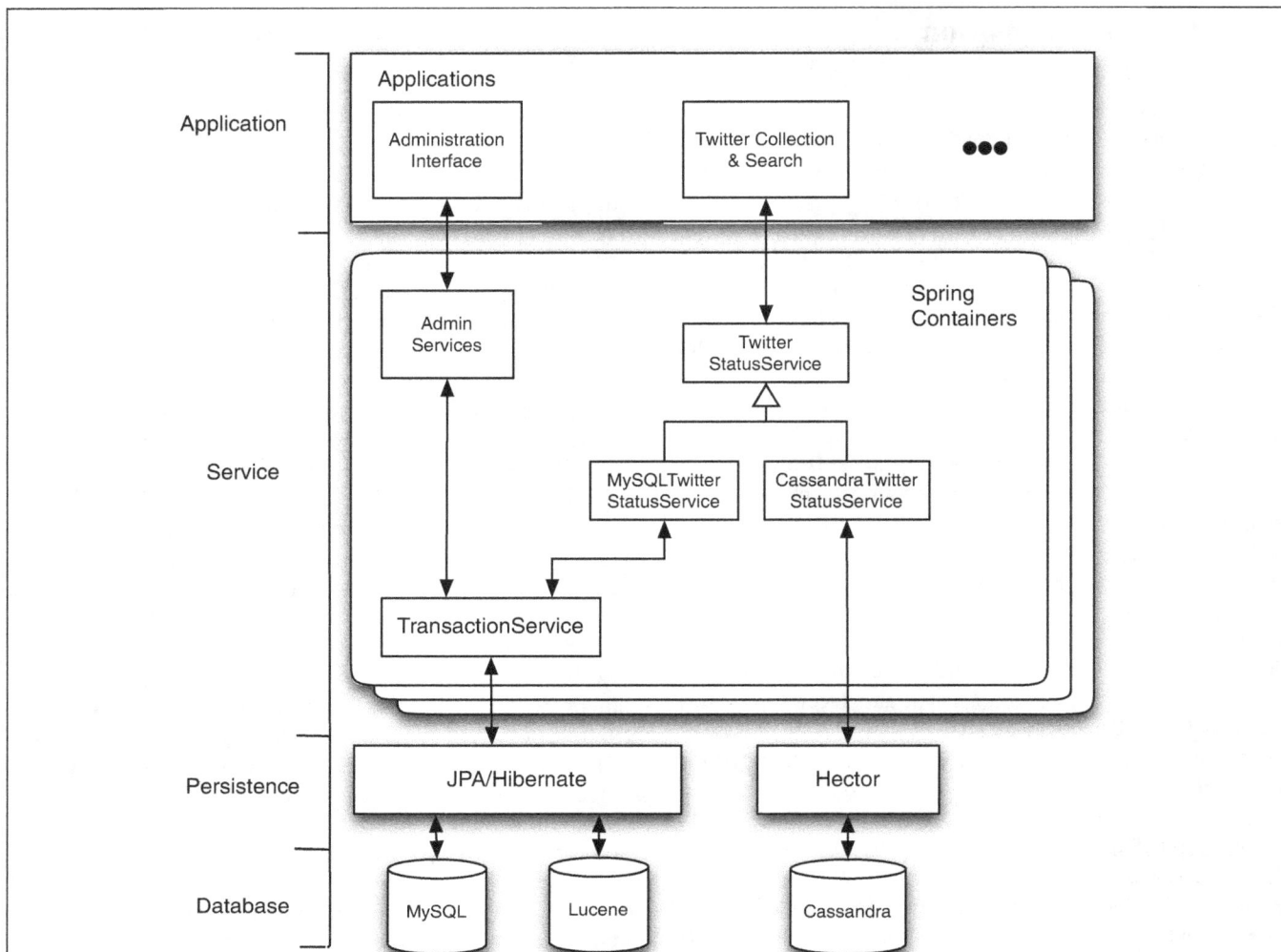

Figure 7. The architecture of the Project EPIC software infrastructure after the addition of Cassandra, a NoSQL data store. This diagram elides details present in Fig. 1 to focus on two important aspects. The first is that none of the services that previously depended on our initial persistence layer have to change. They can continue to store and access data in MySQL and Lucene. The second is that those services that require the scalability and availability guarantees of NoSQL can add an additional implementation of their service interface that stores and accesses data in Cassandra. Due to our use of Spring, we can now flexibly plug-in the service implementations that will meet a wide range of scalability constraints.

Indeed, during the days leading up to and including the first week of the 2012 London Olympics (14 days), our new infrastructure collected 40 million tweets (98.2GB) on a 4 node Cassandra cluster, collecting on 712 user accounts and keywords. At one point during that collection, our system received a burst of tweets that caused our in-memory queue to expand to 40,623 tweets; after the spike, our system cleared that queue in less than two minutes by processing the tweets at a rate of 491 tweets per second. We are quite pleased with the improvements our Cassandra-based system is providing during the collection of truly large-scale "mass convergence" events.

It is important to note that due to the design of our software architecture and our use of Spring, we have the ability to deploy the Project EPIC software infrastructure in a wide variety of configurations: from a single researcher storing Twitter data in JSON files (we have a service not shown in Fig. 1 and Fig. 7 that can persist tweets to a single file) to a research group running the infrastructure on a single powerful server (as Project EPIC did for its first two years) to an even larger research group running a hybrid persistence architecture on a large cluster of machines (as Project EPIC does today). The use of Spring by our software infrastructure allows each of these configurations to be realized in a straightforward manner via the editing of a few configuration files. It is important to note the value of this flexibility as it is sometimes overlooked. The nature of the work done by Project EPIC is inherently multi-disciplinary involving a wide variety of individuals and technical skillsets. Providing an infrastructure capable of enabling any individual involved in the research activities to collect and analyze relevant data is a significant accomplishment.

Having performed this work to add Cassandra to the persistence tier of our software infrastructure, we gain significant options for advancing the research goals of Project EPIC, especially with respect to real-time analysis. Up until this point even providing simple statistics such as the number of data points available in our data sets had proven time consuming and troublesome.

In particular, the move to Cassandra now allows us to develop services that will analyze and index our datasets in parallel. For instance, there is an implementation of Lucene that is built on top of Cassandra. As we collect additional datasets, we will be able to use that variant of Lucene to make sure our index stays up-to-date even as the total number of tweets moves into the billions. Lucene also enables a variety of information retrieval techniques to be applied to our data at scale. Using Lucene to generate term vector representations of our data has proven valuable in applying similarity metrics to tweets, which allows for easy identification of retweets and exploration of the search space.

Finally, there are analysis tools that are being developed for Cassandra that have now become available for use in advancing Project EPIC's research goals. DataStax, for instance, has developed a product that combines Hive, Hadoop and Cassandra such that Hadoop operates directly against Cassandra, effectively mimicking Hadoop's native file system HDFS. Hadoop's MapReduce operations can now be applied directly against data stored in Cassandra column families enabling the use of other Hadoop compatible frameworks to help us scale.

We will be leveraging the Apache project Mahout to apply distributed machine learning and data mining algorithms to our large datasets, enabling a variety of clustering and classification capabilities. The Apache project Hive enables an SQL-like language called QL that can interact directly with data stored in Hadoop. By using DataStax, the data stored in Cassandra can be accessed by Hadoop and, transitively, by Hive giving back some of the advantages of working with a structured query language lost by transitioning to NoSQL. Hive allows our research team to view and store our data in new and interesting ways without requiring even the knowledge of our service tier, translating every query into a set of MapReduce jobs that are executed in parallel across the Cassandra cluster. This can drastically improve the execution time of complex queries, the results of which can be stored and made available to applications through our service tier.

These features will allow us to provide an experimental browsing interface into the data being stored in our Cassandra cluster by our service tier. The set of services created to support this interface can then be used by Project EPIC researchers to understand the types of information that can be extracted from our datasets; this, in turn, would aid the design and implementation of new services and applications that would be directly useful to the research of our NLP and HCC collaborators on Project EPIC.

8. Conclusions

Software engineers are increasingly encountering development situations in which it is straightforward to collect large amounts of data. While NoSQL technologies provide a means for scaling beyond the capabilities of relational databases, they bring a wealth of data modeling challenges that make it difficult for developers to understand how best to migrate data previously stored using a relational schema to the schema-less world of NoSQL. In addition, NoSQL platforms are not meant to replace relational databases, placing pressure on software engineers to create software infrastructures that adopt hybrid persistence architectures that contain both types of technologies. Without the right software architectural approach, these hybrid architectures are difficult to achieve such that the resulting infrastructure is maintainable and straightforward to evolve. In this paper, we present the approach that Project EPIC has adopted to meet the significant data modeling challenges that occur when migrating from a relational approach to the NoSQL approach as well as the software architecture challenges of producing a flexible and extensible software infrastructure. Our data collection infrastructure can now scale in a straightforward manner to handle the increasingly large sets of data that we collect and analyze during times of crisis in support of our crisis informatics research agenda.

Acknowledgments

This material is based upon work sponsored by the NSF under Grant IIS-0910586.

References

[1] Anderson K. M. & Schram A. Design and Implementation of a Data Analytics Infrastructure in Support of Crisis Informatics Research: NIER Track. In *33rd International Conference on Software Engineering,* pp. 844–847. May 2011.

[2] Chang F., Dean J., Ghemawat S., Hsieh W. C., Wallach D. A., Burrows M., Chandra T., Fikes A. & Gruber R. E. Bigtable: A Distributed Storage System for Structured Data. In *7th Symposium on Operating Systems Design and Implementation,* pp. 205–218. Nov. 2006.

[3] Dean, J. & Ghemawat, S. Mapreduce: Simplified Data Processing on Large Clusters. *Communications of the Association of Computing Machinery,* 51(1):107-113. Jan. 2008.

[4] DeCandia, G., Hastorun, D., Jampani, M., Kakulapati, Lakshman, A., Pilchin, A., Sivasubramanian, S., Vosshall, P. & Vogels, W. Dynamo: Amazon's Highly Available Key-Value Store. *ACM SIGOPS Operating Systems Review,* 41(6):205-220. Oct. 2007.

[5] Lakshman, A. & Malik, P. Cassandra: A Decentralized Structured Storage System. *ACM SIGOPS Operating Systems Review,* 44(2):35-40. Apr. 2010.

[6] Malmkjaer, K,The Linguistics Encyclopedia. 2nd Edition. Routledge, 688 pages, 2004.

[7] Palen L., Anderson K. M., Mark G., Martin J., Sicker D., Palmer M. & Grunwald D. A Vision for Technology-Mediated Support for Public Participation & Assistance in Mass Emergencies & Disasters. In *Proceedings of the 2010 ACM-BCS Visions of Computer Science Conference,* pp. 8:1—8:12. Edinburgh, United Kingdom, 2010.

[8] Palen L. & Liu S. B. Citizen Communications in Crisis: Anticipating a Future of Ict-Supported Participation. In *ACM Conference on Human Factors in Computing Systems,* pp. 727–736. San Jose, CA, USA, Apr. 2007.

Automated Trendline Generation for Accurate Software Effort Estimation *

Karthikeyan Ponnalagu & Nanjangud C. Narendra

IBM Research India, Bangalore, India

{karthikeyan.ponnalagu,narendra@in.ibm.com}

Abstract

It is well-known that accurate effort estimation is one of the key factors in deciding the success of a software project. However, as any project manager knows, generating accurate estimates has proven to be extremely difficult in practice. Even well-known estimation techniques such as CO-COMO or SLIM are not guaranteed to work all the time. One key issue in estimation is the selection of the appropriate historical project data set as a frame of reference against which the estimation can be generated. In our experience in working with software projects in IBM, we have found this to be the most crucial deciding factor for the success of a software estimate; indeed, choosing the wrong project data set during estimation could be disastrous for the software project in question. This is because the trendlines (charts of effort vis-a-vis size) generated from the historical data determine the estimate for the software project, and wrong trendlines could result in wrong estimates. To that end, in this paper, we present an automated trendline generation technique for improving effort estimation in software projects. Our technique makes use of a novel data structure that we have designed called *Estimation Key-Map*, which represents project data in a multi-dimensional format. This format enables dynamic analysis and clustering of project data into appropriate subsets that can be selected as historical data for estimation of the software project in question. We present the results of validation of our technique against reported actual data, by evaluating it against a large project data set from IBM; therein, we show how our technique enables the selection of the appropriate trendline, thereby enabling more accurate effort estimates.

---

* Thanks to Subhajit Datta, Bikram Sengupta, Nianjun Zhou and Wesley Gifford for their feedback.

Categories and Subject Descriptors D.2 [*Software Engineering*]: Design - *methodologies*; Design Tools and Techniques - *computer-aided software engineering*

General Terms Design, Experimentation, Human Factors, Verification

Keywords Software Estimation, Trendlines, Custom Application Development

1. Introduction

Successful management of software projects starts with an accurate estimation of development effort. But estimation is a key challenge in complex application software development projects. Inaccurate estimation continues to be a key factor contributing to software project failures. Underestimates lead to schedule pressures compromising the quality of project implementation; whereas, overestimates can result in over priced proposal bids or over staffing of resources. Most failed projects identify planning and estimation as the root cause for failure [12]. By increasing accuracy in estimation, significant cost avoidance in project implementation can be achieved. Accurate estimation can be assisted by the availability of quality historical project data, and most popular estimation models such as COCOMO [5], SLIM [19], Function points [2, 19] are based on historical data.

Software project estimation techniques are designed to convert a size estimate (such as an estimated number of source lines for a system) to an effort estimate (the number of person hours of development effort). A "trendline" is a graph that is generated from historical project information (number of actual source lines and the number of actual person hours for multiple projects). Choosing the right baseline data is critical for successful estimation. Trendlines are created from a subset of available historical project data. We select a subset of the projects that are similar in one or many dimensions such as technology, language, country, organization division, industry sector. etc. The objective of creating specific trendlines is to improve the accuracy of estimation for a candidate project based on the similarity and alignment of its characteristics with the associated dimensions of the available trendlines.

There are well-known limitations of models constructed using historical data [17]. In particular, one limitation is the increased possibility of project failure if a wrong selection of trendline is made or the selected trendline does not contain historical data accurately representing the candidate project's characteristics. For example environmental factors such as development tools, system complexity and development experience are not constant across different development facilities or even in a single development facility over a period of time. So irresepctive of the employed software estimation model, the trendlines need to be validated for data sensitivity on a variety of project data. Thus, one of the major tasks is determining the proper identification of factors from the historical data judged to be relevant to the candidate project to be estimated.

In this paper, we investigate this crucial research issue and present an automated technique for dynamic trendline generation to best suit a candidate project's characteristics. Our key contributions are twofold: (a) a novel data structure called *Estimation Key-Map (EKM)*, that represents project information in a unique multi-dimensional format, and (b) an approach and system architecture for automated trendline generation based on the EKM. Our EKM format enables dynamic analysis and clustering of project data into appropriate subsets that can be selected as historical data for estimation of the software project in question. We present the results of validation of our technique against actual project data from IBM, comprising a data set of 674 projects. Our experimental evaluation demonstrates that our dynamic trendline generation technique can provide accurate effort estimates compared to an estimate based on static one time generated trendline. The initial feedback from project managers who have employed our dynamic trendline generation has shown that they accept the generated trendlines, and they are also motivated to contribute their actual product execution data to the company-wide database used to generate trendlines for other projects.

Our paper is organized as follows. In the next section we will introduce some concepts that we will be using throughout the rest of our paper. Section 3 introduces our EKM model, while our overall approach and system architecture are described in Section 4. The evaluation of our approach against our chosen data set is described in Section 5, along with the results thereof. Our paper is then compared against related work in Section 6. Finally, the paper concludes in Section 7 with suggestions for future work.

2. Preliminaries

To estimate software development effort many models have been developed. If an estimation model predicts development effort using a formula derived from historical data then it is said to be *parametric*. Putnam [19] developed a parametric estimation model known as SLIM. SLIM estimates the cost, effort and schedule of software develop-

ment by using source lines of code (SLOC) as the major input and other productivity impact factors. The general relationship between inputs such as SLOC and environmental and management factors can be determined from historical data. Similarly the Constructive Cost Model (COCOMO) developed by Boehm [5] relates the effort required to develop a software project to Delivered Source Instructions (DSI). COCOMO estimation model also considers factors such as software reliability, platform limitations, resource and staffing quality for adjusting the predicted estimate for a given project. As we can see, these parametric estimation approaches assume that an initial estimate can be provided by a formula that has been adapted with historical data.

Several other estimation techniques are also used in practice. *Expert judgement-based* estimation relies on the experience of domain experts in proposing estimates [18]. A related technique is estimation by *analogy* [15], where effort estimation for a project is derived by reusing and suitably modifying estimates from a similar project implemented in the past.

From our experience in observing the usage of these techniques in IBM, we have noticed that the major weakness of these techniques is their lack of accuracy in terms of grossly under- or over-estimating software effort. One of the primary reasons for this issue is the matching of the project in question with the wrong trendline. Sometimes industry standard trendlines are used for estimation, which turn out to be inappropriate to the project. Indeed, the best trendline is one that is tailored from the project's own development environment. But the challenge is to choose the appropriate trendline that *best represents* the project's characteristics, which is the focus of this paper.

In order to quantify what we mean by *best representation*, we employ the two well-known indicators, viz., R^2, the coefficient of determination [4]; and Magnitude of Relative Error (MRE), which measures the relative error between actual and estimated effort in a project. In this paper, we employ the absolute value of percentage of MRE, which is represented as $MRE = \frac{(E_{act} - E_{est})100}{E_{act}}$; the lower the MRE value, the better, with the ideal MRE value being zero. The R^2 value measures the extent of variability in a data set that is accounted for by the estimation model. A higher value of R^2 indicates that the estimation model is a better fit for the effort data. Additionally, the user could also base their choice of an appropriate trendline depending on the size of the data subset; obviously, subsets with too few data points would not be statistically significant enough.

3. Estimation Key-Map (EKM)

The EKM is a multi-dimensional data structure that models project historical data in terms of specifically defined characteristics and dimensions and it is generated as per the following (manual) procedure:

1. Analyze the project data set and identify its key characteristics, e.g., industry, technology, nature of project (i.e., whether New Development, Maintenance, Enhancement, etc.), project size (small/medium/large as per any consistent predefined norms), etc.

2. Identify the key independent variables that determine project effort, such as deliverable size (either in terms of lines of code, design metrics such as Function Points, etc.), number of defects (whether in-process or post-release), and environmental factors (reliability, extent of reuse, domain expertise of project team)

3. If any of the independent variables are strongly correlated with each other, then combine them via techniques such as principal component analysis [4]. Alternately, remove some of them until the remaining variables are relatively un-correlated. Typically, a metric such as Pearson's Coefficient [4] is used to determine correlation; with a range between -1 and +1, the higher the Pearson coefficient, the greater the correlation. In our experience, we have found a value of 0.6 or greater to denote high correlation.

4. Eliminate those projects that have missing data in any of the key independent variables; optionally, imputation techniques [20, 22] can also be used to "fill in" the missing data

4. Our Approach

4.1 Overview

In our approach, there are two inputs: 1) a candidate project P and 2) a set of historical project data set H. Candidate project P will have a set of predefined dimensions (industry, technology, nature of the project, country, team size, etc.). The process has one output: a trendline generated from projects in data set H that match project P's characteristics in some of the dimensions. The first part of the process (Multi-Level Segmentation) generates a group of different subsets of dimensions to consider. The second part of the process (Trendline Analysis) compares how well each possible trendline fits the historical effort data.

I Multi-level Segmentation:

1. Construct the EKM for H. Let this EKM be $\{M_i\}$, where each M_i is a dimension common to all projects in H. For example, some common dimensions for our illustrative data set described later in Section 5 are Country, Technology, Year.

2. Let the EKM for P be $\{M_i'\}$. Without loss of generality, select only those characteristics of P such that $\{M_i'\} \bigcap \{M_i\}$ is non-empty. (We will discuss the case of $\{M_i'\} \bigcap \{M_i\}$ being empty, later)

3. Let the cardinality of $\{M_i'\} \bigcap \{M_i\}$ be N. Then any number of characteristics $k, 1 \leq k \leq N$, can be selected for filtering the data set H. The total number

of ways in which these characteristics can be selected is $\sum_{k=1}^{k=N-1} \frac{N!}{k!(N-k)!}$, which refers to the number of ways in which k characteristics can be selected from N characteristics. This is done by first selecting a characteristic c_k, and generating a tree (which we also call Estimation Tree), with c_k as the root, thus: each child of c_k is $(c_k, c_j), j \neq k$, each child of (c_k, c_j) is $(c_k, c_j, c_l), l \neq k \ \& \ l \neq j$. Thus this is an exhaustive enumeration of all sub-trees rooted at c_k, and this is iterated for all other characteristics.

4. In case no such subset can be obtained, i.e., if N is zero, then there are two possibilities to consider: (a) either the data set H is not applicable at all and should be dropped, or (b) the existing EKM for H is augmented using some or all characteristics from P, if possible - this is a manual operation on H to be performed by the user. If (b) is implemented, then the procedure moves back to Step 1, i.e., EKM generation, and it is iterated.

II Trendline Analysis:

1. Determine the appropriate data subsets for trendline analysis as per the following criteria: R^2 (coefficient of determination), size of subset, degree of match between the EKM dimensions of the subset and those of the historical data set

2. Perform trendline analysis (to be described in detail in Section 5.2) among all the generated data subsets, and select the best candidate.

3. Record the selection decision for future reuse.

4.2 System Architecture

Our system architecture, which implements our approach, is illustrated in Figure 1. It consists of the following components.

First, the EKM Generator loads the historical project data H from the Project Repository based on the user's selection. The historical data comprises information such as industry, project name, country in which projects are implemented, size of the project's deliverables (e.g., lines of code, function points, etc), technology and language of development. Then for each phase associated in the project such as requirements analysis, design, coding, corresponding project data such as schedule, effort involved, team size are also collected. The implementation quality aspects of the project such as defect density and productivity (as discussed in [1, 19]) are computed and made part of the available data.

Second, the EKM Generator invokes the corresponding Statistical Analyzer tools for the loaded historical data, in order to implement the various statistical analyses selected by the user. To start with, the Structural Analyzer tool is invoked by the EKM Generator to segment the historical data as described in Section 4.1 into multiple clusters. The Quality Analyzer tool is used to validate the data correctness and

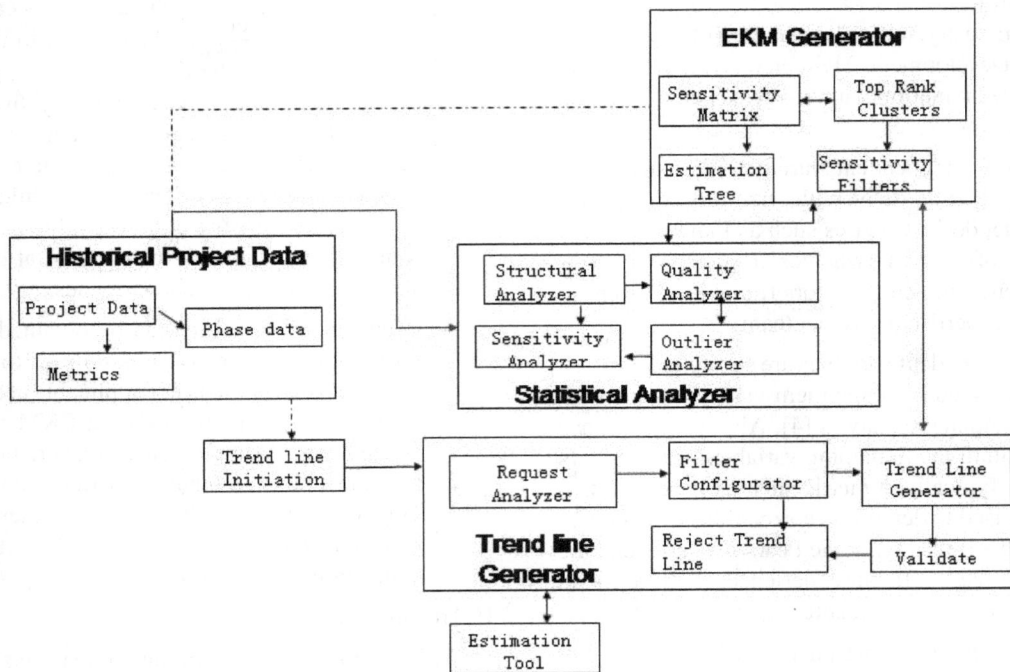

Figure 1. System Architecture

completeness for each cluster belonging to the historical data and to revalidate the clusters accordingly. For example a top level cluster based on technology with poor data quality may be withdrawn from the list of identified clusters in the historical data. Similarly, the Sensitivity Analyzer tool correlates the list of available dependent variables from the historical data against size, identifies the sensitivity factors and accordingly creates and updates the sensitivity matrix for the historical data H. This enables a specific focus on a subset of data variables from H. The Outlier Analyzer employs standard outlier filtering techniques [4] to eliminate outliers from H and also from each of the identified clusters of H. Finally, the results of each of these statistical analyses are retrieved by the EKM Generator, which populates the EKM with the active set of clusters in the historical data. In this paper, we restricted the sensitivity correlation to between size and effort only.

Third, the Trendline Generator accepts the primary input, viz., the project P for which the appropriate trendline is to be generated. Once it identifies the closest matching data cluster from the Estimation Tree, it validates the matching filters based on the user inputs and project characteristics and then creates a specific trendline for the project P. The identified cluster is then converted into the trendline for the estimation tool to use.

5. Evaluation

5.1 EKM Generation from Project Historical Data

We evaluate the ideas in our paper on a project data set from IBM, which we refer to as $H1$, and which consists of 674 projects implemented in IBM locations across several countries. The size vs effort characteristics of all these projects as illustrated in Figure 2 (all trendlines in this paper were generated using the SLIM Metrics tool[1]) imply that a single integrated dataset such as $H1$ can consist of multiple subsets of projects thus contributing to a range of variance in developing applications of similar size. The project dimensions for $H1$, which are inputs for creating the EKM, are presented in Table 1, and they vary in terms of technology involved in project implementation, countries with differing skill sets and developer productivity from which the projects are delivered. In Figure 3 we have shown a subset of the EKM for $H1$, restricted to only two dimensions for ease of display (in some cases, all possible subsets are not shown due to lack of space). In general we focus only on those subsets with size greater than 20.

For our evaluation purpose, we have implemented the EKM as a RDBMS based schema comprising a collection of tables sharing the primary key - child key relationship as follows: The table Dimensions is populated with one record for each of the identified list of dimensions. Thus for our

---

[1] http://www.qsm.com/tools/slim-metrics

evaluation based on Figure.3, the table `Dimensions` will contain three records one each for year, country and technology. The table `DimensionValues` sharing a child relationship with table `Dimensions` will contain one record for each value for a given dimension. For our example, it will contain a total of 11 records. The third table `EKMValues` contains the Number of Projects and the corresponding R-Square values for each unique pair of primary keys from the table `DimensionValues`. This we consider as a flexible design for implimenting EKM adjusting to newer scenarios of historical data interms of data distrubution and subsequent prominence of newer dimensions. We can see that the EKM provides the user with multiple options to choose the appropriate subset for trendline generation. For example, let us assume that the user wants to develop an effort estimate for a project implemented in country E6 which uses client-server technology. They can evaluate the following subsets: E6 only, client-server projects only, E6 projects implemented in 2009, E6 projects implemented in 2008. He/she would reject the last option, since the subset is too small (containing only 2 projects). From the other 3 subsets, they may choose E6 only, since its R^2 value of 0.63 is the highest among the subsets. Also, with 90 projects in that subset, it may be a better choice than the Spain + Client-Server subset with only 14 projects.

Hence the evaluation of our approach is based on the hypothesis that selection of the appropriate subset for trendline generation is primarily dependent on the following factors - goodness of fit of the data in terms of R^2 value, size of the subset (larger the subset, the more statistically significant it is expected to be) and strength of agreement of the EKM dimensions themselves (a subset with the maximal number of matching dimensions is expected to generate a better trendline).

5.2 Trendline Analysis

We now evaluate our hypothesis against 10 candidate projects for which effort estimations were performed. These were client-server projects from the country E1 (country names are anonymized for confidentiality reasons) that were implemented in 2009, hence their EKM was: (Country = E1, Technology = Client-Server, Year = 2009). For each of these projects, based on its reported size, estimates were generated from the following 5 subsets: E1 only, E1 + Client-Server, Client-Server + Year 2009, E1 + Year 2009 and Year 2009. The subset E1 + Client-Server + 2009 was not selected since it has only 10 projects. The MRE value was used to determine the accuracy of effort estimation.

For the subsets that we selected, we see the following characteristics as displayed in Figure 3:

- E1 only: N = 82 and R^2 = 0.71
- E1 + Client-Server: N = 34 and R^2 = 0.59
- Client-Server + Year 2009: N = 118 and R^2 = 0.39

- E1 + Year 2009: N = 28 and R^2 = 0.74
- Year 2009: N = 364 and R^2 = 0.54

From these characteristics, we also notice one obvious result, viz., the subset of larger size would naturally have a lower match among EKM dimensions with the candidate projects, e.g., E1 + Year 2009 and Year 2009 subsets. We also note that in the overall data set, subsets of smaller size possess higher R^2 values. Hence choosing the right subset could be tradeoff between size of subset, its R^2 value and its degree of match to the EKM dimensions of the candidate project.

As a means of evaluating this tradeoff, we mapped the candidate projects against each of the five trendlines above. The results of this mapping is displayed in Figure 4. Due to lack of space, we have only displayed the four best results as trendlines in Figures 5, 8, 6 and 7, representing the (E1 + Client-Server), (Client-Server + Year 2009), (E1 + Year 2009) and (Year 2009) trendlines, respectively. Those figures display the average along with 1-sigma and 2-sigma bounds. In each of those figures, the 10 candidate projects are represented as black squares, superimposed over the red squares representing the projects in the subset. From the Figure 4 data, we notice that the Client-Server + Year 2009 trendline has the lowest relative error (average MRE is 62.1, standard deviation is 35.2), even though its R^2 value is relatively low (R^2 is 0.39). Indeed, most of the candidate projects do lie within the 1-sigma bound, as shown in Figure 8. However, it is a relatively large subset, with 118 points. The next best fit (as can be seen in Figure 7), is from the Year 2009 subset. There are 364 projects in this set, and it has a moderate value of R^2 (R^2 is 0.54).

The worst fit is one of the small-sized subsets, the E1 + Year 2009 subset. It has a high R^2 value (R^2 is 0.74), but the small number of projects (28 projects) in the E1 + Year 2009 subset increases the average MRE values. This is also visible in Figure 6, with one candidate project even outside the 2-sigma bound. Figures 5 and 7 show estimation results between these two extremes.

These results therefore have demonstrated the usefulness of our EKM-based approach, viz., generation of multiple trendlines based on the common EKM dimensions between the historical project data set and the candidate projects for which effort estimates need to be generated. Also our approach is generic enough to hold good against different size and duration based projects (very small to very large projects). If such significant variations on size and duration are available as part of the historical data, they automatically become prominent EKM Values contributing to specific trend lines corresponding to the estimated size or preferred duration of a new project. Hence we conclude that for our hypothesis to hold, the subset that provides the best tradeoff between the three factors - size, R^2 value and degree of match of EKM dimensions - would also provide the best trendline and thereby the most accurate effort estimation.

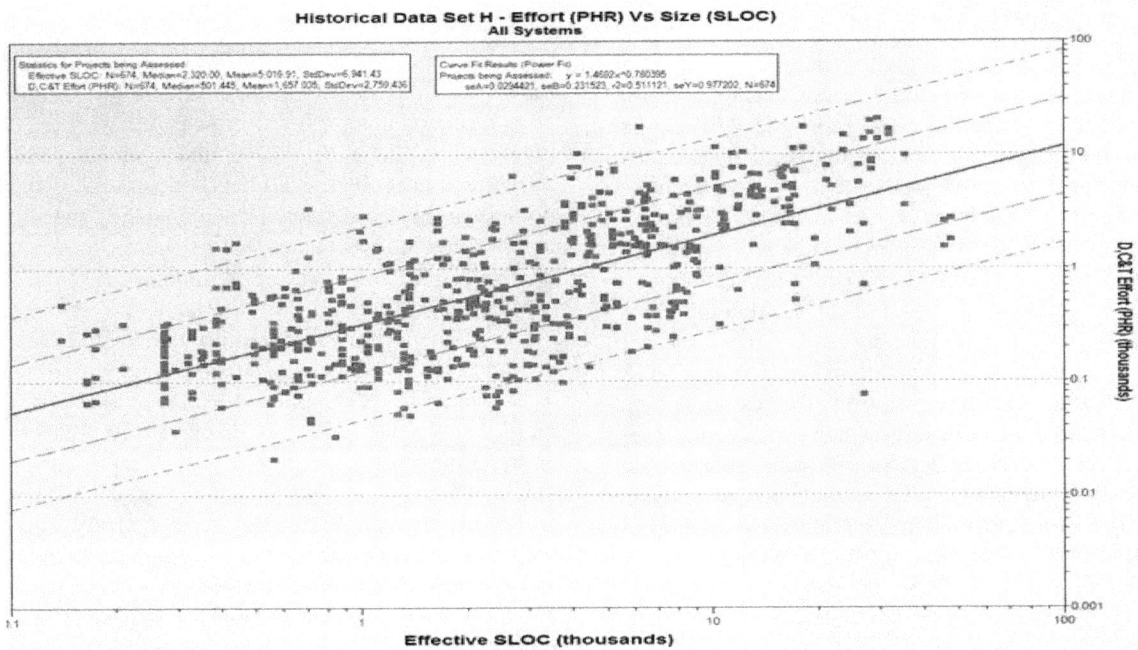

Figure 2. Historical Data set H

Primary Dimension	Category	Secondary Dimension							
			Country					Technology	
		Nil	E1	E2	E3	E4	E5	Client-Server	Mainframe
Year	2009	N = 364 R2 = 0.54	N = 28 R2 = 0.74	N = 102 R2 = 0.31	N = 124 R2 = 0.29	N = 52 R2 = 0.48	N = 38 R2 = 0.71	N = 118 R2 = 0.39	N = 46 R2 = 0.15
	2008	N = 284 R2 = 0.48	N = 50 R2 = 0.73	N = 96 R2 = 0.28	N = 10 R2 = 0.48	N = 32 R2 =0.56	N = 2	N = 66 R2 = 0.49	N = 14 R2 = 0.66
	Others	N = 26 R2 = 0.43	N = 4	N = 4	N = 16 R2 = 0.37	N = 0	N = 2	N = 26 R2 = 0.46	N = 8 R2 = 0.68
Country	E1	N = 82 R2 = 0.71						N = 34 R2 = 0.59	N = 0
	E2	N = 204 R2 = 0.3						N = 80 R2 = 0.27	N = 14 R2 = 0.52
	E3	N = 92 R2 = 0.6						N = 6 R2 = 0.37	N = 8 R2 = 0.87
	E4	N = 30 R2 = 0.41						N = 30 R2 = 0.41	N = 0
	E5	N = 168 R2 = 0.3						N = 42 R2 = 0.1	N = 40 R2 = 0.14
	E6	N = 90 R2 = 0.63						N = 14 R2 = 0.48	N = 6 R2 = 0.56
Technology	Client-Server	N = 210 R2 = 0.44							
	Mainframe	N = 68 R2 = 0.3							

Figure 3. Subset of EKM for Historical Data set H

Table 1. Historical Data Set $H1$

Characteristic	Values
Country	E1, E2, E3, E4, E5, E6 (country names anonymized for confidentiality reasons)
Technology	Client Server, Data Warehouse, Mainframe, Web, Middleware, Mixed
Year	2008, 2009, Before 2008

Project ID	Size (LOC)	Actual Effort (Person Hours)	Estimated Effort (Person Hours)					MRE				
			E1	E1 + Client-Server	Client-Server + Year 2009	E1 + Year 2009	Year 2009	E1	E1 + Client-Server	Client-Server + Year 2009	E1 + Year 2009	Year 2009
1	5,225	2,663	1833	1740	938	2079	1232	31.2	34.7	64.8	21.9	53.7
2	4,015	1,830	1445	1410	787	1641	1007	21.1	22.9	56.9	10.3	45.1
3	2,200	1,394	840	871	527	957	634	39.8	37.5	62.2	31.4	54.5
4	4,235	3,593	1516	1471	816	1722	1049	57.8	59.1	77.3	52.1	70.8
5	7,920	1,068	2667	2427	1237	3019	1697	149.9	127.3	15.9	182.8	58.9
6	5,225	1,626	1793	1707	923	2034	1210	10.3	4.9	43.2	25.1	25.6
7	2,200	690	805	839	511	918	612	16.8	21.8	25.8	33.1	11.3
8	7,920	501	2631	2391	1224	2978	1677	424.9	378.3	144.4	494.1	234.5
9	4,015	1,670	1408	1377	772	1599	985	15.7	17.5	53.8	4.2	41.1
10	4,235	3,485	1537	1489	824	1746	1061	55.9	57.3	76.4	49.9	69.6
								Ave = 82.3	Ave = 67.1	**Ave = 62.1**	Ave = 90.5	Ave = 66.5
								Std Dev = 1271.1	Std Dev = 111.6	**Std Dev = 35.2**	Std Dev = 150.6	Std Dev = 61.9

Figure 4. Estimation Results

5.3 Limitations

There are several limitations to our approach, and we are considering future work that will address these limitations. Our current method relies primarily on the R^2 value as the numerical measure for determining goodness of fit. We would like to explore using other ways to assess goodness of fit. Another limitation of our approach is that it has not been tested on larger and more diverse data sets. We should investigate applying these methods to larger and more diverse data sets in order to fully validate our approach. We know that estimates based on a small set of projects are not as reliable, so we would also like to determine what should be the minimum project set size to consider in this method. In our example, two of the subsets that we considered only had 34 and 28 projects – these project sets might be too small to give us reliable effort estimates. Our current approach is limited to generating trendlines that map project size (in SLOC) to project effort (in person hours of development effort). It would be good to extend the estimation model to include other independent variables: team composition, requirements analysis or design effort, and developer training and expertise. This extension of the estimation model would necessitate adopting different clustering and outlier elimination algorithms to accommodate these extra variables.

6. Related Work

The challenges of software effort estimation has motivated considerable research in recent years. A detailed study of several software projects was reported in [1]. In that paper, it was found that high levels of process maturity, as indicated

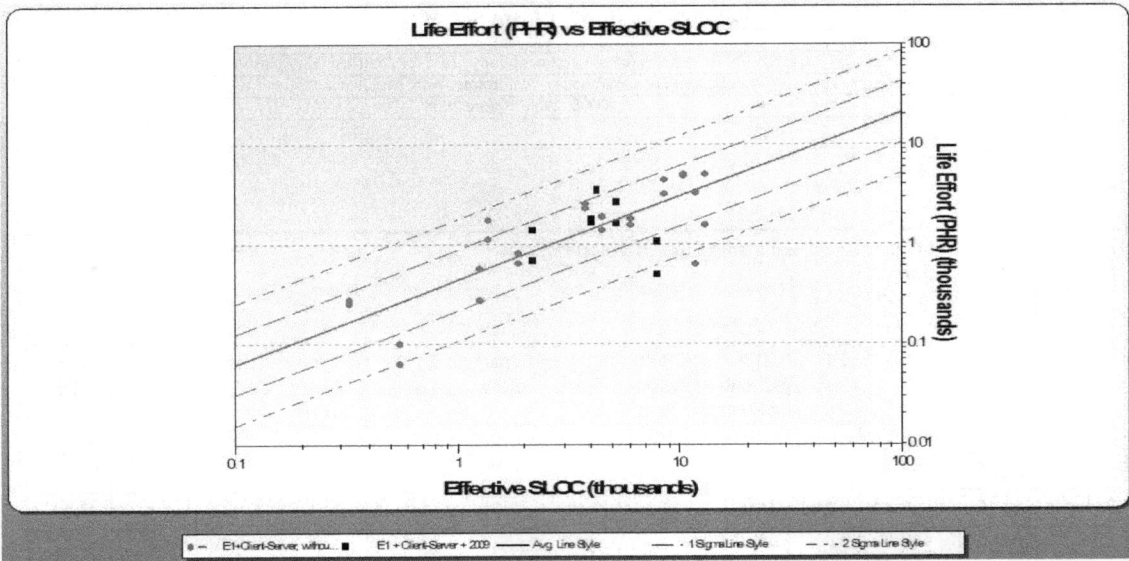

Figure 5. Comparison against E1 + Client Server Trendline

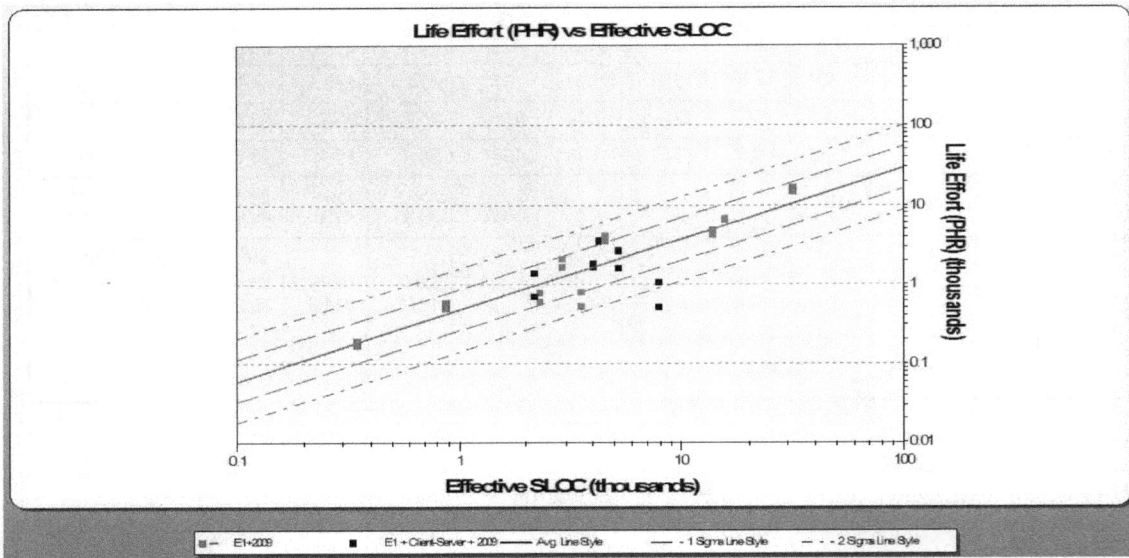

Figure 6. Comparison against E1 + Year 2009 Trendline

by CMM [10] level 5 rating, reduce the effects of most factors that were previously believed to impact software development effort, quality, and cycle time. The only factor found to be significant in determining effort, cycle time, and quality was software size. In [11], the authors report the results of a study that indicates that guesstimates, when aided by low-cost analytical methods, may be the most accurate effort estimation method. Indeed, this study showed that developer-generated guesstimates were more accurate than rigorous analytical methods, leading to the conclusion that effort estimation based on historical data would be the most suitable estimation method. On similar lines, [7] presents an empri-

cal study of effort estimation using a benchmark dataset. A number of machine learning techniques are used to construct an integrated data analysis approach that extracts useful information via visualization, feature selection, model selection and validation. Our approach also aims to provide an integrated system architecture for automated trendline generation for improving effort estimation.

The citation [9] presents an enhanced version of the well-known Grey Relational Analysis (GRA) effort estimation method, which uses similarity-based measures for effort estimation. The approach in [9] presents and demonstrates several variants of a weighted technique for improving on

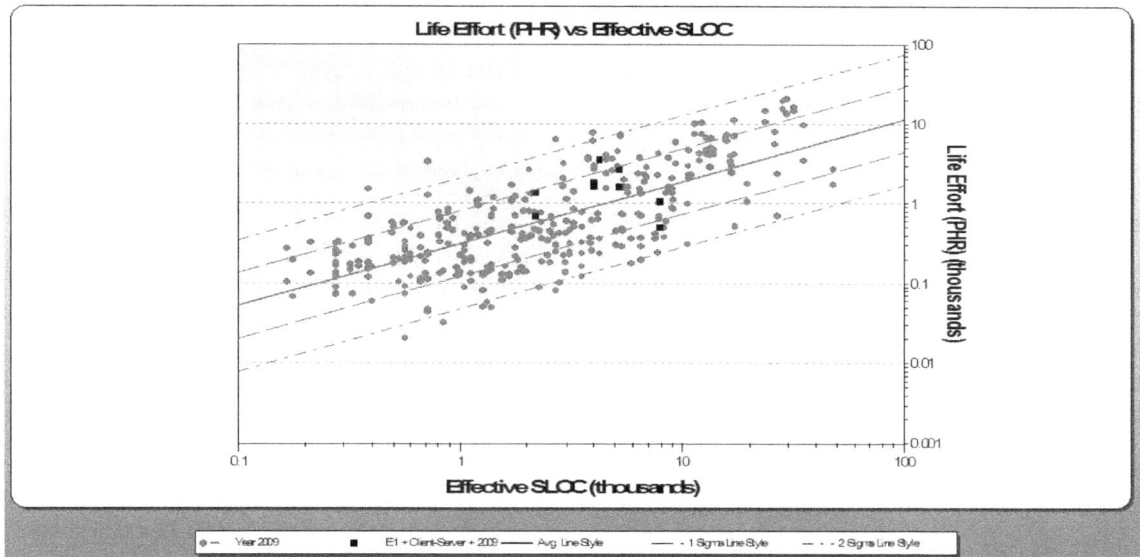

Figure 7. Comparison against Year 2009 Trendline

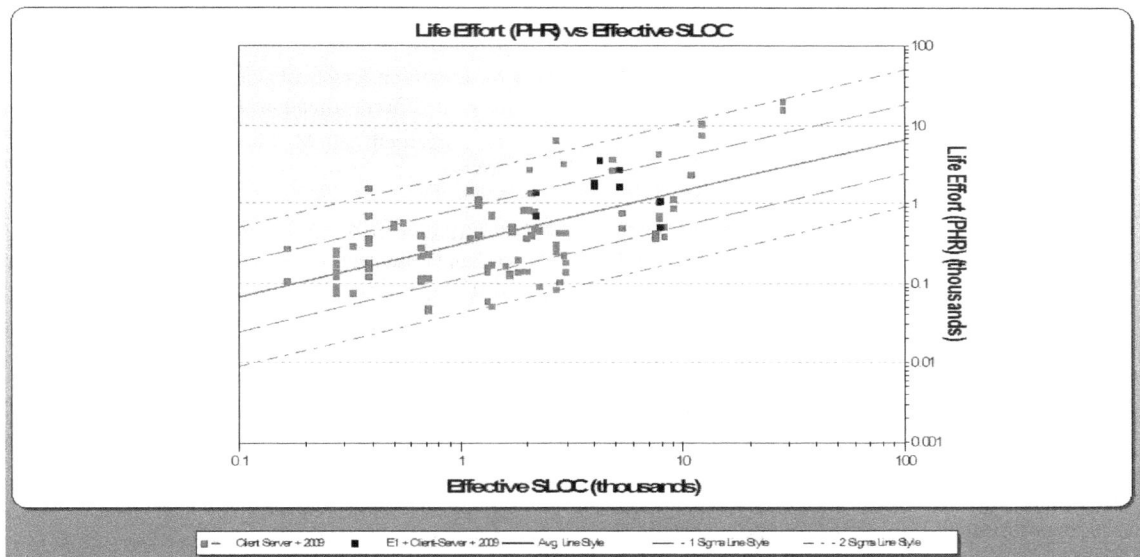

Figure 8. Comparison against Client-Server + Year 2009 Trendline

similarity-based estimates, and shows that the weighted technique out-performs the non-weighted GRA. [3] provide a detailed comparison of well-known estimation models such as COCOMO [5], SEER-SEM[2] and SLIM [19]. Our earlier work [21] addressed the issue of effort estimation of short-duration activities, typically ranging from 1 to 3 days, where we presented a calibratable estimation method based on COCOMO, using historical data.

Validation methods for calibrating software effort estimation models are discussed in [16]. This is done via an exhaustive search over the space of calibration parameters in CO-

COMO. The conclusion of that paper is that software effort estimation models are better calibrated to local data using a so-called "holdout study", i.e., via data not used during calibration. The calibration technique proposed in our paper is also a type of "holdout study".

The citation [13] raises the crucial point that improving software effort estimation is really a matter of accurately capturing the project's context and characteristics, rather than introducing sophisticated estimation models. Our paper aims to implement this recommendation via our EKM-based approach. A later paper by the same author [14] aims to provide a basis for the improvement of software estima-

---

[2]http://www.galorath.com/index.php/products/software/C5/

tion research through a systematic review of previous work. Based on this review, that paper makes some recommendations, in particular, on how to increase the awareness of how properties of the data sets impact the results when evaluating estimation methods. On a different note, [8] argue that the primary issue with software effort estimation is lack of precise terminology regarding what "effort estimate" itself means, and suggest guidelines on how to reduce this lack of clarity and precision in terminology.

Outlier elimination for improving effort estimation accuracy from a historical data set has been presented & demonstrated in [6]. The methodology in that paper makes use of the least of median squares (LMS) regression to uncover such outliers and is applicable irrespective of any subsequent model construction approaches. Our EKM-based technique also incorporates outlier elimination to validate the relationships between the dependent and independent variables of the project data.

7. Conclusions & Future Work

In this paper we have addressed the crucial and difficult issue of accurate software effort estimation, and shown that one of the key issues affecting effort estimation accurary is the selection of the appropriate historical project data set as a frame of reference against which the estimation can be generated. To that end, we have presented and demonstrated a technique for automated dynamic trendline generation. Our technique makes use of our novel construct called Estimation Key-Map (EKM) which characterises the project data set across several orthogonal dimensions. Clustering project historical data based on the EKM and the candidate project to be estimated, helps in generating various categories of subsets from which the best estimate can be generated. We have also demonstrated our method on a data set of 674 projects from IBM.

Future work would involve enhancing our technique by testing our approach on larger and more diverse project data sets, and incorporating additional independent variables apart from size alone for generating trendlines. Additionally, we also plan to extend our approach for schedule estimation in addition to effort estimation.

References

[1] M. Agrawal and K. Chari. Software effort, quality, and cycle time: A study of cmm level 5 projects. *IEEE Trans. Software Eng.*, 33(3):145–156, 2007.

[2] A. Albrecht and J. G. Jr.i. Software function, source lines of code, and development effort prediction: A software science validation. *IEEE Trans. Software Eng.*, 9:639–648, 1983.

[3] S. Basha and D. Ponnurangam. Analysis of empirical software effort estimation models. *CoRR*, abs/1004.1239, 2010.

[4] C. M. Bishop. Pattern recognition and machine learning. *Springer; 1st ed. 2006. Corr. 2nd printing edition*, 2007.

[5] B. W. Boehm. Software engineering economics. *Prentice-Hall*, 1981.

[6] V. K. Y. Chan and W. E. Wong. Outlier elimination in construction of software metric models. In *SAC*, pages 1484–1488, 2007.

[7] D. Deng and M. Purvis. Software metric estimation: An empirical study using an integrated data analysis approach. pages 1 –6, jun. 2007.

[8] S. Grimstad, M. J?rgensen, and K. Mol?kken-?stvold. Software effort estimation terminology: The tower of babel. *Information and Software Technology*, 48(4):302 – 310, 2006.

[9] C.-J. Hsu and C.-Y. Huang. Improving effort estimation accuracy by weighted grey relational analysis during software development. In *APSEC '07: Proceedings of the 14th Asia-Pacific Software Engineering Conference*, pages 534–541, Washington, DC, USA, 2007. IEEE Computer Society.

[10] W. Humphrey. Characterizing the software process: a maturity framework. *Software, IEEE*, 5(2):73 –79, mar 1988.

[11] P. Johnson, C. Moore, J. Dane, and R. Brwer. Empirically guided software effort guesstimation. *Software, IEEE*, 17(6):51 –56, nov. 2000.

[12] C. Jones. Estimating software costs: Bringing realism to estimating. *McGraw-Hill Osborne Media; 2nd edition*, 2007.

[13] M. Jorgensen. Practical guidelines for expert-judgment-based software effort estimation. *IEEE Softw.*, 22(3):57–63, 2005.

[14] M. Jorgensen and M. Shepperd. A systematic review of software development cost estimation studies. *IEEE Trans. Softw. Eng.*, 33(1):33–53, 2007.

[15] E. Kocaguneli, G. Gay, T. Menzies, Y. Yang, and J. W. Keung. When to use data from other projects for effort estimation. In *ASE*, pages 321–324, 2010.

[16] T. Menzies, D. Port, Z. Chen, J. Hihn, and S. Stukes. Validation methods for calibrating software effort models. In *ICSE*, pages 587–595, 2005.

[17] S. Mohanty. Software cost estimation: Present and future. *Software-Pracrice and Experience*, 11:345–361, 1981.

[18] K. Molokken and M. Jorgensen. A review of software surveys on software effort estimation. In *Empirical Software Engineering, 2003. ISESE 2003. Proceedings. 2003 International Symposium on*, pages 223 – 230, sept.-1 oct. 2003.

[19] L. H. Putnam. A general empirical solution to the macro software sizing and estimating problem. *IEEE Trans. Software Eng.*, 4:345–361, 1978.

[20] M. J. Shepperd and M. Cartwright. Predicting with sparse data. *IEEE Trans. Software Eng.*, 27(11):987–998, 2001.

[21] R. Sindhgatta, N. C. Narendra, B. Sengupta, K. Visweswariah, and A. G. Ryman. Timesheet assistant: mining and reporting developer effort. In *ASE*, pages 265–274, 2010.

[22] K. Strike, K. E. Emam, and N. H. Madhavji. Software cost estimation with incomplete data. *IEEE Trans. Software Eng.*, 27(10):890–908, 2001.

Welcome Message from the Workshop Chairs

SPLASH workshops are a great way to improve your knowledge and expand your professional network. The high interactivity of SPLASH workshops provides a creative and collaborative environment to discuss and solve challenging problems related to emerging technologies and research areas with attendees from all over the world. SPLASH workshops complement the OOPSLA, DLS, Onward! and Wavefront tracks of the conference, and provide an opportunity to lead informal, hands-on, or more technical sessions that can result in formal proceedings.

In the last 25 years of OOPSLA/SPLASH, workshops have played an important role in addressing seminal topics that led to significant advances, especially during their formative stages, namely UML, Eclipse, distributed objects, agile software development, new programming languages, and patterns, to mention a few. That tradition continues this year within the new charter for SPLASH, incorporating the visionary focus of Onward! and including hands-on learning through the Wavefront practitioner workshops.

This year, SPLASH offers eleven workshops that represent a diverse set of technology and research topics. Areas covered by the workshops include agents, actors, agile practices, the data-context-interaction paradigm, decentralized control abstractions, domain-specific modeling, education in parallelism, evaluation and usability of programming languages and tools, intermediate languages, foundations of object-oriented languages, free composition, graph databases, multicore and manycore scalability, and virtual machines. The summaries included in this companion provide an introduction to the goals and objectives of each workshop.

We welcome you to these workshops with the hope that the discussions are productive and fruitful, and assist in fostering new collaborations that extend beyond the borders of the conference!

Each workshop proposal received three reviews from the SPLASH Workshop Selection Committee. We would like to thank the members of this committee:

- Bill Opdyke, *JPMorgan Chase, USA*
- Dave Thomas, *Bedarra Research Labs, USA*
- Eric Van Wyk, *University of Minnesota, USA*
- Erik Ernst, *Aarhus University, Denmark*
- Jamie Douglass, *Boeing, USA*
- Jeff Gray, *University of Alabama, USA*
- Jonathan Sprinkle, *University of Arizona, USA*
- Pascal Costanza, *Intel, Belgium*
- Paulo Borba, *Universidade Federal de Pernambuco, Brazil*
- Robert Hirschfeld, *Hasso-Plattner-Institut Potsdam, Germany*

Special thanks to our home institutions for providing needed resources: Universidade do Porto and the University of Southern Denmark.

Ademar Aguiar
Universidade do Porto, Portugal

Ulrik Pagh Schultz
University of Southern Denmark, Denmark

AGERE! Programming with Actors, Agents and Decentralized Control Abstractions

Gul Agha

University of Illinois at
Urbana-Champaign, USA
agha@cs.uiuc.edu

Rafael H. Bordini

FACIN–PUCRS, Brazil
r.bordini@pucrs.br

Assaf Marron

Weizmann Institute of Science, Israel
assaf.marron@weizmann.ac.il

Alessandro Ricci

University of Bologna, Italy
a.ricci@unibo.it

Abstract

The fundamental turn of software into concurrency and distribution is not only a matter of performance, but also of design and abstraction. It calls for programming paradigms that, compared to current mainstream paradigms, would allow us to more naturally think about, design, develop, execute, debug, and profile systems exhibiting different degrees of concurrency, autonomy, decentralization of control, and physical distribution. The AGERE![1] workshop is aimed at focusing on and developing the research on programming systems, languages and applications based on actors, agents and any related programming paradigm promoting a decentralized mindset in solving problems and in developing systems to implement such solutions. The workshop is designed to cover both the theory and the practice of design and programming, bringing together researchers working on models, languages and technologies, and practitioners developing real-world systems and applications.

Categories and Subject Descriptors D.1.3 [*Programming Techniques*]: Concurrent Programming; D.3 [*Programming Languages*]; D.2 [*Software Engineering*]

Keywords actors, agent-oriented programming, asynchronous programming, concurrent programming, event-driven programming, decentralized control

---

[1] *ago, agis, egi, actum,* **agere**. Latin verb meaning to act, to lead, to do—common root for actors and agents

Overview

"The Free Lunch is Over" also for Abstractions

The fundamental turn of software into concurrency, interactivity, and distribution is not only a matter of performance, but also design and abstraction. *The free lunch is over* [14] calls for devising new programming paradigms — possibly as evolution of existing ones — that would allow for natural ways of thinking about, designing, developing, executing, debugging and profiling systems that exhibit different degrees of concurrency, autonomy, decentralization of control, and physical distribution. Almost any application today requires the programming of software components that actively — proactively and reactively — carry out multiple tasks, react to various kinds of events, and communicate with each other. Relevant research questions include: how to properly program these entities and systems of entities, what kinds of programming abstractions can help in systematically structuring complex reactive and proactive behaviors, and what kinds of programming abstractions can be effective in organizing applications as ensembles of relatively autonomous entities working together.

Actors, Agents and Abstractions for Decentralized Control

Given this premise, in SPLASH 2011 the AGERE! workshop [1] was proposed for the first time to investigate the definition of proper levels of abstraction, programming languages, and platforms to support and promote a decentralized mindset [11] in systems development. To this end, *agents* (and multi-agent systems) and *actors* were taken as a starting point, as two main broad families of concepts described in the literature. These abstractions and programming tools explicitly promote such a decentralized-control mindset from different facets, depending on the context in which they are discussed, e.g., concurrent programming or distributed artificial intelligence.

Actors [3] and object-oriented concurrent programming [2, 15] couple object-oriented programming with concurrency, providing a clean and powerful computation model which is nowadays increasingly adopted in mainstream languages, frameworks and libraries. Agents and agent-oriented programming [5–7, 10, 12, 13] provide a rich abstraction layer on top of actors and objects. This approach aims at easing programming of concurrent/distributed systems conceived as societies of autonomous and proactive task-oriented individuals interacting in a shared environment.

The wave of interest on concurrency and distribution in mainstream programming has been clearly witnessed also through the good number of contributions accepted to OOP-SLA and OnWard! in SPLASH 2011 (and in other recent editions) that addresses those same issues. However, the main focus in those contributions (including invited talks and panels) so far has been mainly on issues related to performance, and *mechanisms for extending mainstream paradigms* to effectively exploit the power of e.g. multi-core and many-core architectures. While acknowledging the importance of those objectives, at the same time we argue for the importance of strengthening the research on new paradigms aiming *first* at improving the conceptual modeling and the level of abstraction used to design and program such complex software systems.

With that main objective in mind, AGERE! is organized in SPLASH 2012 to promote the investigation of the features that would make agent-oriented and actor-oriented programming languages effective and general-purpose in developing software systems as an evolution of OOP. Besides actors and agents, the workshop is meant, more generally, to serve as a venue for all programming approaches and paradigms investigating how to effectively specify and structure control when programming reactive systems [4, 8, 9] providing new abstractions for dealing, e.g., with management of asynchronous events and the efficient execution of concurrent activities.

Theory and Practice of Programming with Actors, Agents and Decentralized Control Abstractions

All stages of software development are considered interesting for the workshop, including requirements, modeling, prototyping, design, implementation, testing, and any other means of producing running software based on actors and agents as first-class abstractions. The scope of the conference includes aspects that concern both the theory and the practice of design and programming using such paradigms, so as to bring together researchers working on the models, languages and technologies, as well as the practitioners using such technologies to develop real-world systems and applications.

Finally, the overall perspective of the workshop is what distinguishes this event from related venues (e.g. about

agents) organized in different contexts (e.g. AI) with the intent to hopefully impact mainstream programming paradigms and software development. Another purpose of the workshop is to serve as a forum for collecting, discussing, and confronting related research work that typically appears in different communities in the context of (distributed) artificial intelligence, distributed computing, computer programming, and software engineering.

References

[1] *SPLASH '11 Workshops: Proc. of the compilation of the co-located workshops on DSM'11, TMC'11, AGERE!'11, AOOPES'11, NEAT'11 & VMIL'11*, New York, NY, USA, 2011. ACM.

[2] G. Agha. Concurrent object-oriented programming. *Commun. ACM*, 33:125–141, September 1990.

[3] G. A. Agha, I. A. Mason, S. F. Smith, and C. L. Talcott. A foundation for actor computation. *J. Funct. Program.*, 7(1): 1–72, Jan. 1997.

[4] A. Basu, M. Bozga, and J. Sifakis. Modeling heterogeneous real-time components in BIP. In *Proceedings of the 4th IEEE International Conference on Software Engineering and Formal Methods*, SEFM '06, pages 3–12, Washington, DC, USA, 2006. IEEE Computer Society.

[5] R. Bordini, M. Dastani, J. Dix, and A. El Fallah Seghrouchni, editors. *Multi-Agent Programming Languages, Platforms and Applications - Volume 1*, 2005. Springer.

[6] R. Bordini, M. Dastani, J. Dix, and A. El Fallah Seghrouchni, editors. *Multi-Agent Programming Languages, Platforms and Applications - Volume 2*, 2009. Springer.

[7] R. H. Bordini, M. Dastani, J. Dix, and A. El Fallah Seghrouchni. Special issue on multi-agent programming. *Autonomous Agents and Multi-Agent Systems*, 23 (2), 2011.

[8] D. Harel and A. Pnueli. *On the development of reactive systems*, pages 477–498. Springer-Verlag New York, Inc., New York, NY, USA, 1985.

[9] D. Harel, A. Marron, and G. Weiss. Behavioral programming. *Commun. ACM*, 55(7):90–100, July 2012.

[10] J. J. Odell. Objects and agents compared. *Journal of Object Technology*, 1(1):41–53, 2002.

[11] M. Resnick. *Turtles, Termites and Traffic Jams. Explorations in Massively Parallel Microworlds*. MIT Press, 1994.

[12] A. Ricci and A. Santi. Agent-oriented computing: Agents as a paradigm for computer programming and software development. In *Proc. of Future Computing '11*, Rome, Italy, 2011.

[13] Y. Shoham. Agent-oriented programming. *Artificial Intelligence*, 60(1):51–92, 1993.

[14] H. Sutter and J. Larus. Software and the concurrency revolution. *ACM Queue: Tomorrow's Computing Today*, 3(7):54–62, Sept. 2005. ISSN 1542-7730.

[15] A. Yonezawa and M. Tokoro. *Object-oriented concurrent programming*. MIT Press series in computer systems. MIT Press, 1987.

A Programmatic Introduction to Neo4j

Jim Webber
Neo Technology
42 Southwark Street
London, SE1 1UN
+44 7788 143 121

jim@neotechnology.com

ABSTRACT

In this workshop we provide a hands-on introduction to the popular open source graph database Neo4j [1] through fixing a series of increasingly sophisticated, but broken, test cases each of which highlights an important graph modeling or API affordance.

Categories and Subject Descriptors

E.1 [**Data Structures**]: Graph and networks. E.2 [**Data Storage Representations**]: Object representation. D2.5 [**Testing and Debugging**]: Testing tools.

General Terms

Algorithms, Experimentation.

Keywords

NOSQL, Graph Databases, Neo4j, Java, JVM.

1. INTRODUCTION

Neo4j is a JVM-based NOSQL database. As the leading graph database, its model is intuitive and expressive, mapping closely to your whiteboard domain model. For highly connected data, Neo4j is thousands of times faster than relational databases, making it ideal for managing complex data across many domains, from finance to social, telecoms to geospatial.

2. WORKSHOP AGENDA

This workshop covers the core functionality of the Neo4j graph database. With a mixture of theory and entertaining hands-on coding sessions, attendees will learn how to manage highly connected real-world data [2] and build systems with Neo4j. Specifically we will cover:

- NOSQL and Graph Database overview
- Neo4j Fundamentals and Architecture
- The Neo4j Core API
- Indexing
- Neo4j Traverser API
- Declarative querying with Cypher
- Deployment and operational considerations for large systems

3. METHODOLOGY

Each session comprises a set of practical exercises designed to introduce and reinforce an aspect of the Neo4j stack. The practical parts of the tutorial consist of Koan-style lessons where a specific aspect of the Neo4j stack is presented as a set of failing unit tests that participants will work to fix.

The exercises gradually become more challenging until the attendees are capable of implementing sophisticated graph operations against Neo4j.

Participants will benefit from basic fluency with a modern IDE like Eclipse or IntelliJ to make the most rapid progress, though command-line programmers are encouraged to attend too.

4. REFERENCES

[1] http://neo4j.org

[2] http://www.bbc.co.uk/doctorwho/dw

Evaluation and Usability of Programming Languages and Tools (PLATEAU)

Shane Markstrum

Google

smarkstr@google.com

Emerson Murphy-Hill

North Carolina State University

emerson@csc.ncsu.edu

Caitlin Sadowski

University of California, Santa Cruz

supertri@cs.ucsc.edu

Abstract

Programming languages exist to enable programmers to develop software effectively. But how *efficiently* programmers can write software depends on the usability of the languages and tools that they develop with. The aim of this workshop is to discuss methods, metrics and techniques for evaluating the usability of languages and language tools. The supposed benefits of such languages and tools cover a large space, including making programs easier to read, write, and maintain; allowing programmers to write more flexible and powerful programs; and restricting programs to make them more safe and secure. This workshop gathers the intersection of researchers in the programming language, programming tool, and human-computer interaction communities to share their research and discuss the future of evaluation and usability of programming languages and tools. We are also interested in the input of other members of the programming research community working on related areas, such as refactoring, design patterns, program analysis, program comprehension, software visualization, end-user programming, and other programming language paradigms.

Categories and Subject Descriptors D.3.0 [*Programming Languages*]: Standards; H.1.2 [*User/Machine Systems*]: Human Factors

1. Main Themes and Goals

Following on from the three previous iterations of the PLATEAU workshop at OOPSLA/Onward! and SPLASH, this workshop brings together practitioners and researchers interested discussing usability and evaluation of programming languages and tools with respect to language design and related areas. We will consider: empirical studies of programming languages; methodologies and philosophies behind language and tool evaluation; software design metrics and their relations to the underlying language; user studies of language features and software engineering tools; visual techniques for understanding programming languages; critical comparisons of programming paradigms, such as object-oriented vs. functional; and tools to support evaluating programming languages. We have two goals:

1. Develop and sustain a research community that shares ideas and collaborates on research related to the evaluation and usability of languages and tools.

2. Encourage the languages and tools communities to think more critically about how usability affects the design and adoption of languages and tools.

2. Organizers

* **Shane Markstrum** is currently a Software Engineer at Google in New York, USA. Prior to joining Google he was an Assistant Professor in the Computer Science department at Bucknell University and a Visiting Scholar at Victoria University of Wellington, New Zealand. He received his Ph.D. from the University of California, Los Angeles in 2009. His research interests include domain-specific languages and tools for extensible type systems; and building tool support for non-traditional language constructs.

* **Emerson Murphy-Hill** is currently an Assistant Professor at North Carolina State University, USA. Prior to joining the NCSU faculy he was a postdoctoral researcher at the University of British Columbia in the Software Practices Lab with Gail Murphy. He received is Ph.D. from Portland State University in 2009. His research interests include human-computer interaction and software tools.

* **Caitlin Sadowski** is currently a Software Engineer at Google in Mountain View, USA. She received her Ph.D., focused on dynamic analyses for detecting concurrency errors, from the Computer Science Department of UC Santa Cruz where she was advised by Jim Whitehead and Cormac Flanagan. Her research interests include

the evaluation and usability of programming languages and software, parallelism and concurrency, and computer science education. She was a recipient of a distinguished paper award at OOPSLA 2011 for her paper "Two for the Price of One: A Model for Parallel and Incremental Computation." She was also a Co-Chair for the SPLASH/OOPSLA Transitioning to Multicore (TMC) workshop in 2011 and the ICSE User evaluation for Software Engineering Researchers (USER) workshop in 2012.

3. Program Committee

The following people form the Program Committee (PC) for the workshop:

- Yvonne Coady - University of Victoria, Canada
- Jonathan Edwards - MIT, USA
- Thomas Fritz - University of Zurich, Switzerland
- Philip Guo - Google, USA
- Stefan Hanenberg, University of Duisburg-Essen, Germany
- Ciera Jaspan, Cal Poly Pomona, USA
- Thomas LaToza - UC Irvine, USA
- Portia O'Callaghan - MathWorks, USA
- Chris Parnin, Georgia Institute of Technology, USA
- Philip Wadler, University of Edinburgh, UK

4. Anticipated Attendance

We anticipate the following number of attendees:

- Minimum: 20
- Ideal: 35
- Maximum: 60

5. Advertisement

We advertised this workshop by inviting participants of workshops in the areas of language design, tools, and general usability directly; as well as by emailing related mailing lists, posting on blogs contacting specific people known to be working in this area directly, and through our group mailing list. In addition we maintain a website for presenting organizational information [1].

6. Participant Preparation

Workshop participants submit a paper prior to one month before the workshop. Papers are made available through the workshop website and participants are encouraged to have read the papers before attending the workshop. Participants are also asked to prepare a short presentation to support their paper. The length limit on papers is 10 pages.

We look for papers that describe work-in-progress or recently completed work based on the themes and goals of the workshop or related topics, report on experiences gained, question accepted wisdom, raise challenging open problems, or propose speculative new approaches.

7. Activities and Format

This workshop is run as a full-day workshop at SPLASH and Onward! 2012. We have an introduction and keynote session in the morning followed by the presentation and discussion of workshop papers followed by a breakout session at the end. Table 1 outlines the rough schedule of the format of the workshop.

Time	Activity
0830–0900	Introductions
0900–1000	Key Note Presentation
1000–1030	Morning Break
1030–1200	Presentation of workshop papers
1200–1330	Lunch Break
1330–1500	Presentation of workshop papers
1500–1530	Afternoon Break
1530–1700	Breakout session
1700–1715	Participant Feedback and Organizers Report

Table 1. Workshop Schedule

8. Post-workshop Activities

We hope that our participant's papers, published in the ACM Digital Library, will inspire future researchers. We aim to continue hosting this workshop in subsequent years.

References

[1] https://sites.google.com/site/workshopplateau/

Workshop on Relaxing Synchronization for Multicore and Manycore Scalability (RACES 2012)

Andrew P. Black
Portland State University,
black@cs.pdx.edu

Theo D'Hondt
Vrije Universiteit Brussel,
tjdhondt@vub.ac.be

Doug Kimelman
IBM T. J. Watson Research
Center, dnk@us.ibm.com

Martin Rinard
MIT CSAIL,
rinard@lcs.mit.edu

David Ungar
IBM T. J. Watson Research Center,
davidungar@us.ibm.com

Abstract

Massively-parallel systems are coming: core counts keep rising – whether conventional cores as in multicore and manycore systems, or specialized cores as in GPUs. Conventional wisdom has been to utilize this parallelism by reducing synchronization to the minimum required to preserve determinism – in particular, by eliminating data races. However, Amdahl's law implies that on highly-parallel systems even a small amount of synchronization that introduces serialization will limit scaling. Thus, we are forced to confront the trade-off between synchronization and the ability of an implementation to scale performance with the number of processors: synchronization inherently limits parallelism. This workshop focuses on harnessing parallelism by limiting synchronization, even to the point where programs will compute inconsistent or approximate rather than exact answers.

Categories and Subject Descriptors   D.1.3 [**Programming Techniques**]: Concurrent Programming – parallel programming. D.3.3 [**Programming Languages**]: Language Constructs and Features – concurrent programming structures. D.4.1 [**Operating Systems**]: Process Management – concurrency, synchronization.

Keywords   concurrency; parallelism; synchronization; performance; scalability; manycore; algorithms; data structures; nondeterminism; consistency; approximate computing.

1. Theme and Topics

A new school of thought is arising: one that accepts and even embraces nondeterminism (including data races), and in return is able to dramatically reduce synchronization, or even eliminate it completely. However, this approach requires that we leave the realm of the certain and enter the realm of the merely probable. How can we cast aside the security of correctness, the logic of a proof, and adopt a new way of thinking, where answers are good enough but not certain, and where many processors work together in parallel without quite knowing the states that the others are in? We may need some amount of synchronization, but how much? Or better yet, how little? What mental tools and linguistic devices can we give programmers to help them adapt to this challenge? This workshop focuses on these questions and related ones: harnessing parallelism by limiting synchronization, even to the point where programs will compute inconsistent or approximate rather than exact answers.

This workshop aims to bring together researchers who, in the quest for scalability, have been exploring the limits of how much synchronization can be avoided. We invite submissions on any topic related to the theme of the workshop, *pro or con*. We want to hear from those who have experimented with formalisms, algorithms, data structures, programming languages, and mental models that push the limits. In addition, we hope to hear from a few voices with wilder ideas: those who may not have reduced their notions to practice yet, but who have thoughts that can inspire us as we head towards this yet-uncertain future. For example, biology may yield fruitful insights. The ideal presentation for this workshop will focus on a grand idea, but will be backed by some experimental result.

2. Goals and Outcomes

We will consider the workshop a success if attendees come away with new insights into fundamental principles, and new ideas for improving scaling by limiting synchronization. The goal of this workshop is both to influence current programming practice and to initiate the coalescence of a new research community giving rise to a new subfield within the general area of concurrent and parallel programming. Results generated by the workshop will be made persistent via the workshop website and via the ACM Digital Library.

3. Review and Selection Process

This workshop will employ a novel process for reviewing submissions and selecting those to be presented at the workshop: All reviews will be signed, all submissions and reviews will be posted on the web (unless an author chooses to retract a submission), and the attendees will be the ones selecting which papers will be presented.

In a bit more detail: At least three committee members will review each submission, and each review will be signed. Once all the reviews for a submission are in, they will be sent to the author, who can decide to retract the paper if so desired. Then, all submissions (except any that are retracted) will be posted on the workshop website, along with all reviews and a net score determined for each submission by the program committee.

At that point, prior to the workshop, all registered attendees will be invited to read the submissions and the reviews, and vote on which of the papers they want to see presented at the workshop.

A separate and more conventional process will be employed for selecting papers to be included in published proceedings in the ACM Digital Library.

Additional detail and the rationale for these processes is presented at http://soft.vub.ac.be/races/call-for-participation/#review-process

4. Program Committee

Andrew P. Black, Portland State University
Yvonne Coady, University of Victoria
Tom Van Cutsem, Vrije Universiteit Brussel
Theo D'Hondt, Vrije Universiteit Brussel
Phil Howard, Portland State University
Doug Kimelman, IBM Research
Eddie Kohler, Harvard SEAS
Jim Larus, Microsoft Research
Stefan Marr, Vrije Universiteit Brussel
Tim Mattson, Intel
Paul McKenney, IBM
Hannes Payer, University of Salzburg
Dan Prener, IBM
Lakshmi Renganarayana, IBM
David Ungar, IBM Research
Martin Vechev, ETH Zurich

6th Workshop on Virtual Machines and Intermediate Languages (VMIL'12)

Hridesh Rajan

Iowa State University, USA

hridesh@iastate.edu

Michael Haupt

Oracle Labs, Potsdam, Germany

michael.haupt@oracle.com

Christoph Bockisch

Universiteit Twente, The Netherlands

c.m.bockisch@cs.utwente.nl

Steve Blackburn

Australian National University, Australia

Steve.Blackburn@anu.edu.au

Abstract

The VMIL workshop is a forum for research in virtual machines and intermediate languages. It is dedicated to identifying programming mechanisms and constructs that are currently realized as code transformations or implemented in libraries but should rather be supported at VM level. Candidates for such mechanisms and constructs include modularity mechanisms (aspects, context-dependent layers), concurrency (threads and locking, actors, software transactional memory), transactions, etc. Topics of interest include the investigation of which such mechanisms are worthwhile candidates for integration with the run-time environment, how said mechanisms can be expressed at the intermediate language level, how their implementations can be optimized, and how virtual machine architectures might be shaped to facilitate such implementation efforts.

Categories and Subject Descriptors D.3.4 [*Programming Languages*]: Processors—runtime environments

Keywords virtual machines, intermediate languages

1. Motivations and Themes

An increasing number of high-level programming language implementations is realized using standard virtual machines. Recent examples of this trend include the Clojure (Lisp) and Potato (Squeak Smalltalk) projects, which are implemented on top of the Java Virtual Machine (JVM); and also F# (ML) and IronPython, which target the .NET CLR.

Making diverse languages–possibly even adopting different paradigms–available on a robust and efficient common platform leverages language interoperability. Also new languages with many kinds of mechanisms and concepts researched in various communities are mostly reflected in high-level language and library design. AspectJ, Scala and JPred are examples of languages originally compiled for the JVM platform.

Vendors of standard virtual machine implementations have started to adopt extensions supporting this trend from the run-time environment side. For instance, the recent release of the Oracle standard JVM includes the *invokedynamic* instruction, which facilitates a simpler implementation of dynamic programming languages on the JVM.

The observation that many language constructs are supported in library code, or through code transformations leading to over-generalized results, has led to efforts to make the core mechanisms of certain programming paradigms available at the level of the virtual machine implementation. Thus, dedicated support for language constructs enables sophisticated optimization by direct access to the running system. The workshop's main goal is the discussion of compilation techniques, intermediate languages and execution environments that more naturally support such constructs even within compiled programs. This support will, e.g., facilitate new dynamic optimization, incremental compilation, and improve debugging. It can be expected that language constructs benefit from a more efficient execution and better integration into the development process: increased efficiency and improved integration will raise the acceptance of the concepts which in turn activates further research at the conceptual level.

The main themes of this workshop are to investigate which programming language mechanisms are worthwhile candidates for integration with the run-time environment, how said mechanisms can be declaratively (and re-usably)

expressed at the intermediate language level (e.g., in byte-code), how their implementations can be optimized, and how virtual machine architectures might be shaped to facilitate such implementation efforts. Possible candidates for investigation include modularity mechanisms (aspects, context-dependent layers), concurrency (threads and locking, actors, software transactional memory), transactions, paradigm-specific abstractions, and combinations of paradigms.

The areas of interest include, but are not limited to, compilation-based and interpreter-based virtual machines as well as intermediate-language designs with better support for investigated language mechanisms, compilation techniques from high-level languages to enhanced intermediate languages as well as native machine code, optimization strategies for reduction of run-time overhead due to either compilation or interpretation, advanced caching and memory management schemes in support of the mechanisms, and additional virtual machine components for managing them.

2. Workshop Format

The planned workshop agenda interleaves presentations of accepted papers, invited talks from experts in the research area, and discussions to stimulate participants. The accepted workshop papers should act as motivation for new researchers to include the topics of this workshop into their research. To accomplish this, authors of accepted papers will be required to prepare a presentation, and all prospective workshop participants will be asked to read all accepted papers. For this purpose, all papers will be made available on the workshop web page.[1]

3. About the Organizers

Hridesh Rajan is an Associate Professor of Computer Science at the Iowa State University. He received his Ph.D. from the University of Virginia in 2005. He is the recipient of a 2009 US National Science Foundation CAREER award, a 2010 ISU LAS Early Achievement in Research award, and a 2012 Big-12 Fellowship. He was also co-organizer of the 2007-2011 edition of this workshop. His research on programming language and verification support for modular program design has been funded by the US National Science Foundation. He is a member of IEEE, IEEE Computer Society, ACM, SIGSOFT, and SIGPLAN.

Michael Haupt is a researcher and software developer in the Virtual Machine Research Group at Oracle Labs. His research interests are in improving the modularity of complex software system architectures as well as in implementing programming languages, in which latter area his main focus is on faithfully regarding programming paradigms' core mechanisms as primary subjects of language implementation effort. Michael holds a doctoral degree from Technische Universität Darmstadt, where he has worked on the Steam-

loom virtual machine to provide run-time support for AOP languages. He has published papers on this and other AOSD-related subjects in the L'Objet and IEEE Software journals as well as in the AOSD, VEE, OOPSLA, and ECOOP conference series. Michael has served as PC member for ECOOP 2008 and 2010, as reviewer for TAOSD, and has been supporting reviewer for the AOSD, ECOOP, ICSE, FSE, MODELS, and VEE conference series. He has co-organized the Dynamic Aspects Workshop series in conjunction with the AOSD conferences, and the previous three editions of the VMIL. Michael is a member of the ACM.

Christoph Bockisch is an assistant professor on Software Composition with a research focus on the design and implementation of programming languages with advanced dispatch mechanisms. He received his doctoral degree from the Technische Universität Darmstadt in 2008. To provide virtual machine support, Christoph researches extensions to high-performing Java virtual machines based on just-in time compilation. He furthermore researches meta-models for the definition of arbitrary dispatch mechanisms to act as a first-class representation. He is co-founder and co-organizer of the workshop series on Virtual Machines and Intermediate Languages (VMIL) and Free Composition (FREECO). He is Student-Events Co-Chair and PC member of the AOSD'13 conference.

Stephen M. Blackburn is a Professor at the Australian National University (ANU). He was Program Committee Chair for VMIL'11. He has served on numerous SIGPLAN program committees, including ECOOP'12 and ISMM'12. He is an organizer of the EVALUATE workshop series. His research interests include programming language implementation, architecture, and performance analysis. He received his PhD from the ANU. He is a Distinguished Scientist of the ACM.

4. Program Committee

- David Grove (chair), IBM Research
- Daniel Frampton, Microsoft
- Kawachiya Kiyikuni, IBM Research
- Chandra Krintz, UCSB
- Prasad Kulkarni, University of Kansas
- Christian Probst, Technical University of Denmark
- Ian Rogers, Google
- Jeremy Singer, University of Glasgow
- Witawas Srisa-an, University of Nebraska
- Christian Wimmer, Oracle Labs

Acknowledgments

Hridesh Rajan was supported in part by the US National Science Foundations under grants CCF-11-17937, CCF-10-17334, and CCF-08-46059.

---

[1] See http://design.cs.iastate.edu/vmil/2012/.

Workshop: What Drives Design?

Dennis Mancl

Alcatel-Lucent
Murray Hill, NJ, USA
dennis.mancl@alcatel-lucent.com

Steven D. Fraser

Cisco Systems
San Jose, CA, USA
sdfraser@acm.org

Gail E. Harris

Instantiated Software
Toronto, Canada
Gail.Harris@instantiated.ca

Bill Opdyke

JP Morgan Chase
Chicago, IL, USA
opdyke@acm.org

Abstract

Designers are busy people, and they are getting busier. In today's world designers must deal with three competing pressures:

- A relentless avalanche of changes in end-user technologies and applications domains,
- An insatiable marketplace that demands rapid delivery of innovative products and services, and
- A parade of improvements in implementation technologies: languages, tools, and prototyping environments.

The job of design is becoming more frantic. Designers have less time to think. Managers have already sold the customers on the next innovation to the system, and the developers have already started hacking. Can we really think that fast?

Maybe there is a silver bullet design methodology. There have been a number of attempts to *drive* design from responsibilities, features, tests, models, behavior, domains, and contracts. Could these be a good place to start? Do any of these approaches (RDD, FDD, TDD, and so on) offer any help to the busy designer?

This workshop will attempt to gather the evidence for effective design principles. Should we consider adopting a single approach, or should we consider taking inspiration from several methods? The workshop will discuss benefits and pitfalls.

Categories and Subject Descriptors D.2.2 [**Software Engineering**]: Design Tools and Techniques – object-oriented design methods.

Keywords Design methodologies

1. What Drives Design?

Software development is getting more demanding. Today's software designers are facing a kind of Attention Deficit Disorder: all of the demands to design faster are making us lose our focus.

How do we stay focused? Maybe we need to pick a set of core design principles. Maybe we need to have a way to *drive* our design work based on something other than customers' demands and managers' whims.

At the OOPSLA 2008 conference, Rebecca Wirfs-Brock presented a thought-provoking talk titled "What Drives Design?" [1] The talk gave a survey of several popular ways of organizing design work – "driven" by:

- responsibilities, features, tests
- models, behavior, domains, contracts

Each of the methods has strengths and weaknesses, depending on who is using the methods and what kinds of problems they are trying to solve.

This workshop will explore how we can profit from using some of the proposed design principles. The workshop participants are invited to share their experiences:

- Positive and negative experiences with one of the xDD methods (RDD, FDD, TDD, MDD, BDD, and so on)
- Design experiences where the designers "borrowed some ideas" from one or more of the xDD methods

This workshop will also try to address some questions about modern challenges in design:

- How do new languages and development environments affect the design process? For example, do scripting languages like Javascript and Ruby promote design or "non-design?" Is Eclipse-based Java development just another video game?
- Should we do our design thinking in pictures or words? MDD is mostly driven by pictures (UML diagrams), whereas DDD tries to do design in linguistic terms (ubiquitous language).
- Are there some key architecture requirements areas (such as security or reliability) that are mostly ignored by the xDD methods?
- How strictly should we follow the proposed design approaches?

- How should we teach design to junior staff members?
- One criticism of many of the xDD design approaches is that they "drive out" much of the creativity, innovation, and fun. What are some design principles and practices that we should consider using to reinforce and reward innovation?
- There is an ongoing battle over what is the right volume of design documentation. Can xDD principles help designers find the balance between anarchy and process obsession?

The workshop discussion will explore some things to consider when choosing the appropriate design approach, depending on the problem area or design team.

2. Organizers

- Dennis Mancl, Alcatel-Lucent, Murray Hill, NJ 07974, USA

- Steven D. Fraser, Cisco Research, San Jose, CA, USA
- Gail E. Harris, Instantiated Software, Toronto, Canada
- Bill Opdyke, JP Morgan Chase, Chicago, IL, USA

3. Post-workshop Poster

A post-workshop poster summarizing the most significant ideas shared and questions generated during the session is posted on the workshop website:

http://mysite.verizon.net/dennis.mancl/splash12/index.html

References

[1] Wirfs-Brock, Rebecca, "What Drives Design?" Video recording of an OOPSLA 2008 invited talk on the InfoQ site, http://www.infoq.com/presentations/What-Drives-Design-Rebecca-Wirfs-Brock

The Data, Context and Interaction Paradigm

James O. Coplien

Gertrud & Cope
cope@gertrudandcope.com

Trygve Reenskaug

Dept. of Informatics, University of Oslo
trygver@ifi.uio.no

Abstract

This is a design track overview tutorial that provides a foundation for exploring and applying the DCI (Data, Context and Interaction) paradigm. DCI is a means to supporting full object orientation that restores much of the original object vision that has been lost by class-based design and programming. DCI focuses on objects and their relationships to the roles of human mental models by which end users and programmers reason about them generally. DCI leads to an architecture that extends contemporary object-oriented programming from its data-centric structure to focus more on the business value of system-level operations.

DCI captures the structure of the system data as classes, which spawn objects at run time. Classes are tied together by data references and by method invocations that run along those data references. The Context augments these relationships on a per-use-case basis with connections that bind together objects in a use case according to their dynamic interaction. The Context is the locus of use case enactment in the architecture: a new concept that encapsulates the roles that define system dynamics. It also encapsulates the knowledge of how to choose objects and bind them to roles to set up these dynamic per-use-case relationships.

This computational model facilitates a design where stable data design can be reasoned about in its own right in terms of classes, and where use case logic also has first-class standing. The Context weaves together these two perspectives at run time under program control. The system has a new dynamic architecture for each use case enactment. The basic building blocks are run-time modules that are created dynamically according to business needs.

In spite of its greatly increased flexibility over traditional object orientation, DCI can conveniently be implemented in most modern programming languages. The addition of traits or other modest and conservative reflection features make DCI possible not only in languages at the end of the spectrum where we find Python and Ruby, but also at the end of the spectrum where we find C++ and .Net, as well as many

interesting languages in between. The traits of Scala in particular are a natural expression of much of DCI semantics.

DCI preserves and amplifies the crucial object properties of object-oriented programming: identity, encapsulation, reflection of human mental models, and more. The workshop will illustrate these principles through examples. Some of these examples show how DCI upholds object principles in ways that supersede recently published work such as [3].

This tutorial (it is not a classic workshop) will teach roles and contexts as fundamental new building blocks of object-oriented programs. DCI is a paradigm that more faithfully lives up to the original goals of the object paradigm in its basis in stakeholder mental models, its proximity to end user concerns, and its dynamic computational model, than one finds in class-oriented programming.

Categories and Subject Descriptors C.5.m [**Computer System Implementation**]: Language Constructs and Features – abstract data types, polymorphism, control structures.

General Terms Algorithms, Management, Documentation, Design, Human Factors, Languages, Theory, Verification.

Keywords context; roles; use case; restricted OO; full OO; mental models; reflection.

References

[1] Reenskaug, Trygve. The common sense of object-oriented programming.
http://folk.uio.no/trygver/2009/commonsense.pdf
(2009).

[2] Coplien, James, and Gertrud Bjørnvig. Lean Architecture for Agile Software Development. Wiley (2010).

[3] Hermann, Stephan. Demystifyng object schizophrenia. MASPEGHI Workshop (MechAnisms for SPEcialization, Generalization and inHerItance), at ECOOP'10, Maribor, Slovenia.

Developing Competency in Parallelism: Techniques for Education and Training

Richard A. Brown

St. Olaf College
Northfield, MN 55057
rab@stolaf.edu

Edward F. Gehringer

North Carolina State University
Raleigh, NC 27695-8206
efg@ncsu.edu

Abstract

With the increasing penetration of parallelism into computing, programmers of all stripes need to acquire competencies in concurrent programming. This workshop will concentrate on discussing and disseminating resources for gently introducing parallelism into programmers' skill sets. It will provide a venue for the developers and vendors of programming languages to showcase their facilities and training materials. It will seek short "killer" parallel application examples that can be used in academic or training environments. Another focus will be on short modules that can be used in short courses for practicing programmers, or dropped into academic courses dealing with some aspect of programming. Finally, it will provide a forum for showcasing tools for visualizing and/or teaching parallelism in programming.

Categories and Subject Descriptors K.3.2 [**Computers and Education**]: Computer and Information Science Education; D.1.3 [**Programming Techniques**]: Concurrent Programming.

General Terms Algorithms, Performance, Design, Languages.

Keywords CS education, education, curriculum, applications, exemplars, LittleFe, CSinParallel, parallelism, parallel computing, multicore, parallel programming, distributed computing, scalability

1. Main Theme and Goal

By now, we all understand the need to teach more parallel and distributed computing (PDC) in computer science at the undergraduate level. Practicing programmers know they need to develop and improve their own PDC skills and comprehension, in response to the exponential increase in the number of cores per CPU and the broad adoption of network-based application technologies such as cloud computing. How shall we teach and/or learn the principles and practices of PDC? This workshop will gather educators and practitioners with compelling examples and strategies for PDC teaching, along with others seeking to apply such elements in their teaching and training activities, in order to present and obtain hands-on experience with PDC assignments, tools, and other resources, and to consider how to adopt and add to them. Approaches based on applications and on programing languages and systems will particular attention.

2. Organizers

Dick Brown is a professor at St. Olaf College, where he served as Director of Computer Science for 18 years and has introduced ten new courses in the CS curriculum. He is co-director of the NSF-funded CSinParallel project (csinparallel.org), dedicated to producing and disseminating modular teaching materials for incrementally introducing parallel and distributed computing throughout the undergraduate CS curriculum, and directs the HiPerCiC project, which develops interdisciplinary applications of high-performance computing for any disciplines. He serves as Treasurer of EAPF.

Ed Gehringer is an associate professor at North Carolina State University. He is a veteran of all 26 OOPSLA/SPLASH conferences. He has chaired the Educators' and Trainers' Symposium at SPLASH 2010 and 2011, the latter of which focused on teaching parallelism. He has taught parallel computer architecture for over 20 years, and has chaired the 10 most recent Workshops on Computer Architecture Education, which have been increasingly devoted to topics involving parallelism.

3. Anticipated Attendance

Workshops devoted to teaching parallelism at other conferences in the past couple of years have attracted from 25 to 50 participants. We believe that is a realistic range for this workshop.

4. Advertisement

The workshop will be advertised to the CS-education community via the SIGCSE-members e-mail list, which has approximately 1100 subscribers. It will also be promoted through the proposer's Workshop on Computer Architecture Education mailing list, which contains several thousand active e-mail addresses. We will also announce it via LinkedIn, where both of us have several hundred contacts.

5. Participant Preparation

Participants will receive an advance list of PDC technologies (languages, libraries, and applications) to be included in hands-on workshop exercises, with an invitation to bring their own access and/or implementations of those technologies. Also, all participants will receive experience with available computational resources for teaching PDC, such as Intel's Manycore Testing Lab and a LittleFe system.

6. Activities and Format

This workshop will offer multiple types of sessions.

One kind of session will present EAPF Exemplars and CSinParallel modules, followed by hands-on activities with some of the Exemplars and modules, an activity in applying Exemplars and LittleFE in teaching and training, and concluding with a group discussion. The Exemplars focus on teaching PDC through applications, which range from simple numerical-integration calculations to compelling topics such as computational drug design. Each exemplar offers numerous implementations, thus providing explained example code in a variety of programming platforms for adoption and comparison. CSinParallel modules present concepts of PDC in flexible units intended brief (1- to 3-day) insertions into various courses in undergraduate CS curricula. LittleFE is a portable Beowulf cluster kit that supports multicore, distributed, GPU-accelerated, and hybrid computation, designed for undergraduate PDC education.

Another type of session will have un-conference format, where attendees gather in groups to discuss questions submitted in advance or proposed during the workshop. Example questions: What approach or what tool provides the clearest explanation of a race condition? What tools can be used to visualize the execution of a parallel program? What techniques are most useful in debugging nondeterministic parallel programs?

Submitted papers will constitute a third type of session. The combination of session types will provide multiple avenues for addressing the challenge of incrementally introducing PDC into programming education.

7. Post-workshop activities

Exemplars, CSinParallel modules, and LittleFE are already being disseminated on the websites eapf.org, csinparallel.org, and littlefe.net. Suitable new materials that may emerge from the workshop will be added to those sites.

8. Special requirements

None.

The 12th Workshop on Domain-Specific Modeling

Juha-Pekka Tolvanen

MetaCase
Ylistonmaentie 31
FI-40500 Jyvaskyla, Finland
jpt@metacase.com

Jonathan Sprinkle

University of Arizona
ECE Department
1230 E. Speedway Blvd.
Tucson, AZ

sprinkle@ECE.Arizona.Edu

Matti Rossi

Aalto University School of Business
Runeberginkatu 22-24
FI-00100 Helsinki, Finland

Matti.Rossi@aalto.fi

Jeff Gray

University of Alabama
Department of Computer Science
Box 870290
Tuscaloosa, AL

gray@cs.ua.edu

Abstract

Domain-Specific Modeling (DSM) has proven to be a viable solution to the challenges related to abstraction mismatches between the problem and solution spaces. In many cases, DSM assists in the generation of final products from high-level models that are specific to a domain in terms of abstractions and representation. This automation is possible because both the language and generators are tailored for one domain. This paper introduces DSM and describes the related workshop at SPLASH 2012 (22 October 2012, Tucson, AZ).

Categories and Subject Descriptors D 3.2 [**Languages**]: Specialized application languages, very high-level languages; D 2.2 [**Design Tools and Techniques**]: *Computer-aided software engineering* (CASE)

Keywords Modeling Languages; Metamodeling; Domain-Specific Languages; Code Generation

1. Introduction

The primary drawback of most software and systems modeling tools is that they are constrained to work with a fixed notation. At the same time most users desire a customized modeling environment that can be easily tailored to contain the concepts needed in the user's problem domain. DSM languages (DSMLs) and tools provide viable solutions for making the development experience more flexible, faster and easier.

Industrial experiences of DSM consistently show it to be several times faster than current practices, including current UML-based implementations of MDA. As Booch et al. [1] state, "the full value of MDA is only achieved when the modeling concepts map directly to domain concepts rather than computer technology concepts." Accordingly, in DSM the models are constructed using concepts that represent things in the problem domain, not concepts of a given programming language. The modeling language follows the domain abstractions and semantics, allowing developers to perceive themselves as working directly with domain concepts. The models represent

simultaneously the design, implementation and documentation of the system. In a number of cases, the final products can be generated automatically from these high-level specifications with domain-specific code generators. This automation is possible because of domain-specificity: both the modeling language and code generators correspond to the requirements of a narrow domain, often in a single company.

This paper introduces DSM by describing a general framework for defining domain-specific modeling languages and code generators for a specific purpose. This is followed by describing the focus and topics of the 12th workshop on Domain-Specific Modeling.

2. Defining and using DSMLs

Three things are necessary to achieve full automatic code generation from domain modeling: firstly, a modeling tool supporting a domain-specific modeling language; secondly, a code generator; and lastly, a domain-specific framework. Figure 1 shows these three elements at two levels: the definition level and the use level.

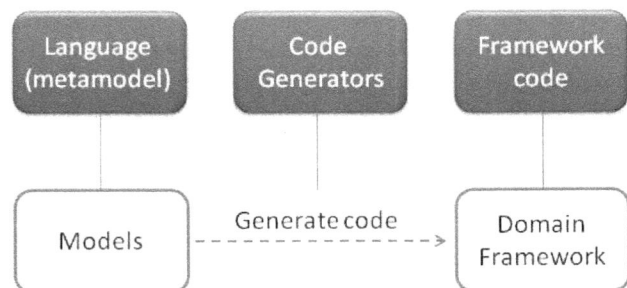

Figure 1. Framework for domain-specific modeling

The top-level (representing the definition) is made once by the organization for a given domain. Normally, one or two experts will define the modeling language (i.e., a metamodel) and related code generation, normally with a metamodeling tool [3, 5]. The metamodel is the implementation of the DSML, and includes the concepts and rules directly from the domain. The framework code will often be created by developers in earlier projects in the domain, with some being added or modified specifically for the DSM creation project.

The bottom-level process represents the use of a domain-specific modeling language and code generator. This level is performed many times, once for each product, by developers. Development time can often be further reduced by reusing parts of the model that are common to several products. The code generation and use of a domain framework or platform services require no effort by the developer. Together, these savings form the primary payback of the DSM approach amortized over each use.

This is unlike many visual modeling languages that are fixed to a specific notation that maps to semantically well-defined concepts of programming languages (like UML, SA/SD). With those languages, developers must leap straight from requirements into implementation concepts, and map back and forth between domain concepts, UML concepts, and program code. This requires significant time and resources, and can lead to errors.

In DSM, the specification models are built from instances of the domain concepts [4]. The code generator walks through the model and transforms the concept structures into code. In some cases, the code will be fully self-contained; more often, significant parts of the code will be calls to reusable components and the domain framework. Because the code is generated, syntax and logic errors do not normally occur, and the resultant improvement in quality forms a significant secondary payback of the DSM approach [2].

3. Workshop Focus and Topics

DSM has been successfully applied in many different domains. There are general characteristics about these domains that suggest useful DSM application scenarios. Each of these examples represents a type of configuration problem with numerous choices. Furthermore, each of these examples is based upon an underlying execution platform, or API, that may change. This makes a system brittle because of the tight coupling to the execution platform. Moreover, these systems are constantly evolving by virtue of changes in the hardware and software platform, and due to changes in requirements. Therefore, there is a need to incorporate several degrees of concern separation through higher levels of system representation.

The goals of the workshop are to collect and exchange experiences related to building and using DSM; continue building and extending the DSM community; and address in focus groups the issues raised in the presented papers and at previous workshops. The workshop examines DSM in different ways, including: 1) Full papers describing

either practical or theoretical ideas; 2) Experience reports on applying DSM; 3) Position papers describing work in progress or an author's position regarding current DSM practice; 4) DSM demonstrations describing a particular language, generator or tool.

The presentations of papers and demonstrations form the basis for discussion in the group work sessions. The results of the group work sessions, along with presentation slides, will be made available on the workshop website [6] together with the papers. The topics addressed in the workshop include:

- Industry/academic experience reports describing success/failure in implementing and using DSM
- Approaches to identify constructs for DSM languages
- Novel features in language workbenches/DSM tools
- Approaches to implement metamodel-based languages
- Metamodeling frameworks and languages
- Modularization technologies for DSM
- Novel approaches for code generation from DSM
- Issues of support/maintenance for DSM-based systems
- Evolution of languages along with their domain
- Organizational and process issues in DSM
- Demonstrations of working, or in-progress, DSM solutions (languages, generators, frameworks, tools)
- Identification of domains where DSM can be most productive in the future

References

[1] Booch, G., Brown, A., Iyengar, S., Rumbaugh, J., and Selic, B., *MDA Journal*, May 2004.

[2] Gray, J., Tolvanen, J.-P., Kelly, S. Gokhale, A., Neema, S., and Sprinkle, J,, "Domain-Specific Modeling," *CRC Handbook on Dynamic System Modeling*, (Paul Fishwick, ed.), CRC Press, 2007.

[3] Kelly, S., Rossi, M., and Tolvanen, J.-P., What is Needed in a MetaCASE Environment?, *Journal of Enterprise Modelling and Information Systems Architectures*, Vol 1., 1, 2005.

[4] Kelly, S., and Tolvanen, J-P, *Domain-Specific Modeling*, Wiley, 2008.

[5] Lédeczi, A., Bakay, A., Maroti, M., Völgyesi, P., Nordstrom, G., Sprinkle, J., and Karsai, G., Composing Domain-Specific Design Environments, *IEEE Computer*, November 2001.

[6] Workshop on Domain-Specific Modeling (DSM'12), http://www.dsmforum.org/events/DSM12

19th International Workshop on Foundations
of Object-Oriented Languages (FOOL'12)

Workshop Summary

Jonathan Aldrich

Carnegie Mellon University

jonathan.aldrich@cs.cmu.edu

Jeremy Siek

University of Colorado at Boulder

jeremy.siek@colorado.edu

John Boyland

University of Wisconsin-Milwaukee

boyland@cs.uwm.edu

Abstract

The search for sound principles for object-oriented languages has given rise to considerable research during the last few decades, leading to a better understanding of the key concepts of object-oriented languages and to important developments in type theory, semantics, program verification, and program development. The purpose of this workshop is to provide a forum for discussing new ideas in the foundations of object-oriented languages and provide feedback to authors. Submissions to this workshop were invited in the general area of foundations of object-oriented languages, object-oriented languages, including integration with other paradigms and extensions, such as aspects, components, and meta-programming.

Categories and Subject Descriptors D.3.1 [*Programming Languages*]: Formal Definitions and Theory

General Terms Languages, Security, Theory, Verification

Keywords foundations, object-orientation, programming languages, type theory, semantics, analysis, verification, concurrency, distributed systems, databases, security

1. Main Theme and Goals

The theme of the workshop is the general area of foundations of object-oriented languages, including integration with other paradigms and extensions, such as aspects, components, meta-programming. Topics of interest include language semantics, type systems, program analysis and verification, formal calculi, concurrent and distributed languages, databases, software adaptation, and language-based security issues. Papers are welcome to include formal descriptions and proofs, but these are not required; the key consideration is that papers should present novel and valuable ideas relating to foundations for object-oriented languages. The main focus in selecting workshop contributions will be the intrinsic interest and timeliness of the work, so authors are encouraged to submit polished descriptions of work in progress as well as papers describing completed projects. In addition to the sharing of research ideas, another goal of the workshop is to provide feedback to the authors, helping them prepare their papers for submission to top-tier conferences.

2. Papers and Activities

FOOL is a 1-day workshop that includes presentations of accepted papers as well as invited speakers and other technical sessions.

FOOL does not have formal proceedings, to enable authors to present preliminary work that they wish to later publish formally in a conference venue. Papers are peer-reviewed by the program committee above, however, and are posted online at the FOOL workshop site as an informal record of the workshop. Many past FOOL papers have had significant influence on object-oriented programming language research and revised versions appear in prominent conferences and journals. The home page of FOOL is at

```
http://www.cs.cmu.edu/~aldrich/FOOL/,
```

and the web page for FOOL'12 will be avialable soon.

3. Location at SPLASH/OOPSLA

After many editions held in conjunction with POPL, the steering committee felt that the the object-oriented research community that is centered on OOPSLA and SPLASH would also provide a strong positive research community. Furthermore, FOOL fills a need for a foundational language workshop at SPLASH. Hence, this year we look forward to a FOOL hosted at SPLASH and continuing to improve the synergies between these communities.

4. Organization

FOOL is guided by a steering committee as follows:

- Jonathan Aldrich (Carnegie Mellon University)
- Viviana Bono (Universitá di Torino)
- Atsushi Igarashi (Kyoto University)
- James Noble (University of Wellington)
- Jeremy Siek (Chair, University of Colorado)
- Elena Zucca (Universitá di Genova, Italy)

The program committee for FOOL'12 will be decided on soon.

3rd International Workshop on Free Composition (FREECO)

Christoph Bockisch, Lodewijk Bergmans
& Steven te Brinke

University of Twente
{c.m.bockisch, bergmans, s.tebrinke}
@cs.utwente.nl

Ian Piumarta

Viewpoints Research Institute
ian@vpri.org

Abstract

The history of programming languages shows a continuous search for new composition mechanisms to find better ways for structuring increasingly complex software systems into modules that can be developed and reused independently. Composition mechanisms can address various types of dependencies among modules, e.g., inheritance, delegation, aggregation, design patterns, contracts, explicit protocols, or domain-specific compositions.

However, most languages adopt a fixed set of composition mechanisms, usually with explicit notation and predefined semantics. In case a language does not provide any mechanisms with the desired compositional behavior, programmers may need to write workarounds or introduce the new composition mechanism through macros, libraries, frameworks or language extensions.

This workshop intends to stimulate research in programming languages and software development by exploring the notion that today's languages with their limited set of composition mechanisms is insufficient. Instead we should allow compositions that support more flexibility, adopt a wide variety of compositions, domain-specific and tailored compositions, or programmable compositions of various program artifacts.

Categories and Subject Descriptors   D.2.2 [*Software Engineering*]: Design Tools and Techniques

General Terms   Design

Keywords   composition, decomposition, free composition, open composition mechanisms, programming languages, design languages

1. Themes

The theme of the workshop is the *future of composition techniques and modularity in programming languages*; this workshop aims at pushing the limits of language designs to offer developers more flexibility in decomposing and composing their software into independent modules.

Examples of topics targeted by this workshop include, but are not limited to:

- flexible, tailorable composition mechanisms
- unified techniques for expressing a wide range of compositions
- new composition mechanisms
- new module systems
- modularity & modularization limitations and capabilities
- modularization & composability metrics
- tools and case studies
- techniques for expressing/introducing domain-specific compositions
- general concepts/theories underlying generic composition techniques
- languages that are extensible with new composition mechanisms
- conflict detection and/or resolution when combining composition mechanisms
- formal models for expressing generic or flexible composition mechanisms
- design techniques for supporting a wide range of composition mechanisms

2. Format

FREECO is a full-day workshop that solicits papers of up to 5 pages in ACM style. These papers are peer-reviewed by our program committee and will be published in the workshop's post-proceedings. We allow participation in the workshop without an accepted or even submitted paper. All participants are encouraged to formulate a position statement of maximal one page ACM style. These position statements are not reviewed and not published in the workshop proceedings, but will be made available on the workshop's homepage[1] before the workshop. All papers will also be published in advance on the homepage. Participants are encouraged to read all papers and position statements before the workshop.

The planned workshop agenda interleaves presentations with technical content and interactive, plenary activities to stimulate participants. We intend to have an invited talk from an expert in the field and the following interactive activities:

- Sessions consisting of either group discussion, lightning talks and/or break-out groups to elaborate on interesting research questions. These questions will be distilled from the technical presentations and their ensuing discussions.

- Authors of accepted papers can choose between:

  - A traditional presentation (15 minutes), followed by a question and answer session (5 minutes).

  - A writer's workshop discussion (45 minutes).

The purpose of the writer's workshop is particularly to improve the quality of papers for submitting extended versions as conference papers in the future. We will follow the format discussed at `http://www.cs.wustl.edu/~schmidt/writersworkshop.html`, in short this is:

- Authors will cite one paragraph from their paper which they consider most representative of their work.

- All authors choosing the writer's workshop format are required to read and prepare all writer's workshop other papers; other participants are requested to read and prepare at least one such paper (but we strongly encourage them to read all).

- One or two participants familiar with the paper summarize it from their perspective. In the plenary discussion, the key points of the paper are identified.

- Participants discuss what they liked, i.e. what are the strengths of the paper, and give constructive suggestions for improving the paper or the approach.

- The authors can ask questions to the other participants to clarify their statements.

- The discussion of a paper—including the authors citation of one paragraph—in this format will be allocated a time slot of 45 minutes.

3. Organizers

Christoph Bockisch is an assistant professor on Software Composition with a research focus on the design and implementation of programming languages with advanced dispatch mechanisms. He received his doctoral degree from the Technische Universität Darmstadt in 2008. Christoph au-

thored and co-authored several papers about programming languages published amongst others by the ECOOP, OOP-SLA and AOSD conferences. He is co-organizing the workshop series on Virtual Machines and Intermediate Languages (VMIL) and Free Composition (FREECO), was program chair of the European Summer School on AOSD 2009; he is Students-Event co-chair and PC member of the AOSD 2013 conference.

Lodewijk Bergmans is a (part-time) assistant professor at the TRESE group at the University of Twente, where he focuses on software composition. He has over 20 years of experience in the field of object-oriented and aspect-oriented software development, and has published well over 50 refereed articles in international books, journals, conferences and workshops. He holds M.Sc. and Ph.D. degrees in Computer Science, both from the University of Twente. He has served on the PC of e.g. the ECOOP, AOSD and NODe conferences. He was the AOSD workshop chair at AOSD 2002. He has also (co-)organized many workshops in a wide range of conferences.

Steven te Brinke is a Ph.D. Assistant in Software Engineering at the TRESE group of the University of Twente. He received his M.Sc. degree with honors from the University of Twente in 2011 entitled "First-order Function Dispatch in a Java-like Programming Language". Steven co-authored several papers about programming languages design and composition, among which were publications in both previous editions of the FREECO workshop.

Ian Piumarta is a senior computer scientist at Viewpoints Research Institute with over 25 years of experience in dynamic languages and their implementation. His research interests are centered on making computing systems that are open, reflexive, dynamically self-implementing and understandable at a deep level by non-experts. He holds a B.Sc. (hons) and Ph.D. in Computer Science from the University of Manchester (UK) and has published more than 30 papers and articles. He has served on the programme committees of more than a dozen workshops and conferences, and served three times as co-chairman of international conferences sponsored by the ACM or IEEE.

3.1 Program Committee

- **Uwe Assmann**, University of Dresden, Germany
- **Harold Ossher**, IBM Research, USA
- **Michael Haupt**, Oracle Labs, Germany
- **Roel Wuyts**, University of Leuven, Belgium
- **Ian Piumarta**, Viewpoints Research Institute, USA
- **Christoph Bockisch**, University of Twente, The Netherlands
- **Lodewijk Bergmans**, University of Twente, The Netherlands
- **Steven te Brinke**, University of Twente, The Netherlands

---

[1] `http://trese.ewi.utwente.nl/workshops/FREECO/FREECO-SPLASH2012/`

Developing a Coding Scheme for the Analysis of Expert Pair Programming Sessions

Mark Zarb

School of Computing
University of Dundee
Dundee, UK
markzarb@computing.dundee.ac.uk

Abstract

Communication occurs constantly within pair programming, however, little is known about this communication, and how it changes according to skill or experience. This research presents the creation of a coding scheme, used for the analysis of expert intra-pair communication.

Categories and Subject Descriptors D.1.5 [**Programming Languages**]: Object-oriented Programming.

Keywords pair programming; XP; communication; video analysis; grounded theory; collaboration; analytic coding

1. Research Problem and Motivation

Pair programming is a method for software development "that favours both informal and immediate communication over [...] traditional design methods" [1]. It is primarily a coding activity during which two programmers collaborate continuously on the same program, usually at the same computer. The pair takes on different roles: one, the driver, has full control of the keyboard, whereas the other (the navigator) is in charge of reviewing the code and performing continuous analysis and design. It is common practice for partners to switch roles frequently. Pair programming encourages programmers to talk to each other – this 'pair pressure' results in greater enjoyment and increased knowledge distribution [2], as well as quality improvement.

Communication is an integral factor to pair programming [3]; however, it is also regarded as being one of the main factors leading to failure in pair programming [4]. Little is known about the nature of this communication, and how it impacts pair programming success. The goal of this research is to gain an understanding of the different communication topics that occur within the pair.

This approach and the results arising from the overall research project shall benefit novice pair programmers. The improved understanding in the way expert pairs communicate within successful projects could lead to the creation of communication patterns and guidelines. Novice pairs can be trained in these patterns to emulate expert methods of dealing with pair programming issues (e.g. how to break silence, regain focus, or recover from an interruption) in order to improve the way they aid each other whilst pairing.

2. Background and Related Work

Existing studies show that pairs who experienced a high rate of communication did not necessarily experience high satisfaction, nor a high level of confidence with the final outcome of their work [5]. Communication within the pair should stay on-topic to drive the work forward.

There are several studies that focus on analysing pair programming videos, however, many of them use both novices and experts to create their concepts [6, 7]. Furthermore, these studies focus on the *process* of pair programming, rather than on the types of communication. As such, there is no well-studied catalogue of communication techniques for pair programming. This initial investigation presents an analysis of several sessions from an expert pair of programmers, with the aim of creating a robust coding scheme for understanding pair programming success.

3. Approach

The coding scheme presented is a general coding scheme that can be applied to expert pairs, primarily to understand the various topics of communication that relate to software development, but also to gather data that will allow for the development of communication patterns.

An initial set of 60 videos (the *pairwith.us* project [8], with each video lasting approximately 30 minutes) showing the same pair of expert programmers working on an incre-

Copyright is held by the author/owner(s).
SPLASH'12, October 19–26, 2012, Tucson, Arizona, USA.
ACM 978-1-4503-1563-0/12/10.

mental software project have been acquired for the development of these codes. Twenty-nine videos were eliminated from the set due to problems which would hinder the investigation: most of the initial videos had bad audio-visual quality, several videos had no video feed, and some videos featured a distracting echo. The remaining 31 videos were re-watched and analysed using Grounded Theory.

During this analysis, the author observed various verbal and non-verbal (mouse pointing, gesturing, finger-drumming, grunting) instances of communication, as well as several notable behaviours (such as the programmers' constant awareness of their goals, and use of jokes to lighten the mood and regain focus). For every video watched, the author listed the key observations of these trends.

4. Results and Contributions

The communication trends were continuously compared and condensed to create a list of ten common analytic codes (keywords that categorise segments of the audiovisual data) that could be seen to occur throughout all the videos: *talking about previous work; continuous review of the expected goal; explaining; silent instances; discussion; unrelated conversation; jokes; switching of roles; high 5; distraction.*

In order to verify the validity of the coding scheme, a sample of five videos from the original set of 31 was selected and fully transcribed. The videos were then re-watched, and the transcription was coded. The researcher noticed that certain codes were too vague. For example, a *Discussion* was difficult to pinpoint and thus was split up into *Explanation*, *Suggestion* and *General*. Furthermore, it was clear that there was a distinction between conventional 'quiet' silence, and muttering (e.g. whilst typing, or figuring out code logic). Thus, the codes were adapted with each viewing of the five videos, until a set of codes that could be applied to all instances was achieved.

The author ran inter-rater reliability tests to assess the new version of codes – increased to 11. The inter-rater reliability for the raters was found to be Kappa = 0.56 (p < 0.001), indicating a moderate agreement with the way the author coded the video. The data showed an overlap between certain codes, such as *Joke* and *Off-Topic*, as well as *Planning* and *Suggestion*, suggesting that raters were confused by similar codes.

To reduce the potential degree of error, and to ensure that the coding scheme could be used to analyse other pairs, it was decided to collapse the codes with the most variability. This resulted in a refined set of codes, ordered below by their frequency of occurrence across the sample videos:

- Suggestion
- Silence
- Off-Topic
- Explanation
- Review
- General
- Muttering
- Distraction
- Switch

The videos were re-coded, and preliminary inter-rater reliability tests resulted in Kappa = 0.71 (p < 0.001), indicating a higher agreement that was more substantial, with a closer match of the analytic codes. The data also indicates that the codes for *Distraction* and *Switch* are behaviour-led codes rather than communication-based – this shall be reviewed in later experiments. The author expects to test these codes on videos produced by other expert pairs. Future experiments shall also test the inter-rater reliability.

This paper presents a set of communication topics used within the pair. These codes can be used to gather data on the way expert pairs communicate between themselves: this is the first step towards discovering communication patterns that lead to success in pair programming.

Acknowledgements

The research work disclosed in this publication is funded by the Strategic Educational Pathways Scholarship (Malta). The scholarship is part-financed by the European Union – European Social Fund (ESF) under Operational Programme II - Cohesion Policy 2007-2013, "Empowering People for More Jobs and a Better Quality of Life".

The author would like to thank Dr Janet Hughes and Prof John Richards, for their attention and support.

References

[1] Williams, L., et al., *Strengthening the Case for Pair Programming*. IEEE Software, 2000. **17**(4): p. 19-25.

[2] Bryant, S., P. Romero, and B. du Boulay, *The Collaborative Nature of Pair Programming*, in *Extreme Programming and Agile Processes in Software Engineering*, P. Abrahamsson, M. Marchesi, and G. Succi, Editors. 2006, Springer Berlin/Heidelberg. p. 53-64.

[3] Cockburn, A. and L. Williams, *The costs and benefits of pair programming*, in *Extreme programming examined*. 2001, Addison-Wesley Longman Publishing Co., Inc. p. 223-243.

[4] Sanders, D., *Student Perceptions of the Suitability of Extreme and Pair Programming*, in *Extreme Programming Perspectives*, M. Marchesi, et al., Editors. 2002, Addison-Wesley Professional. p. 168-174.

[5] Choi, K.S., F.P. Deek, and I. Im, *Pair dynamics in team collaboration*. Computers in Human Behavior, 2009. **25**(4): p. 844-852.

[6] Cao, L. and P. Xu. *Activity patterns of pair programming*. 2005: IEEE.

[7] Salinger, S. and L. Prechelt. *What happens during pair programming?* in *Proceedings of the 20th Annual Workshop of the Psychology of Programming Interest Group (PPIG '08)*. 2008. Lancaster, England.

[8] Marcano, A. and A. Palmer. *pairwith.us*. 2009 [cited 2012 31 July]; Available from: http://vimeo.com/channels/pairwithus.

Benchmarking Typestate-Oriented Programming Languages

Benjamin W. Chung

Carnegie Mellon University

bwchung@andrew.cmu.edu

Abstract

The performance of typestate-oriented programming languages is difficult to evaluate as existing benchmarks do not exercise the unique features of these languages. We address this by developing a new benchmark suite specifically designed to evaluate typestate-oriented functionality. These benchmarks model projected applications, providing overhead and memory loads similar to actual applications.

Categories and Subject Descriptors D.2.8 [*Software Engineering*]: Metrics; D.3.3 [*Programming Languages*]: Language Constructs and Features

General Terms Performance, Experimentation

Keywords Typestate, Protocols, Benchmarks, Performance, Dynamic Behavior

1. Introduction

Typestate-oriented programming languages raise the level of abstraction by directly expressing protocols, while maintaining a similar underlying structure to that of other dynamic languages. As dynamically modified interfaces are widely used in many applications, such as many Javascript applications and some virtual machines [2, 4], protocol alteration is a very important part of programming in dynamic languages. However, even in existing dynamic programming languages, interface alteration after object creation remains unexamined by many leading benchmark suites [5].

2. Plaid

Plaid is a new programming language being developed to support the idea of first-class state [6]. Each state can have fields and methods, and methods can transition the receiver. This enables several new design concepts that are little used in more traditional object-oriented languages.

```
1  state Socket {
2    val identifier;
3  }
4  state ClosedSocket case of Socket {
5    method open() {
6      this <- OpenSocket;
7    }
8  }
9  state OpenSocket case of Socket {
10   method read() { ... }
11   method write() { ... }
12   method close() {
13     this <- ClosedSocket;
14   }
15 }
```

Figure 1. A basic Plaid program

An example of Plaid code can be found in Figure 1, which models a simple socket representation with two states, ClosedSocket and OpenSocket. Socket can transition between the two states via the open and close methods, and both expose custom functionality depending on the state they are in.

3. Existing Benchmarks

Existing benchmark suites are focused primarily on determining the speed of a system at performing certain algorithms, such as manipulating a splay tree[1]. It has been shown that these standard metrics are not representative of real-world application speed, and that optimizations targeting these benchmarks do not always improve speed of applications [1, 3]. In addition, little work has been done towards a benchmark suite for a typestate-oriented language such as Plaid. Two suites, DaCapo and V8, are particularly relevant for our project, as they represent commonly used benchmark suites for large programs and dynamic languages, respectively.

DaCapo DaCapo is a benchmark suite written to analyze the performance of Java Virtual Machines (JVMs) in actual use cases. It uses a selection of benchmarks that are common applications for the JVM, primarily based on large open-source software projects. This core causes the suite to represent the performance of a large number of Java applications,

SPLASH'12, October 19–26, 2012, Tucson, Arizona, USA.
ACM 978-1-4503-1563-0/12/10.

---

[1] http://v8.googlecode.com/svn/data/benchmarks/v7/run.html

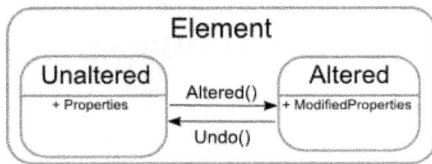

Figure 2. State diagram for implementation of the action pattern.

as many applications either use the frameworks that make up DaCapo or use similar algorithms and memory structures to them [1]. However, this same functionality makes it difficult to apply the DaCapo suite to the typestate-oriented model, as it is highly Java specific.

V8   The V8 benchmark suite was written by the V8 team to act as a measure of the speed of the V8 Javascript engine. The V8 benchmark uses algorithmic benchmarks to arrive at a composite number, such as the DeltaBlue constraint solver[2]. Despite this popularity, V8 has significant disadvantages, focusing primarily on mathematical speed, rather than dynamic functionality.

4.   Design Goals

Benchmarks that accurately represent the performance of a real application are hard to create by using small programs that a single algorithms. To mitigate this issue, we will create programs that perform tasks that are similar to those that a actual user might need. These programs should run algorithms that are reasonable use cases for the language, and should run in a reasonable amount of time. The use of a typestate-oriented language also imposes some requirements on the type of benchmarks used, so benchmarks should use state change regularly to evaluate the performance of protocol dynamism in Plaid.

5.   Proposed Benchmarks

We have several benchmarks planned for the suite, that analyze several categories of application. We will be using a basic transactional database as well as heavily modified traditional benchmarks, such as sorting benchmarks and a subset of V8. These will benchmark different aspects of a potential real application.

Transactional Database   A transactional database has features that can be modeled easily via typestate, such as the underlying tree data structure and the actions on the database. This benchmark will preform a large number of sequential operations on a B-tree data structure. Typestate can be used to implement the transaction system via a modification state, which tracks whether a particular node in the B-tree has been modified. This system can allow rollbacks of a transaction simply by changing the state of the affected nodes within the tree. A diagram of this model can be seen in Figure 2.

---

² https://developers.google.com/v8/design

Benchmark	Plaid	Javascript	Java
Shell Sort	4.19	.131	.022
Binary Search Tree	1.09	.41	.0017
Splay Tree	18.26	.28	.11

Table 1. Preliminary comparison of execution times in seconds

Algorithmic   We also plan on porting traditional benchmarks from the V8 suite into Plaid, to analyze the speed of the Plaid runtime at executing standard algorithms, despite the limitations discussed above. In addition, we have created two more benchmarks to provide simpler, garbage collector intense operations. This reuse of traditional benchmarks also enables comparison of Plaid to the original language. In many cases, the more traditional benchmarks can be modified to take advantage of typestate oriented functionality. The Richards and BST benchmarks both use state change extensively. This is caused by the prevalence of state and state-like patterns in traditional object-oriented code.

6.   Results

Current Benchmarks   At the present time, we only have a small subset of the V8 suite, as well as our new algorithmic benchmarks. Javascript versions of all of our current benchmarks exist, allowing us to compare the existing performance of Plaid to V8.

Results   Using our preliminary benchmarks, we have determined that Plaid is approximately 1 order of magnitude slower than the equivalent JavaScript program, and 2 orders slower than the equivalent Java program, as seen in table 1. All of the preliminary benchmarks were highly algorithmically centered, with large memory usage and extreme repetition and recursion. Results were gathered on a computer running the 1.6 JRE on Windows 7 with a Intel Core i7-2760QM CPU at 2.40GHz, and 8.00 GB DDR3 PC3-10600 RAM.

References

[1] S. M. Blackburn, R. Garner, B. Wiedermann, and et al. The Da-Capo benchmarks: Java benchmarking development and analysis. In *OOPSLA '06*.

[2] A. Gal, B. Eich, M. Shaver, D. Anderson, and et al. Trace-based just-in-time type specialization for dynamic languages. In *ACM SIGPLAN 2009*, PLDI '09.

[3] M. Maass and I. Shafer. Instrumenting V8 to measure the efficacy of dynamic optimizations on production code. 2012.

[4] G. Richards, S. Lebresne, B. Burg, and J. Vitek. An analysis of the dynamic behavior of javascript programs. In *ACM SIGPLAN 2010*, PLDI '10, 2010.

[5] G. Richards, A. Gal, B. Eich, and J. Vitek. Automated construction of javascript benchmarks. *SIGPLAN Not.*, 2011.

[6] J. Sunshine, K. Naden, S. Stork, J. Aldrich, and E. Tanter. First-class state change in plaid. In *OOPSLA '11*.

Author Index

www.ingramcontent.com/pod-product-compliance
Lightning Source LLC
Chambersburg PA
CBHW061401210326
41598CB00035B/6063